9.25   WEST. NEWS   10%

SIR ROBERT HOWARD

SIR ROBERT HOWARD

(1626-1698)

A Critical Biography

by

H. J. OLIVER

DUKE UNIVERSITY PRESS

Durham, North Carolina

1 9 6 3

Library of Congress Catalogue Card number 63-17327

Cambridge University Press, London N.W.1, England

Printed in the United States of America
by the Seeman Printery, Inc., Durham, N. C.

Preface

THERE was, perhaps, no person of greater importance and influence in the earlier days of the Restoration theatre than the sixth son of the first Earl of Berkshire, Sir Robert Howard." This opinion, expressed by Montague Summers in 1935, in his *Playhouse of Pepys*, is demonstrably correct; yet no full critical biography of Howard has ever been published, and literary historians therefore know him only as John Dryden's brother-in-law; as the man who (so they unfairly put it) "collaborated" with Dryden in the first popular Heroic play, *The Indian Queen*; and as Dryden's opponent in the famous controversy on the question whether plays ought to be written in blank verse or in rhyme (and the implication always seems to be that this was to Howard's discredit, although Dryden himself afterwards admitted to having been in the wrong).

To the general rule that scholars have been interested in Howard merely for his connection with Dryden, there have been some honorable exceptions, including Montague Summers, Allardyce Nicoll, Alfred Harbage, E. S. de Beer, and Florence R. Scott. Unfortunately, however, only an abstract of Miss Scott's thesis on Howard was published, together with a few notes and brief articles (so that the principal value of her work appears now to have been to point to important sources of information); and Summers, Nicoll, Harbage, and de Beer were able to give Howard little more than passing mention in histories of the theater or other comprehensive works.

I hope that my own full study has succeeded not only in revealing Howard's importance as a dramatist and in giving an accurate account of his relations with Dryden, but also in drawing attention to his writings in non-dramatic verse and prose, to his considerable influence in Parliament and Council during the reigns of Charles II and of William and Mary, to his work behind the scenes for the Restoration of Charles II and for the Revolution of 1688, and to his prominence in matters of state finance, both as Auditor of the Receipt in the Exchequer and as the associate and friend of the great City financiers of his day.

I am sadly aware that a parliamentary or economic historian might have been able to make better use of some of my material, and that there may be sins of omission in some parts of the book. I make no apology, however, for the absence of any attempt to psychoanalyze Howard; from the facts as I have presented them, each reader is free to make his own inferences.

Quotations are given in the original spelling, except that I have disregarded the long *s*, have made the modern distinction between *i* and *j*, and between *u* and *v*, and have expanded the crossed *p*. A few misprints have been silently corrected. Titles of works widely known and reprinted in our time—such as *The Indian Emperor*—have been modernized, in accordance with what seems to be current academic practice, but the titles of seventeenth century pamphlets, for example, are given in the original form. All quotations are from first editions, unless otherwise noted; for ease of reference, however, the text of Howard's plays is normally quoted from the collected edition of 1692, the first to include *The Duke of Lerma*. It will be understood, of course, that documents cited from the Calendars of State Papers and from the Reports of the Historical Manuscripts Commission have already been slightly modernized or paraphrased by the editors of those volumes; and that the Parliamentary speeches quoted from Grey or from the Journals are summaries and not verbatim transcripts. Except in quotations, my English spelling and punctuation have been altered by the publisher to accord with American conventions and with "house style."

My research has led me to many of the great libraries of the English-speaking world and I should like to acknowledge my indebtedness to the officials of the British Museum, the Bodleian, the Public Record Office, the Victoria and Albert Museum, the Birmingham Public Library; the Libraries of Harvard, Yale, Princeton, and Duke Universities, and of the University of Texas; the Huntington and William Andrews Clark Memorial Libraries in Los Angeles; the New York Public Library; the Fisher Library of the University of Sydney; and the Public Libraries of Victoria and N.S.W.

It is also a pleasure to express my sincere gratitude to Sir Ralph and Lady Eastwood for hospitality at Vasterne, Howard's old home, and for assistance in tracing its history; to Mr. Levi Fox, Director of Shakespeare's Birthplace, Professor E. Robertson, Librarian of the John Rylands Library, Manchester, and Mr. L. E. Tanner, Keeper of the Muniments and Library in Westminster Abbey, for prompt and helpful answers to enquiries; to the Reverend Canon G. H. Jeudwine, of Church Oakley, Basingstoke, Hants, and the Reverend R. L. Sharp, of Wootton Bassett, Swindon, Wilts., for permission to consult and to quote from their parish registers; to Mr. L. J. Downer, of the University of Melbourne, for assistance with legal Latin; and to Professor G. P. Shipp, of the University of Sydney, for characteristic kindness in reading my pages on Howard as translator, and checking my Latin there.

Three other forms of assistance are even more difficult to define and to acknowledge with anything like adequacy. Dr. James M. Osborn, of Yale, went to great trouble to place at my disposal his invaluable collection of Clayton Manuscripts, and generously gave me permission to quote from them whatever I needed; A. W. G. Lowther Esq., F.S.A., of Ashtead, Surrey, who has in preparation a history of the Ashtead Estate, exchanged information with me, and, most unselfishly, drew my attention to sources that I might otherwise have overlooked; and my wife contributed so much to the book at all stages of its preparation, that I am sorry she would not agree to have her name on the title page as joint author.

Finally, I should like to record my indebtedness to the Australian

Humanities Research Council for a generous subsidy towards the publication of the book, and to Duke University Press, for even greater generosity in undertaking the publication of work that is not only highly specialized but is also by an author from another country.

H. J. OLIVER.

The University of N.S.W.
 1962

Abbreviations

The following standard abbreviations are used in the footnotes and text:

B.M. MSS	British Museum Manuscripts
Bod. MSS	Bodleian Manuscripts
Cal. Proc. Comm. Ad. Mon.	Calendar of the Proceedings of the Committee for Advance of Money
C.S.P.	Calendar of State Papers
C.S.P., Col.	Calendar of State Papers, Colonial Series
C.S.P.D.	Calendar of State Papers, Domestic
C.T.B.	Calendar of State Papers, Treasury Books
H.L.Q.	Huntington Library Quarterly
H.M.C.	Historical Manuscripts Commission
Inst. Hist. Res. Bull.	Institute of Historical Research Bulletin
J.E.G.P.	Journal of English and Germanic Philology
M.L.N.	Modern Language Notes
M.L.R.	Modern Language Review
M.P.	Modern Philology
N. & Q.	Notes and Queries
P.M.L.A.	Publications of the Modern Language Association
P.R.O.	Public Record Office
R.E.S.	Review of English Studies
S.P.	Studies in Philology
S.R.	Stationers' Register
T.L.S.	Times Literary Supplement

Contents

SIR ROBERT HOWARD

Chapter one. BEFORE THE RESTORATION

IT is certain that Charles II did not always reward most generously those to whom he owed most; it is also true that he was not always forgetful of services done for him and was willing, within his means, to put money and sinecures at the disposal of families who had remained loyal to the Stuarts in the Civil War and during the period of the Commonwealth. There was, then, nothing surprising in the royal beneficence that helped to make Sir Robert Howard wealthy and influential after the Restoration. The illustrious Howard family had not been unanimous in its allegiance to the Crown, but Charles II knew well that Sir Robert personally and several other members of the Berkshire branch of the family had given distinguished service in the field and had been willing to risk life as well as property in the Stuart cause; in extending favor to any one of them, the King was acknowledging, however inadequately, the loyalty of many.

Among those who had lost heavily in the Civil War was Robert's father Thomas Howard (1587-1669), second son of Thomas, Lord Howard of Walden and First Earl of Suffolk, Earl Marshal of England, and Lord High Treasurer from 1614 to 1619. The younger Thomas, who inherited the estates of his mother's family at Charlton in Wiltshire, married in 1614 Elizabeth, daughter of William, Lord Burleigh. In 1622 be became Baron Howard of Charlton and Viscount Andover, and in 1626 Earl of Berkshire. Before the Civil War he was wealthy; the King had given him annuities of at least £1200 and the profits from patents for his inventions (he seems to have been an amateur scientist of some originality); he had also been granted, with Viscount Wallingford, the lease of the Post Fines, which brought them a constant income of at least £1600 per annum.[1] In return, he performed such duties as were required of him and held responsible positions (he was, for example, "steward of the town of Oxford") and in 1639, at the time of the troubles with the Scottish Covenanters, he became a Privy Counsellor.[2] He was involved in some of the

1. *Calendar of State Papers Domestic*, 1625-1626, pp. 57, 556; 1635, p. 25; 1637-1638, p. 236; 1625-1626, p. 537; *C.S.P., Treasury Books* 1696-1697, p. 119; *C.S.P.D.*, 1656-1657, p. 313. For Post Fines, see below pp. 9-11.
2. *C.S.P.D.*, 1627-1628, p. 549; 1635-1636, p. 388; 1639, pp. 5, 319.

earliest of the fighting, in August, 1642, and was soon captured and committed to the Tower; his estates were duly confiscated.[3]

Of his consequent pitiful condition even after his liberation, perhaps the most vivid account is that given by Anthony à Wood in a later letter: "You do not mention his great sufferings for the kings cause, his going poor and bare all the broken times and had it not been for his ribban would have been very despicable beholding to a friend for a pint of sack or meals meat."[4] In 1657 he had to borrow against his rights under the grant of the Post Fines before he had received a penny from them, "haveing very pressing occasions for the use of money for the supply of my urgent and necessary affaires"; even in 1662 he was negotiating for the sale of Berkshire House to Charles II to mend "a broken fortune, occasioned by the persecution of his [the King's] enemies," "his personal estate being in danger of forfeiture"; and as late as 1667 there is official reference to "the great extremity of the Earl's affairs," a grant of £8,000 made to him by the King not having been paid.[5]

A few further examples of the family's part in the Civil War will suffice to fill in the background. Charles, the eldest son, who succeeded to the titles of Lord Howard of Charlton and Viscount Andover when his father was created Earl of Berkshire, had been chosen by the King in January, 1642, as his next Ambassador to Venice. The outbreak of the Civil War in August, however, meant that instead of going to Venice he defied Parliament by following the King to York (impeachment having already been preferred against him on 20 July).[6] He remained under suspicion during the Interregnum, and, like his father, was almost entirely dependent on royal bounty after the Restoration: in 1663 he was petitioning the King "for some compensation in lieu of the embassy to Venice, to which he was appointed by Charles I, though prevented going by the troubles; is now in too ill health to solicit for it, being almost ruined by losses contracted in the service of the late King," and in 1664 he was " 'upon the uttermost

3. C.S.P.D., 1641-1643, p. 373; C.S.P. Venetian, 1642-1643, pp. 135-136.
4. B. M. Harl. MS 1056, f. 15, first cited by H. K. S. Causton, The Howard Papers (London, 1862), p. 507.
5. A deed of 10 November 1657, in the James M. Osborn Collection, Clayton MSS, Yale University; C.S.P.D., 1661-1662, p. 606; C.S.P.D., 1666-1667, p. 58.
6. C.S.P. Venetian, 1640-1642, p. 269; C.S.P.D., 1641-1643, p. 357.

confines of starving' for want of money due to him."[7] He became Earl of Berkshire on his father's death in 1669, and free gifts of £500 in 1669, £1,000 in 1670, and £3,000 in 1673 were ordered to be paid to him;[8] but he died in poverty in the hospital of La Charité in Paris in 1679. (None of his sons survived him, and the title passed to his brother Thomas.)

Another of Berkshire's family, the third son, Henry, won fame for his gallantry as colonel commanding the garrison of Malmesbury after it had been recaptured from the Parliamentary forces; the fifth son, Edward, fought on the Royalist side in the West in 1643.[9] One of the daughters, Lady Mary Howard, was arrested by order of the Council of State in July 1659, on suspicion of being implicated in the somewhat premature plot to restore Charles immediately to the throne (she was even said to have carried to England a Commission from the King and to have negotiated with Lambert); she was kept prisoner in the Tower for at least two weeks.[10] On the day of Lady Mary's arrest President Whitelock also ordered Colonel Okey "to search the house of the Countess of Berkshire, at Charlton, for arms and papers, and if you can find any papers of importance, send them up to Council, and send the Countess."[11] The seventh son, Philip, was also arrested, and released only on a bond of £1,000.[12]

Against this family background of constant endeavor in the Royalist cause, the career of Sir Robert Howard may be seen in the right perspective.

Robert, born in January 1626, was the sixth son of the Earl of Berkshire. He was baptized in St. Martin-in-the-Fields on 19 January;[13] presumably he was named after one of his father's brothers, as four of the older children had been; and the fact that for about twenty-seven years there were thus two Robert Howards and for some

---

7. *C.S.P.D.*, 1648-1649, pp. 147-148, 150-151, 185, 243; *C.S.P.D.*, 1650, pp. 557, 517; *C.T.B.*, 1660-1667, pp. 231, 503; *C.S.P.D.*, 1663-1664, p. 93; 1664-1665, p. 22.

8. *C.T.B.*, 1669-1672, pp. 229, 667, 692; 1672-1675, p. 88.

9. See his *Caroloiades*, 1689, p. 177 n. (Reference from Edward Howard, *The Change of Crownes*, ed. F. S. Boas, London, 1949, p. 1.)

10. Godfrey Davies, *The Restoration of Charles II* (London, 1955), p. 133 n. 62.

11. *C.S.P.D.*, 1659-1660, pp. 48, 50, 158, 189, 194, 230.

12. Davies, *op. cit.*, p. 133.

13. J. L. Chester, ed., *The Marriage, Baptismal, and Burial Registers of the Collegiate Church or Abbey of St. Peter, Westminster* (London, 1876), p. 243.

nine of them two Sir Robert Howards has caused considerable difficulty for historians: the indexes to the Calendars of State Papers, for
example, are hopelessly confused and attribute to the uncle instead
of the nephew even grants made after the former's death in 1653.
The elder Sir Robert, like his sister Frances, won notoriety for the
family because of a love affair, but inasmuch as he, too, was an ardent
Royalist, it was not a name of which the nephew need have been
ashamed as he grew into manhood.[14]

Of the younger Robert's early years there is little record. He was
probably the "Mr. Robert Howard" who appears in a list of "the young
Lords and Noblemens Sonnes" who took part in Carew's masque
Coelum Britannicum on 18 February 1634 (the two sons of the Earl
of Bridgwater who also took part were rather older, being about
twelve and thirteen).[15] Of his university career there is no formal
record whatever at either Cambridge or Oxford; but Venn's attempt
to connect him with Magdalene College, Cambridge, is unconvincing,
although often repeated by later authorities. Anthony à Wood more
plausibly connects him with Magdalen at Oxford, describing Howard
as "of *Magd.* Coll. under the tuition of Dr. *Edw. Drope*, as he himself
used frequently to say; (yet he occurs not matriculated) which, I
presume, was about 1641."[16] His father's association with Oxford and
the fact that his own son Robert matriculated at St. Edmund Hall on
25 November 1663 lend some support to Wood.[17] But he himself
did not graduate, no doubt because of the outbreak of the Civil War,
in which he was soon personally involved; since he is later referred
to with some respect as a classical scholar, he must have built on his
university education by further study.

On Saturday 29 June 1644, according to the manuscript diary of

14. Frances had married Robert Carr, Earl of Somerset, after the infamous
divorce from her first husband, Robert Devereux, Earl of Essex; her brother
had been imprisoned in the Fleet for his romantic liaison with Lady Purbeck.
Details of the legal consequences, and of the elder Sir Robert's conversion to
Catholicism under the influence of Lady Purbeck, are given in (for example)
R. T. Petersson, *Sir Kenelm Digby* (London, 1956), pp. 139-142. The elder
Sir Robert was governor of Bridgnorth Castle when it surrendered in 1646; he
had previously been expelled from the House of Commons; and, of course,
his estates, like his brother's, were sequestered.

15. *The Poems of Thomas Carew*, ed. Rhodes Dunlap (Oxford, 1949), p. 185.

16. *Alumni Cantabrigienses* (Cambridge, 1922), II, 416; *Athenae Oxonienses*
(1721), II, 1018.

17. Cited by H. S. H[oward], *N. & Q.*, CLXXVII (1939), p. 7.

Richard Symonds, "Mr Robt. Howard son to ye Earle of Berks, & Leiften^t Colonel to his brother of horse was knighted for his gallant service ag^t ye rebells [when] we came over ye passe."[18] Clarendon gives an account of this battle in his *History of the Rebellion* but, probably because he so strongly disliked Howard by the time the book was written, he gives the credit for the day's achievements to the Earl of Cleveland, without mentioning Howard once.[19] Other contemporary accounts, such as those by Symonds and by William Sanderson, make the picture clearer. The Parliamentary leader, Waller, sent a body of cavalry (Clarendon says 1,500 strong) to go some distance along the River Cherwell, cross it, and attack the Royalist rearguard. Howard saw the move, and with a successful charge forced the Parliamentary cavalry to recross the river. Howard also rescued Lord Wilmot, who, according to Symonds, had been hit in the arm. Symonds adds that Howard was knighted "neare Banbury in ye feild."[20]

His active share in the warfare must have ended soon afterwards, and the only biographical information for the following ten years concerns his marriage and the births (and deaths) of his children. The parish registers of Church Oakley, Basingstoke, Hants, give the following facts:[21]

1645   "Sr Robert Howard son of ye Earle of Berks and Mrs Anne Kingsmyll second daughter to Sr Richard Kingsmyll of Malshanger [i.e., Malhanger] were married ye first of february 1644" [i.e., 1645]

1646   "Robert Howard sonne of Sir Robert howard was baptized . . . in februarie 1645" [i.e., 1646]

1647   "William Howard sonn of Sr Robert Howard was baptized April"

1649   "Dorothy Howard daughter of Sr Robert Howard was baptized the 6th of July"

1651   "Thomas Howard sonn of Sr Robert Howard was baptized ye twentie first of february 1650" [i.e., 1651]

18. B. M. Add. MS 17062, f. 76. The diary was printed by the Camden Society in 1859, edited by C. E. Long.

19. For Howard's share in the impeachment of Clarendon, see below, pp. 133-136.

20. Sanderson, *A Compleat History of the Life and Raigne of King Charles* (London, 1658); Symonds f. 8. See also F. E. Paget, *Some Records of the Ashtead Estate, and of its Howard Possessors* (Litchfield, 1873)—the account in Appendix 3 by W. H. E. McKnight.

21. Some, only, of the information in the registers has been cited, inaccurately, by Miss Florence R. Scott, "The Marriages of Sir Robert Howard," *M.L.N.*, LV (1940), 411-415.

1653 "Dorothie Howard daughter of Sr Robert Howard was buried ye twentie sixt of December"

1654 "Dorothie Howard daughter of Sr Robert Howard baptized January ye 20"

1656 "Ellizabeth Hooward the daughter of Sir Robert Hooward was buried the 17 daie of August 1656"[22]

In notes about his family and himself, written for Elias Ashmole probably in 1674 or 1675, Thomas Howard wrote that "my second brother was kild at Tangeir."[23] This must mean that William's death was before 1669, because Robert, who died on 23 July in that year, is called by Thomas his "onley" brother, meaning, presumably, the only one surviving at that time. At any rate, Thomas alone survived his father, and that by less than three years (he died on 4 April 1701).

Thomas also told Ashmole that his mother died "about 18 years since"—i.e., in 1657 or thereabouts. Little else is known about her. It is probable, however, that she brought Sir Robert a good jointure on her marriage.[24] Certainly Robert did not share the poverty of other members of the Howard family; on the contrary he was soon in a position to lend his father money. Interestingly, too, forty-four years after this first marriage, and some years after his third wife had died, Howard was still trying to obtain a favor for a kinsman of his first wife; on 25 June 1689 he wrote to "the right Hono^{ble} the Lord Godolphin":

My Lord

my sonne not being well desires mee to beg your Lo^p to continue your Charity to endeavor to gett m^r Henry Kingsmyll A hundred or if you cannot 50 li to releeve his present nescessitys, to which my Lord I am very willinge to adde my humble request havinge soe neer A relation to him.

Ro: Howard[25]

22. These records make it clear that the Mary Howard who was born on 28 December 1653 and died at Rouen in 1735, "Mary of the Holy Cross" and author of *The Chief Points of Our Holy Ceremonies*, cannot have been Sir Robert's daughter. (Many historians of the Howard family have been in error here.) Thomas Howard recorded that his *only* sister (presumably the second Dorothy) died in 1668.

23. Bodleian Ashmole MS 243, f. 273.

24. Her father was assessed by the Committee for Advance of Money at £500 on 25 November 1644, some two months before the wedding, and at £600 on 1 January 1646.

25. P.R.O. Treasury Papers 11, Vol. IV (June-Aug. 1689), No. 18. Here and elsewhere I have followed the modern conventions concerning *u* and *v*. Howard's own use of these letters is quite arbitrary. I have preserved other peculiarities, including the capital "A"—always a feature of his script.

By 1656 or 1657 Howard was able to commence negotiations with the Government for the renewal of the valuable 1625 grant to his father and to Viscount Wallingford, of the lease "of the Post Fines, parcel of the Green Wax, answerable in the Exchequer, for 48 years, at the rent of 2,272 l. 8 s. per annum."[26] Briefly, a Post Fine was a fee paid to the Crown in return for the royal license to levy a fine; the Greenwax, taking its name from the seal of green wax used on documents delivered by the Exchequer to sheriffs, was the fine or amerciment levied by the sheriff under the authority of such document. What Wallingford and Andover had paid £2,272/8/0 a year for, then, was the right to collect in the King's name, through agents, all such fines. Preliminary enquiries concerning the Post Fines were already being made before April, 1656, no doubt in the hope that the Council could be persuaded to grant Berkshire a renewed lease;[27] and on 17 March 1657 the Council considered a report from the Treasury Commissioners "on the Earl of Berkshire's proposals for reforming post fines—that in the 3 years from Michaelmas 1648, the post fines yielded 3,070 l. 3 s. 0 d. a year on an average; that the late King, by lease of 13 Jan. 1640/1, granted all the said profits to the Earl for 31 years, at the rent of 2,275 l.; and that Sir Robert Howard, the Earl's son, has offered for the lease 500 l. yearly more rent"; and the Commissioners were ordered "if they find it to the State's advantage to farm the fines," to "grant the said Earl a new lease, on terms advantageous to the State."[28] The Howards knew that the farming of the Post Fines was worth more than twice as much as the £795 per annum implied in the report of the Treasury Commissioners, and were prepared to bid higher for a renewal of the privilege, if necessary; and in September the Commissioners reported to the Council that "Sir. R. Howard is willing to advance the yearly rent of 2,275 l. to 3000 l., if the Earl may have a grant of all the post fines for the rest of the term hitherto granted"; and Oliver Cromwell in person ordered that the tender should be accepted.[29] Since Berkshire's share of the cost of obtaining the grant was agreed to be £393/16/3, it would seem that what we should call bribery was certainly involved.[30]

26. *C.S.P.D.*, 1625-1626, p. 537. Other documents give the rent as £2,276/8/0.
27. *Cal. Proc. Comm. Ad. Mon.*, 1642-1656, I, 640, III, 1388.
28. *C.S.P.D.*, 1656-1657, p. 313.
29. *C.S.P.D.*, 1657-1658, pp. 93-94.
30. Deed of 10 November 1657, Osborn MSS, Yale.

That Sir Robert's own interest in these negotiations was not purely filial is suggested by a number of deeds in which father and son (or their representatives) made formal financial arrangements about the proceeds. In an indenture of 1 September 1656 Berkshire first agreed that Robert should arrange for the new lease of the Post Fines on the understanding that one-third of the profit was to be Robert's for undertaking the negotiations for renewal; Berkshire was to be paid either two-thirds of the profit after the costs had been deducted or £1,000 a year, in either case less £100 a year for three years as repayment for £300 which Robert had lent to his father in advance.[31] The transactions added considerably to the son's wealth, but in less than two years the father, through incautious borrowing and acceptance of dangerous legal conditions, had transferred all his rights to Robert Abbott, for only £1440 in cash.[32]

The story of Robert Abbott, whose name appears prominently in these negotiations, is told by Evelyn, years later, in his diary. Abbott was a noted Royalist "one who was condemn'd to die (but escaped) at the beginning of the Troubles 40 years past, as concerned in the Commission of Aray, for K. Char[les] I",[33] as Evelyn noted in 1679, referring to Abbott's part in Waller's plot of 1643; and it may well have been because of their common interest in restoring the King that he and Howard first met. He was also a wealthy "scrivenor" or financier: "I often used his assistance in mony matters," adds Evelyn, calling him "an honnest worthy man." Abbott's wealth was inherited in 1658 by his nephew and apprentice Robert Clayton (1629-1707), later to become Sir Robert and Lord Mayor of London (1679-1680), and also to figure in the Howard story. Evelyn relates how, on Abbott's death, Clayton became "so prodigiously rich & opulent, that he was reckoned one of the welthiest Citizens." The wealth was further added to when Clayton inherited the estate of his fellow apprentice and later partner, John Morris (whose name also enters the Howard story); and Evelyn refers more than once to Clayton's magnificent homes in the City and at Morden and relates how he took the Countess of Sutherland to dine at Clayton's home in 1679 while he was Lord Mayor, "that she might see the pomp & ceremonie of this Prince of

31. Osborn MSS, Yale.
32. Indentures of 10 November 1657 (with memoranda) and 27 May 1658, Osborn MSS, Yale.
33. *The Diary of John Evelyn*, ed. E. S. de Beer (Oxford, 1955), IV, 186.

Citizens, there never having ben any, who for the statlinesse of his Palace, prodigious feasting & magnificence exceeded him."[34] Evelyn adds that Clayton was suspected of "hard-dealing, especialy with the Duke of *Buckingham*, much of whose estate he had swallow'd: but I never saw any ill by him, considering the trade he was off: The reputation, & known integrity of his Unkle Abbot, brought all the Royal party to him, by which he got not onely greate credite, but vast riches; so as he passed this Office with infinite magnificence & honor."

It was, then, through Abbott and later Clayton and Morris that Howard negotiated the cash advances for his father on the Post Fines; but the frequency and the informal nature of their correspondence make it seem probable that the relations were not merely of principal and client and that it was through his association with these wealthy scriveners that Howard himself came to play a part in the financial affairs of the kingdom, perhaps gaining the experience that made him better qualified than has sometimes been thought for his later position as Auditor of the Receipt in the Exchequer.

It is also interesting to find Howard connected with such noted Royalists in the years before the Restoration; and in view of this, and his family's loyalty, it is not surprising that, although the Council had granted him a sympathetic hearing when he approached them for a renewal of a financial arrangement not disadvantageous to the State, he was still under suspicion; and in 1657 or 1658 he was arrested and imprisoned. The evidence is in the Preface "To the Reader" of Howard's *Poems*, published in 1660. Referring particularly to the "Panegyrick to the King," which is the first poem in the collection, Howard says that: "It was written when the King deserved the Praise as much as now, but separated farther from the Power; which was about three years since, when I was Prisoner in *Windsor-Castle*, being the best diversion I could then find for my own condition; to think, how great his Vertues were for whom I suffered, though in so small a measure compar'd to his own, that I rather blush at it, than believe it meritorious."[35] The exact date of the imprisonment is not known: it may well have been in 1658 when many suspected Royalists were taken into custody as the death of Cromwell appeared imminent and when the leading Royalist John Mordaunt was brought to trial for treason and escaped conviction only on the casting vote of the President of the

34. *Ibid.*, IV, 185. 35. *Poems* (1660), sig. A3^v.

High Court of Justice.[36] From the fact that Howard was able to spend his time writing verse, it would seem that the imprisonment was not unduly severe; but that it was justified is suggested not only by the story of the continuing Royalist activities of the Howard family, but also by a letter from Robert to John Mordaunt dated June, 1659. Mordaunt was in direct correspondence with Charles II at the time and was leader of the "Trust" in England empowered to negotiate for his return. A transcript of Howard's letter reads:

1. I shall in London expect youre returne!

2. Hitherto all my proceedings doe more then answer my expectations, especially the businesse in Staffordshire; which by my friend there, is grown to a considerable greatnesse.[37]

3. At your return, I shall dispose of my self as the king's interest will best require mee. I only desire you, that a right use may be made of the distractions they are in here. Their own ruines, which is visible before them, may invite them, more then their consciences, to think of an accommodation; the managing of which is to put our selves in a capacity to enforce more then perhaps they entend; so that if they meane no deceit, wee are not lesse capable of judging; and their falsnesse will not have much power, if wee prepare in the worst expectation; and wee shall never have so free leave againe to arme our selves. But, without dispute, the King must at first appeare in person. Where that shall bee, I shall advise with you when you come, that wee may in the safest way hazzard him that is our all."[38]

A man may always sincerely believe that he is more influential in inner councils than, in fact, he is; but this letter—written during the confused days of the Rump Parliament at the time when the Royal return was planned for as early as July (1659)—reads like that of a trusted man of some importance who has been sounding public opinion, is in a position to offer good advice concerning the time to act and the method, is prepared once again to take arms if necessary on behalf of the King, and can safely assume that he will be listened to when he discusses the movements of the King himself.

In short, when the King did return to London at the end of May in 1660, Sir Robert had every reason to believe that a new day had dawned for England, and for the Howard family in particular.

36. Davies, *Restoration of Charles II*, p. 125.

37. The "friend" may well have been Sir Charles Wolseley, who undertook to bring Staffordshire under the Royal banner. See Davies, *op. cit.*, p. 130.

38. *H.M.C.*, 10th Report, part VI, Peck MSS, p. 210.

BEFORE the King's return, Howard was preparing for publication a collection of the poems that he had been composing for the past three years or more. The volume was entered on the Stationers' Register on 16 April 1660 and must have been published soon afterwards, for in June it was being advertised in *Mercurius Publicus*.[1] The title-page reads:

POEMS,

viz.

1. A PANEGYRICK to the KING.
2. SONGS and SONNETS.
3. THE BLIND LADY, a COMEDY.
4. The Fourth Book of VIRGIL,
5. STATIUS his ACHILLEIS,
   with ANNOTATIONS.
6. A PANEGYRICK to GENERALL MONCK.

By the Honorable
Sʳ ROBERT HOWARD.

The publisher was Henry Herringman, who brought out John Dryden's "Astræa Redux" in the same year (having printed his "Heroique Stanzas" in 1659) and with whom Dryden was probably living at the time.[2]

The Preface "To the Reader" was not of the kind most likely to stifle adverse criticism, for Howard began by decrying "the usuall custom" of alleging that a volume was published only at the insistence of friends—and went on to assert that his poems were published only at the insistence of his bookseller: "I had not stock of confidence enough to shew these things privately to many friends, much lesse to be furnish'd with enough, to make them publick to all indifferent persons, had not the desires of the Book-seller prevail'd with me: to whose civilities I believ'd my self so far engag'd, as to deny him nothing that he thought a kindnesse, which could not be severely prejudiciall to my self: Yet I doubted not, but that I should receive the censures of many." Even if Howard was in fact already on friendly

1. Sybil Rosenfeld, "Dramatic Advertisements in the Burney Newspapers," *P.M.L.A.*, LI (1936), 123-152; J. M. Osborn, *John Dryden: Some Biographical Facts and Problems* (N.Y., 1940), p. 171.
2. *The Medal of John Bayes.* See below, p. 65.

terms with Herringman—and in view of the close relationship of each with Dryden this is quite probable—his preface could easily have begun in a more winning tone. "Yet," he proceeded, "I wish that it may so far give satisfaction to all, that they may as little repent the reading, as I did the writing; whilst in these gentle studies I found a diversion from greater follies."

He went on to explain, that "two or three copies of Verses onely excepted" all the poems had "layn by me these many years" and that all would have been put aside, now that he was older and wiser, had it not been for the bookseller's request; but he hoped that a poem in praise of the King would "be received willingly by all, since . . . man's largest invention has been excell'd by His actions," although he would have hesitated to print the panegyric had it not been clear to the reader that it was written earlier, in fact "about three years since, when I was Prisoner in *Windsor-Castle*, being the best diversion I could then find for my own condition; to think, how great his Vertues were for whom I suffered, though in so small a measure compar'd to his own, that I rather blush at it, than believe it meritorious."

Howard's "Panegyrick to the King" also provided Dryden with a key for his complimentary verses "To my Honored Friend, Sr Robert Howard, On his Excellent Poems" (lines which were reprinted, with minor variations of spelling and punctuation, in the 1693 *Poems on Several Occasions*). Forcing his logic but adapting his compliment both to Howard and to the times, Dryden wrote that

> Of Morall Knowledge Poesie was Queen,
> And still she might, had wanton wits not been. . . .
> Like some brave Captain, your successful Pen
> Restores the Exil'd to her Crown again;
> And gives us hope, that having seen the days
> When nothing flourish'd but Fanatique Bays,
> All will at length in this opinion rest,
> "A sober Prince's Government is best.

Then, after commending Howard as translator, Dryden hailed him as a prophet, since he both foretold the greatness of Charles II and ended his volume with the "Panegyrick to Generall Monck":

> But to write worthy things of worthy men
> Is the peculiar talent of your Pen:
> Yet let me take your Mantle up, and I
> Will venture in your right to prophesy.

"This Work by merit first of Fame secure
"Is likewise happy in its Geniture:
"For since 'tis born when *Charls* ascends the Throne,
"It shares at once his Fortune and its own.

Already Dryden was showing his Jonsonian art of adapting the tribute to the receiver; even if the compliment was not deserved, it was, on the whole, neatly paid.

In fact Howard's "Panegyrick to the King" lacks even the fluency that Dryden attributed to it. The phrasing is contorted; word order is twisted to fit the sense into the couplet; and the constant striving for epigram produces some odd results:

> To fair days, storms succeed; to storms, the fair:
> We know but what we are by what we were.
> And Mans condition's valu'd more or lesse,
> By what he had, not what he does possesse

—which, as Euclid might have remarked, is absurd. The poem tries to develop the contrast between the great virtues of the King and his ill fortunes (and England's) and argues that misfortune has made Charles seem only firmer, brighter, and more "refin'd"; he is compared to the bright sun about to burst through the clouds (an obvious metaphor that Dryden also had used in his poem on the Restoration, "Astræa Redux"). But it is with ingenuity that Howard explains away Charles's failure in an earlier attempt to regain his kingdom, "Comming in with the *Scots*, who were before Conquer'd by the *English* at *Dunbar*" (as the footnote makes clear):

> Once for your Kingdome's sake you durst oppose
> Your Laurel'd Enemies with your conquer'd foes.
> Yet Heaven from your assistance then was staid,
> Lest the ill Act the good had over-weigh'd;
> And in the Victory those *Scots* had found
> Their Crimes together with your Vertues crown'd.

He adds that the English although victorious suffered most; indeed they hardly know how great their sufferings are, so blunted are their faculties. They can only blame each other, and civil dissension is inevitable, until the King is restored:

> Thus the great Power of all, having first chose
> To make your Vertues great and safe by Woes,
> Will, by as unexpected ways, restore
> Your ravish'd Crowns, as they were lost before.

The poem has, then, the virtue of trying to base its prediction of the King's restoration on what the poet's judgment of the political situation tells him to be probable; and the conclusion has the merit of returning to the theme of the opening lines, the idea that the King's present and past distresses are the best guarantee of his future successful reign. Even if the reasoning is sometimes specious, one might say that the poet has his eye on the poetic subject. The obvious comparison is with Dryden's "Astræa Redux"; and it is only fair to Howard to point out that his poem is free from the worst excesses of Dryden's, such as

> The joyful *London* meets
> The Princely *York*, himself alone a freight;
> The *Swift-sure* groans beneath great *Glouc'sters* weight

or, of the month of May,

> A month that owns an Interest in your Name:
> You and the Flow'rs are its peculiar Claim

(and similar absurdities recur in Dryden's "To His Sacred Majesty, a Panegyrick on His Coronation" in 1661). It is also true, of course, that the artistry of Dryden's crescendo in the final stanzas of "Astræa Redux," with the repeated personal pronouns and the climax on the word "*You*," was—and was to remain—quite beyond Howard's poetic range.

The "Panegyrick to Generall Monck" which ends the volume is briefer than the "Panegyrick to the King" but is of exactly the same order of poetic merit. It also is in heroic couplets; and again Howard tries to achieve the epigrammatic force to which the couplet is perhaps best adapted. He does succeed, albeit a little clumsily, in stating an interesting theme:

> 'Tis not your pow'r, that has inspir'd my muse,
> T'were mean to praise that which you scorn to use.
> 'Tis that above the reach of pow'r in you
> I praise, Victorious over Conquest too.
>   Yet you more truly glorious will appear,
> To dispose Scepters, than you could to wear.
> For ravish't Crowns are still another's due,
> But thus bestow'd, they are all ow'd to you.

This theme, however, he is quite unable to develop. He can only restate it, comparing Monk's action in restoring the King, with Neptune's when he calmed the waves to assist the journey of Aeneas (Lambert even becomes "that Wave which to the vastest swelling rose"); and so, through tributes to Monk's ancestry and the reasonable claim that only a man of Monk's particular temper could have managed the restoration so well and without bloodshed, Howard comes to his trite climax of the comparison of Monk also to the rising sun which, he alleges, seems at first hardly to move but nevertheless shines and warms:

> May you still shine, as now at your full height,
> Till you to greater glory passe through fate.
> You that a KING a Scepter gave to sway,
> And taught rebellious Subjects to obey;

(and the poem and the volume do thus end, not with a bang but with a semicolon).

Of the second section of his volume, the "Songs and Sonnets," Howard wrote in his Preface: "I must professe they were never directed to any particular Beauty, which may (to the Amorous Reader at least) be a just excuse, if they want Perfection, to remember I wanted Passion, and had onely my own warmth, unassisted by the influence of a Mistresse. Nor shall I envy him that writes better, by being much in love, if he must purchase the advantage of Wit by the losse of Freedom." This declaration that one's love verses were not sincerely felt but were only a poetic exercise is strange to modern ears, but it was conventional in the seventeenth century—had, indeed, been so ever since Thomas Watson's similar disclaimer in his *Hecatompathia* (1582), the first of the Elizabethan sonnet sequences.[3] Howard's disavowal of personal experience is no doubt little more than a continuation of the Cavalier tradition, that poetry was something a gentleman wrote casually; to take either love or poetry seriously was beneath aristocratic dignity.

A little of the Cavalier grace remains in the best of Howard's lyrics, but on the whole they are not distinguished for originality of phrasing or of sentiment. The eighteenth-century anthologist George Ellis, whose *Specimens of the Early English Poets* (1790, and often reprinted) shows him to have been a good judge of the poetry of the later seventeenth century, chose to represent Howard by stanzas from two songs which are Howard's closest approximation to the manner

3. Compare Dr. Johnson's comment on Cowley's *The Mistress*, in *Lives of the Poets* (World's Classics edition, 1938, I, 35).

of such better poets of a slightly later time as Rochester, Sedley and Dorset. The first is "To the unconstant Cynthia. A Song":

> Tell me once, Dear, how it does prove
> That I so much forsworn could be?
> I never swore always to love,
> I onely vow'd still to love thee:
>   And art thou now what thou wert then?
>   Unsworn unto by other men?
>
> In thy fair Breast, and once-fair Soul,
> I thought my Vows were writ alone;
> But others Oaths so blurr'd the Scrole,
> That I no more could read my own.
>   And am I still oblig'd to pay,
>   When you had thrown the Bond away?
>
> Nor must we onely part in Joy,
> Our tears as well must be unkind:
> Weep you, that could such truth destroy;
> And I, that could such falseness find.
>   Thus we must unconcern'd remain
>   In our divided Joys and Pain.
>
> Yet we may love, but on this diff'rent score,
> You what I am, I what you were before.

There are weaknesses of expression (notably in the second line of the third stanza, which doesn't say exactly what Howard means); but the fashionable paradox is neatly stated and the words are admirably calculated for singing. That these are mostly "songs" in the narrower sense is proved by the title of one of them "Song at Amaranta's Command, set to the Tune of 'Archibella'" and by the fact that at least two of the others are found in contemporary song-books, with their musical settings. "The Opinion" ("Long have I thought,/It was in vain") is in *Catch that Catch can: or The Musical Companion* (1667), set to music by Henry Cooke; and "Amaranta, to the God of Love" ("Ah, mighty Love, what power unknown") is in *Select Ayres and Dialogues* (1669), set by no less an artist than Henry Lawes.[4] There is evidence that Howard continued to write songs for music until near the end of his life.[5]

4. Day and Murrie list these songs in their *English Song-Books 1651-1702* (Bibliographical Society, London, 1940 for 1937) but are unaware of Howard's authorship.

5. See below pp. 137 and 302. Day and Murrie also list (No. 3747) a song

In the second lyric chosen for Ellis's collection, "The Resolution," ("No *Cynthia,* never think I can / Love a divided heart and mind") there is less to admire: it is not so much that the poem has many faults as that it lacks any real poetic virtues. Rochester would have made the same point in one third of the number of lines, in words that would have put Cynthia more firmly in her place and would have been memorable for at least one unexpected (and perhaps shocking) image.

There are fifteen lyrics in this section of the *Poems.* Five are addressed to Amaranta, four to Cynthia, and one to Celia; and of these ten, only two others are worthy of further comment. "To Amaranta. The Fate of Scorn" arouses a mild interest by its reminder to the scornful mistress that an aging soldier "preserves his fame, / Not by those wounds he gave, but those he bears," and the second of the poems "To the unconstant Cynthia" contains one or two credit-able couplets, such as the one summarizing the lover's refusal to regret a mistress who has been unfaithful:

> Yet sure I meant not long to sit about
> The ashes, when the fire was quite burnt out

and the final request

> Then blush not that you quench'd this am'rous flame,
> But blush with me, if we two love again.

Of the remaining five, two are undistinguished love songs of the same kind; one is in the conventional "dialogue" form, being a conversa-tion between Thirsis and Charon concerning the fate of lovers and their mistresses in Hades (it reaches a conventional conclusion, but holds attention by the briskness of the interchange); and the other two are complimentary verses, not good enough to remember but no doubt competent enough to give pleasure to the ladies to whom they were addressed.

Of Howard as a lyric poet, then, the most that could be said would be that he had skill in writing verses for music but that he was wise in not devoting much of the space in this volume of his collected poems to the lighter trifles of this kind.[6]

"When I drink my heart is possessed," music by John Blow and words at-tributed to Howard, in *The Theater of Music* (1667) and subsequent collections.

6. The poems in B.M. Add. MS 38001, once attributed to Howard, can no longer be claimed for him; earlier scholars were misled by the portrait bound

Almost half the volume is in fact taken up by his translations, of Virgil and Statius. Of the Virgil he was apologetic in his Preface, where he explained that he had published only one book (the Fourth), "not judging it convenient to perfect those other Books of his *Æneid's*, which I have rudely gone through, having long since laid aside all designes of that nature; and this little of it rather grew publick from accident, than designe, the Mingle it had with my private Papers, was the greatest cause, that it received its share in the publick Impression." Yet for this Dryden reserved perhaps his neatest compliment, when he wrote in his commendatory verses that

> *Elisa's* griefs, are so exprest by you,
> They are too eloquent to have been true.
> Had she so spoke, *Æneas* had obey'd
> What *Dido* rather then what *Jove* had said.
> If funerall Rites can give a Ghost repose,
> Your Muse so justly has discharged those.
> *Elisa's* shade may now its wandring cease,
> And claim a title to the fields of peace.

It is now known that when Dryden came to make his own translation of Virgil (1697), he kept his eye on earlier English verse translations, "particularly those that were written in heroic couplets" and from them "often took rhymes, stray phrases, even whole lines and passages."[7] A more recent critic puts it more strongly still: "Dryden's procedure is intelligible only if we presume that he was seeking a definitive version, constantly embodying in his own work what he thought had been well done, and constantly measuring himself against the best version he could find of any given passage."[8] From Howard, however, Dryden borrowed only one or two phrases and perhaps an occasional rhyme—but a certain similarity is inevitable when two poets are translating a Latin author into the poetic idiom of a particular period, and some of the rhymes are found in other seventeenth-century translations as well.

In spite of his complimentary verses, then, Dryden probably had no high opinion of Howard's translation. He failed to mention it in the

---

up with the manuscript (and it was even claimed that the corrections were in the hand of Dryden).

7. J. M. J. Bottkol, "Dryden's Latin Scholarship," *Modern Philology*, XL. (1943), 243. Mr. Bottkol does not, however, mention Howard's translation.

8. L. Proudfoot, *Dryden's 'Aeneid' and its Seventeenth Century Predecessors* (Manchester, 1960), p. 267.

long Dedication to his own translation of the *Æneid*, addressed to the
Earl of Mulgrave, though he did admit that "Some of our Country-
men have translated Episodes, and other parts of *Virgil*, with great
success" and added that "'tis the utmost of my Ambition to be
thought" the equal of Denham, Waller, and Cowley, "or not to be
much inferiour to them, and some others of the Living." Nor did he
make any amends at all—although he obviously intended to do so—
when he added to his notes on the *sixth* book of the *Æneid* the comment "Sir *Robert Howard* in his Translation of this *Æneid*, which was
Printed with his Poems in the Year 1660; has given us the most
Learned, and the most Judicious Observations on this Book, which are
extant in our Language."[9] As if it were not enough to say that Howard
translated the sixth book when in fact he translated the fourth, Dryden has obviously confused the Virgil, on which there are no notes,
with the annotations on the Statius! Perhaps it was just as well that
Howard was then old and too near death to worry about his brother-
in-law's well-intentioned blundering.

Howard does, however, receive one mention in Dryden's preface.
Dryden writes: "Of his [Jupiter's] power to deferr the blow [which
killed Pallas], I once occasionally discours'd with that Excellent Person Sir *Robert Howard*, who is better conversant than any Man I know,
in the Doctrine of the Stoicks, and he set me right; from the concurrent testimony of Philosophers and Poets, that *Jupiter* cou'd not
retard the effects of Fate, even for a moment. For when I cited *Virgil*
as favoring the contrary opinion in that Verse,

> *Tolle fugâ Turnum, atq; instantibus eripe fatis.*

He reply'd, and I think, with an exact Judgment, that when *Jupiter*
gave *Juno* leave to withdraw *Turnus* from the present danger, it was
because he certainly fore-knew that his Fatal hour was not come: that
it was in Destiny for *Juno* at that time to save him; and that he himself obey'd Destiny, in giving her that leave."[10] These words, written
when Howard and Dryden were both old, apparently refer rather to
the years of their intimacy around 1663 than to the period when
Howard was translating Virgil. To the relevant lines of his translation, X. 661-663, where Jove is made to say:

9. *The Works of Virgil* (1697), sig. (e)3; p. 631.
10. *Ibid.*, sig. (c)1ʳ.

My own *Sarpedon* fell beneath his Foe,
Nor I, his mighty Sire, cou'd ward the Blow.
Ev'n *Turnus* shortly shall resign his Breath . . .

Dryden has added a note: "I have mention'd this Passage in my Preface to the *Æneis*; to prove, that Fate was superior to the Gods . . . Sir *Robert Howard* has since, been pleas'd to send me the concurrent Testimony of *Ovid*; 'tis in the last Book of the Metamorphoses";[11] and this obviously refers to the period just before 1697. Dryden's tributes to his brother-in-law's classical knowledge give further reason for believing that Howard had more than the usual familiarity with Roman literature and philosophy.

Howard's own translation of Book IV of the *Æneid* is both original (making little, if any, use of the earlier seventeenth-century versions) and reasonably accurate (even if, more than Dryden, perhaps, he tends to sidestep the difficulties presented by single words); it is also readable. Nevertheless it inevitably suffers in comparison with Dryden's own; Book IV was one of those in which Dryden humbly thought that he had "succeeded best."[12] The difference becomes apparent in the first few lines, when Virgil's

cum sic unanimam adloquitur male sana sororem

is rendered less than adequately by Howard as

The Love-sick Queen thus to her Sister said (p. 142)

and is slightly expanded by Dryden into the more satisfactory but still incomplete

Her Sister first, with early Care she sought,
And thus in mournful Accents eas'd her Thought.   (ll. 9-10)

Dryden continues to elaborate in his translation of Dido's ensuing speech. Howard's version of this is:

My *Anna*, of what dreams am I afraid?
What guest is this with unaccustom'd charms?
How noble in his Soul? how brave in Arms?
I think (nor vainly) he's of heavenly kind;
'Tis fear that argues a degenerate mind.
What various fates he told, with Battles mixt!
Were it not in my breast for ever fix'd,
Never the Marriage Fetters more to prove,

11. *Ibid.*, p. 637.   12. *Ibid.*, sig. (e)3ᵛ.

Since so deceiv'd by fate of my first Love;
Did I not loath those Rites a second time,
I might perhaps yield to this tempting crime.
For I confess, since (slain by fratricide)
Sichæus fell, whose blood the Altars di'd,
This onely has enclin'd my thoughts; again
I feel impressions of an antient flame.
But may the earth first snatch me to her womb,
And to the shades *Jove*'s Thunder whirle me down;
To Hell's dark shades whose night admits no fate,
E're shame and vertues rites I violate.
He who first made my heart Love's sacrifice,
Still has it, in his grave it buried lies.   (p. 142)

Dryden's translation (29 lines as against the 21 of Howard and the
Latin) is:

My dearest *Anna*, what new Dreams affright
My lab'ring Soul; what Visions of the Night
Disturb my Quiet, and distract my Breast,
With strange Ideas of our *Trojan* Guest?
His Worth, his Actions, and Majestick Air,
A Man descended from the Gods declare:
Fear never harbours in a Noble Mind,
But Modesty, with just Assurance join'd.
Then, what he suffer'd, when by Fate betray'd,
What brave Attempts for falling *Troy* he made!
Such were his Looks, so gracefully he spoke,
That were I not resolv'd against the Yoke
Of hapless Marriage; never to be curs'd
With second Love, so fatal was my first;
To this one Error I might yield again:
For since *Sichæus* was untimely slain,
This onely Man, is able to subvert
The fix'd Foundations of my stubborn Heart.
And to confess my Frailty, to my shame, ⎫
Somewhat I find within, if not the same, ⎬
Too like the Sparkles of my former Flame. ⎭
   But first let yawning Earth a Passage rend;
And let me through the dark Abyss descend;
First let avenging *Jove*, with Flames from high, ⎫
Drive down this Body, to the neather Sky, ⎬
Condemn'd with Ghosts in endless Night to lye; ⎭
Before I break the plighted Faith I gave; ⎫
No; he who had my Vows, shall ever have; ⎬
For whom I lov'd on Earth, I worship in the Grave. ⎭ (ll. 11-39)

Both versions occasionally fall flat (Dryden's most notably in the unnecessary "Somewhat I find within, *if not the same*, / Too like the Sparkles of my former Flame") but Howard's more often does so. It is difficult even to make sense of his "Hell's dark shades whose night admits no fate"; and "What various fates he told, with Battles *mixt*" is almost ludicrous. Again, while not even Dryden can quite rise to the superb final words of the Latin, "ille habeat secum servetque sepulchro," it is a sound poetic instinct that leads him to make "Grave" the final word and give it a special stress because it completes the triple rhyme. One understands why he said "I have endeavor'd to follow the Example of my Master: And am the first *Englishman*, perhaps, who made it his design to copy him in his Numbers, his choice of Words, and his placing them for the sweetness of the sound."[13] Yet in all justice we must admit that Howard's version is closer to the *meaning* of the Latin and that many of his faults arise from an attempt, probably mistaken, to translate the Latin line by line. (Dryden himself, on rereading, apparently preferred one of Howard's lines to his own, for in the second edition of his *Virgil*, in 1698, in which he made very few alterations, he changed lines 17-18 to read:

> Fear ever argues a degenerate kind,
> His Birth is well asserted by his Mind.)

Another revealing example of the difference between the two English poets is provided by their versions of Virgil's famous lines (78-79)

> Iliacosque iterum demens audire labores
> exposcit, pendetque iterum narrantis ab ore.

Howard writes:

> Again (distracted) asks to hear *Troy*'s fate,
> And on his moving lips her eyes still wait   (p. 144),

Dryden:

> Still on his Face she feeds her famish'd sight;
> She longs again to hear the Prince relate
> His own Adventures, and the *Trojan* Fate:
> He tells it o're and o're; but still in vain;
> For still she begs to hear it, once again.
> The Hearer on the Speaker's Mouth depends,
> And thus the Tragick Story never ends.   (ll. 108-114)

13. *Ibid.*, sig. (e)1.

That the *total effect* of the Dryden lines is the better need hardly be
questioned; but this effect is gained only by liberal paraphrase and is
justified only by Dryden's professed aim "I have endeavour'd to make
Virgil speak such English, as he wou'd himself have spoken, if he had
been born in *England*, and in this present Age."[14] Howard keeps his
eye firmly on the Latin; and his image, if not exactly that of the Latin
"pendet ab ore," is as vivid as, and perhaps expressed in more idio-
matic English than, Dryden's penultimate line.

Sometimes, to be sure, Howard simply omits important words of
the Latin. Virgil's description of Dido's suicide

> dixerat; atque illam media inter talia ferro
> collapsam aspiciunt comites, ensemque cruore
> spumantem, sparsasque manus   (ll. 663-665)

is rendered, with restraint but inadequately, as

> This said, she thrust the sword into her breast,
> And flowing blood the wretched act exprest.   (p. 167)

Dryden does try to reproduce each detail in the original but perhaps
comes unduly close to bathos in the final line as a result:

> She said, and struck; Deep enter'd in her side
> The piercing Steel, with reeking Purple dy'd:
> Clog'd in the Wound the cruel Weapon stands;
> The spouting Blood came streaming on her Hands.   (ll. 951-954)

One notices also that it is Dryden (writing, of course, nearly forty
years later) who is the more inclined to "poetic diction" of the kind
that has unfortunate connotations for a modern reader lacking the
historical sense. So Iarbas' bitter complaint to Jove about the success
of Æneas with Dido:

> et nunc ille Paris, cum semiviro comitatu,
> Maeonia mentum mitra crinemque madentem
> subnixus,[15] rapto potitur: nos munera templis
> quippe tuis ferimus, famamque fovemus inanem   (ll. 215-218)

appears in Dryden as:

> And now this other *Paris*, with his Train
> Of conquer'd Cowards, must in *Affrick* reign!
> (Whom, what they are, their Looks and Garb confess;
> Their Locks with Oil perfum'd, their *Lydian* dress:)

14. *Ibid.*, sig. (f)1.   15. "Subnexus" is the reading of some editions.

He takes the Spoil, enjoys the Princely Dame;
And I, rejected I, adore an empty Name.   (ll. 314-319)

Howard's version reproduces the scorn of the original just as well, and
has the merit of not sounding "poetic" in the wrong sense of that
word:

This *Paris* with his troope that scarsly are
Like men, in their soft robes and perfum'd hair,
Enjoys my passion's object, whilst we raise
In vain to thee our offerings and our praise.   (p. 150)

One could perhaps sum up Howard's translation of Book IV of
the *Æneid* by saying that he has made a reasonably conscientious attempt to render Virgil's Latin in English heroic couplets and has set
himself an impossible task by allowing normally only one English
iambic pentameter to give the full meaning and the poetic implications
of each Latin hexameter (and those hexameters the work of a poet
noted for succinctness). At its worst Howard's language is bathetic,
and many a colorful phrase in the Latin remains untranslated or is
mistranslated, or leads to an English line that hardly makes sense, as
when Dido's call on Hecate:

nocturnisque Hecate triviis ululata per urbes   (l. 609)

is paraphrased, inaccurately:

and *Hecate*, whose howls fills night and wayes.[16]

Noticeably Howard is not successful in lending dignity to Æneas'
answers to Dido:

At length replies, Fair Queen, I cann't deny
Your words or merits, nor shall ever I
Unwillingly admit *Eliza*'s name
Unto my thoughts, whilst life inspires this frame. . . .
                         (p. 154, Virgil ll. 333-336)

16. P. 165. Dryden's version of this line, "Thou *Hecat*, hearken from thy
dark abodes" (l. 875), has been defended by William Frost on the not fully
convincing reasoning that it "achieves a rapidity appropriate to the feverish speech
of the love-tormented queen, a rapidity doubtless impossible had the full sense
of 'nocturnisque', etc., been given. Here Dryden imitates less what Vergil actually said than the fact that he said it in *lines*" (*Dryden and the Art of Translation*, New Haven, 1955, p. 52). As I have shown, Howard is more entitled
to this defense—if it is one—than is Dryden, whose translations are often better
precisely because he will sometimes take two or more lines to render one of
Virgil's.

But he does catch something of the pathos of her speeches to him:

> For thee, my early and unspotted fame
> Is lost, which once to Heaven bore my name.
> To what am I now dying left? Ah guest,
> In that, all *Hymen*'s Titles now must rest.
> But why do I delay? Is it to see
> My Brother ruine all? or till I be
> Led captive by *Hyarbas*? If I might
> Have had a young *Æneas* ere thy flight . . .
>
> (p. 154, Virgil ll. 321-329)

The run-on lines and the variations in the placing of the accent do achieve the illusion of genuine emotion, even if the finest poetic effects are beyond Howard. Dryden was not being a hypocrite when he found something to admire in passages such as these.

Of his translation of Statius' unfinished *Achilleid*, Howard wrote in the preface to the *Poems*: "For this piece of his, I confesse I chose it as most pleasing to me," adding that "there wants not ingenious men who preferr'd it before his other Poems." Then, self-consciously referring to the lengthy prose notes which follow each of the five "Books" of his Statius translation,[17] he goes on: "The *Annotations* may in some places perhaps be judged too large; yet, had I omitted any thing, it is probable that the same persons would have censur'd me for ignorance: so that being equally sensible of these extreams, I judg'd it the testimony of the greatest modesty, By omitting little, to shew my self not at all secure in the world's opinion."

Dryden, in his Complimentary verses, also divided his attention between the translation itself and the Notes:

> But if *Æneas* be oblig'd, no lesse
> Your kindnesse great *Achilles* doth confesse,
> Who dress'd by *Statius* in too bold a look,
> Did ill become those Virgin's Robes he took.
> To understand how much we owe to you,
> We must your Numbers with your Author's view;
> Then we shall see his work was lamely rough,
> Each figure stiffe as if design'd in buffe;
> His colours laid so thick on every place,
> As onely shew'd the paint, but hid the face:

17. Howard was working from an edition which, based on one of the later Statius manuscripts, divided Book I into four "Books"; it also included some additional lines of doubtful authenticity.

> But as in Perspective we Beauties see,
> Which in the Glasse, not in the Picture be;
> So here our sight obligeingly mistakes
> That wealth which his your bounty onely makes.
> Thus vulgar dishes are by Cooks disguis'd,
> More for their dressing than their substance priz'd.
> Your curious Notes so search into that Age,
> When all was fable but the sacred Page,
> That since in that dark night we needs must stray,
> We are at least misled in pleasant way

—and the context forbids one to see any sly ambiguity in Dryden's "misled," tempting as such an interpretation may be.

Howard's notes, which are not unlike those in many modern school editions of Greek and Latin texts, provide further evidence of his classical knowledge, even if they are open, as he himself suspected, to the charge of being overfull and pretentious. He takes the opportunity of translating into English verse other Latin and also Greek poetry, and makes a great parade of authorities (he leans particularly on the learned Selden). He similarly shows a tendency to pronounce confidently on any subject that comes up—a tendency that was later to lead to Shadwell's amusing caricature of him as "Sir Positive At-All." So, after producing some evidence of the pagan belief in the enviousness of God, he adds: "I forbear to produce further Testimonies, to prove, there was such an opinion among the Heathen, I do not think them needfull; since it is certain, the Devill would let slip no occasion of raising prejudice against God, and charging him with his own crime" (p. 201); perhaps there is also a notable lack of humor in the conclusion of a discussion on the possibility of "Beasts having copulation with Women," when, after referring to Suetonius and to Leviticus, he adds: "Besides, if it be possible, we need no farther proof than the unsatiable nature of some women" (p. 208). On the other hand, Howard is to be commended for his understanding that Greek myths need not be taken literally and for his attempts to interpret them; and, although he may reach some wrong conclusions, he is already trying to make that connection between pagan and Christian myth which was to be one of the main threads in his later *History of Religion*. So he writes: "I have in some of these Notes, given short intimations, that there was nothing in the worship of *Dæmons*, which was not an imitation of the worship of the true God: Larger proofs whereof, time perhaps may favour my intentions to produce" (p. 239); and he accepts the identification of Saturn with Noah and comments on the similarity between religious ceremonials mentioned in Juvenal and Suetonius and some referred to in the Old Testament (pp. 277-279).

Some excuse for the length of the notes is given by Statius' own fondness for learned allusions and geographical names; and it is not Howard's fault that these tend to clutter the verse translation as well. In spite of them, however, he does manage to write a poem that carries the reader along because of its narrative power and the interest of the conflicts of character involved.

Of Howard as a translator, little need be added to what has been said already. His version of Statius, like that of Virgil, includes an occasional mistranslation but would be more easily criticized for its frequent inadequacy, in lines where only the general sense of the Latin is given and no attempt made to translate every word. For example, the opening of Statius' address to Domitian:

> At tu, quem longe primum stupet Itala virtus
> Graiaque   (I. 14-15)

is watered down to

> But Thou by *Greeks* and *Romans* all-renown'd   (l. 15)

and many of the picturesque details of Statius'

> nox trahit in somnos, saxo conlabitur ingens
> Centaurus blandusque umeris se innectit Achilles,
> quamquam ibi fida parens, adsuetaque pectora mavult
> (I. 195-197)

are missing in Howard's

> Night now laid on her heavy charms the while.
> *Achilles* the kind Centaur's shoulder took,
> And his affecting Mother's breast forsook.   (I. 224-226)

The confusing word-order of I. 224 here ("laid on her" or "her heavy charms"?) is also characteristic.[18]

As with the Virgil, one feels that Howard is setting himself an impossible task in trying, for the most part, to translate each Latin hexameter in one English pentameter; it is notable that when he does occasionally allow himself more room, he is not unsuccessful. So,

18. The wrong punctuation that makes nonsense of I. 125-130 is presumably the printer's.

Statius' laconic line of comment on the promises of Achilles to bring back to Deidamia captives and spoils from the siege of Troy

> inrita ventosae rapiebant verba procellae   (I. 960)

retains its force and loses none of its suitability as the conclusion of a Book in Howard's couplet

> His fruitlesse words thus strove to ease her care,
> And his vain promise lost it self in air.   (IV. 309-310)

Perhaps, then, criticism should wonder most at how much of Statius' meaning, and tone, Howard is able to retain in his shorter English verse lines. (No doubt Statius was an easier project in this respect than was Virgil.)

Here, for example, are the lines describing the appearance of Achilles to his mother Thetis in the cave of Chiron whither she has come in search of him:

> The Youth arriv'd, loaded with dust and sweat,
> And wearied with his arms and labours; yet
> His snowy looks, the rosy blushes stain'd;
> His hair the shining Gold with glittering sham'd.
> Upon his cheeks no Down yet seem'd to rise:
> A gentle lustre in his sparkling eyes
> Still shin'd; his face, those charming beauties wore,
> Which his admired Mother had before.
> So shews young *Phœbus*, when he doth retire
> From *Lycia*, and for shafts assumes his lyre.
> By chance he came in pleas'd, (O how much more
> It added to what was so well before!)
> For under *Pholoe* in a Cave he slew
> A Lionesse, and took the young ones too,
> Which in his arms he bore. But the lov'd prey,
> At his dear mother's sight he threw away;
> By *Chiron* now embrac'd, and then again
> Doth in his mother's jealous arms remain.   (I. 183-199)

(Among the best lines here are, interestingly, those translating—inaccurately—the characteristic Statius parenthesis, "o quantum gaudia formae adiciunt!" [I. 167-168]. Another example would be his "Who finds out fraud when 'tis a God deceives?" [II. 186] for Statius' "quis divum fraudibus obstet" [I. 364].)

At the end of Book III Howard conveys much of the pathos of the situation of Deidamia when Achilles must leave her for the glory that awaits him at the siege of Troy; there is also genuine understanding of the feelings of both Thetis and Achilles when she persuades him to don woman's apparel that he may escape the fate foretold him, in the speech (II. 64-92) ending:

> Why dost thou frown, and turn away thy face?
> Needst thou to blush? Is gentlenesse disgrace?
> By our known streams, I do assure thee too,
> *Chiron*, nor doth, nor shall know what we doo.

Finally, a few lines from Achilles' account to Ulysses and Diomed of his training under Chiron may serve as illustration of Howard's skill in verse narrative:

> My tired limbs, a soft bed never press'd:
> I with my Master on a stone took rest.
> When now almost to twice six years I came,
> He taught me to pursue the swiftest game.
> And the fierce Lapithæ; and when I threw
> My darts, to overtake them. Sometimes too,
> *Chiron* would follow me through fields and plains,
> Till age deni'd; and tired with my pains,
> Would lay me on his neck. He made me bold
> To passe the frozen Rivers bound with cold.
> These were my youthfull sports . . .
> And now my Age, and *Chiron*, did designe
> My arms for nobler Wars . . .
> I scarce remember all. I learn'd the art
> To leap vast dikes, whose banks were far apart;
> And the high tops of airy hills to gain,
> To get me breath and swiftnesse for the plain.
> Then, the true image of a fight to yield,
> He made me take huge milstones on my shield;
> To enter burning hovells, and with force
> And speed, to stay swift Horses in their course.
> Once I remember, how dissolved snow,
> And constant showres had swel'd Sperchios so,
> That with its furious stream it drove a throng
> Of torn-up Trees, and rowling stones along:
> Then where the waves, the horrid'st force express'd,
> He bad me to oppose my youthfull breast,
> And stop the swelling billows as they run;
> Which he with all his feet could scarce have done.
> Nor could th'impetuous stream a conquest gain,
> Whilst *Chiron* threatned, urging still my shame . . .
>   (V. 127-137, 147-148, 157-174)

Neither students of classical poetry in translation nor historians of English literature seem to know of Howard's version of the *Achilleid* (though they note that both Pope and Gray translated portions of the *Thebaid*); and Sir Walter Scott, "justly" according to the *Dictionary of National Biography*, described *Poems 1660* as "productions of a most freezing mediocrity."[19] But were there so many poets writing in 1660 who had an equal mastery of the couplet and could do as much to vary its theoretically monotonous rhythm?[20]

In spite of the inclusion of some of his poems in anthologies, however, and although the *Poems* were reissued in 1696, Howard's literary reputation in his own time depended rather on his plays. Unfortunately by 1803 George Ellis could truthfully say, echoing Theophilus Cibber, that "Sir Robert is chiefly known to posterity by his controversy with his brother-in-law Dryden";[21] but Howard's contemporaries were right, as will be shown, in thinking that as a dramatist he deserved better than that. And because of his later work in drama, a special interest attaches to the only play in *Poems 1660*, namely *The Blind Lady, A Comedy*, undistinguished as it is.

The story of *The Blind Lady*, perhaps traceable to Peter Heylyn's *Cosmography*,[22] tells of the rivalry between Phylanter, son of the Vaivode of Ruthenia, and Mironault, Vaivode of Lithuania, for the hand of the Princess Mirramente, daughter of the King of Poland. Phylanter with his forces attacks and attempts to kill Mironault in the presence of the Princess herself, falsely alleging knowledge of treachery plotted against her; but Mironault, with his two companions, Hippasus and Pysander, fights his way out through the ranks of the besieging army. The three are forced to take refuge in the home of the blind lady, Cæca, where again they are besieged by Phy-

19. *The Works of John Dryden* (London, 1808), XI, 6. Edward Phillips, in his *Compendiosa Enumeratio Poetarum* (1669) noted that Howard had translated the *Thebaid* but this must, I think, be an error.

20. Eighteenth-century anthologies (for example, those of Giles Jacob and Nichols) also attribute to Howard a translation (nearly two hundred lines) from Lucretius, Book V, which they call "Nature's Changes." It is not without merit, in its use of the couplet, but it invariably suffers in comparison with Dryden's superb translation of the latter part of Book III. For Howard's poem, "Against the Fear of Death," also printed by Nichols and Jacob, see below, chap. vi.

21. *Specimens of the Early English Poets* (3rd edition, 1803), III, 304. For Cibber, see p. 317.

22. D. E. Baker, *Biographia Dramatica*, cont. Isaac Reed and Stephen Jones (London, 1812), II, 61.

lanter; but this time the Princess herself comes with a rescuing army, gives her hand to Mironault and pardons the repentant Phylanter at the request of Mironault's sister Amione, who has, conveniently, both fallen in love with him and become the bosom friend and confidante of the Princess (an ending which certainly deserves Carryl N. Thurber's description of it as "anti-climactic").[23]

A "comic" subplot centers on Mironault's two friends, particularly Pysander, and concerns the events in Cæca's house just before and during the incredible siege. Pysander pretends to make love to the aged Cæca, that her servants may be persuaded to defend the house, and defend him as her future husband; he further pretends love to her elderly maid Quinever. But after the rescue of them all by the Princess, the tables are turned and Pysander is ordered to carry out his promise to marry Cæca, while Hippasus must marry Quinever. When, therefore, at the end of the play Mironault can speak to his Princess of

> Those joys are falling now upon me,
> Which neither time or age can ever lessen;
> For still your Virtues like *Medea*'s charms
> Shall bring fresh beauties to my happy arms

Pysander can only look at his octogenarian bride and say

> We Bridegrooms disagree, for every day
> Will oblige most that adds to your decay.

Nevertheless the comedy based on the decay of the physical powers of Cæca (and her maid) is in questionable taste; and understandably Alfred Harbage finds it "ugly and callous unless we consider her no more than a symbol of jade Fortune."[24] Such an interpretation is tempting, and Pysander perhaps invites it when he says as they first enter Cæca's house:

> Here we shall find
> Good Fortune sure, for that whore too is blind.   (II.iii)

One might even argue that Fortune is courted by the one who is reckless and without cares and finally won only when she is no longer sought. It is to be feared, however, that such a sophistication is over-flattering to Howard's play, which seems to stop short of consistent

23. *Sir Robert Howard's Comedy, "The Committee,"* ed. Carryl Nelson Thurber (University of Illinois Studies in Language and Literature, No. 7, 1921) p. 21.
24. *Cavalier Drama* (London, 1936), p. 246.

allegory or symbolism. Nor does he deal consistently with what sometimes promises to be a principal theme—that of the qualities of the
just ruler, who, like the King of Poland and unlike his daughter's
servants, should be incapable of deriving pleasure from the suspicion
cast on a trusted follower.

The play remains, then, a comedy or tragi-comedy—more than
half-way between Jacobean tragedy and Heroic drama. Interestingly
it seems to have been written with a stage like that of the Elizabethan
public theater in mind, for it demands no scenery and requires only
one upper level (on which characters can appear "above," as they
frequently do, and from which they can "descend") and a "vault"
(into which Cæca can be thrust and from which she can call out and
be heard by those on the main stage). There is no record of its ever
having been produced, but those who criticize its structure and its
"too rapid shift of scene"[25] fail to allow for the theater for which it
was intended.

The Blind Lady resembles Caroline drama and the later Heroic
plays in having a great deal of undramatic (and indeed unnecessary)
narrative: nothing is ever implied or said once if saying it twice will
do. The characters constantly explain themselves, even to themselves,
and not only in soliloquy; and they too often strike attitudes. The
dialogue similarly is often no more than a mouthing of platitudes,
particularly on Love and Honor:

> Whither does Love thus hurry me?
> A Tyrant that denies the smallest hopes,
> Where he gives largest wishes!
> The greatest Beauties are like greatest Wealths,
> Subjects for all mens wishes, not their hopes.
> Fears share with Love the Empire of the heart,
> Rendring alike the Lover and the Coward   (I.ii)

and so on (frequently at moments, as in the besieged castle, when
speedy action is essential). The characters do indeed address each
other as if they were addressing a public meeting.

As a result, they remain cardboard figures and any real dramatic
sympathy with them is out of the question. One cannot believe in, let
alone admire, a woman who asks her lover

> Is there a possibility to know
> Your meaning then?   (I.ii)

25. Thurber, p. 21.

or a warrior who proclaims

> They fought it nobly, though, if my ears
> Deceive me not, I hear some comming.   (I.v)

Phylanter alone promises at times to hold our attention, as a study of
the basically worthy soldier who is a victim of his passions; one who,
being tempted, rationalizes to find excuses for doing what he wants
to do, and discovers that soon, like Macbeth, he is

> Stepped in so far, that should I wade no more,
> Returning were as tedious as go o'er.

Howard, who had obviously been studying his Shakespeare as well
as his Fletcher and, I suspect, Ford,[26] can do no more than repeat this
sentiment many times, not only through the mouth of Phylanter himself, as in

> I know it, and now must sink or else go on. . . .
> We cannot hope ere to return again
> Back on our fancies to our first conditions   (IV.ii)

but also through his father Albertus:

> it is the fate of guilty men,
> That such should seek at safety through more crimes. (II.i)

Development of character, at this stage of his career, was beyond
Howard's powers.

The erratic versification is perhaps adequately illustrated from the
opening dialogue:

> *Albertus.* But upon what injury, *Phylanter?*
> *Phylanter.* Love and Ambition, Sir, those two great injuries
>   Of mens seduced minds, which fill the thoughts
>   Full of Revenge, not with the justnesse of it.
>   What *Mironault* has done, moves not my hate;
>   But what he may, my fears. By her, a Kingdom, Sir;
>   And, with her self, a World—
>   Falls in my arms. How slow you are to crown
>   Me and your self with happinesse?
>   You can love neither, and deny.
> *Albertus.* But are you sure he comes?
> *Phylanter.* I am certainly inform'd so.

26. His Princess seems to owe something to Calantha of *The Broken Heart*;
and Cæca's servant Peter, "thou ingratefull piece of wise formality" (III.ii), is
often very like Ford's "wise formalitie" Iohn a Water, Mayor of Cork, in
Perkin Warbeck.

From this it is impossible to extract any verse pattern, other than a basic iambic stressing. The number of syllables in the lines varies from six to twelve, and the number of stresses, so far as one can judge, from three to six; and while one or two commendable effects are attained by the reversal of the normal stress (for example, "Falls in my arms"), in other lines it is difficult to know where the stress should be. As a result, the reader is constantly stumbling and never knows when a stress on a most unimportant word may be required, to make a line into verse. It is indeed not easy to believe that lines like the following were intended as verse at all:

> I owe the world so much: I'le think on't
> When I can pay it. *Lycespes*, welcome,
> I was resolved just now to seek you.   (I.i)

In writing such "verse" as this, Howard was in the tradition of the Cavalier drama. Alfred Harbage has shown that, particularly before the Civil War, the form regularly employed in plays was "rhythmic prose, usually (though not in Montague) masquerading as blank verse" and has found that "there is usually at least a dim echo here and there of the old pentameter."[27] Thomas Killigrew for one did not seem to care whether the printers set up some of his work as verse or prose; sometimes, Harbage suggests, they set up prose to look like verse, and it is an interesting fact that the compositor who set up the 1692 reprint of Howard's plays, working from the 1665 volume, began by setting up as prose what in his copy text was printed as verse; then at the foot of page 4 he apparently decided that perhaps it was verse after all and from that point on he followed the lineation of his copy. Howard, if he even noticed the difference, presumably did not care. Instead of saying with *The Dictionary of National Biography* simply that Howard's "blank verse is execrable," we ought rather to note that he was writing in the tradition of a mistaken belief as to what form dramatic dialogue must take—and we should add that in some of his later plays the blank verse is much better. Rhyme, incidentally, is also used in *The Blind Lady*, but seems to be thought appropriate only for soliloquy, although it is not used consistently even there.

The language of *The Blind Lady* certainly does not raise to the level of "poetry" what might otherwise be branded as merely verse.

27. *Cavalier Drama*, p. 38.

The imagery, often conventional, is sometimes also absurd, and the dramatist's striving for originality is all too obvious in Phylanter's

> Love for the Princesse too,
> For whose fair sake, Who'd not attempt
> The angry billows swell'd with horrid storms,
> The Sea-gods Pyramids, when every wave
> Bears too, like those, within its womb a grave,
> Or dangers yet unheard of? (I.i)

After language such as this, a return to ordinary speech can produce only bathos.

Of the comparatively few critics and historians of drama who have mentioned the play, only two have a good word for it—C.N. Thurber and Montague Summers (always ready to see merit in the literature of his beloved Restoration). Thurber grants it "some good rough fun" (p. 21) and Summers finds that "the comic episodes are very good, and, if in some measure derivative, well-written and decidedly amusing."[28] "Occasionally amusing" would have been a juster verdict, since the humor is nearly all in the words of Pysander,[29] complaining of his wounds:

> Would I were a Dog, and could lick my self whole.
> I shall be as fly-blown, as a ruine cheese (II.iii)

and appropriately wooing the ancient horror who thinks

> he speaks as well
> As any that I knew these six King's Reigns (III.i)

with the compliment that

> many a man
> Has travailed many miles, and tedious wayes,
> To see a lesser monument. (III.i)

Perhaps the best that can be said for *The Blind Lady* is that in flashes such as these it shows some faint glimmering of the gift for comedy that was to be demonstrated in *The Committee*; and that in its attempts to reproduce some of the situations and effects of the better Elizabethan and Jacobean tragedies, it began the experimenting that led to *The Duke of Lerma*.

28. *The Playhouse of Pepys* (London, 1935), p. 169.

29. In Act II. Sc. iii he becomes, suddenly, Pysenor, apparently by a compositor's error.

Chapter three. AT THE RESTORATION

THE preface to the *Poems* concluded with an apology, of a kind, for the author's inability to check his volume carefully:

I have thus, ingenuous Reader, given you a clear and true account of my Self and Writings, not opprest with apprehension, nor rais'd by neglect; but preserv'd by an indifferency, that destroys not my civilitie to others, nor my own content; desiring not to engrosse, but share satisfaction. If in any thing I justly need, or designe to ask pardon, 'tis for Errors that probably the Reader may meet with; having been reduc'd to the strait of neglecting this, or businesse. I confesse my Interest prevail'd with me though, not wholly to neglect the Reader, since I prevail'd with a worthy Friend to take so much view of my blotted Copies, as to free me from grosse Errors. Having thus set down all my designe and reasons, I leave the Reader with as little Concern to use his, as I have shewed him mine.

It is not quite clear whether Howard used the services of his friend before or after the work went to the printer: the wording would perhaps suggest the former, the context the latter. (If the duties of the worthy friend were to read the proofs, then he fell down on the task rather badly.) I do not think that we can go so far as to say with J. M. Osborn that "this friend was unquestionably Dryden," although Dryden's connections with both Howard and Herringman make the identification tempting.[1] What is clear is that Howard certainly had "businesse" enough to occupy him after the Restoration—business, for example, in seeking from the King grants which promised a better return than did the careful rereading of mere literature.

On 16 June 1660 there is note in the Docquet Book of a "warrant for a grant to Sir Robert Howard, of the office of Serjeant Painter to the King"; and that he did in fact fulfil some at least of the administrative obligations of the position is shown by orders to pay him in January 1662 £300, and in February of the same year £450 "in full" "for gilding, painting, and adorning the King's yacht."[2] (Perhaps it was also in this capacity that he received on 30 July 1661 £500 "for service done," the money "to be accounted for in the office of works.")[3] This position he surrendered on 28 February 1663, when it is described

1. Osborn, *John Dryden*, p. 171.
2. *C.S.P.D.*, 1660-1661, p. 55; 1661-1662, pp. 236, 256, 270, 277.
3. *C.S.P.D.*, 1661-1662, p. 19; *C.T.B.*, 1660-1667, pp. 267, 289.

in greater detail as "the office of Serjeant Painter of all the King's works, palaces, barges, coaches, etc."[4]

More profitable would have been another grant made to him in June, 1660, that of Clerk of the Patents in Chancery; and after he was invested and sworn in by Clarendon, "upon the petition of the said Lord Chancellor Clarendon and Sir Robert Howard this grant was made to Sir Robert Howard for life." But, no doubt for a consideration, he surrendered it after four years, when it was granted to Thomas Vyner.[5]

At least as important, if probably more burdensome, was his appointment in October, 1660, with Sir John Grenville (soon to become Earl of Bath) and five others, "to take examination on and treat and compound for all lands etc. received before May 25, 1660, belonging to the King and discovered by them." This task, of deciding exactly what should be done about all the grants of Royal property made during the Interregnum and what financial settlements should be made by all who had "unjustly detained goods, jewels, money, forfeitures etc. due to the Crown" (simply by their ownership under what had become, by the very fact of the Restoration, a false title), was one of the major problems facing Charles II's administrators; and it is not surprising that by May of the following year the seven commissioners were petitioning for "ampler commission for Recovery of the vast sums now fraudulently detained from His Majesty; the present being defective in power and number of persons."[6] The King could hardly have shown greater faith in Howard than by appointing him to act on this commission, and, seventeenth-century methods being what they were, it would be difficult not to assume that a great deal of money was made by the seven officers. Howard's father would seem either to have been another of the commissioners or to have acted on his son's behalf; there are many entries in the Treasury Books concerning his discovery of "concealed lands" and on one occasion (May, 1663) he was granted "15,000 l. moiety of 30,000 l. discovered by him"—but there is no evidence that he received it.

Naturally, in view of these duties as a commissioner, Howard would

4. *C.S.P.D.*, 1663-1664, p. 58.
5. *C.S.P.D.*, 1660-1661, p. 76; *H.M.C.* 79, MSS of the 12th Earl of Lindsey, pp. 180-181 (notes about the office, endorsed by Danby); *C.S.P.D.*, 1663-1664, p. 677.
6. *C.S.P.D.*, 1660-1661, pp. 323, 607.

know that one of his own principal sources of income, the lease of the Post Fines, was now of doubtful value in so far as it depended on the 1657 grant by Cromwell and his Council; and he and his father took immediate steps to have a new lease granted, virtually as a continuation of that allowed by Charles I in 1641 (renewing the original grant of 1625). The Earl of Berkshire, as has been shown, had sold his share of the lease of the Post Fines outright to Abbott; but it was obviously in the interests of Abbott's successors, Clayton and Morris, to support the application for the new lease, on which they could have *some* claim, in equity if not in law, rather than to allow all to go to another.[7]

Consequently, on 29 April 1661, there is record of the "Demise to Thomas Earl of Berkshire and Sir Rob. Howard, his son, for 48 years, of the Post Fines in the Court of Common Pleas; rent 2,276 l., with allowance of such defalcations as were granted in a former lease now surrendered, and of Post Fines since Michaelmas 1657, pardoned by the Act of Oblivion, and power to defalk the surplus of the fines above the rent from Michaelmas 1657, to June 24, 1660, which they would have received but for the said surrender." (In September, 1664, £4814/ 17/6 of the rent was in fact remitted "in defalcation of and consideration for post fines pardoned and discharged by the late Act of General Pardon.")[8]

At the same time Berkshire and Howard made good their other claim, to the Greenwax, by petitioning "for a warrant to stop any grant of pardon or remission of fines which may be prejudicial to them as farmers, at a great rent, of the casual revenue called Greenwax . . . until the surveyor or farmers of Greenwax be heard thereon"; and in August of the same year John Brewster was appointed on Berkshire's nomination "Receiver and Surveyor of the Greenwax in the Exchequer; all profits to be paid to the Earl of Berkshire and Sir Rob. Howard, reserving 577 l. 5 s. 5 d yearly to the King." This grant of the Greenwax was for thirty-one years.[9]

7. For evidence that Clayton and Morris remained on friendly terms with Howard, see, e.g., Howard's note of 6 March 1661, Osborn MSS, Yale.

8. *C.S.P.D.*, 1660-1661, p. 577; *C.T.B.*, 1660-1667, p. 619.

9. *C.S.P.D.*, 1660-1661, p. 577; *C.S.P.D.*, 1661-1662, p. 72; *C.T.B.*, 1660-1667, pp. 136, 274; *C.S.P.D.*, 1666-1667, pp. 412-413 (where the relevant document, like many others in this volume, is wrongly dated; for "1666?" read "1661"). From the two sums of £2,276 and £577.5.5, £1200 per annum was to be paid direct to the Queen for life; a pension of £500 to Dame Barbara Villiers,

The rights of Clayton and Morris to the Post Fines (but not to the Greenwax) under the new grant were secured by private deeds. Howard's share was one quarter of the proceeds and he did nothing to prejudice this, but Berkshire's half soon became a quarter, and Clayton and Morris's quarter a half, in return for "a certen competent sume." A note from Berkshire on 9 April 1662 asks Sir Robert and Brewster to pay William Howard £60 from the Greenwax receipts, probably in repayment of another loan; and Sir Robert's annotation suggests that he was not allowing his father or brother any more than they were entitled to: "pray Mr Clayton, lett my brother William have £50 upon this note the other tenn must be payd to mee and it shall be discounted in the money wee are to supply my Lord wth" (and William's receipt is for fifty pounds, not sixty). No doubt because of Berkshire's need, not Howard's, they even mortgaged to Morris and Clayton for £1000 their rights to nominate Brewster's successor as Receiver of the Greenwax.[10]

The father was not only impecunious; he was also growing old (he was born in 1587). Lacking his son's ability to make money, he pathetically relied on petitions to the King. Probably in vain, he asked in 1660 not only "for the office of Custos Brevium in the Court of Common Pleas" but also "for a patent of a new invention of which he is informed, for the boiling of potashes for making soap" and for part of "the royalty of the sea between Runswick and Yarm, co. York, and the tenancy of all the weed which grows and is driven by the waves of the sea to the shore, called sea-wreck or sea-weed, and also certain pible stones useful to burn the said sea-weed within the dominion of England, Wales and Scotland."[11] Eventually, in 1662, "for his many losses in the late King's cause," Charles II granted him £8000 from the excise, £3000 of which was allotted to his daughter Elizabeth (and probably given to her by her father as her dowry

---

widow of Sir Edward, was also charged against these rents—and not always paid promptly. *C.S.P.D.*, 1660-1661, p. 430; 1661-1662, pp. 490, 491, 566; 1663-1664, p. 670; *C.T.B.*, 1660-1667, pp. 577, 637-638, 702. Brewster's salary as Receiver for the Howards was £40 per annum.

10. MSS and deeds (25 June, 29 June, 25 July 1661, and 21 May 1662) in the Osborn MSS, Yale. It may be worth noting here that an entry in *C.S.P.D.*, 1660-1661, p. 497 relating to "Sir Robert Howard's lighthouse at Dungeness" is an error, taken over from the original license (P.R.O., S.P. 38, Vol. 19, p. 79), for "Sir Edward Howard."

11. *C.S.P.D.*, 1660-1661, pp. 243, 385, 188; *C.T.B.*, 1660-1667, p. 17.

when she married John Dryden in 1663); the £8000 was to be paid by yearly instalments of £1000 but by 1665 the grant had "brought in nothing" and "on account of the great extremity of the Earl's affairs, the money is now to be assigned upon the receiver general of rents."[12] In fact the grant had been mortgaged for £5000 ready cash in the year in which it was given. After Berkshire's death in 1669 his widow was again asking "for a grant of 3,000 l. promised to her late husband, on a petition a little before his death," only £5000 of the £8000 having been paid even then.[13]

In comparison Sir Robert was luckier, more astute, or less given to spending; and with one minor exception, his career was for a few years after the Restoration one of unqualified success. In the military sphere, he was soon (9 November 1660) commissioned as colonel of a regiment of infantry in the Hampshire militia;[14] in the political sphere, he was elected Member of Parliament for Stockbridge in Hampshire, for the parliament beginning in May 1661. (There was question of who should sit as his fellow-member, but his name was on both returns.)[15] With the exception of James II's 1685 Parliament, of which he would have considered it no credit to be a member, he sat in every parliament after his first election until his death in 1698; and though he changed both his constituency (he represented Castle Rising in Norfolk from 1679) and some of his principles, his parliamentary service was exceptional not only for its length but also, as I hope to show, for the influence he exercised.

There is further evidence of the regard in which he was held during these early years of Charles II's reign, in his appointment under the act of 2 May 1662 (14 Charles II.c.2) as one of the twenty-one Commissioners for reforming the streets and buildings of London and for supplementing existing services. John Evelyn, who was another of the Commissioners, mentions his own appointment with what sounds like justifiable pride, and notes that "There were divers Gent: of quality in this Commission." Evelyn records a meeting of

12. *C.S.P.D.*, 1661-1662, p. 288; 1665-1666, p. 138; 1666-1667, p. 58.

13. *C.S.P.D.*, 1661-1662, p. 523; 1668-1669, pp. 20, 640; *C.T.B.*, 1667-1668, p. 160.

14. *C.T.B.*, 1660-1667, p. 82; see also B. M. Sloane MS 3299, f.24 (a letter from Howard to one of his officers, Sir Andrew Henley: "You see what strictnesse must be used; the oath of Aleageance must be constantly tenderd; and all the Conventicle meetings of the Phanatiques disturbd & prevented.")

15. *Commons Journals*, VIII, 252-253.

the Commissioners on 31 July, when "we ordered the Paving of the Way from st. *James's* north, which was a quagmire, & also of the *Hay-market* about *Piqudillo*, and agreed upon Instructions to be printed & published for the better-keeping the Streetes clean"; but there are few or no other records of meetings.[16]

The one setback to Howard's career in these years of advancement and prosperity came in August, 1661. On the thirteenth of that month, Sir William Morice, as Secretary of State, issued to Sir John Robinson, as Lieutenant of the Tower, warrants "for the imprisonment of Sir Rob. Howard, knt, James and Philip Howard, esqs., Sir Rob. Killegrew, knt., and Henry Killegrew, esq." Just what was the connection between Sir Robert Killigrew (father of Thomas, William, and Henry) and the Howard brothers, it is difficult to say, although it almost certainly had something to do with the theater. At any rate, the trouble was not unduly serious, for a week later (on 21 August) Morice issued a second warrant, "for the discharge of the said five prisoners."[17]

Four months later Howard was associated with another Killigrew, Sir Robert's better-known son Thomas, in a venture that was to prove very important indeed in the development of the Restoration theater. The story has been told by at least three authorities and may be retold very briefly here.[18] On 20 December 1661, an agreement was drawn up between (1) the Earl of Bedford; (2) Thomas Killigrew and Sir Robert Howard, in association with the eight actors, Hart, Burt, Lacy, Mohun, Robert Shatterell, Clun, Cartwright, and Wintershall; and (3) William Hewett and Robert Clayton. Under this agreement, the Earl leased to Hewett and Clayton, in trust for the others, for forty-one years, at a rent of £50 per annum, a plot of land (approximately 112' × 58') between Bridges Street and Drury Lane; on this was to be erected a theater which (as a condition of the lease) must cost at least £1500. In a further agreement, on 28 January 1662, Hewett and Clayton made over the land to Howard, Killigrew, and the actors, as a theater company. The building shares were divided into thirty-six

16. Evelyn, *Diary*, ed. de Beer, III, 319 and n. 1, 328 and n. 5.

17. *H.M.C.*, 11th Report, Pt. 7 (Danby papers) p. 3.

18. Leslie Hotson, *The Commonwealth and Restoration Stage* (Cambridge, Mass., 1928); Montague Summers, *The Playhouse of Pepys*; Allardyce Nicoll, *A History of English Drama 1660-1900*, Vol. I (Cambridge, 1952: 4th edition, revised).

parts, of which Killigrew and Howard had nine each, Lacy four, and the other seven actors two each; and on the same day the eight actors, and others, were tied to the proposed theater by an agreement between them and Howard and Killigrew, under which the actors undertook not to play elsewhere, and the acting company agreed to pay the building sharers a rent of £3/10/0 for each acting day. Howard, then, was advancing one quarter of the cost of the new theater (which actually cost £2400 in all) for a minimum return of 17/6 for each day on which it was used. There were other possible profits: for example, on 10 February 1663 Howard and the other sharers, for a license fee of £100 and a rental of 6/8 per day, granted to Orange Moll (Mistress Mary Meggs) the sole right for thirty-nine years to sell oranges and lemons and such dainties in the theater except in the Upper Gallery (but she stole the agreement, and did not pay with any regularity).[19] The theater, occupied in May 1663, was known as the Theatre Royal in Bridges Street; it was burnt down on 25 January 1672—ironically, by a fire said to have begun "under the stairs where Orange Moll keeps her fruit"[20] and was replaced by the new "Theatre Royal in Drury Lane" in 1674.

The Bridges Street theater, which permitted elaborate scenery, was to provide dramatists with an opportunity for gorgeous spectacle, an opportunity that Howard certainly took in *The Indian Queen* in 1664. But until it was built, Killigrew's company acted in the so-called "first" Theatre Royal, in Vere Street, which did not allow such elaborate effects and, although roofed, was probably closer in type to the Elizabethan "public" theater familiar to students of Shakespeare; and it was here that Howard first saw successfully produced two of his plays, *The Surprisal* and *The Committee*. He had certainly become in a period of less than two years a man of many parts, indeed a man of distinction.

19. Hotson, p. 291; Montague Summers, *The Restoration Theatre* (London, 1934), pp. 82-83.
20. Summers, p. 82, quoting a newsletter of 27 January 1672.

Chapter four. TWO COMEDIES AND A POEM

HOWARD'S second play, *The Surprisal*, was acted by the King's Company at the Vere Street theater on 23 April 1662. It had some success, as is made clear by a reference to it in a doggerel newsletter from a man about town to a country friend, included in a miscellaneous collection of state papers and letters in the British Museum:

> ffor the surprizall it was a good proofe
> By its getting them mony it took well enough
> Without which Divell take the Play
> Be it never so good the Actors say
> But they may thanke God with all their hart
> That Lacy plaid Brankadoros part.[1]

Further evidence that it was not considered worthless is provided by revivals in 1667 and 1668, when Pepys saw it at least five times. To be sure, he was not enthusiastic. On 8 April 1667 he was in time only for "the latter end," "wherein was no great matter, I thought, by what I saw there. Thence away to Polichinello, and there had three times more sport than at the play." He saw the full performance on 26 August, "a very mean play, I thought: or else it was because I was out of humour," and he was more interested in Orange Moll's news that Lord Buckhurst and Nell Gwyn had parted company. Then on 26 December Nell's acting in it as Samira only added to his disappointment: "saw 'The Surprizall'; which did not please me today, the actors not pleasing me; and especially Nell's acting of a serious part, which she spoils." He attended yet another performance on 17 April of the following year, when the singing was mostly "base" but the tedium was relieved when his beloved Mistress Knepp (who played the part of the second, more serious, heroine, Emilia) came to eat oranges with him in the pit. Two weeks later (1 May) he saw it again, without comment.[2]

In spite of these revivals (and there was still another at Drury Lane in 1715)[3] and the various printings (in *Four New Plays*, 1665, in the

1. B.M. Add. MS 34217, f.31b (I have expanded the contractions), first cited by Hotson, p. 246.

2. *The Diary of Samuel Pepys*, ed. H. B. Wheatley (London, 1923), VI, 249; VII, 77, 233, 375; VIII, 1.

3. John Genest, *Some Account of the English Stage, from the Restoration in 1660 to 1830* (Bath, 1832), II, 559.

four issues of *Five New Plays* at the end of the century and, according to Genest, in 1722), later critics have, understandably, endorsed the verdict of Pepys.[4] One may grant Howard's right to compose in the traditional loose verse that he had already used, or abused, in *The Blind Lady*, but one cannot overlook his inability to create a plausible plot; and if a retelling of the story of *The Surprisal* makes it sound not only old-fashioned and uninteresting but also absurd, then the fault is the dramatist's.

Miranzo, returning to Sienna from travel abroad, learns that his aged uncle Castruccio, who is also his guardian, is to be married to the young, beautiful, and dutiful Emilia. As Miranzo's sister, Samira, puts it, "I do believe she thinks choice were a sin." Samira herself is loved by Miranzo's friend Cialto; but Cialto, having lost all his property to the grasping senator Brancadoro (Senior), now "shuns all occasions" of seeing her and behaves in a most "disordered" way (his disorder is indeed such as to forbid any possibility of our sympathizing with him, as apparently we are supposed to do). The further complication arises that Castruccio, never doubting Samira's consent, has "provided" a husband for her, in Brancadoro Junior, the son of the very man to whom is due her lover Cialto's distress. All this, to be fair, we learn quickly—but in an exposition that is static and, because undramatic, rather dull.

As soon as Samira, Miranzo, and Castruccio have left the stage, the foolish younger Brancadoro enters, in conversation with his tailor. (Like *The Blind Lady* and *The Committee*, *The Surprisal* demands no scenery; as on Shakespeare's stage, "scene" succeeds scene in unbroken continuity, with variation only in the use of an upper stage from which characters can speak and from which they can move, out of sight of the audience, to reappear on the main stage through the curtains at the back of it.) Brancadoro provides, if unwittingly, the further necessary plot complication when he takes into his service the villain Villerotto, envious of Cialto because "cashiered" by Cialto from his command. (The rather blatant stealing of motive and type from Shakespeare's Iago is interesting additional evidence of Howard's close knowledge of his predecessors; similarly Brancadoro seems to owe something to Shakespeare's Slender of *The Merry Wives* and still

4. See, e.g., Genest, I, 56; Thurber, p. 22; Nicoll, I, 214; Harbage, *Cavalier Drama*, p. 247; John Downes, *Roscius Anglicanus*, ed. Montague Summers (London, [1928]), p. 144; *The Playhouse of Pepys*, p. 170.

more to John Ford's Bergetto in *'Tis Pity*; Emilia's later questioning of her governess concerning the identity of the men in the masque and procession is derived either from the "ball" scene in *Romeo and Juliet* or from Ford's adaptation of that in *'Tis Pity*, or from both; and the type of plot is imitated, presumably, from the Fletcher or Massinger tragi-comedy.)

Villerotto next hires some discontented soldiers to murder Cialto (one is uncomfortably aware now of the echoes from Macbeth's hiring of the murderers of Banquo); and an attempt by Miranzo to frighten Brancadoro by challenging him to a duel with Cialto fails because Brancadoro has just wit enough to fix for the duel a time after what he knows to be the probable hour of Cialto's murder. Brancadoro's folly has already provided some dramatic relief from the heroics of the love story; now there is a further interlude in a masque with which Castruccio woos Emilia on her wedding day—but which is also the occasion for Miranzo's falling in love with Emilia.

At this point (the end of Act III, scene i) the outcome of the plot is perfectly clear, but we are brought to it only through nearly three acts of escapes, escapades, and disguises that it would be tedious to relate in full. Briefly, both Samira and Emilia decide to take refuge in a nunnery; neither reaches it, because Villerotto captures them both. Miranzo, in a friar's habit, saves Cialto from Villerotto and his assassins; and eventually Samira and Emilia are also rescued when they are on the point of committing suicide rather than meet the fate worse than death with which Villerotto (somewhat implausibly) is threatening them both. Brancadoro is blackmailed into restoring Cialto's estate, on threat that his share in the proposed murder will otherwise be divulged; Villerotto, still like Iago, is unrepentant to the last; and Castruccio and Emilia's father are so relieved to see Samira and Emilia safe that ready consent is given by all to the marriages of the young lovers.

Only fine poetic language or interesting characterization could save a play built on such a story; Howard can hardly be praised for either. His language is undistinguished, and when the dialogue is not rant, it is generally flat (it was the first four pages of this play that the compositor of the 1692 edition understandably set up as prose until he decided that he had better follow his copy and print as the blankest of blank verse). Contemporary opinion was right in feeling that

Brancadoro alone of the characters is worth remembering. The villain, as we have seen, is a bad copy of Iago; and the heroes never come to life. "What storm tosses his noble Soul!" Miranzo once says of Cialto —and proceeds to develop a very similar storm himself. At this stage of his career, Howard cannot show a character in distress: he can only make him say that he is distressed (or have him try to convince others of the fact by the very absurdity of his conduct). Nevertheless we can well believe that Brancadoro provided Lacy with a playable part; and an audience not acquainted with Brancadoro's more distinguished predecessors might get many laughs from his foolish attempts to strike the right level of wisdom and bravery in a society into which he is most uncomfortably thrust by his wealth. While prepared to act in accordance with the conviction that there is no woman "so simple to refuse me," he is beneath passion and, like Bergetto, he doesn't really care for the girl at all, or for anybody except himself:

> I care not for *Cialto*, nor her neither;
> I can let her alone, if there be such ado about her. (Act I)

Again like Bergetto, and Slender, he has no idea of how to woo, beyond relating tales of his own prowess and telling jokes:

> I'le tell you a pretty Jest, Mistress;
> A Friend of mine would have had me married
> A Kinswoman of his . . .   (II.i)

(compare Bergetto: "Sirrah *Sweet-heart*, I'le tell thee a good jest . . . ," II. 1057). A skilful actor would make comical both Brancadoro's cowardly fears, when he has to woo Samira in the presence of his fierce-looking rival, Cialto, and his bravado as soon as Cialto has gone; but it must be confessed that Howard is not as wise as Shakespeare and Ford, who used their witless clowns very sparingly. Nor does he pack as much into the dialogue. An occasional phrase, such as

> As I live and breathe,
> I never took more pains a Squirrel-hunting,
> Than I have done in seeking her,   (III.iii)

is amusing in itself, but mostly Howard relies on the actor to bring out the humour in the situation and the basic ideas.

Even this, however, implies good sense of the theater; and perhaps because of his close association with the actors involved in the Bridges Street agreement, an association that presumably also gave him special opportunities to watch all plays being performed or rehearsed, he does seem to have developed, very rapidly, knowledge of what will go well on the stage. He was also quick to sense which way the dramatic wind was blowing; already in *The Surprisal* there is some attempt at the analysis of Love that was to prove so popular a feature of Heroic Tragedy; there is some of the jesting at old age and particularly at the absurdity of old men in love that was to be one of the mainstays of Restoration comedy (even in Congreve); and Miranzo's disguise as a Friar is an early example of the particular kind of disguise that was to be repeated *ad nauseam* in Restoration drama. A play like *The Surprisal* is of no aesthetic value but it does show Howard in the role of a dramatic pioneer.[5]

Probably between the date of the first performance of this comedy and the opening of *The Committee*, he composed some commendatory verses for his friend Dr. Walter Charleton's extraordinary *"Chorea Gigantum, or, The Most Famous Antiquity of Great Britain, Vulgarly called Stone-Heng, Standing on Salisbury Plain, Restored to the Danes."* (This was not published until 1663, but the imprimatur is dated 11 September 1662.) Charleton's thesis is well enough described in the heading of Howard's poem, "To my worthy Friend, D^r. Charleton, on his clear Discovery of *Stone-Heng* to have been a DANISH Court-Royal, for the Election of Kings, and not a *Roman Temple*, as supposed by Mr *Inigo Jones*"; and Howard's lines, which immediately follow the dedication to the King and precede the complimentary verses by Dryden, are as follows:

> How much obliging is Your learned Care!
> Still busie to *preserve*, or to *repair*;
> Which unto *Men* not onely life can give,
> But makes their *Monuments* themselves to live.
> *Health* comes to them by Your immortal aim:
> And to their Actions *Truth*, the health of Fame.
> The sickly World seems thus Restor'd by Thee;
> Whilst thy large *Soul*, like its *Eternity*,
> On wasting *Time* atchievs new Victories,
> Which buried now in its own ruins lyes.
>
> Nor wert Thou to engage with *Time* alone;
> But that which kept the Wonder more unknown,

5. I can see no reason, however, for believing with F. E. Paget that it must have been in Sheridan's mind when he wrote *The Duenna* (*Some Records of the Ashtead Estate, and of its Howard Possessors,* p. 45).

Mens Errors; which are still the greatest crime,
And more destroy the truth of things, than Time.
For, if unskilful hands too rashly rake
In antique rubbish, every bold mistake
Hides what they seek, and loses it far more,
By the new ruine, than the old before.

Nor is Thy STONE-HENG a less Wonder grown,
Though once a *Temple* thought, now prov'd a *Throne*:
Since we, who are so blest with *Monarchy*,
Must gladly learn, from Thy Discovery,
That great *Respects* not onely have been found
Where *Gods* were *Worship'd*, but where *Kings* were *Crown'd*.

Rob. Howard.

If Howard can hardly be blamed for not knowing more about Stonehenge than did Charleton and Inigo Jones, he is once again open to the charge that he need not have rushed in quite so confidently where angels, and even historians, fear to tread. A possible defense is that he accepts Charleton's premise only to make a political point. Dryden, in his set of complimentary verses, carries the process much further; for the sake of an elaborate political analogy, he is prepared to argue that the world might never have progressed beyond the ideas of Aristotle had it not been for Columbus and Englishmen like Bacon, Gilbert, Boyle, Harvey—and Charleton. In fact, a reader not knowing of the subsequent development and reputations of the two poets might not have been sure that he could choose between them at this stage, although he would have perceived that Dryden was attempting a greater complexity of thought.[6] Certainly Howard's versification would have given no cause for complaint. Its regularity is further reason for agreeing with Harbage that the irregularity of the verse in his early plays is the result of conscious if mistaken choice, not of incompetence; it also shows that all theories which divide the authors' shares in the slightly later *Indian Queen* on the supposition that Dryden could write regular verse but Howard could not, are simply wrong.

Presumably the success of *The Surprisal* encouraged him to continue writing for the stage; and his next play, *The Committee*, was to be one of the most popular of all Restoration comedies. It was first produced, at the Theatre Royal in Vere Street, in October or

6. The Dryden poem has been interpreted fully by Earl R. Wasserman in *The Subtler Language* (Baltimore, 1959).

November of this same year, 1662, and was revived countless times during the following years and in the eighteenth century—for example, in 1663 (at the new theater in Bridges Street), 1667, 1668, 1669, 1676, 1686 and until at least 1788. Then in the adaptation by Knight under the title of *The Honest Thieves* (first acted at Covent Garden in 1797) it held the stage into the nineteenth century. *The Committee* was also often printed: in *Four New Plays* (1665) and *Five New Plays* (1692), in at least three eighteenth century editions, and then often again in Bell's *British Theatre*.[7] It has had the further distinction of being one of the only two of Howard's plays (the other is *The Duke of Lerma*) to be reprinted in the twentieth century.[8]

In his Epilogue, Howard asks us to:

> Accept this half years purchace of his Wit,
> For in the compass of that time 'twas Writ

and in the Prologue he stresses a certain novelty in what he has written:

> However his design was well enough,
> He try'd to shew some newer fashion'd Stuff.
> Not that the name *Committee* can be new,
> That has been too well known to most of you:
> But you may smile, for you have past your doom;
> The Poet dares not, his is still to come.

The reference is to the political satire that provides the play both with its title and with its novelty (although the possibilities of making drama from the situation of the years just before the Restoration, and from the penniless Cavaliers and the Puritans who had acquired their estates, may have been brought home to Howard by Abraham Cowley's *Cutter of Coleman Street*—a reworking of his old play *The Guardian*—acted at Lincoln's Inn Fields in December, 1661). Howard's plot centers on the Committee for Sequestrations, of which, as he says,

7. It had sufficient fame also for its story to be told in *A Companion to the Theatre . . . Containing the Stories of the most Celebrated Dramatic Pieces*, printed for F. Cogan and J. Nourse (London, 1740); and as late as 14 January 1789 W. Powell acknowledges receipt of £1/1/0 from Lowndes "for Corrected Bookes of The Committee & Every Man in his Humour" (B.M. Add. MS 38729, f.205).

8. Edited by C. N. Thurber, University of Illinois Studies in Language and Literature, No. 7 (1921). For rather perverse reasons, Thurber based the text on a prompt copy of 1776. *The Indian Queen* has also been reprinted, but only because of Dryden's association with it.

many of his audience would have had unhappy memories dating from the days before the Restoration when the Committee demanded that Royalists "take," or subscribe to, the Presbyterian Covenant as the price of being allowed to "compound" for their own property, otherwise liable to be sequestered or confiscated. Such satire would naturally have a special appeal for a Royalist audience after the Restoration, and for the King himself; he attended a special performance at the Theatre Royal on 13 May 1667, and another at Court on 8 February 1669.[9] The topicality of the play is also the point of Steele's (or Addison's) amusing reference to it over forty years later: "My friend Sir Roger de Coverley . . . told me that he had a great Mind to see the new Tragedy with me, assuring me at the same Time, that he had not been at a Play these twenty Years. The last I saw, says Sir Roger, was the *Committee*, which I should not have gone to neither, had not I been told before-hand that it was a good Church of *England* Comedy."[10]

Topical interest, however, is not what makes a play last on the stage: it may even be a disadvantage. Genest went so far as to say in 1832 that "the political part of it, which no doubt contributed to its popularity originally, now hangs as a dead weight upon it, as the greater part of an audience is not acquainted with the history and manners of the time a little preceding the Restoration"—but he added that the comic roles of Teg and Obadiah "have singular merit" such as could still make the play worth while. There is a similar comment in Baker's slightly earlier *Biographia Dramatica*: "even in our time, when the species of character against which the satire of it is principally aimed . . . is totally abolished and forgotten among us, [it] has been frequently performed, and never made its appearance without giving satisfaction to the audience, and producing all the effects which the true *vis comica* ever has on the mind: a certain sign that the piece must possess some, if not a capital, share of wit."[11]

In spite of Genest, I question whether the political satire can ever have been "a dead weight" upon the play; indeed that some of it seemed relevant to later periods is proved by Jacob's note early in the eighteenth century that "The *Committee* has lately been forbid to be acted, the Audience turning some Scenes of it, by Party Interpretations,

9. P.R.O., L/C. 5/139, p. 129, and 5/12, p. 17, cited by Nicoll, pp. 343-344.
10. *Spectator,* 25 March 1712, No. 335.
11. Genest I, 56; Baker, I, 375-376.

to Times they never were intended to represent."[12] Any theater-goer
would be amused by the portrayal of the hypocrisy of the members
of the Puritan committees; and although the special viewpoint of the
dramatist is, naturally enough, that of the Royalist who had suffered
from just such misappropriation of property as is shown in his play,
no special knowledge of seventeenth-century history is needed for an
appreciation of the development of the theme announced by the
Coachman on the first page: "Plague on this new Gentry, how liberal
they are." An audience not aware of the resentment at the Puritan
abolition of the Prayer Book might not fully appreciate Arbella's
jibe at the studied performance of stupid Abel Day, jocularly coached
by Ruth to impress Arbella by pretending that he is immersed in
affairs of State:

> *Abel* Pardon, Mistress, my profound Contemplations,
>   In which I was so hid that you cou'd not see me.
> *Arbella* This is a set Form,—they allow it
>   In every thing but their Prayers

but there is no missing the point of their later conversation:

> *Abel* I know Parliament-men, and Sequestrators;
>   I know Committee-men, and Committee-men know me.
> *Arb.* You have great acquaintance, Sir?
> *Abel* Yes, they ask my opinion sometimes.
> *Arb.* What weather 'twill be; have you any skill, Sir?
> *Abel* When the weather is not good, we hold a Fast.
> *Arb.* And then it alters.
> *Abel* Assuredly.
> *Arb.* In good time. . . .
> *Abel* Our profound Contemplations
>   Are caused by the conservation of our Spirits
>   For the Nations good, we are in labour.
> *Arb.* And I want a deliverance.   (Act II)

All the satire is aimed at the smug hypocrisy with which the Puritans
carry out their misdeeds, notably their sequestration of Royalist lands:

> *Obadiah* The order is, that the Composition arising out of
>   Mr. *Lashley*'s Estate, be and hereby is invested and allow'd to
>   The honourable Mr. *Nathaniel Catch*,
>   For and in respect of his sufferings and good service.
> *Mr. Day* It is meet, very meet, we are bound
>   In duty to strengthen our selves against the day of trouble,

12. *The Poetical Register*, I, 143.

When the common Enemy shall endeavour to raise
Commotions in the Land
And disturb our new built *Zion*.   (Act II)

Had there been any to challenge this, the standard charge against the Puritans in the literature of the Restoration, the Royalist authors could have pointed to the avowal in the Parliamentary *Souldiers Catechisme* of 1644 wherein the Parliamentary soldier was taught to affirm that he fought not against the King but "to rescue the King out of the hands of his and the Kingdomes enemies; and to maintaine his Honour and just Prerogatives." This is exactly the line of attack followed by Samuel Butler in *Hudibras*, Part I of which was published about this very time, early in 1663.

In its context in *The Committee*, Mr. Day's hypocrisy is even worse than the quotation above makes it seem, since he is indulging in reciprocal bribery, by which he persuades the Committee of Sequestrations to place Arbella's estate in his hands, in return for the favors he has meted out to the other members, who are content "to take the burthen" upon them "and be Stewards to the Nation." One of the "Committee-men" caps this with the sanctimonious:

Now verily it seemeth to me
That the work goeth forward, when Brethren
Hold together in Unity

and later informs the Royalist Colonel Careless:

Know, we must keep our rules, and instructions, lest we
Lose what providence hath put into our hands.

The committee scene from which these quotations are taken, in Act II, is perhaps the best in the play. Unfortunately Howard could not really go on beyond this point, and again his invention fails him, particularly in the last act, but not only there.

The plot tells of the adventures of two heroes, Colonels Blunt and Careless, and two heroines, Ruth and Arbella, who are all in the clutches of the Committee. Blunt and Careless have come up to London to compound for their estates (but refuse to take the Covenant as the price of being allowed to do so); Ruth, who is really Annice, daughter of the late Sir Basil Throughgood, has been brought up by the Chairman of the Committee, Mr. Day, as his daughter, only that he may profit from her estates; and Arbella, "a rich Heir of one that di'd in the/King's Service, and left his Estate under Sequestration," has unluckily been a fellow-passenger with Mrs. Day in the coach from Reading to London and is now firmly in that worthy's clutches, as a bride for her doltish son Abel. A fully satisfactory plot would surely show the *outwitting* of the Puritans by the Royalists; but the happy ending depends in fact on a lucky accident, when Mr. Day leaves his keys unattended and Ruth is able to steal not only the deeds of her own and Arbella's estates but also dishonorable letters with which she can blackmail the Days into agreeing to her marriage to Careless, and Arbella's to Blunt, and to the return of all their estates to the rightful owners. This, eked out by the arrest of Careless and his rescue from prison, and the escapades of his Irish servant, Teg, is hardly enough for a full five-act play. But at least Howard has abandoned his heroics, and the play remains on the level of comedy nearly all the time.

The stagecraft (again on the Elizabethan-type stage, with the "unlocalized scene" and constant movement and action) is quite competent; and the dialogue, if not witty *enough* (particularly in comparison with what was later to be written by Etherege, Wycherley, and Congreve), does not fall flat. Howard is not at his best when dramatizing the wit-combats of the sexes, but at least there is humor in the conquest by beauty of the misogynist Blunt, and in the contrast between Blunt's scenes with Arbella and the much sprightlier exchanges of his friend Careless and the pert Ruth.

The characterization is always adequate and often much better than that. Blunt, Careless, and the grasping Day may all be "types" but each is amusing in a different way; and Ruth and Arbella, in their campaign against the Days, have just a little of the gaiety of the Shakespearian comic heroines and a similar likable honesty in knowing what they want and setting out to get it (with an occasional more serious note, as when they suddenly realize that they have taken it for granted that they are in love with *different* men and have an anxious moment or two until they check up). Certainly actresses of the caliber of Mrs. Barry and Anne Bracegirdle, who played these parts in 1706, would have made something of them and particularly of the scenes in which Ruth, at Mrs. Day's request, instructs Abel Day how to woo Arbella. One is reminded of the joke played on Malvolio, as Ruth tells Abel that he must be very dignified like his father's clerk

Obadiah, and produces results even better than she could have hoped
for, as in Abel's announcement (in Act IV):

> An important affair hath call'd my Honourable Father
> And Mother forth, and in the absence of *Obadiah* I am enforced
> To attend their Honours, and therefore I conceiv'd it right
> And meet to acquaint you with it; lest in my absence you
> Might have apprehended, that some mischance had befallen
> My person: therefore I desire you to receive consolation;
> And so I bid you heartily farewel.   *Exit*
> *Arb*. Given from his mouth this tenth of *April*.

The best female part in *The Committee*, however, is almost certainly Mrs. Day. She is a non-stop talker and busybody; and such
characters can become as tiresome in a play as they are made to seem
to the other characters. Howard avoids this danger of monotony very
skilfully indeed, in at least four ways. First, we are kept interested by
the variety of her topics: nobody can mention a subject which does
not give her "a new Theam," as Blunt quickly recognizes to his cost.
Secondly, the sheer vulgarity of her attempts to impress is amusing:
the plot discloses that she was once kitchen maid to Careless's father,
and everything she says is consistent with such a background. A good
example would be the anecdote with which she tries to impress Blunt,
of the time she was one of eleven passengers on a coach journey:

> There was, in the first place, my self,
> And my Husband, I shou'd have said first; but his Honour
> Wou'd have pardoned me, if he had heard me;
> Mr. *Busie* that I told you of, and his Wife;
> The Mayor of *Redding*, and his Wife;
> And this *Ruth* that you see there, in one of our Laps—
> But now, where do you think the rest were?
> *Col. Blunt* A top o'th' Coach sure.
> *Mrs. Day*   Nay, I durst swear you wou'd
> Never guess—why—
> '   Wou'd you think it;
> I had two growing in my Belly,
> Mrs. *Busie* one in hers, and Mrs. Mayoress of *Redding*
> A chopping Boy, as it proved afterwards in hers;
> As like the Father as if it had been spit out of his mouth;
> And if he had come out of his mouth, he had come
> Out of as honest a Mans Mouth as any in forty Miles
> Of the head of him:
> For wou'd you think it,

> At the very same time when this same *Ruth* was sick,
> It being the first time the Girl was ever coach'd,
> The good Man Mr. Mayor,
> I mean, that I spoke of,
> Held his Hat for the Girl to ease her Stomach in.   (Act I)

(This, I think, catches the idiom and the rhythm of the speaking voice splendidly.) Thirdly, our interest is held by the discomfort of those forced to listen to Mrs. Day, particularly those who are so unwise as to try to get a word in or to express an opinion. She has the trick of imputing to others the introduction of the subject on which she has chosen to expatiate ("And now you talk of/This same *Abel*, I tell you but one thing . . ."—to people who would rather talk of anything else); and her chief victim, her husband, is mercilessly snubbed even for trying to be gracious:

> *Ruth* Your pleasure, Sir.
> *Mr. Day* Nay, 'tis my Wife's desire that—
> *Mrs. Day* Well, if it be your Wife's, she can best tell
>   It her self, I suppose: d'ye hear, *Ruth*, you may . . . (Act I)

Also, her prolixity is only part of her character; and as we listen to her talk, we watch at the same time the disclosure of her avaricious schemes, the product of cunning but not of high intelligence.

Another memorable comic character is the chief tool of the Days, the pompous Puritan Obadiah, Clerk to the Committee of Sequestrations. Obadiah takes himself very seriously indeed: "my care and circumspection," he solemnly believes, are necessary for the running of the State. He can never be hurried, either in speech or in his walk: "I am a Rogue," Careless avows, "if I have not seen a Picture / In hangings walk as fast" (Act II) and one can imagine the laugh a good actor would get when, sent on an errand by Abel, Obadiah gravely moves off the stage announcing "I shall use expedition" (Act IV). Certain of success also would be the scene in which Teg gets him drunk and he appears "with nothing fix'd / About him but his Eyes" —and is seduced into singing Cavalier songs of riotous anti-Puritan abuse. Fortunately we have Colley Cibber's tribute to Underhill's performance in the part later in the seventeenth century: "In the solemn formality of *Obadiah* in the *Committee* . . . he seemed the immoveable Log he stood for! a Countenance of Wood could not be more fixt than his, when the Blockhead of a character required it"

—and Cibber mentions the role in the same breath as *The Squire of Alsatia*, as one well known and well worth playing.[13]

Yet it was none of these parts that first made the play famous. Evelyn saw it on 27 November 1662: "a ridiculous play of Sir *R: Howards* where that Mimic *Lacy* acted the Irish-footeman to admiration"; on 12 June 1663 Pepys found it "a merry but indifferent play, only Lacy's part, an Irish footman, is beyond imagination"; on 13 August 1667 he noted: "Sir W. Pen and I to the King's house, and there saw 'The Committee', which I went to with some prejudice, not liking it before, but I do now find it a very good play, and a great deal of good invention in it; but Lacy's part is so well performed that it would set off anything"; and Downes confirms that it was one of Lacy's greatest roles, when, speaking of *The Rehearsal*, he quotes the doggerel rhymes:

> For his Just Acting, all gave him due Praise,
> His Part in The Cheats, *Tony Thump*, *Teg* and *Bayes*,
> In these Four Excelling; The Court gave him the *Bays*.[14]

Remembering Lacy's success as Brancadoro in *The Surprisal*, one is tempted to say that Howard owed him a lot; but Lacy might well have said that the debt was the other way. Anthony Leigh, Quin and Macklin, among others, also had success in the part, although, because it lent itself to gags, it sometimes got the players into trouble (Leigh in the role offended James II at Oxford in July 1686).[15] Thurber goes so far as to say that possibly Teg is "the prototype . . . of the comic Irishman of the stage today" and Summers mentions the Teague of Farquhar's *Twin-Rivals* as among the imitations; but there were comic Irishmen in English drama before Howard, notably in Shakespeare (and at least one of them had been called Teague) and it would be difficult to trace direct lines of descent.[16] Family tradition alleges that the character was based on one of Howard's own servants.

13. *An Apology for the Life of Mr. Colley Cibber, Comedian, and Late Patentee of the Theatre-Royal. With an Historical View of the Stage during his Own Time. Written by Himself* (London, 1740), p. 92.

14. Evelyn, *Diary*, III, 345; Pepys, *Diary*, III, 155, VII, 62-63; John Downes, *Roscius Anglicanus, Or an Historical Review of the Stage . . . from 1660 to 1706* (London, "1708" [1711?]), pp. 15-16.

15. Downes, *Roscius Anglicanus*, ed. Summers, p. 146.

16. Thurber, *The Committee*, Preface, p. 7; Summers, *Playhouse of Pepys*, p. 266 n.109. The earlier Teague was in *The Welsh Ambassador*, probably by Dekker and Ford.

So Charles Howard, in his *Historical Anecdotes of Some of the Howard Family*, tells how "When Sir Robert was in Ireland, his son was imprisoned here by the parliament" and how Sir Robert sent one of his domestics to work through friends for his son's release; the servant reappeared with good news but not until he had spent several days in Dublin, and being asked why, "the honest Hibernian answered, with great exultation, that he had been all the time spreading the news, and getting drunk for joy among his friends." "From this, Sir Robert took the first hint of that odd composition of fidelity, and blunders, which he has so humourously worked up in the character of Teague."[17] Charles Howard gives no source for the story, and Paget naturally asks whether before the Restoration any of Sir Robert's sons was old enough to be worth imprisoning (the eldest would have been only 13 in 1659).[18]

It is doubtful whether the search for an original of Teg is worth while. The character is not subtle or complex, but all depends on Teg's being "simply honest." He is completely literal-minded; to him taking the Covenant means stealing a copy of it from a Bookseller (and this, in his master's presumed interest, he proceeds to do). He is quite unaware of his own limitations; and being asked by Careless where his first master is, gravely replies

> He's dead, Mastero, and left poor *Teg*;
> Upon my soul, he never serv'd poor *Teg* so before. (Act I)

He knows that Mrs. Day is no lady by birth; accordingly when he is sent on an important mission to flatter her, although he does as he is told, he laughs every time he uses the form of respectful address and the interview reaches its inevitable conclusion:

> *Abel* Sirrah, we that are at the head of affairs
>   Must punish your Sauciness.
> *Teg* You shall take a knock upon your Pate, if you are
>   Saucy with me, that I shall; you Son of a Roundhead, you.
> *Mrs. Day* Ye Rascally Varlet, get you out of my Doors.
> *Teg* Will not I give you my Message then?
> *Mrs. Day* Get you out, Rascal?
> *Teg* I prethee let me tell thee my Message?
> *Mrs. Day* Get you out, I say.

17. London, 1769, pp. 111-113.
18. *Some Records of the Ashtead Estate*, p. 44 n.

Teg Well then I care not neither; the Devil take
Your Ladyship, and Honourship, and Kitchenship too: there now.
Exit. (Act III)

No doubt a still better dramatist would have put more into the language itself; but while *it* is no more than adequate, the opportunities
afforded for fun, and for good fooling on the stage, are numerous, and
Lacy and others took them.

When we think of Restoration comedy, we tend to do so in terms
of Wycherley and Congreve, and forget that it was some years after
the return of Charles II before drama reached their standard. *Love
in a Wood*, Wycherley's first play, belongs to 1671 and his master-
piece *The Country Wife* to 1675, while Congreve's *The Old Bachelor*
can hardly have been written before 1689 or 1690. Even Etherege's
Comical Revenge, generally said to have begun the great revival of
drama, belongs to 1664, the year after Dryden's first play, *The Wild
Gallant*; and *The Comical Revenge*, it should be remembered, has,
alongside its witty subplot of the Comedy of Manners type, a "main"
plot (written in verse) which is of the kind that Howard had included in *The Blind Lady* and *The Surprisal* but had practically
abandoned in *The Committee*. If, indeed, *The Committee* were
printed in prose, as it nearly all could be, so that the loose "verse"
form (which it shares with such plays as Cowley's) did not disguise
its true character, then it might be seen for what it is, a unified and
amusing comedy, new in its time, and probably the first good play to
be written after the Restoration.

Chapter five

TWO HEROIC PLAYS—AND JOHN
DRYDEN

IN view of the success of *The Committee*, it is surprising that Howard
did not attempt to follow it up with another satirical comedy. Instead
of doing so, however, he turned to a different kind of play altogether
and helped to lead the way in a new, and to us not so desirable, direction, by writing what has sometimes been called the first English
"Heroic play," *The Indian Queen.*

The best definition of the new literary form was to be given by
Dryden, when he wrote that "an Heroick Play ought to be an imitation, in little of an Heroick Poem; and, consequently . . . Love
and Valour ought to be the Subject of it."[1] Dryden had come to this
conclusion, he tells us, from a study of Ariosto and Tasso among
others; and from such sources (and Aristotle's dicta about the tragic
hero) there developed the theory, later expressed in the Prefaces to
The State of Innocence and Fall of Man and *Troilus and Cressida*,
that whereas a tragedy must be "more than barely possible," must
have "a likeness of truth" and be "probable," "an heroic poet is not
tied to a representation of what is true, or exceedingly probable." The
hero of the Heroic play, as of the Heroic poem, must far exceed in his
magnanimity (in the older sense) any virtue to which the ordinary
mortal might aspire. He was, in effect, an ideal; and the contemporaries of Dryden and Howard admired the heroes of such literature
for precisely this reason—the reason for which we lose interest in
them, since the modern preference is, generally speaking, for psychological reality, and for *development* of character in dramatic terms,
whether towards greater virtue or less. Tasso and Ariosto also provided precedent for the use of chivalrous love as the motive of the
plot (as it had not been in the literature of the Romans and the
Greeks). The plot, although frequently based on history, would normally progress through a series of surprises, including reversals of
fortune and unexpected revelation of identity, to an ending that need
not be tragic (even in the sense of demanding the deaths of the prin-

1. "Of Heroique Plays. An Essay," prefixed to *The Conquest of Granada
by the Spaniards* (1672). See also A. E. Parsons, "The English Heroic Play,"
M.L.R., XXXIII (1938), 1-14, to which I am indebted for much in this paragraph, and Bonamy Dobrée, *Restoration Tragedy 1660-1720* (Oxford, 1929).

cipal characters); and in the English form an exotic setting was preferred. The rhyming heroic couplet, while not obligatory, would
generally be the meter used; and the heroic prose romances would be
the most popular sources (particularly those of La Calprenède and
Scudéry).

It is clear that in this use of source material and in other ways,
French literature contributed a great deal to the Heroic play. The
growing fashion for rhyme in drama was itself, of course, in imitation
of the French plays; and in so far as the English Heroic play tended
to become an analysis, in something like a series of verse debates, of
a situation involving conflicting motives (especially love and honor)
it was an adaptation of French tragedy—not the tragedy of Racine,
whose first work belongs to 1664, but, as Allardyce Nicoll pointed out,
that of Corneille.[2] Perhaps one might even say that the English Heroic
play most often pursued the same kind of debate as in French tragedy,
to the opposite conclusion—not the triumph of reason over passion,
as in *Bérénice*, but the triumph of love.

In spite of this French influence, there is no longer any doubt that,
as Alfred Harbage has shown, all the elements of the Heroic play of
the Restoration were present in the drama written before the closing
of the theaters in England in 1642, especially in Cavalier drama but
not only there: Heroic drama is, in a sense, a development of the
tragi-comedy of Fletcher and Massinger; and Dryden himself emphasized the importance, in this development, of the work of Sir
William Davenant and particularly of his *Siege of Rhodes* (1656).[3]
(In fact, most of the elements are already present in Davenant's earlier
Love and Honor.) Nicoll also shows how close to Cavalier drama,
on the one hand, and to Heroic drama proper, on the other, is such
a play as George Cartwright's *The Heroick-Lover*, printed in 1661.[4]
Here—and, significantly, in rhyme—we already have the bombastic
Restoration hero choosing between love and duty:

> My love to fair *Francina*, bids me not;
> My duty to my *Prince*, can't be forgot

although this hero decides that duty must come first and so, quite
implausibly and unnecessarily, kills himself, that the Prince may have

2. *English Drama*, I, 97.
3. *Cavalier Drama*, chap. iii. Nicoll (p. 93) draws attention also to Rochester's
rewriting of Fletcher's tragi-comedy *Valentinian*.
4. *Op. cit.*, I, 104.

no rival in his attempts to win the lady—attempts which turn out to be in vain.

I should further agree with Nicoll, and with W. S. Clark, in suspecting that at first the most important figure in the development of the Heroic play was Roger Boyle, Earl of Orrery. As Harbage has demonstrated, Orrery did not invent the form, as was once argued,[5] and he was more attracted to French classicism than were his friends and rivals, but he may have been influential in showing what could be done with the older form in the new theater. His play *The General* (originally, and later again, known as *Altamira*) was not produced in London until after Howard's *Indian Queen*; but it was acted in Dublin in October, 1662, and known in manuscript at Court before that. Orrery married Sir Robert Howard's cousin Margaret, daughter of Theophilus Howard, Earl of Suffolk, brother of the Earl of Berkshire; and in the dedication to *The Rival Ladies* in 1664 Dryden specifically acknowledged an indebtedness to Orrery, not as the originator but as the reviver of the heroic couplet. Both Howard and Dryden, then, may well have benefited from Orrery's experience when they themselves experimented with Heroic drama.

What is certain is that it was the success of *The Indian Queen* at the Theatre Royal in Bridges Street in January 1664 that led to the vogue of this kind of drama on the Restoration stage. How much of the credit for the play belongs to Howard is, however, uncertain.

That the problem may be seen in the right perspective from the beginning, the main facts should be briefly stated. They are, that *The Indian Queen* was published in Howard's *Four New Plays* in March, 1665, with a title-page describing all four of them as "Written by the Honourable Sir *Robert Howard*," and republished in his *Five New Plays* in 1692, reissued in 1700; that Dryden, in the "argument" distributed to members of the audience on the first night of his *Indian Emperor,* a sequel to *The Indian Queen* and acted in the following year, referred to the earlier play and added in parenthesis "part of which poem was wrote by me"; that he nevertheless did not include *The Indian Queen* in the list of his plays published with his *King Arthur* in 1691, although he did include *The Tempest* which he adapted in collaboration with Davenant; and that *The Indian Queen* was not included in the Collected Edition of Dryden's plays in 1701.

5. Notably by Clark, who edited Orrery's *Dramatic Works* (Cambridge, Mass., 1937) and wrote a series of articles on him in *M.L.R.* and elsewhere.

Yet no less an authority than Allardyce Nicoll at least twice calls the play "Dryden's *The Indian Queen*"![6] I cannot help wondering how seriously Howard's claim to authorship would have been taken had it depended on one parenthetical remark and had the play been published in Dryden's collected works and never in Howard's. If it be argued that Howard was later to be accused of using another's brains without adequate acknowledgment, in *The Duke of Lerma*, it is also true that one contemporary, Clifford, thought it to Dryden's discredit that he based his Almanzor on the character of Montezuma in *The Indian Queen*,[7] and another accused Dryden of stealing *The Wild Gallant* from Howard.[8] At any rate, it should be clear that on the external evidence alone, no strong case could be made out for a large share by Dryden.

I must also question the validity of Dryden's *later* works as evidence of his authorship of *The Indian Queen*, since what those later plays have in common with the earlier one could always be the result of what Dryden learnt from Howard.[9] One must rely rather on what one can discover about the characteristics of the work of the two *before* their collaboration in this play—and again the facts have been grossly misinterpreted. Scott, for example, writes that "the versification of this piece, which is far more harmonious than that generally used by Howard, shews evidently, that our author [Dryden] had assiduously corrected the whole play, though it may be difficult to say how much of it was written by him."[10] What Scott, who had read *Poems 1660*, should have remembered was that Howard could write heroic couplets quite competently when he chose; and like most who

<hr/>

6. *English Drama*, I, 96 n. 1 and 118. Similarly C. L. Day (*The Songs of John Dryden*, Cambridge, Mass., 1932) attributes to Dryden two of the songs from *The Indian Queen*, on the ground of their similarity to the incantation scene in the later *Indian Emperor*, and also prints as his, "You to whom Victory we owe," while remarking "there is no way of telling, apparently, whether the song is by Dryden or Howard" (p. 142). James Kinsley, *The Poems of John Dryden* (Oxford, 1958) prints the Prologue, Epilogue, and Songs, but does admit in a note that "none of the pieces printed here can be certainly attributed to him, or to him alone" (IV, 1825).

7. *Notes upon Mr. Dryden's Poems* (1687), also cited by Scott, I, 83.

8. "The Session of the Poets, to the Tune of Cock Lawrel," printed in *Poems on Affairs of State* at the end of the century but probably composed at least twenty-five years earlier: cited in *The Works of John Dryden*, ed. E. N. Hooker and H. T. Swedenberg (Berkeley, 1956), I, 255 n. 2.

9. I differ here from Nicoll, *English Drama*, I, 110.

10. *The Works of John Dryden*, Introduction, I, 83.

have discussed the problem (perhaps all except Harbage), Scott was misled by the irregular verse of Howard's three earlier plays—verse which, as has been demonstrated, is written in the mistaken belief that such irregularity was appropriate in a certain kind of play—and drew the erroneous conclusion that Howard's verse without Dryden's help would not even have scanned.

There is no doubt that the two men were in close contact at this time. Indeed, towards the end of 1663 Dryden and Howard were living in the same house, as is shown by a letter from Sir Andrew Henley dated from Bramshill 8 October 1663 and addressed to Howard "In Lincols In feilds the sixth Doore from Turnstyle Holborne Row London." It seems that Howard was about to purchase from Henley a house (in which he had already lived as Henley's tenant) together with some of the contents, but Henley was retaining certain pieces of furniture, including "the serge Bed Mr Dreiden useth."[11] Dryden's residence with Howard at this period is confirmed by the anonymous author of "The Medal of John Bayes" (1682), when, after tracing Dryden's career to the point at which he became "Journey-man" to "Mr. Herringman," the Bookseller, "who kept him in his House for that purpose," he continues:

> Then by th' assistance of a Noble *Knight*
> Th' hadst plenty, ease and liberty to write

(and a footnote explains: "Sir *R.H.* who kept him generously, at his own House"). Shadwell (if he was the author) goes on:

> First like a *Gentleman* he made thee live;
> And on his Bounty thou didst amply thrive.
> But soon thy Native swelling Venom rose,
> And thou didst him, who gave thee Bread, expose.
> 'Gainst him a scandalous Preface didst thou write,
> Which thou didst soon expunge, rather than fight.
> (When turn'd away by him in some small time)
> You in the Peoples ears began to chime,
> And please the Town with your successful Rime. . . .

The reference to the later controversy over rhyme in drama does not concern us for the minute; but it is clear that in Shadwell's eyes Howard was Dryden's benefactor, and a generous one.

11. B. M. Sloane MS 813 f. 71, first printed by W. S. Clark, *M.L.N.*, XLII (1927), 16-20. That the reference is to John Dryden was questioned by C. E. Ward, *R.E.S.*, XIII (1937), 298-300, but Clark defended his interpretation, in *R.E.S.*, XIV (1938), 330-332.

Then on 1 December of this same year (1663), Dryden married Howard's sister, Elizabeth. The marriage must, in one sense at any rate, have seemed an act of favor on the part of the Howards; the lady's father was an Earl (albeit not a wealthy one) and therefore she was far above Dryden in social standing. Perhaps this was why years later, in 1682, some of Dryden's enemies were anxious to suggest in their lampoons that it was a forced marriage, and an unhappy one.[12]

At any rate, during these months just before the first performance of *The Indian Queen* in January, 1664, Howard could have had the assistance of his guest and future brother-in-law while working on his play. That Dryden did have a share in it we acknowledge, because Dryden said so; but he himself claimed no more than that, and I cannot believe that during the following years when he and Howard were publishing their controversy over drama and when Dryden did not hesitate to question the authenticity of Howard's *Duke of Lerma*, he would not have asserted his own authorship of whole scenes or more of *The Indian Queen* if he had in fact been entitled to the credit.[13]

12. The evidence is inconclusive: what is known is that there were three children of the marriage, of whom the eldest, Charles, was not born until 1666, and that Lady Elizabeth was still living with her husband when he died in 1700. (Soon after his death, she became insane; she lived until 1714.) See G. R. Noyes, ed., *The Poetical Works of Dryden* (Cambridge, Mass., 1909, revised 1950), "Biographical Sketch," p. xx, and references given there. In a letter to Malone of 18 May 1799, Lady Dryden spoke of Lady Elizabeth's "having, to bad conduct before marriage, united bad conduct afterwards, & having used Mr. Dryden very indifferently"; and Honor Pigott in the same year recorded the family tradition that Dryden and his wife "were very Unhappy, for she was of a most sad temper" (the letters are given by J. M. Osborn, *op. cit.*, pp. 245-246 and 250).

13. I also suggest that an attempt such as J. H. Smith's to distinguish Dryden's share in the play is doomed to failure from the start, since some of the premises are wrong ("The Dryden-Howard Collaboration," *S.P.*, LI (1954), 54-74). Where Smith is right is in asserting that at the time of the composition of *The Indian Queen*, Howard, as the author of *The Committee* and *The Surprisal*, was both the more experienced and the more famous of the two writers, *The Wild Gallant* being the only play by Dryden to have been already produced, and that a failure. "Thus," as Smith well says, "it would seem likely that Sir Robert would have felt entitled to take the lead not only in proposing any collaboration but also in deciding what sort of play he and his prospective brother-in-law should do together, and in planning the same" (p. 56). Unfortunately the conclusions he draws—that Dryden went further than Howard intended when collaboration was first proposed, and wrote Act I, Act II Sc. i and Act III—depend on a belief that Howard could not write fluent verse unaided; on imaginary biography; and on the supposition that any scene of *The*

It seems to me that literary history must treat *The Indian Queen* as Howard's, while recognizing the probability that Dryden showed an interest in it and contributed to its success in some indefinable but not major way.

The beginning of the play indicates immediately the author's desire to move away from the continuous action of the unlocalized Elizabethan-type stage, and to experiment with the facilities for scenery and spectacle offered by the new theater. Davenant, for one, had experimented with scenery in the theater before this, but he had used it rather for background and as decoration than for its own sake or for what it could contribute to the action. Howard goes much further. "As the Musick plays a soft Air," says the stage direction for the Prologue, "the Curtain rises softly, and discovers an *Indian* Boy and Girl sleeping under two Plantain-Trees; and when the Curtain is almost up, the Musick turns into a Tune expressing an Alarm, at which the Boy wakes and speaks." The costumes were most lavish (Mrs. Behn said in her *Oronooko* in 1688 that she had given to the King's Company for use in *The Indian Queen*, presumably in Act V, a set of feathers presented to her in Surinam);[14] and that audiences were impressed even more by the spectacle than by the play itself is implied by the references to it of Pepys and Evelyn. Pepys noted on 27 January 1664: "to Covent Garden, to buy a maske at the French House, Madame Charett's, for my wife; in the way observing the streete full of coaches at the new play, 'The Indian Queene'; which for show, they say, exceeds 'Henry the Eighth'";[15] and Evelyn confirms this on 5 February: "I saw acted the *Indian Queene* a Tragedie well written, but so beautified with rich Scenes as the like had never ben seene here as

---

Indian Queen in which there is no obvious parallel to Howard's other plays must have been written by Dryden, even though there is no parallel to Dryden's other work either. All that Smith proves is that Howard's share was certainly *not* minor.

As further evidence against Mr. Smith's divisions, it might be worth mentioning that he tends to give Howard scenes containing inexact rhymes, on the theory that Howard's ear was bad; yet he says nothing of the presence in Act III (given to Dryden) of rhymes like "bear"—"her," "upon"—"alone" and "less"—"increase." The heroic quatrains in Acts II and III are also not good evidence of Dryden's authorship; they merely show, as Harbage pointed out, the lasting influence of Davenant (*Cavalier Drama*, p. 65) and, of course, the desire for variety.

14. Noted by Genest, I, 57-58.   15. *Diary*, IV, 23.

happly (except rarely any where else) on a mercenarie *Theater*."[16]
Evelyn's distinction here between the "mercenarie" or commercial
theater on the one hand and, presumably, the private and Court
theaters on the other, is significant. Howard was developing what had
been done in the Elizabethan private theater and was transferring to
the public stage the kind of lavish presentation that had been customary
in masques and (to a lesser extent) in Italian opera; and it may help
a modern audience to appreciate the play if it is remembered that part
of the pleasure the Restoration audience had from it was almost precisely the pleasure that we derive from our later but no more realistic
operas. (Towards the end of Howard's life Purcell did in fact turn
The Indian Queen into an opera, as will be seen.) Pepys testifies also
to the skill with which it was performed; on 1 February, after mentioning that he had been told that the King had been to see it, he
continues: "so home to dinner, and took my wife out immediately
to the King's Theatre, it being a new month, and once a month I
may go, and there saw 'The Indian Queene' acted; which indeed is
a most pleasant show, and beyond my expectation; the play good, but
spoiled with the ryme, which breaks the sense. But above my expectation most, the eldest Marshall [Anne] did do her part [Zem-
poalla] most excellently well as I ever heard woman in my life; but
her voice was not so sweet as Ianthe's [Mrs. Betterton's]; but, however, we came home mightily contented."[17]

The Prologue is interestingly used not only for atmosphere but also
to prepare the audience to accept the characters of the main play as
godlike, above ordinary mortal concern:

> *Boy* Wake, wake, *Quevira*; our soft rest must cease,
> And fly together with our Country's Peace. . . .
> By ancient Prophecies we have been told
> Our World shall be subdu'd by one more old;
> And see that World already's hither come.
> *Quevira* If these be they, we welcome then our Doom.
> Their Looks are such, that Mercy flows from thence,
> More gentle than our Native Innocence.

16. *Diary*, III, 368-369. But the alternative reading "or happly except rarely
any where else" would seem to make better sense. The scenery of *The Indian
Queen* was so successful that it was called for often afterwards in other plays,
by Dryden and others. See T. B. Stroup, "Scenery for the *Indian Queen*,"
M.L.N., LII (1937), 408-409.

17. *Diary*, IV, 27-28.

Boy Why should we then fear these are Enemies,
    That rather seem to us like Deities?
Quevira By their protection let us beg to live;
    They came not here to Conquer, but Forgive.
    If so, your Goodness may your Pow'r express;
    And we shall judge both best by our success.

Even if in this way the lines are neatly turned into the customary
flattery of the audience, the entry of the Ynca of Peru with his magnificent general Montezuma, prisoners and attendants, has been well
prepared for.

The tone of the play is set by the very first speech, that of the
Ynca to Montezuma:

> Thrice have the *Mexicans* before us fled,
> Their Armies broke, their Prince in Triumph led;
> Both to thy Valour, brave young Man, we owe;
> Ask thy Reward, but such as it may show
> It is a King thou hast oblig'd, whose Mind
> Is large, and like his Fortune unconfin'd.

If this were realistic dialogue, one might have to brand the Ynca an
egoist and a braggart; but it is not. It is a kind of declamation, a
dramatic proclamation; and as in all later Heroic drama, the function
of the characters is to strike attitudes and to mouth sentiments (almost as in a Richardson novel). Their method of expressing themselves, and of drawing attention to their own virtues, is no more to
be used as evidence against them than is the speech of an actor in a
pageant. So, when Montezuma adds in an aside

> He sees my Service is above
> All other payments but his Daughters Love

the audience are meant to accept the dramatic fact, that Montezuma's
service is great, but it is not to occur to them to ask whether Montezuma ought to be the one to say so. Nor, of course, if the modern
reader is to enjoy the play, is he to quibble about the terms in which
the Restoration Superman describes his love: "our mutual Fires" is
the conventional phrase and we need expect no other.

At the opening of the play, then, the hero Montezuma, who has
come to the Peruvian court as a stranger, has by his own great powers
defeated the Mexican enemies of Peru and hopes to be rewarded with
the hand of the Ynca's daughter, Orazia:

> I beg not Empires, those my Sword can gain;
> But for my past and future Service too,
> What I have done, and what I mean to do;
> For this of *Mexico* which I have won,
> And Kingdoms I will Conquer yet unknown;
> I only ask from fair *Orazia*'s Eyes
> To reap the Fruits of all my Victories.

Genest was probably the first to point out (I, 57) that it was these lines that Fielding had in mind when in his immortal skit on seventeenth- and eighteenth-century heroics, *The Tragedy of Tragedies, or, The Life and Death of Tom Thumb the Great,* he made Tom Thumb proclaim:

> I ask not kingdoms, I can conquer those;
> I ask not money, money I've enough;
> For what I've done, and what I mean to do,
> For giants slain, and giants yet unborn,
> Which I will slay—if this be called a debt,
> Take my receipt in full: I ask but this,—
> To sun myself in Huncamunca's eyes   (I.iii)

—Huncamunca similarly being the daughter of the King for whom Thumb is General.

The Ynca's refusal to bestow his daughter on a stranger and his struggle to hold back his rage are presented in the same stagey manner:

> *1st Peruvian* Our *Ynca*'s Colour mounts into his Face.
> *2nd Peruvian* His Looks speak Death

and he offers Montezuma another chance to request the towns and kingdoms he deserves, only to be told:

> Thou giv'st me only what before I gave.
> Give me thy Daughter.

The next character to speak in this idiom is the captured Mexican Prince, Acacis, who urges Montezuma to show restraint:

> No, I must your Rage prevent,
> From doing what your Reason wou'd repent;
> Like the vast Seas, your Mind no limits knows,
> Like them lies open to each Wind that blows—

and here yet another characteristic of the Heroic style is clearly seen: the simile taken from the most obvious aspects of nature and applied quite mechanically and tritely, but always with the implication that the argument from analogy is valid unless refuted by another analogy.

This is one of the many characteristics of Heroic drama that Samuel Butler parodied so delightfully in his "Repartees between Cat and Puss at a Caterwalling in the Modern Heroic Way";[18] Fielding also had great fun with it in *Tom Thumb*, for example in the marriage blessing by the Parson:

> Long may they live, and love, and propagate,
> Till the whole land be peopled with Tom Thumbs!
> So, when the Cheshire cheese a maggot breeds,
> Another and another still succeeds:
> By thousands and ten thousands they increase,
> Till one continued maggot fills the rotten cheese.   (II.ix)

Acacis' speech succeeds only in making Montezuma resolve that since he must not kill the father of his beloved, he will join the Ynca's enemies, the Mexicans. A. E. Parsons has seen in this an equivalent of the withdrawal of the epic hero Achilles from battle, but probably Coriolanus would provide a nearer parallel. (In fact Howard's principal source, freely adapted, is one of the French romances to which his success turned many English dramatists for their new material, the "Histoire de Zelmatide heritière de l'Empire des Incas, et de la Princesse Izatide," in De Gomberville's *Polexandre*, probably in the translation by William Browne.)[19] What is more significant than any literary parallel, however, is the absence of any real mental conflict on the part of the Heroic hero: if he has a struggle of conscience, the result is merely announced; and the main function of the plot is to place the character in one dilemma after another and make the audience wonder which of the two possible courses of action he will pursue. For the statement of resolves and the announcement of fixed policies, the couplet is the best literary medium; and its use, of course, helps to make the dialogue of the Heroic play sound like a series of epigrams (or truisms). One of the few forms of variation possible is curtness in rejoinder and reply: and then we have, in effect, the Elizabethan Senecan stichomythia, as in the ensuing dialogue of Montezuma and Acacis:

> *Acacis* Your Honour is oblig'd to keep your trust.
> *Montezuma* He broke that Bond in ceasing to be just.

18. *Satires and Miscellaneous Poetry and Prose*, ed. René Lamar (Cambridge, 1928), pp. 137-138.

19. Parsons, *op. cit.*, p. 9. The main source was pointed out by Clark, *R.E.S.*, IV (1928), 55-57 and by Summers, *Playhouse of Pepys*, p. 174.

Acacis Subjects to Kings shou'd more Obedience pay.
Montezuma Subjects are bound, not Strangers, to obey.

If it were an Italian opera, this would be a duet for tenor and baritone; and Samuel Butler again found it rather absurd:

Cat Force is a rugged Way of making Love.
Puss What you like best, you always disapprove.
Cat He that will wrong his Love will not be nice,
    T'excuse the Wrong he does, to wrong her twice.
Puss Nothing is wrong, but that which is ill meant.
Cat Wounds are ill cured with a good intent. . . .[20]

At any rate, within a few minutes the characters have been speedily, if neither subtly nor convincingly, maneuvered into the first of many paradoxical situations: Montezuma is fighting with the Mexicans against the father of his beloved Orazia, while Acacis the Mexican is staying with the Peruvians to protect Orazia and her father from the Mexican attacks.

The next character to be introduced is Zempoalla, the usurping Queen of Mexico, mourning her supposedly dead son Acacis and vowing in the presence of her general Traxalla that all her future prisoners shall be sacrificed to the God of Vengeance. One notices again how the chief difficulty of the language of the Heroic play is not to rise to a climax but (and in this it is like much early Elizabethan tragedy) to sink to the level of the normal. Zempoalla's "Hark, hark, what noise is this that strikes my Ear" is a good example. We have previously had

Montezuma Hark, hark.
Acacis What noise is this invades my ears?

In a realistic play, such a line would be bathetic and fatal to all illusion; in stylized recitative it is inadequate, but apparently Mrs. Marshall was able to prevent its sounding absurd.

At the beginning of Act II Montezuma triumphantly captures Orazia and her father; but one speech from Orazia is enough to make him repent:

But I'll redeem my self, and act such things,
That you shall blush *Orazia* was deny'd;
And yet make Conquest, though with wearied Wings,
Take a new flight to your now fainting side.

20. *Op. cit.*, p. 137.

It was of just such decisions that Shadwell must have been thinking when in his epilogue to *The Virtuoso* (1676) he wrote:

> But of those Ladies he despairs to day
> Who love a dull Romantick whining Play;
> Where poor frail Woman's made a Deity,
> With senseless amorous Idolatry;
> And sniveling Heroes sigh, and pine, and cry.
> Though singly they beat Armies, and huff Kings,
> Rant at the Gods, and do impossible things;
> Though they can laugh at danger, blood, and wounds;
> Yet if the Dame once chides, the milk-sop Hero swoons.
> These doughty things, nor Manners have nor Wit;
> We ne're saw Hero fit to drink with yet.[21]

In this respect, of course, the Heroic play is at the opposite extreme from the classical epic—as nobody would know better than Howard, having translated the Dido section of Virgil's *Aeneid*.

When Acacis again does the noble thing, by allowing Montezuma to retain control of his captives, it is Zempoalla's turn to be placed in a dilemma: either she must claim them or break her vow of sacrifice. Acacis now confesses to Montezuma that he also is in an impossible position: his mother has no right to her throne, having won it by treachery when Traxalla slew her brother; the rightful Indian Queen is Amexia, of whom nothing is known. Then the positions of the pieces on the chessboard are immediately changed again: word comes that Traxalla has seized Orazia and her father, and so the two potential rivals for her hand, Acacis and Montezuma, must join forces to save her. Montezuma's distress at the news of the capture, incidentally, is again announced, by Montezuma himself, and not demonstrated:

> *Orazia* forc'd away! What tempests roul
> About my thoughts, and toss my troubled Soul?

Clearly, the interest of the audience must be held by the changing situation and not by such psychology as this.

Situations continue to change rapidly in Act III, but first the audience is entertained with more spectacle. "*Zempoalla* appears seated upon her Slaves in Triumph, and the Indians as to celebrate the Victory, advance in a Warlike Dance; in the midst of which

21. *The Complete Works of Thomas Shadwell*, ed. Montague Summers (London, 1927), III, 181; also cited by Nicoll, p. 85 n. 3.

Triumph, *Acacis* and *Montezuma* fall in upon them. *Zempoalla* descends from her Triumphant Throne, and *Acacis* and *Montezuma* are brought in before her." If this sounds like the scenario for a Hollywood musical named "Anna and the King of Peru," perhaps the comparison has its virtues: it serves to remind us that today also there are forms of entertainment ostensibly dramatic in kind which enthrall devotees not by any coincidental resemblance to any living being but by spectacle, music, dancing, exotic scenery, glamorous personages, and exciting situations instead. Such virtues, plus perhaps a certain verbal charm, are precisely what *The Indian Queen* offered in the theater of Charles II (nor was this the first or last upper-class audience to have literary tastes that were in one sense unsophisticated).

Another good illustration of this is afforded by the scene later in Act III in which Zempoalla visits the prophet and sorcerer Ismeron (an incident that A. E. Parsons would compare with the visit of the epic hero to the underworld). She begins the scene with a purple passage, like an aria, on a Shakespearian theme:

> He stirs not; ha, in such a dismal Cell
> Can gentle Sleep with his soft blessings dwell?
> Must I feel tortures in a humane Breast,
> While Beasts and Monsters can enjoy their Rest?
> What quiet they possess in sleeps calm bliss!
> The Lions cease to roar, the Snakes to hiss. . . .

Ismeron soon breaks into song with the incantation "You twice Ten Hundred Deities," and the God of Dreams rises and refuses to tell Zempoalla what lies in the future. To soothe her in her rage and disappointment, the conjurer next summons Spirits of the Air, who sing to her:

> Poor Mortals that are clog'd with Earth below
> Sink under Love and Care,
> While we that dwell in Air
> Such heavy Passions never know . . .

and the scene closes with Zempoalla threatening to burn all the temples of all the prophets unless Montezuma can be inspired with love for her (her love for him having previously been announced, by her, and shown to have placed her in yet another dilemma:

> Does he command in Chains? what wou'd he do
> Proud Slave, if he were free, and I were so?

> But is he bound, ye Gods, or am I free?
> 'Tis love, 'tis love, that thus disorders me:
> How Pride and Love tear my divided Soul!
> For each too narrow, yet both claim it whole.)[22]

Act IV makes use of a different scene again, Montezuma's prison cell, into which Traxalla brings Orazia. Montezuma will be killed unless Orazia yields to Traxalla, and the sword is drawn; then "enter *Zempoalla* hastily, and sets a Dagger to *Orazia's* Breast," threatening to kill *her* (whom Traxalla loves) if Traxalla kills Montezuma (whom Zempoalla loves). Here, surely, is *the* typical scene of the play: a tableau in which the various conflicts as they are at that moment are symbolized by the positions of the four characters on the stage; and just as typically, the next move is a reversal of the positions, as each tries to protect the loved one directly: "He [Traxalla] puts her [Zempoalla] by and steps before *Orazia*, and she [Zempoalla] runs before *Montezuma*." The dialogue takes the form of the operatic quartet:

> *Traxalla* Can fair *Orazia* yet no pity have?
>   'Tis just she shou'd her own Preserver save.
> *Zempoalla* Can *Montezuma* so ungrateful prove
>   To her that gave him Life, and offers Love?
> *Orazia* Can *Montezuma* live, and live to be
>   Just to another, and unjust to me?

attaining its climax in Montezuma's joyful cry when Orazia is thus brought to confess her love for him. Significantly, too, the action has almost reached a stalemate: none of the characters can make the first move! The stalemate is averted only by the entrance of the jailer.

Zempoalla now orders Montezuma to be confined in darkness, and decides to join forces again with Traxalla and to offer up the other captives to sacrifice; and it is Orazia's turn to explain the paradox of *her* situation:

> How are things ordered, that the wicked shou'd
> Appear more kind and gentle than the good!
> Her Passion seems to make her kinder prove,
> And I seem cruel through excess of Love:
> She loves, and wou'd prevent his Death; but I
> That love him better, fear he shou'd not die.

22. Again to Fielding's amusement. See *Tom Thumb*, I, vi.

This conflict is solved by Acacis, who liberates them both; but then announces that, having thus repaid his debt to Montezuma, he can now admit his rivalry for the love of Orazia—and demands that they fight for her! This reversal of the expected thus places Montezuma in yet another dilemma, which he proceeds to describe:

> Oh Tyrant Love, how cruel are thy Laws!
> I forfeit Friendship, or betray thy Cause.
> That Person whom I wou'd defend from all
> The World, that Person by my hand must fall.

The duel, however, like all duels except one in Howard's plays, is inconclusive, although Acacis is wounded: it is interrupted by Orazia, and soon all are again in the power of Zempoalla and Traxalla, leaving Acacis with yet another problem on his hands:

> Now, *Montezuma*, since *Orazia* dyes,
> I'll fall before thee, the first Sacrifice;
> My title in her death shall exceed thine,
> As much as in her life, thy hopes did mine:
>   And when with our mixt blood the Altar's dy'd,
>   Then our new Title let the Gods decide.

Never in the history of drama can the act-curtain have fallen on a question to which the audience had less chance of predicting the answer.

Act V is the most spectacular of all. "The Scene opens, and discovers the Temple of the Sun all of Gold, and four Priests in habits of white and red Feathers, attending by a bloody Altar, as ready for Sacrifice. Then Enter the Guards, and *Zempoalla*, and *Traxalla*; *Ynca*, *Orazia*, and *Montezuma* bound; as soon as they are plac'd, the Priest sings."

The Ynca, precisely because his forgiveness can have no real result, now forgives Montezuma for his presumption in loving Orazia. Acacis, having pleaded with Zempoalla for the life of Montezuma and having been "forgiven" by Orazia, carries the play's particular brand of reasoning to its "logical" end:

> You said, you did both Pity, and Forgive;
> You wou'd do neither, shou'd *Acacis* live.
> By Death alone, the certain way appears,
> Thus to hope Mercy, and deserve your Tears. *Stabs himself.*

Again, however, the intrusion of an outsider is necessary to avoid the stalemate; messengers arrive announcing an invasion by Amexia and an army:

> King *Montezuma* their Lord shouts Proclaim,
> The City rings with their new Sovereign's Name;
> The banish'd Queen declares he is her Son,
> And to his succour all the people run

and we are apparently to overlook the bathos while we marvel at the new irony of this information for Zempoalla:

> Can this be true? O Love! O Fate! have I
> Thus doated on my mortal Enemy.

Even now there must be a further surprise: "She sets a Dagger to *Montezuma*'s Breast" as if to kill him:

> Dye then, ungrateful, dye; *Amexia*'s Son
> Shall never triumph on *Acacis* Throne:
> Thy death must my unhappy flames remove;
> Now where is thy defence—against my love?
> > *She cuts the Cords, and gives him the Dagger*
> *Traxalla* Am I betrayed? *He draws and thrusts at* Montezuma,
> > *he puts it by and kills him.*
> *Montezuma* So may all Rebels dye.

(The irony of that pronouncement, coming from Montezuma, is apparently unintentional.)

Amexia enters with her army, and the identity of Montezuma as her son is soon confirmed. The following account of the upbringing of Montezuma by Garrucca is based on Howard's translation of Statius' account of the training of Achilles by Chiron—and probably intended to suggest the heroic parallel:

> *Montezuma* I owe him all that now I am,
> He taught me first the noble thirst of fame,
> Shew'd me the baseness of unmanly fear,
> Till th'unlick'd Whelp I pluck'd from the rough Bear,
> And made the Ounce and Tyger give me way,
> While from their hungry Jaws I snatch'd the Prey:
> 'Twas he that charg'd my young arms first with toils,
> And drest me glorious in my Salvage spoils.—
> *Garrucca* You spent in shady Forest all the day,
> And joy'd returning to shew me the Prey.
> To tell the story, to describe the place,
> With all the pleasures of the boasted chase.

Montezuma, Orazia, Amexia and the Ynca are prepared to forgive Zempoalla; but, voicing still another paradox, she kills herself:

> The greatest proof of Courage we can give,
> Is then to dye when we have power to live.

It cannot be accidental that the closing speech of Montezuma stresses the ironies and contradictions of life:

> So strange a fate for Men the Gods ordain
> Our clearest Sun shine shou'd be mixt with rain;
> How equally our joys and sorrows move!
> Death's fatal triumphs join'd with those of Love.
>   Love Crowns the dead, and death Crowns him that lives,
>   Each gains the Conquest which the other gives.

Clearly, if one may adapt the words of the Poet Laureate, of these have the songs been fashioned, the tales been told; and if they have not been fashioned and told to the finest dramatic effect, it is because it is the business of the best drama to explore one conflict fully rather than to pile as many novel conflicts as possible one on the other. Significantly, it is the novelty and the ingenuity of *The Indian Queen* that the Epilogue stresses:

> You see what Shifts we are inforc'd to try
> To help out Wit with some Variety . . .
> You have seen all that this old World cou'd do,
> We therefore try the fortune of the new . . .
> 'Tis true, y'have marks enough, the Plot, the Show,
> The Poet's Scenes, nay, more, the Painter's too. . . .

For these qualities, *The Indian Queen* was an overnight wonder; but one spectacle can always be outdone by another, and in the following year Dryden was to cap Howard's play with a kind of loose sequel, *The Indian Emperor* (the connection being in the character of Montezuma, with the addition of his two sons and daughter, and the son and two daughters of Zempoalla and Traxalla, and also the ghosts of Traxalla, Acacis and Zempoalla). *The Indian Emperor* is—let us not mince words—far more absurd than *The Indian Queen*; and Dryden lived to say in the Epistle Dedicatory to *The Spanish Friar* (1681), that the only defense for the more extravagant passages of all his Heroic plays "is, that I knew they were bad enough to please, even when I writ them." That he had learnt the exact formula for pleasing is shown in the Prologue to *The Indian Emperor* when he writes ironically:

> We neither promise you one Dance, or Show,
> Then Plot and Language they are wanting too:

and that formula had been made popular by *The Indian Queen*. "Unnatural but never dull" was Genest's just verdict on Howard's play; but its only hope of revival today, and this also is just, would be in the full operatic version of Purcell.[23]

The Vestal Virgin, Or, The Roman Ladies. A Tragedy was apparently Howard's attempt to follow up the success of his first Heroic play, and perhaps is also evidence of his desire to write a true tragedy (*The Indian Queen* had been called one, on the title-page, and certainly the Queen, Zempoalla, had committed suicide, as had the noble Acacis; but hero and heroine, Montezuma and Orazia, had survived). *The Vestal Virgin* is an inferior play and may not have had a very long run in the theater: neither Evelyn nor Pepys mentions it, and Downes includes it only in a list of "divers other plays" by modern authors acted by the King's Company (although since such stage-successes as *The Country Wife, Love in a Wood, The Rehearsal* and *The Committee* are on the same list, this is not in itself evidence of failure).[24] It is thus possible that Shadwell is referring to it specifically when in Act III of *The Sullen Lovers* he has Sir Positive, his caricature of Howard, prepare a statement, to be signed by one of his critics, "that the Play of Sir *Positive Att-All* Knight, called the Lady in the Lobster, notwithstanding it was damn'd by the Malice of the Age, shall not onely read, but it shall act with any of *Ben Johnson's*, and *Beaumont's* and *Fletcher's* Plays."[25] On the other hand, Shadwell may have been thinking not of *The Vestal Virgin* in particular but of Howard's plays in general. "The Lady in the Lobster," meaning, strictly, the calcareous structure in the stomach of the lobster (supposed to resemble in shape a seated woman), would seem to have become proverbial for something in which there was only a small core of substance, in proportion to a large amount of flabbiness (Swift similarly chose the phrase in *The Battle of the Books* to ridicule Dryden's inability to wear Virgil's armor with distinction: "For, the

23. Genest, I, 57; for Purcell, see later, pp. 299-303.
24. *Roscius Anglicanus*, ed. Summers, p. 15.
25. The suggestion is made by J. H. Smith, *op. cit.*, p. 63.

Helmet was nine times too large for the Head, which appeared Situate far in the hinder Part, even like the Lady in a Lobster, or like a Mouse under a Canopy of State, or like a shrivled Beau from within the Pent-house of a modern Perewig."[26] The name might, then, be applied in scorn to any or all of the plays of a dramatist one wished to ridicule as having a minimum of sense.

The Vestal Virgin was published in the *Four New Plays* of 1665, and that it had already been acted is shown by the formula: "Just as the last Words were spoke, Mr. *Lacy* enter'd and spoke the *Epilogue*" (which follows). The play's chief claim to fame is that, like Suckling's *Aglaura,* it has an alternative comic ending and could be acted, presumably on successive days, in two different forms. The comic version also has an "*Epilogue* Spoken by Mr *Lacy,* who is suppos'd to enter as intending to speak the Epilogue for the *Tragedy.*

> By your leave, Gentlem—How! what do I see!
> How! all alive! Then there's no use for me. . . ."

This form of the Epilogue contains a reference that helps to date the play:

> All that I wish is that the *Dutch* may fight
> With as ill fortune as we Poets write—

although, as J. H. Smith points out, it does not necessarily date it after the official declaration of war against Holland on 4 March 1665: indeed it cannot do so, for the play was published in *Four New Plays* in March 1665. Pepys, for one, thought of the war as beginning in 1664.[27]

Mr. Smith goes on to work out an elaborate theory that *The Vestal Virgin* was first written in loose blank verse before *The Indian Queen* and rewritten in couplets after it. "Demonstrating this would take too long to be feasible here," he writes; "instead of doing so, I offer the reader the choice of taking my word for it, or reading the play himself."[28] It is a fair offer—and I reach the opposite conclusion. Mr. Smith argues that the alleged failure of *The Vestal Virgin* turned Howard against rhyme and so led him to quarrel with Dryden's Epistle Dedicatory to *The Rival Ladies* championing rhyme, and thus begin the famous controversy. I think he is quite unfair to Howard

---

26. *"A Tale of a Tub" With Other Early Works,* ed. Herbert Davis (Oxford, rep. 1957), p. 157.
27. Smith, *op. cit.,* pp. 59-60.   28. *Ibid.,* p. 60.

and misrepresents the controversy, which, as will be shown, did not involve any ill feeling at all in the early stages. Although *The Indian Queen* was a success, Howard is equally likely to have believed sincerely that unrelieved rhyme was a mistake, however popular: this, at any rate, was what he *said,* and continued to say. It would then be to Howard's credit that he did not rest on the laurels of *The Indian Queen* but decided to write another play, a tragedy, in which rhyme would be used alongside the free blank verse he had relied on in his earlier plays. The experiment was, in our eyes, a failure; perhaps it was so in his also, although his only other play, *The Duke of Lerma* (1668), occasionally varies blank verse with passages of rhyme. And in the preface to *The Duke of Lerma*, so far from resenting Dryden's superior skill in rhyme, he went out of his way to admit it: "speaking of Rhyme in Plays, he desires it may be observ'd, That none are violent against it, but such as have not attempted it, or who have succeeded ill in the attempt; which as to my self and him I easily acknowledge; for I confess none has written in that way better than himself, nor few worse than I." This acknowledgment is also quite consistent with the earlier explanation in the Preface to *Four New Plays*: "But while I give these Arguments against Verse, I may seem faulty that I have not only writ ill ones, but writ any; but since it was the fashion, I was resolv'd, as in all indifferent things, not to appear singular, the danger of the vanity being greater than the error; and therefore I follow'd it as a Fashion, though very far off."

There is, then, no call for such a rearrangement of dates and such a theory of rewriting as Mr. Smith proposes. Already in *The Indian Queen* Howard had tried to break the monotony of the rhyming couplets not only with quatrains but also with half-lines or incomplete lines unrhymed. In *The Vestal Virgin* there are many more of these freedoms, particularly for quick exchange of dialogue (Howard was to say, and with reason, in his controversy with Dryden that he found rhyme particularly absurd in question and answer, comment and rejoinder); it is the "set" or longer speeches that tend to be written in rhyme, although it is not confined to them (and on the whole the rhymed sections are the worst).

The play may be treated more briefly than *The Indian Queen*. The story involves three pairs of lovers, Sertorius and Marcellina, Tiridates and Hersilia, Artabaces and Verginia; but it is some time before these pairings sort themselves out. The prime mover of the action is the villain Sulpitius, brother of Sertorius; and his chief tool is Mutius, "One that had been a Lieutenant of a Province, a Lover of War." The play begins with Sulpitius trying to create discord by informing his brother Sertorius (who is at this stage in love with Hersilia) and his friend Tiridates, separately, that Hersilia does not wish to see them for a few days. The motive, of course, is his own love for Hersilia, revealed in a melodramatic soliloquy:

> Where must my wild beginnings find an end?
> Nature and Friendship; Brother too, and Friend!   . . .
> Yet all those ties keep not their hold so fast,
> As to oppose unshaken but one blast
> Of Love's unruly storm; great Trees fall so,
> Pulling up all about 'em where they grow.

Perhaps a character's being torn between love and honor was sufficient to gain him the interest and even the sympathy of the Restoration audience; but neither he nor the hero wins much of our respect as the former weaves his childish plots and the latter "droops":

> *Sulpitius* Why do you droop? fie, fie, do not give way
>   To your encroaching Griefs; hope and obey. . . .
> *Tiridates* My hopes are only rais'd by thy kind Charms,
>   O let me always hold thee in my Arms   *Embrace*

—enough, one would have thought, to justify Genest's "Howard seems to have been superlatively ignorant of Roman manners," although Summers found this verdict "rather hard."[29] Even classical scholars of Howard's standing, apparently, forgot all they had learnt of Roman codes of behavior, as soon as Love raised its ugly head on the Heroic stage; or perhaps it would be fairer to say that no real attempt has been made to adapt to a Roman setting incidents taken from Scudéry's *Artamène*[30] and perhaps other similar romances. Howard's Romans, Mexicans and Peruvians speak in the same idiom.

It is also characteristic of Heroic drama that Howard should not be prepared to rely on the intelligence of his audience. We may hear Sertorius and Tiridates told that it is Hersilia's wish that they should

---

29. Genest, I, 58; Summers, *Playhouse of Pepys*, p. 175.

30. Howard probably knew the English translation of 1653 and perhaps also Killigrew's adaptation of the story in *Cicilia and Clorinda*. Compare Harbage *Cavalier Drama*, pp. 247-248; Smith, *op. cit.*, p. 57 n. 8; Summers, *Playhouse of Pepys*, p. 175.

seem reserved, we may see them "bow and stand still" when she
speaks to them, but she must still say in an aside to Marcellina

> —Ha—*Marcellina*, a word.
> D'ye not observe what an unusual distance
> Prince *Tiridates*, and *Sertorius* keep?

And Marcellina must reply

> I both observe and wonder.

Also noteworthy is the number of inconclusive duels. One sometimes
feels that Heroic drama is more concerned to show people being put
in odd positions (for example, friend feeling that he ought to fight
friend) than to bring about any immediate results; and so although
Sertorius and Tiridates come to blows, they are parted by Sulpitius,
who, to be consistent, ought to be glad to see one of them dead.
(Instead he assures Sertorius that Hersilia would necessarily hate the
victor—and receives the unanswerable, if hardly moving, reply

> She's cruel now; if she her hate should show
> When I am dead, 'tis more than I shall know!)

Similarly, when Sertorius and Tiridates discover the treachery of
Sulpitius, they must debate at length the question of which of them
has the greater right to challenge the common enemy; but in the
long run neither fights him, since they decide that it is for Hersilia to
choose between them. The Act may then end with the dramatist drawing attention to his new and ingenious paradox:

> *Sertorius* How meanly we must part! never before
> Honour and Love shew'd such strange properties,
> To keep all safe by being Enemies;
> With their own niceness they themselves betray,
> And while they both Command they both obey.
> *Exeunt at several doors*

Act II introduces Verginia, the Vestal Virgin of the title, who has
returned to the home of her father Emilius (she is Hersilia's sister)
and is seeing a man for the first time. This, of course, is another of
the unique situations that the dramatist will use to catch the attention
of his audience, and the plot is quickly developed to that end. Sulpitius
schemes with Mutius to set fire to the house of Emilius and have
Hersilia carried off by Mutius and his discontented veterans as she
tries to escape from it (this being the method Mutius has found always

to work with coy "Damsels"). News of the fire comes to Sertorius and Tiridates just in time once again to stop a duel that we had hoped against hope might rid the story of one of them. (Sertorius has previously conducted this edifying conversation with his servant Caska:

> *Sertorius* If I shou'd fall by *Tiridates* Sword,
>   Carry the News thy self unto *Hersilia*,
>   And watch her as thou woud'st an Arrow shot,
>   To see whether it hit or no.
> *Caska* To what purpose, Sir?
> *Sertorius* If she had any pity for me living,
>   Her sorrow for me dead, will shew it.
> *Caska* But how, Sir, shou'd I send you word?
> *Sertorius* 'Tis true. . . .)

Act III gave theater-goers a new kind of spectacle. "The *Scene* appears a Burning-house" and into it plunges Artabaces ("Prince of *Armenia*, driven from his Country by the *Romans*" and elder brother of Tiridates), newly arrived in Rome. From the burning house he emerges "with *Verginia*, vail'd, and in a swoon," proclaiming

> Here's something yet, she was well sindg'd,
>   And had been over-roasted presently.

The humor is presumably deliberate; it is certainly misplaced. There is more of it in their ensuing dialogue, which must have been intended to appeal for its novelty, as the Vestal Virgin regains consciousness in the arms of a creature she can only assume to be another man and therefore another father. Artabaces, of course, is overcome by her purity and innocence, and willingly goes back into the fire to attempt to rescue her father and sister. The irreverent modern reader is more likely to be amused by it all, since the love duet continues at length as the house continues to burn, but Crowne's burning temple in the second part of *The Destruction of Jerusalem* suggests that at least one of Howard's contemporaries was so impressed as to wish to imitate.

After further melodramatic adventures (Howard certainly seems to have been at a loss for plausible complications of plot) both Artabaces and Verginia are captured by Mutius; Sulpitius carries off Hersilia; Sertorius rescues Marcellina (who has one extraordinarily inept soliloquy beginning

> —What shall I do, my thoughts are tir'd, I find,
>   With tedious Journeys up and down my mind);

and Tiridates rescues Emilius. Sertorius and Tiridates draw and are about to fight yet again; this time they defer the quarrel until they have both looked for Hersilia. This is presumably variation within a pattern.

In Act IV, after further complications tedious to relate, Marcellina, trying to aid Sertorius in a fight against Sulpitius and his men, is fatally wounded; and Sertorius, also wounded, discovers his love for her as they die hand in hand.

Act V is a tissue of horrors. Artabaces is blinded by order of Mutius, Tiridates is slain by Sulpitius; the brothers are however reunited before their deaths, and Tiridates indeed expires in his brother's arms:

> What hand or chance shut up those Eyes of thine?
> While I enquire the cause death closes mine.   *Dies*

Artabaces, although blind, manages to kill Mutius and then in turn dies in the presence of Verginia:

> *Verginia* Are you not dying too? O, let me know.
> *Artabaces* Yes, all the while I liv'd, I have been so. . . .
> We have no right in Time to come, no more
> Than we had Title to the Time before. . . .
> I cou'd have smil'd at loss of Life and Crowns,
> But at the loss of you—I dye—in Frowns.   *Dyes*

Perhaps the kindest words ever used of *The Vestal Virgin* were written by Charles Lamb of Verginia's ensuing speech. "There is," he wrote in his essay "The Superannuated Man," "a fine passage . . . in a Tragedy by Sir Robert Howard, speaking of a friend's death" and he quoted Verginia's

> . . . 'Twas but just now he went away;
> I have not since had time to shed a Tear;
> And yet the Distance does the same appear,
> As if h'ad been a thousand years from me.
> Time takes no measure in Eternity.[31]

Lamb's admiration for the sentiment is understandable; yet even here, where the rhyme is for once not unduly obtrusive, the expression as a whole cannot escape the charge of flatness.

It remains for Hersilia and Verginia to kill themselves, after a

31. Lamb, *Complete Works and Letters* (New York, 1935), p. 175.

little competition to see who shall do so first; for the unrepentant Sulpitius to be captured and condemned to be flung from the Tarpeian rock; and for Emilius in the closing speech to announce that he will pause only to revenge the deaths of his daughters and then die too.

The published play also gives the alternative happy ending, introduced with the words "Thus it was Acted the Comical way; the Alteration beginning in *Act IV*. towards the latter end. . . ." In this version Marcellina's intervention saves the life of Sertorius in the fight with Sulpitius and his men; and in the different Act V Mutius' servant Corbulo, after being shown heating the irons for the blinding of Artabaces (an incident which, oddly enough, is not in the tragic version), apparently remembers that Mutius has struck him (as he does not remember it in the tragedy) and instead of blinding Artabaces, provides him with a sword; and in the end everybody is saved except Mutius. As J. H. Smith has shrewdly pointed out, only in the comic version is the Corbulo motif completed and the pact made by Sertorius and Tiridates (that neither will avow his love to Hersilia until the other is present) carried out; and it would thus seem that the comic was the original version, even though the two epilogues make it clear that it was customary to act the tragedy first.[32] There is nothing to choose between them: so little of the action arises from character—indeed there is so little character—that one ending is no more arbitrary than the other.

Perhaps enough has been said to show that the play sinks to depths greater than those of *The Indian Queen*, and has not even the interest of the exotic, or pseudo-exotic, to compensate for its deficiencies. It could appeal, if at all, for a few ingeniously contrived situations and the discussion to which they give rise—discussion of problems arising from the conflict of two immovable forces, or of two irreconcilable emotions in one man's mind (in fact, of what is nowadays called "ambivalence"); but Howard is again unable to explore those conflicts or find moving language in which to state them.

He did not think easily in the images that we consider natural to great poetry; rather he seemed to think in commonplaces, to which he added mechanical similes in an attempt to make them poetic. One such simile, to be sure, has become proverbial in English, through another's use of it. As Thomas Stroup has pointed out, Verginia's

32. *Op. cit.*, p. 59.

Mind's like smooth Paper never writ upon,
When folded up, by some Impression,
Marks will remain it never had before,
And ne'er return to former smoothness more   (III.i)

may have suggested Locke's famous comparison of the mind to a white piece of paper in the *Essay concerning Human Understanding* (1690), although it is possible that the idea itself came to either Howard or Locke, or to both, from their reading of Hobbes.[33] I may add that Howard certainly did not mind an occasional plagiarism from Shakespeare: Emilius' lament over his dead daughters—"Death like a Frost on a too early Spring, /Stole on thy Blossoms"—being perhaps the most glaring. (Compare Capulet's "Death lies on her like an untimely frost / Upon the sweetest flower of all the field," in *Romeo and Juliet* IV.v. 28-29.)

The effect of *The Vestal Virgin*, for the modern reader, is, too often, bathos; one can only hope that for the Restoration audience the statement of theoretical problems of conduct and the performance of popular (and distinguished) actors and actresses, in parts that gave them ample opportunity to strike attitudes and to declaim, were enough to make the play seem worth while (as modern film audiences will excuse in a musical any plot that allows the star to perform the set dance or song). Probably, however, *The Vestal Virgin* did fail; and although Howard was prepared to publish it soon after its appearance in the theater, he did not attempt anything further in the kind. In that at least he was wiser than many of his contemporaries.

33. Thomas B. Stroup, "Philosophy and the Drama," *T.L.S.*, 19 January 1933, p. 40. The use of Hobbes in *The Indian Queen* II. iii—noted by Louis I. Bredvold, *The Intellectual Milieu of John Dryden* (Ann Arbor, 1934, rep. 1956), p. 67 n. 51—is thus not a reason for suspecting Dryden's authorship. On Dryden's alleged debt to Hobbes, see also J. A. Winterbottom, "Hobbesian Ideas in Dryden's Tragedies," *J.E.G.P.*, LVII (1958), 665-683.

MANY students of English literature who have not read a line of *The Surprisal, The Committee* and *The Vestal Virgin* nevertheless know of the volume, *Four New Plays*, in which they, together with *The Indian Queen*, were published in March, 1665; for in the Preface which he printed in this volume, Howard joined issue with his brother-in-law John Dryden on the question whether English plays ought to be written in rhyme. He thereby first took part in the so-called controversy for which, ironically enough, his name is still best known.

It would seem, on Dryden's own admission, that the discussion (and it *was*, originally, no more than that) began when "in my Epistle Dedicatory, before my *Rival Ladies*, I had said somewhat in behalf of Verse [rhyme], which he was pleased to answer in his Preface to his Plays."[1] This Epistle Dedicatory was printed with *The Rival Ladies* in 1664 and perhaps, though not necessarily, written before the play was entered on the Stationers' Register in June of that year. But there is no reason to believe with J. H. Smith that Howard had begun a "quarrel" with Dryden on the subject of rhyme before this.[2] It is true that at the conclusion of this epistle in which he dedicates *The Rival Ladies* to the Earl of Orrery, Dryden writes:

> I must remember 'tis your Lordship to whom I speak; who have much better commended this way by your Writing in it, than I can do by Writing for it. Where my Reasons cannot prevail, I am sure your Lordship's example must. Your Rhetorick has gain'd my cause; at least the greatest part of my Design has already succeeded to my Wish, which was to interest so noble a Person in the Quarrel, and withall to testifie to the World how happy I esteem my self in the honour of being,
> > My Lord,
> > > Your Lordship's most
> > > Humble, and most
> > > > Obedient Servant,
> > John Driden.

1. "A Defence of an Essay of Dramatique Poesie, being an Answer to the Preface of *The Great Favourite, or the Duke of* Lerma." (This was published in some copies of the second edition of *The Indian Emperor* in 1668.) See below, p. 108.
2. *Op. cit.*, pp. 61-62.

We surely need not assume that Dryden had already joined issue *with Howard* on the question of rhyme. "Quarrel" would more naturally mean the general discussion that had presumably been going on at least since the Restoration on the question whether English plays should, like the French, be written in rhyme; Dryden himself traces the discussion back to Sir Philip Sidney. All he is saying to Orrery, then, is that he is glad to be able to cite Orrery's practice as justification for his own play and his own theory. This in turn means that if there is no reference to Howard in Dryden's words here, Mr. Smith's whole case for the revision of *The Vestal Virgin* collapses on that ground also, because its first premise is wrong; and it is odd to force so limited an interpretation on the word "quarrel" and yet to accuse Dryden in effect of inaccuracy in his later specific statement that the exchange of opinion with Howard began with the Epistle Dedicatory to *The Rival Ladies*. Indeed, so far as Dryden was concerned, there was no personal "quarrel" *until Howard replied* to this, as is shown by the full passage from the "Defence of an Essay of Dramatic Poesy." It is: "But I gave not the first occasion of this difference in opinions. In my Epistle Dedicatory, before my *Rival Ladies*, I had said somewhat in behalf of Verse, which he was pleased to answer in his Preface to his Plays: that occasioned my Reply in my Essay, and that Reply begot this rejoynder of his in his Preface to The Duke of *Lerma*. But as I was the last who took up Arms, I will be the first to lay them down. . . ."

The Epistle Dedicatory to *The Rival Ladies* is, indeed, little more than a statement of a position: the avowal by an innovator that he has good precedent, and good reason, for his "New way . . . of writing Scenes in Verse." "Though, to Speak properly," he goes on, " 'tis not so much a New way amongst us, as an Old way new reviv'd: For many Years, before *Shakespears* Plays, was the Tragedy of Queen *Gorboduc* in *English* Verse, written by that famous Lord *Buckhurst*. . . ." Fortunately Dryden's argument does not depend on this remarkable display of ignorance. Even if rhyme had not previously been known in English drama, he goes on to say, England ought not to be as different in its plays as it is in its pronunciation of Latin from "the most polish'd and civiliz'd Nations of *Europe*." The difficulty is, he admits, the strength of the other English tradition, blank verse, which he (quite erroneously) thinks to have begun with Shakespeare:

"Shakespear (who with some Errors not to be avoided in that Age, had, undoubtedly a larger Soul of Pœsie than ever any of our Nation) was the first, who to shun the pains of continual Rhyming, invented that kind of Writing, which we call Blanck Verse, but the *French* more properly, *Prose Mesurée:* into which the *English* Tongue so naturally Slides, that in writing Prose 'tis hardly to be avoided."

"The only inconvenience with which Rhyme can be charged," he believes, is the occasional necessity to alter the natural word order for the sake of a rhyme (in blank verse, he maintains, the temptation is easily resisted by any writer of any ability at all). When rhymed verse is written without such dislocation, "it must then be granted, Rhyme has all the advantages of Prose, besides its own." Waller first showed "the Excellence and Dignity of it" and the advantages of closing the couplet. "This sweetness of Mr. *Wallers Lyrick* Pœsie was afterwards follow'd in the Epick by Sir *John Denham,* in his *Coopers-Hill*: a Poem which your Lordship knows for the Majesty of the Style, is, and ever will be the exact Standard of good Writing. But if we owe the Invention of it to Mr. *Waller,* we are acknowledging for the Noblest use of it to Sir *William D'avenant*; who at once brought it upon the Stage, and made it perfect, in the Siege of *Rhodes.*"

Dryden thinks it unnecessary to name all the advantages "which Rhyme has over Blanck Verse." One, mentioned by Sidney, is the help it gives in memorizing lines; another (and this was to provide one of the main sources of contention between himself and Howard) is that "in the quickness of Reparties, (which in Discoursive Scenes fall very often) it has so particular a Grace, and is so aptly Suited to them, that the suddain Smartness of the Answer, and the Sweetness of the Rhyme, set off the Beauty of each other." The greatest of all advantages, however, is that rhyme "Bounds and Circumscribes the Fancy." The poetic imagination "must have Cloggs tied to it, least it out-run the Judgment." Blank verse leads to verbosity; rhyme is not a mere embroidery but "when the difficulty of Artfull Rhyming is interpos'd, where the Poet commonly confines his Sence to his Couplet, and must contrive that Sence into such Words, that the Rhyme shall naturally follow them, not they the Rhyme; the Fancy then gives leisure to the Judgment to come in; which seeing so heavy a Tax impos'd, is ready to cut off all unnecessary Expences." One proviso Dryden does make—that a fit subject should be chosen. "Neither must the Argument alone, but the Characters, and Persons be great and noble. . . . The Scenes, which, in my Opinion, most commend it, are those of Argumentation and Discourse, on the result of which the doing or not doing some considerable action should depend."

Dryden has not said *enough* to convince anybody who doubted the validity of rhyme in English drama; and indeed his opinion hardly carried sufficient weight as yet to cause any admirer of blank verse to feel that his cause was lost or in danger of being lost. To Howard, however, it seemed that the theoretical case for rhyme was weak, particularly in so far as it depended on the argument that English drama ought not to lag behind the European in style; and so, although he himself had tried writing in rhyme "since it was the fashion" and "not to appear singular," he was now prepared to put the case for blank verse.

He did so in the Preface "To the Reader" printed with his *Four New Plays*. (This volume, containing the two comedies and the two "tragedies" all "As they were Acted by His Majesties Servants at the Theatre-Royal," was published by Herringman, and bears L'Estrange's *Imprimatur* "March 7. 1664/5.") The preface begins in the self-conscious style of the preface to the *Poems 1660*. Howard, asserting that he is very sensible of the danger of overrating one's own works, assures his readers that "these Follies were made publique as much against my Inclination as Judgment: But being pursu'd with so many Sollicitations of Mr *Herringman*'s, and having received Civilities from him if it were possible exceeding his Importunities; I at last yielded to prefer that which he believed his Interest, before that which I apprehended my own Disadvantage . . . there are few that know me but will easily believe I am not much concern'd in an unprofitable Reputation."

After this preliminary cough, he begins well: he is not concerned to defend his own plays, "yet I shall presume to say somthing in justification of our Nations Plays, though not of my own; since in my Judgment, without being partial to my Country, I do really prefer our Plays as much before any other Nations, as I do the best of ours before my own." Drama, he points out, is constantly changing: Terence and Plautus, for instance, would not necessarily draw audiences nowadays; nor is the contemporary French fashion for narration instead of action necessarily right, although it has won English admirers "who possibly believe well of it more upon the account that what the *French* do ought to be a Fashion, than upon the Reason of the thing." The Ancients themselves observed the rule because the kind of action they wrote about, such as "Heracles burning upon his own Funeral Pyle," could not be shown on the stage; "the *French* . . . without the necessity, somtimes commit the Error"; and, after all, Horace himself maintained "that every thing makes more impression Presented than Related." Howard adds that if there were not general agreement with Horace on this, there would be no more plays.

This is all true enough, and is a shrewd answer to Dryden's unsound argument for the use of foreign models (and that Dryden was not concerned only to point out that any style successful abroad was worth trying in England is shown by his repetition, in the *Essay on Dramatic Poesy*, of the argument that "the universal consent of the most civilized parts of the world ought in this, as it doth in other customs, to include the rest"). Howard's premises are right; and "if these Premises be granted," he continues, " 'tis no partiality to conclude, That our *English* plays justly challenge the Preheminence." This does not mean that they are perfect; Howard is inclined to think that English dramatists, except Ben Jonson, have been wrong in "mingling and interweaving Mirth and Sadness through the whole Course of their Plays" and now believes "that it is most proper to keep the Audience in one entire disposition both of Concern and Attention," since they may not otherwise make the necessary adjustments quickly enough, however mixed mirth and sadness may be in life. On this question, then, he admits having changed his mind; his own breaking of the unities in, for example, *The Surprisal* he would presumably now have criticized (just as he was to say he had been wrong in writing *The Indian Queen* and *The Vestal Virgin* mainly in rhyme). Perhaps he had been impressed by Samuel Sorbière's criticism of English neglect of the unities, in his *Relation d'un voyage en Angleterre* (1664), but he was with Sprat, who wrote a reply on behalf of the Royal Society (1665), in refusing to admit that his own nation's plays were necessarily inferior because of this, and he was with Sprat and against Sorbière on the question of blank verse.[3]

The mere fact, then, that the French fashion is for rhyme in drama

3. George Williamson, "The Occasion of *An Essay of Dramatic Poesy*," *M.P.*, LXIV (1946), 1-9, has drawn attention to the relevance of the works of Sorbière and Sprat in this connection.

does not seem to Howard very important. "This is the dispute betwixt many ingenious Persons, Whether Verse in Rhime, or Verse without the sound, which may be call'd Blank Verse, (though a hard Expression) is to be preferr'd? But take the Question largely and it is never to be decided, but by right application I suppose it may; for in the general they are both proper, that is, one for a Play, the other for a Poem or Copy of Verses; a Blank Verse being as much too low for one, as Rhime is unnatural for the other: A Poem being a premeditated form of Thoughts upon design'd Occasions, ought not to be unfurnish'd of any harmony in Words or Sound: The other is presented as the present Effect of Accidents not thought of." He therefore thinks rhyme to be particularly inappropriate when a reply completes the couplet, that is, when the thought is most clearly unpremeditated; and we may do him the justice of believing that his own practice in *The Indian Queen* had brought this to his attention—as it had not been brought to Dryden's, since Dryden, as has been seen, actually mentioned rhymed repartee for the way in which "the suddain Smartness of the Answer, and the Sweetness of the Rhyme, set off the Beauty of each other." Howard had common sense on his side and (although he may not have welcomed the ally) Samuel Butler too.

Nor is Howard impressed by Dryden's argument that rhyme curbs a "luxuriant Phansie": "this is no Argument for the Question in hand; for the dispute is not which way a Man may write best in, but which is most proper for the Subject he writes upon." Blank verse, as used in Beaumont and Fletcher, for example, is itself not the speech of everyday life; but these are all questions of *degree*, and rhyme is less life-like still. It is worst "when a Servant is call'd, or a Door bid to be shut in Rhime."

To Dryden's complimentary citing of Orrery's plays as proof of the success of rhyme in drama, Howard neatly replies that there rhyme does seem natural; but this "does not convince my Reason, but employ my Wonder." Then, after apologizing for his own attempts at rhyme,[4] he gives it as his opinion that the Italian plays mentioned by Dryden are inconsiderable, and the Spanish ones mostly only dramatized novels—and this is not *enough*. If his own practice is said to be no better, and is held against him, "in this I resemble the greatest

4. Quoted before. See p. 81.

part of the World, that better know how to talk of things than to perform them, and live short of their own Discourses."

In all this there was surely a good deal of common sense. Indeed, it is interesting to compare Howard's arguments for the more "natural" blank verse with what Mr. T. S. Eliot has been saying in our own day. Mr. Eliot has pointed out that good dramatic prose such as Congreve's is itself not "natural," not the speech of everyday life: but at least prose is not regarded by a member of the audience "as a wholly different language from that which he himself speaks." "And . . . the audience, its attention held by the dramatic action, its emotions stirred by the situation between the characters, should be too intent upon the play to be wholly conscious of the medium."[5] That was surely Howard's argument against rhyme; and it is a valid one.

It should also be clear that, so far at any rate, there was nothing like a personal quarrel between Dryden and Howard. Nothing had been said that either could have resented; and in fact in the very next year, 1666, Dryden prefixed to his *Annus Mirabilis* a letter to Howard which is eloquent testimony to their continuing friendship. It begins:

> I am so many ways oblig'd to you, and so little able to return your favours, that, like those who owe too much, I can onely live by getting farther into your debt. You have not only been careful of my Fortune, which was the effect of your Nobleness, but you have been sollicitous of my Reputation, which is that of your Kindness. It is not long since I gave you the trouble of perusing a Play for me, and now, instead of an acknowledgment, I have given you a greater, in the correction of a Poem. . . . I should not have written this but to a Person, who has been ever forward to appear in all employments, whither his Honour and Generosity have call'd him. . . .

Dryden adds that Howard can bear witness that the poem was written in a place where the poet could not so much as converse with a seaman to check the naval terms used; the letter is subscribed "From *Charleton* in *Wiltshire, Novem.* 10. 1666." Dryden and his wife, driven from London by the plague, which had closed the theaters on 5 June 1665, had gone down to the home of Lady Elizabeth's father, the Earl of Berkshire, and, although there were differences of opinion over Lady Elizabeth's dowry, remained there for more than a year.

That Sir Robert had been on the side of his sister and his brother-

---

5. *Poetry and Drama: The Theodore Spencer Memorial Lecture 1950* (London, 1951), pp. 13, 12.

in-law in the dispute with Berkshire is shown by a letter from the Drydens to Sir Robert Long, on 14 August of this year:

Since you have been pleasd thus farr to give Your self a trouble in our businesse, the whole profit of which we owe originally to you, when you wrought my Lord to Assign the patent, we hope you will so much own your former Kindnesse as to keep what money you receive for us in your hands till we come up. As for the unreasonable proposition my Lord Berkshyre made, & writ us word that you approv'd it, we well know it was only to be rid of his importunityes[.] we have sent an Acquittance signd by us both with this inclos'd; & a letter which Sir Robert Howard has done us the favour to write to you, on purpose that the money might be receiv'd by no other then your self in whom we absolutely confide.[6]

Sir Robert Long was at the time Auditor of the Receipt in the Exchequer; Howard had recently resigned the office of Clerk of the Patents, in which capacity he would have worked with Long. It will be remembered that £3000 out of the "patent" referred to, the grant of £8000 made to Berkshire in 1662, had been assigned to Elizabeth Dryden; that none of it had been paid; and that in 1666 the grant had therefore been newly assigned on the receiver of rents. What Dryden scholars have not known, I believe, is that Berkshire had mortgaged the money in advance; and my suggestion would be that his "unreasonable proposition" was that Elizabeth's share also should go to pay off the mortgage. At any rate, Howard stepped in and arranged with Long on 13 August 1666 that the money should be held for his sister and her husband.[7] Nor did Howard leave the matter there; on 21 August of the following year, 1667

Sir Robert Howard moves the confirmation of a warrant of the late Lord Treasurer on behalf of his sister the Lady Draydon, viz. for 3000 l., whereof part is paid. Ordered that the unpaid remainder be put into the 8000 l. for the Earl of Berkshire on the Eleven Months' Tax: and that the order for her remainder be put into Sir George Downing's hands to be assigned by the Earl of Berkshire to her.[8]

The money was eventually paid in full.

There is, then, no lack of evidence of the good will felt for each other by Dryden and Howard in the early days of the "controversy"; and, to resume the story of *Annus Mirabilis*, in 1666 Sir Robert, although not living in London, was apparently in London at least often

6. *The Letters of John Dryden*, ed. C. E. Ward (Durham, N. C., 1942), pp. 6-7.

7. *Ibid.*, p. 145.   8. *C.T.B.*, 1667-1668, p. 68.

enough to be entrusted with the task of thus correcting Dryden's proofs, and even, if he took his final instructions literally, Dryden's style.

Dryden, after saying that he is sure he has Howard's "approbation" for the choice of quatrains, goes on to discuss the style appropriate for his poem: "But I am sensible I have presum'd too far, to entertain you with a rude discourse of that Art, which you both know so well, and put into practice with so much happiness." The imitation of Virgil has been noticed by Howard: "Upon your first perusal of this Poem, you have taken notice of some words which I have innovated (if it be too bold for me to say refin'd) upon his *Latin*"; and Dryden, after explaining why he wrote in that way, adds a series of compliments that can surely not all be insincere:

In conclusion, I must leave my Poem to you with all its faults, which I hope to find fewer in the printing by your emendations. I know you are not of the number of those, of whom the younger *Pliny* speaks, *Nec sunt parum multi qui carpere amicos suos judicium vocant*; I am rather too secure of you on that side.

He begs Howard "to make my Poem fairer by many of your blots" and concludes:

But since the reproach of my faults will light on you, 'tis but reason I should do you that justice to the Readers, to let them know that if there be any thing tolerable in this Poem, they owe the Argument to your choice, the writing to your encouragement, the correction to your judgment, and the care of it to your friendship, to which he must ever acknowledge himself to owe all things, who is,
              Sir,
          The most obedient and most faithful of your Servants,
              John Dryden.

It is almost an anti-climax to note, with Hugh Macdonald, that apparently the proof-correcting was not done as well as it could have been; but Dryden was generous enough to add a note "To the Readers" relieving Howard of the blame: "Notwithstanding the diligence which has been used in my absence, some faults have escap'd the Press."[9]

When, therefore, Dryden sat down at Charlton to amuse himself

9. Hugh Macdonald, *John Dryden. A Bibliography of Early Editions and of Drydeniana* (Oxford, 1932), p. 13.

by drafting an *Essay of Dramatic Poesy*, he certainly did not think of Howard as his enemy or even as his opponent. They had taken different sides in a discussion on the place of rhyme in drama, a discussion in which Sorbière and Sprat had also participated; but they were on the same side so far as the status of English drama was concerned, each refusing to believe that French drama was superior. Dryden's preface "To the Reader" makes all this quite clear:

The drift of the ensuing Discourse was chiefly to vindicate the honour of our English Writers, from the censure of those who unjustly prefer the French before them. This I intimate, least any should think me so exceeding vain, as to teach others an Art which they understand much better than my self. But if this incorrect Essay, written in the Country without the help of Books, or advice of Friends, shall find any acceptance in the world, I promise to my self a better success of the second part, wherein the Vertues and Faults of the English Poets, who have written either in this, the Epique, or the Lyrique way, will be more fully treated of, and their several styles impartially imitated.

The famous *Essay* was, then, an attempt at further clarification of the issues ("all I have said is problematical"); and for such a clarification the dialogue form, which had proved so useful in manuals of instruction for hundreds of years, would have seemed natural and right.

The *Essay* was not entered on the Stationers' Register until August, 1667, and it was not published until 1668; and Dryden in his Epistle Dedicatory to Buckhurst speaks of finding it among "loose Papers," long since forgotten. He also says he has discovered "many things in this discourse which I do not now approve." It is to Dryden's discredit that the Epistle also contains one gratuitous phrase which could not have failed to give offense, namely the remark that "none are very violent against it [rhyme], but those who either have not attempted it, or who have succeeded ill in their attempt." Howard had spoken with proper modesty of his own failure in writing rhyme and had rightly said that his theory was independent of his practice. Dryden's phrase, even if one believes that it was written thoughtlessly rather than maliciously, was unworthy of him; and surely it was this that introduced the first note of bad feeling into what had previously been a friendly discussion of literary principles. Howard was entitled to resent it; and recognition of the significance of Dryden's slur on Howard proves invalid the usual histories of the controversy and such assertions as F. L. Huntley's that "Only when forced to, does Dryden become personal in his attack."[10]

Whether Howard also wondered about the propriety of Dryden's putting arguments into the mouths of characters who might be identified with his circle of acquaintances we do not know. It will be remembered that the *Essay* takes the form of a discussion among four friends, Eugenius, Crites, Lisideius, and Neander, who on "that memorable day, in the first Summer of the late War, when our Navy ingag'd the Dutch" (3 June 1665) hired a barge and were rowed down the Thames towards the noise of battle; their discussion of the bad poems that will be an outcome of victory becomes an assessment of the state of contemporary poetry and, by agreement, of drama in particular, including the question of rhyme.[11]

Dryden's own explanation of his dialogue method is given to Buckhurst in the Epistle Dedicatory. "For my own part," he writes, "if in treating of this subject I sometimes dissent from the opinion of better Wits, I declare it is not so much to combat their opinions, as to defend my own, which were first made publick." ("First" would seem to be a reference to the Epistle Dedicatory of *The Rival Ladies*.) "And yet, my Lord," Dryden continues,

this war of opinions, you well know, has fallen out among the Writers of all Ages, and sometimes betwixt Friends. Onely it has been prosecuted by some, like Pedants, with violence of words, and manag'd by others like Gentlemen, with candour and civility. Even *Tully* had a Controversie with his dear *Atticus*; and in one of his Dialogues makes him sustain the part of an Enemy in Philosophy, who in his Letters is his confidant of State, and made privy to the most weighty affairs of the Roman Senate. And the same respect which was paid by *Tully* to *Atticus*, we find return'd to him afterwards by *Cæsar* on a like occasion, who answering his Book in praise of *Cato*, made it not so much his business to condemn *Cato*, as to praise *Cicero*.

"This allusion," remarks Mr. Williamson, "applied to no one so well as to Howard."[12] Williamson, however, did not notice the previous sneer at those who had criticized rhyme. If this reference to Atticus

10. F. L. Huntley, *On Dryden's "Essay of Dramatic Poesy"* (Ann Arbor, 1951), p. 57.

11. Williamson (*op. cit.*, p. 9 n. 43) points out that the phrase "the late war" indicates revision of the *Essay* in 1667. Nichol Smith in his edition of the *Essay* (London, 1900) also drew attention to Dryden's mention of the plays written in the "seven years" since the Restoration.

12. *Op. cit.*, p. 6.

were intended to soothe Howard, it probably came too late; I think it at least as likely that it does not refer to Howard at all and that we should therefore be suspicious of the traditional identification of Howard with Crites, one of the characters in the *Essay*.

Dryden's own explanation of his method is given in his next paragraph. In full, it reads:

But that I may decline some part of the encounter with my Adversaries, whom I am neither willing to combate, nor well able to resist; I will give your Lordship the Relation of a Dispute betwixt some of our Wits upon this subject, in which they did not onely speak of Playes in Verse, but mingled, in the freedom of Discourse, some things of the Ancient, many of the Modern wayes of writing, comparing those with these, and the Wits of our Nation with those of others: 'tis true they differ'd in their opinions, as 'tis probable they would: neither do I take upon me to reconcile, but to relate them: and that as *Tacitus* professes of himself, *Sine studio partium aut ira*: without Passion or Interest; leaving your Lordship to decide it in favour of which part you shall judge most reasonable, and withall, to pardon the many errours of,
>   *Your Lordships most obedient humble Servant,*
>   JOHN DRYDEN.

Although there have been one or two dissentients, it has been customary to identify the four speakers in Dryden's *Essay*, Eugenius, Lisideius, Crites and Neander ("three of them persons whom their witt and Quality have made known to all the Town; and whom I have chose to hide under these borrowed names, that they may not suffer by so ill a relation as I am going to make of their discourse") with, respectively, Lord Buckhurst (afterwards Earl of Dorset), Sir Charles Sedley, Sir Robert Howard, and Dryden himself. It must be objected, however, that the dedication of the *Essay* makes the Eugenius-Buckhurst identification most improbable: Buckhurst is spoken of not as a participant in the debate but as the one who must adjudicate on it.[13] Similarly, as G. R. Noyes has pointed out, there are one or two things in the *Essay* itself that speak against the identification of Crites with Howard: namely, that Crites champions the ancient dramatists, whereas Howard had spoken up for the contemporary playwrights, in his Preface to the *Four New Plays*; and that when Crites does give Howard's arguments against rhyme, he specifically says that he is quoting

13. F. L. Huntley, *op. cit.*, p. 10, points out that on 3 June 1665, the date of the naval battle off Lowestoft which is given as the day of the debate recorded in the *Essay*, Buckhurst was with the Fleet.

somebody else. One need not urge this last point too strongly, or agree with Noyes's alternative identification of Crites with Roscommon, to feel that the case for the Howard-Crites identification is not fully convincing.[14]

It is time to summarize the *Essay* itself. After the gradual diminution of the noise of the naval battle is taken as an indication that the enemy has been driven out to sea, the spate of "ill verses" that will follow the victory is smilingly mentioned by "*Crites*, a person of a sharp judgment, and somewhat too delicate a taste in wit, which the world have mistaken in him for ill nature." When Lisideius says he knows poets who have prepared in advance both panegyrics upon the victory and elegies on the English commander, the Duke of York, "*Crites*, more eager then before, began to make particular exceptions against some Writers." The strictures of Crites are agreed to be justified, but he seems to be portrayed already as the most captious of the group.

Eugenius, admitting the justice of the criticisms by Crites of certain living poets, nevertheless feels that modern poetry in general can be defended; and "all of them were thus far of *Eugenius* his opinion, that the sweetness of English Verse was never understood or practis'd by our Fathers; even *Crites* himself did not much oppose it." Crites is next presented, however, as the champion of the ancients in drama; and this, as Noyes has rightly insisted, does make difficult the identification of Crites with Howard. Crites offers a reasonable defense of the ancient drama, largely by stressing the logic of the unities of time, place, and action; "*Eugenius* who had waited with some impatience" replies at length that the ancients did not in fact observe the unities and criticizes certain features of their drama, sometimes wittily, as in his account of the typical plot of a Roman comedy, sometimes most unconvincingly, as in his complaint that Greek tragedies were all on known stories, or his lament that the playwrights did not always dispense poetic justice. Crites finally interrupts him to say that Eugenius maintains that "the Moderns have acquir'd a new perfection in writing, I can onely grant they have alter'd the mode of it." "This moderation of *Crites*, as it was pleasing to all the company, so it put an end to that dispute; which, *Eugenius*, who seem'd to have the better of

14. G. R. Noyes, " 'Crites' in Dryden's *Essay of Dramatic Poesy*," *M.L.N.*, XXXVIII (1923), 333-337. Noyes's further suggestion, that Eugenius uses some of Howard's arguments against Crites, is not as readily acceptable.

the Argument, would urge no farther." That Eugenius had the better of the argument may not seem certain; but one agrees that enough has been said about the ancients, and welcomes the question Lisideius puts to Eugenius: "why he prefer'd the English Plays above those of other Nations? and whether we ought not to submit our Stage to the exactness of our next Neighbours?"

Lisideius, by invitation, begins this discussion by saying how much he prefers the contemporary French observance of the unities to the multiple plots of the typical English tragi-comedy; this, it will be remembered, is what Howard had said in the Preface to *Four New Plays*. In fact, nothing Crites has said so far is as close to Howard's views as are these ideas developed by Lisideius. He also touches on the question of narration, raised by Howard; but that Lisideius does not represent Howard becomes clear when he maintains that the French dramatists narrate only such actions as cannot be presented adequately on the stage, and distinguishes between such narration and recapitulation (which ought not to be necessary). Moreover, he concludes by saying briefly that he does approve of rhyme.

The defense of the English plays is now undertaken by Neander, speaking for the first time. We should remember that according to Dryden's preface "To the Reader," this vindication of contemporary English drama was the chief aim of the *Essay*; and the success of Neander's argument has not, I think, been questioned among English critics. Granting the greater regularity of the French plots and of their observance of "the decorum of the Stage (to speak generally)," Neander nevertheless contends that tragedy and mirth can be blended successfully in a plot because "contraries when plac'd near, set off each other," and so English tragi-comedy is for him "a more pleasant way of writing for the Stage then was ever known to the Ancients or Moderns of any Nation." He easily refutes all the previous arguments that had depended on the alleged "unnaturalness" of English drama and demonstrates, for example, that "if we are to be blam'd for showing too much of the action, the French are as faulty for discovering too little of it." "By their servile observations of the unities of time and place, and integrity of Scenes, they have brought upon themselves that dearth of Plot, and narrowness of Imagination, which may be observ'd in all their Playes . . . if you consider the Plots, our own are fuller of variety, if the writing ours are more quick and fuller of spirit." There follow the famous appreciations of Shakespeare, Beaumont and Fletcher, and Ben Jonson ("the most learned and judicious Writer which any Theater ever had . . . I admire him, but I love *Shakespeare*"); and Jonson's *The Silent Woman* is examined in detail before Neander concludes that "our present Poets . . . have far surpass'd all the Ancients, and the Modern Writers of other Countreys."

"*Lisideius*, I think, was going to reply, when he was prevented thus by *Crites*: I am confident, said he, the most material things that can be said, have been already urg'd on either side; if they have not, I must beg of *Lisideius* that he will defer his answer till another time, for I confess I have a joynt quarrel to you both, because you have concluded, without any reason given for it, that Rhyme is proper for the Stage." (It will be seen that the question of rhymed drama is taken up only at a late stage of the *Essay* and as part of a larger discussion.) Crites does not wish to discuss whether rhyme is native to English drama or came from France; he does not deny that Shakespeare and Beaumont and Fletcher and Jonson sometimes used it; but he does insist that the successful use of blank verse by such dramatists is an unanswerable argument in its favor, and he believes that popular opinion will agree with him in this. Nevertheless, he says, "I will not on this occasion, take the advantage of the greater number, but onely urge such reasons against Rhyme, as I find in the Writings of those who have argu'd for the other way"—that is, for blank verse (and he proceeds to summarize Howard's arguments from the Preface to *Four New Plays*). These words, Noyes has said, "would not naturally be put into the mouth" of Howard himself; but although it would be odd, it would not be impossible for Dryden to have Crites speak thus if Crites were in fact a portrait of Howard.[15]

The arguments by Howard that Crites now uses against rhyme are its unnaturalness in dialogue that represents unpremeditated thought (but it is proper for non-dramatic poetry); its inappropriateness in repartee ("no man ever was deceiv'd but with a probability of truth"); and its inability to express the greatest thoughts naturally or the lowest gracefully ("for what is more unbefitting the Majesty of Verse, then to call a Servant, or bid a door be shut in Rhime?").

15. Noyes, *M.L.N.*, XXXVIII, 333-337.

Crites also repeats Howard's argument against Dryden[16] that while it is true that some men write better in verse, this does not prove that verse is more natural in a particular context. He adds, with examples, that "he who wants judgment to confine his fancy in blank Verse, may want it as much in Rhyme."

Neander's reply begins with a series of sentences that present their own problems. "It concerns me less then any," says Neander, "to reply to this Discourse; because when I should have prov'd that Verse may be natural in Playes, yet I should alwayes be ready to confess, that those which I have written in this kind come short of that perfection which is requir'd. Yet since you are pleas'd I should undertake this Province, I will do it, though with all imaginable respect and deference both to that person from whom you have borrow'd your strongest Arguments, and to whose judgment when I have said all, I finally submit." Again Dryden seems to be distinguishing between Howard and Crites. Even if he is, however, how could Dryden have reconciled the compliment with the remark in the dedication that those who had opposed rhyme "either have not attempted it, or . . . have succeeded ill in their attempt"? Could he really have believed that Howard would overlook one because of the other? I suspect that the two inconsistent remarks belong to two different periods: the compliment to the days when the *Essay* was first composed, in 1665, the sneer to the time of the dedication, at least two years later, when for some reason Dryden felt differently about his brother-in-law. Had the family disputes over money finally, in 1668, involved them all, as such disputes will? (In 1667, as has been shown, Howard was still going out of his way to do Dryden a good turn.) Perhaps the remark in the dedication was not meant to apply to Howard at all; but Howard could hardly be blamed for thinking that it did. Again if he did suspect Crites of being a portrait, he may have resented the suggestions of loquaciousness, "somewhat *too* delicate a taste in wit" and a fondness for personal attacks. Perhaps Dryden did not mean these to apply to Howard, either; but then Marston probably began another famous theatrical quarrel with a portrait of Jonson that was *intended* to be complimentary.

However this may be, Neander's development of the case for rhyme is more reasonable than was Dryden's first statement on the question.

16. Nichol Smith points out (*op. cit.*, p. 112) that it is Dryden and not Neander who is being answered here.

Comedy is expressly excluded; it is admitted that blank verse has its
uses; and all that is asserted is that "in serious Playes where the subject
and characters are great, and the Plot unmix'd with mirth . . . ,
Rhyme is there as natural, and more effectual then blank Verse."
Nevertheless—and it is no service to Dryden to deny this—Neander
has the worst of it. It is true, as he says, that there can be contortion
of word order in blank verse as well as in rhyme and that repartee can
sound forced in blank verse also; it is true that you can, when writing
rhymed couplets, occasionally write hexameters or vary iambics with
other "Lyrique numbers" or even "break off in the *Hemystich*, and begin another line." Precisely because "variety of cadences is the best
rule," however, these are poor arguments in favor of rhyme. Moreover,
it is simply not true that *throughout a play* "rhime might be made as
natural as blank verse, by the well placing of the words, &c."; and it
is not true that, because accent has replaced quantity in the pattern
of verse, blank verse "at most" is "but a Poetick Prose, a *Sermo ped-
estris*" and that the addition of the "sweetness of Rhyme" is necessary
before a formal verse pattern is established. Yet another of Neander's
arguments, that the English dramatist ought to adopt "the Universal
consent of the most civiliz'd parts of the world" and, like the French,
Italian, and Spanish tragedians, write in rhyme, Howard had already
answered. Four hits Neander does perhaps score against Crites, or
Howard. One is in his declining to accept popular opinion as a literary
test, another his refusal to be too impressed by what has been done
in another age; Dryden was always persuasive on this theme, and it
is here that he makes the oft-quoted remark, of his great Elizabethan
and Jacobean predecessors: "not onely we shall never equal them, but
they could never equal themselves, were they to rise and write again
. . . For the Genius of every Age is different." The third is his
demonstration that the argument from what is "natural" is misleading:
what is in question, he submits, is the "nature" of *serious drama*, in
which "the Plot, the Characters, the Wit, the Passions, the Descrip-
tions, are all exalted above the level of common converse, as high as
the imagination of the Poet can carry them, with proportion to ver-
isimility." (From this premise, however, which itself conceals an
ambiguity, Dryden drew exactly the wrong conclusion; it was to be
some time before he saw that rhyme does not necessarily, or indeed
often in drama, "exalt.") The fourth point that is well made is the

affirmation that "our language is noble, full and significant; and I know not why he who is Master of it may not cloath ordinary things in it as decently as the Latine; if he use the same diligence in his choice of words." To such heights of rhetoric Howard could not aspire; but he could still feel, and with reason, that "the calling of a servant, or commanding a door to be shut" sounded ridiculous in rhyme as often as not—and Neander admits as much when he suggests that the difficulty is best avoided altogether in an Heroic play.

When, finally, Neander comes to answer, none too convincingly, the arguments against Dryden's original contention that "Rhyme bounds and circumscribes an over-fruitful fancy," he says to Crites: "To this you answer'd, that it was no Argument to the question in hand, for the dispute was not which way a man may write best; but which is most proper for the subject on which he writes." It has not, I think, been noticed that *Crites* said no such thing: *Howard* said it, in the Preface to *Four New Plays*. Yet it is not quite certain that Crites and Howard were one in Dryden's mind even here, for it would have been an easy slip for Dryden to think that he had put this particular argument of Howard's into the mouth of Crites along with so many others; and only a few sentences later Neander is referring to the other part of the same argument which carries weight because Crites has taken it "from a most acute person," who is, of course, Howard.

The question whether Dryden *intended* Crites to be a portrait of Howard is, I suggest, unanswerable: whether because of change of intention or not, the evidence is conflicting, and even if one does believe that Crites is Howard, it is difficult to say just how critical the portrait was meant to be. (Perhaps it is only fair to note that in the final paragraph of the *Essay*, after the memorable description of the return of the four men to Somerset Stairs, Dryden writes that they parted, "*Eugenius* and *Lysideius* to some pleasant appointment they had made, and *Crites* and *Neander* to their several Lodgings"; at least it is implied that Crites did not share the taste that Buckhurst and Sedley, if these were they, had for lighter company, presumably female.) What is certain is that the *Essay* is what Nichol Smith has claimed it to be, "our first example, and an example that would have been very notable at any time, of what in our days has come to be called comparative criticism"; it also proves Dryden to have been "our first great master of appreciative criticism."[17] Even so, he had not really succeeded in stating a convincing case for the use of rhyme in drama—and he had, intentionally or not, given Howard some reason to feel that he had been slighted and that he ought to reply.

That Dryden's slight had in fact touched Howard on the raw is shown by his specific reference to it in his reply to the *Essay of Dramatic Poesy*. This is in his Preface to his own new play, *The Great Favourite, or, The Duke of Lerma*, published by Herringman in the same year, 1668. Towards the end of his Preface "To the Reader," Howard writes:

> I had almost forgot one Argument, or Observation, which that Author has most good fortune in; It is in his *Epistle Dedicatory*, before his *Essay* of *Dramatick Poesie*; where, speaking of Rhyme in Plays, he desires it may be observ'd, That none are violent against it, but such as have not attempted it, or who have succeeded ill in the attempt; which as to my self and him I easily acknowledge; for I confess none has written in that way better than himself, nor few worse than I: Yet, I hope, he is so ingenuous, that he would not wish this Argument should extend further than to him and Me; for if it should be received as a good one, all *Divines* and *Philosophers* would find a readier way of Confutation than they yet have done, of any that should oppose the least Thesis or Definition, by saying, they were denied by none but such as never attempted to write, or succeeded ill in the attempt.

Dryden deserved the rebuke; and had Howard left it at that, more of the honors would have rested with him. But like many a man who is in the right, he had the knack of putting himself in the wrong, and perhaps did so here by the tone of the rest of his Preface. Indeed there are times during this controversy when one is reminded of the famous remark by Hobbes describing an earlier quarrel between distinguished men, that of Salmasius and Milton over the execution of Charles I: "they are very good Latin both, and hardly to be judged which was better; and both very ill reasoning, hardly to be judged which is worse." The difference is, ironically, that Howard, the classical scholar, was to commit a silly blunder in his Latin that was to give Dryden an opening for further gibes.

To be fair, there are three different causes of the petulant tone of the Preface to *The Duke of Lerma*. One, as has been shown, was Dryden's gratuitous comment about bad rhymesters; the second, as

17. *John Dryden* (Cambridge, 1950), p. 18 (but pp. 12-22 should all be read, as forming probably the finest appreciation we have of Dryden's *Essay*).

will be seen later,[18] was that Howard was on edge because it had been asserted that *The Duke of Lerma* showed him guilty of plagiarism; the third, and probably most important, was that he was indeed at the time, as he claimed, "fetter'd in Business of most unpleasant Natures," for these were the days when in the House of Commons he was not only impeaching Sir William Penn but also defending himself against vexatious actions brought by his second wife, the Lady Honoria.[19] Had Sir Walter Scott known these facts, he would not have been so certain that "The Preface to *The Duke of Lerma* is written in the tone of a man of quality and importance, who is conscious of stooping beneath his own dignity, and neglecting his graver avocations, by engaging in a literary dispute."[20]

In the Preface, after some account of the history of his own new play, Howard writes: "I must ingenuously confess, that the manner of *Plays*, which now are in most esteem, is beyond my power to perform." He does not object to what generally pleases: "I rather blame the unnecessary Understanding of some that have labour'd to give strict Rules to Things that are not Mathematical," for example, by defining exactly the difference between Tragedy and Comedy, or Comedy and Farce. He thinks that poets are not bound to "strict Reason" and that they "must infringe their own Jurisdiction, to profess themselves oblig'd to argue well"; he will therefore not attempt to give any explanation other than "Chance, which waited upon my present Fancy" for his having written some scenes of *The Duke of Lerma* in rhyme, some in blank verse. This subject, of course, brings him to Dryden.

I cannot therefore but beg leave of the *Reader,* to take a little notice of the great pains the *Author* of an *Essay* of *Dramatick Poesie* has taken, to prove *Rhime* as natural in a serious *Play*, and more effectual than *blank Verse*: Thus he states the Question, but pursues that which he calls *Natural* in a wrong Application; for 'tis not the Question, whether *Rhime* or not *Rhime*, be best, or most Natural for a grave and serious Subject; but what is nearest the nature of that which it presents.

In fact Howard *had* previously said, in the Preface to *Four New Plays*, "the dispute is not which way a Man may write best in, but which is most proper for the Subject he writes upon"; he could not then afford

18. See chap. viii, pp. 139-141.
19. See below, chap. vii, pp. 127-129.
20. *The Works of John Dryden*, I, 97.

to declare this line of reasoning irrelevant now, even if he did think the other premise, that rhyme could never give the illusion of natural speech, more important. Moreover, in developing this second argument, he carelessly, in his haste, referred to the words of Seneca that Dryden had quoted as evidence that commonplace things, such as an order to close the door, could be said in poetry provided the poetry were good enough. So Howard now writes of "*Seneca*, loftily expressing such an ordinary thing, as, *Shutting a Door*. '*Reserate clusos Regii postes Laris*'"—but "reserate," of course, means "open." Going on to claim that the line from Seneca was beside the point where English rhymed verse was concerned, Howard unfortunately added: "I have heard that a Gentleman in *Parliament*, going to speak twice, and being interrupted by another *Member*, as against the Orders of the *House*, he was excused by a Third, assuring the *House* he had not yet spoken to the Question."

After this it is too late for Howard to say that some of the argument about the unities is really rather absurd, since "if strictly and duly weigh'd, 'tis as impossible for one Stage to present two Houses, or two Rooms truly, as two Countreys or Kingdoms; and as impossible that five hours, or four and twenty hours should be two hours and a half, as that a thousand hours or years should be less than what they are. . . . Impossibilities are all equal, and admit no degrees." He wisely suggests that such doctrines as that of the three unities ought to be considered "Propositions" rather than "Confident Laws, or Rules made by Demonstration" and urges that each poet must follow his own fancy. It is then that he makes mention of Dryden's remark about the bad writing of those who have attacked rhymed verse; he adds that he is in fact pleased with most of the Propositions in Dryden's *Essay* but cannot allow false reasoning to go unnoticed.

Dryden's famous answer was in his *Defence of "An Essay of Dramatic Poesy,"* issued as a preface to the second edition of *The Indian Emperor* but omitted from later editions. It will be remembered that the author of "The Medal of John Bayes" alleged that Dryden withdrew the preface rather than accept a challenge from Howard:

> 'Gainst him a scandalous Preface didst thou write,
> Which thou didst soon expunge, rather than fight . . .

and the author of the *Letter from a Gentleman to the Honourable Ed. Howard Esq.* was also to maintain that Sir Robert had received a "cold Answer" to a challenge.[21] The evidence, particularly that addressed to Sir Robert's own brother, is not easily overlooked, although one would prefer to believe that Dryden withdrew the Preface because his good sense and his heart told him that personalities in literary argument are to nobody's credit. The author of "The Medal of John Bayes" further implies that Howard left Dryden to his own resources after this Preface and that this was why Dryden took to writing plays. That is hardly likely to be true; but it is very doubtful whether friendly relations between the brothers-in-law were resumed as soon as some biographers of Dryden have believed: I know of no evidence suggesting close contact again until they were old men, in the 1690's.

Dryden explains, in the second paragraph of the *Defence*, that while he was preparing the new edition of *The Indian Emperor*, *The Duke of Lerma* came into his hands: "the Author of which, a noble and most ingenious Person, has done me the favour to make some Observations and Animadversions upon my *Dramatique Essay*." Dryden congratulates Howard on undertaking the weaker cause—weaker "as combating the received Opinions of the best Ancient and Modern Authors"; and the sarcasm intensifies as he adds:

For my own concernment in the Controversie, it is so small, that I can easily be contented to be driven from a few Notions of Dramatique Poesie; especially by one, who has the reputation of understanding all things: and I might justly make that excuse for my yielding to him, which the Philosopher made to the Emperour; why should I offer to contend with him who is Master of more than twenty Legions of Arts and Sciences? But I am forc'd to fight, and therefore it will be no shame to be overcome.

There is an unkind reference here to Shadwell's caricature of Howard as Sir Positive At-All, in the comedy *The Sullen Lovers*, first produced at Lincoln's Inn Fields on May 2 of this year; and Dryden's next paragraphs, while claiming not to bother with *The Duke of Lerma* itself, contain scathing references both to the fact that the play was not entirely Howard's and to its literary weaknesses.[22] Coming to the real issue, Dryden admits that Howard "attacques me on my

21. See below, p. 117. Gerard Langbaine, who disliked Dryden for personal reasons, also says of the *Defence* that "upon some considerations our Author was obliged to retract it" (*An Account of the English Dramatick Poets*, Oxford, 1691, p. 165).

22. See below, chaps. viii and ix.

weakest side, my defence of Verse" but justly points out that Howard
had changed his ground on the question of what is meant by "natural":
"I still shall think I have gain'd my point," Dryden rightly says, "if
I can prove that Rhyme is best or most natural for a serious subject.
. . . I wonder he should think me so ridiculous as to dispute
whether Prose or Verse be nearest to ordinary Conversation." Perhaps, he adds—unwilling to leave personalities out of it—Howard himself will now be suspected to be the gentleman he mentioned *"who
was allowed to speak twice in Parliament, because he had not yet
spoken to the Question"*—as he was certainly the man "who, as 'tis
reported, maintain'd a contradiction *in terminis*, in the face of three
hundred persons."

Dryden points out that the very fact that prose is nearer discourse
than is verse could be a reason for *not* using prose in drama. A work
of art is not merely a representation of nature; rhyme "seems to have
succeeded Verse by the general consent of Poets in all Modern Lan-
guages"—which at least shows that it works, and does please; and
"I confess my chief endeavours are to delight the Age in which I live"
(even to the extent of writing comedy if that is what his age wants,
though he is by nature unsuited to it).

Dryden next maintains that Howard has misrepresented that part
of his argument which depended on his quotation from Seneca, *reserate
clusos regii postes laris*; he cited this as an instance not of the placing
of words, but of the choice of them and quoted "that Aphorism of
Julius Cæsar, Delectus verborum est origo Eloquentiæ." "But," he
adds

> *delectus verborum* is no more Latine for the placing of words, than *Reserate*
> is Latine for shut the door, as he interprets it, which I ignorantly construed
> unlock or open it.
>
> He supposes I was highly affected with the sound of those words; and
> I suppose I may more justly imagine it of him: for if he had not been
> extreamly satisfied with the sound, he would have minded the sense a
> little better.

Dryden has to admit that a list of *errata*, issued ten days after the
first publication of *The Duke of Lerma*, corrected the *reserate* error

> which it seems, was the Printers fault. I wonder at his modesty, that he
> did not rather say it was *Seneca's* or mine, and that in some Authors
> *Reserare* was to *shut* as well as to *open*. . . . Yet since he has given the
> *Errata*, I wish he would have inlarged them only a few sheets more, and

then he would have spar'd me the labour of an Answer: for this cursed Printer is so given to mistakes, that there is scarce a sentence in the Preface, without some false Grammar, or hard sense in it. . . .

One may perhaps say of this, as Sir Walter Scott said of the whole *Defence*, that "it would be difficult to point out deeper contempt and irony, couched under language so temperate, cold, and outwardly respectful";[23] but after all it was not for Dryden to take one slip, and that afterwards corrected, as proof that Howard knew no Latin: Dryden had already elsewhere complimented him on his classical scholarship and, in his Preface to his translation of Virgil, he was to do so again. Howard, who had many other things on his mind at the time, may not even have been coy or absurd when he attributed the error to the printer; after all, before Seneca had come into the question, Howard's example of an idea it would be difficult to express in rhyme was the *shutting* of a door.[24]

What the quotation from Seneca should have suggested to Howard, as Dryden goes on to say, "is only this, that if *Seneca* could make an ordinary thing sound well in Latine by the choice of words, the same with the like care might be perform'd in English." But he cannot let well alone, and is soon sneering at Howard's statement that he will not write plays, or critical essays again, "since that little Fancy and Liberty I once enjoy'd, is now fetter'd in Business of more unpleasant Natures": "the Muses have lost him," quips Dryden, "but the Commonwealth gains by it; The corruption of a Poet is the Generation of a Statesman." Dryden, who must have known perfectly well that Howard was referring to legal troubles with his second wife, earns no credit for this; and perhaps in the long run the joke was on him, for Howard, if never a great statesman, was at least to prove himself a very influential and capable politician and public servant.

After further skirmishing, on the question of "taste," Dryden comes to the problem of the unities. He maintains that he was discussing only the best *means* of achieving in art an agreed *end*, the imitation of nature, and that he was not claiming to lay down the law; on the contrary, he was writing an *Essay* and "my whole Discourse was Sceptical." Nevertheless, he will defend his position, supported by the

23. *Op. cit.*, II, 264.
24. Macdonald (*Dryden. A Bibliography*, p. 187) points out that Howard did not even bother to correct the mistranslation when *The Duke of Lerma* was reprinted, in his lifetime, in *Five New Plays* (1692).

authority of Aristotle and Horace, Ben Jonson and Corneille; and he begins by quoting Howard's remarks on the unity of place, "That 'tis as impossible for one Stage to present two Rooms or Houses truly, as two Countries or Kingdoms . . . impossibilities are all equal, and admit of no degree." This, Dryden says, amounts to the proposition "that the Stage being one place, cannot be two. This indeed is as great a Secret, as that we are all mortal."

The reference here is to a famous or notorious poem by Howard entitled "Against the Fear of Death." It does not appear in *Poems 1660* but is printed as Howard's in eighteenth-century anthologies; and the fact that the same gibe, based on the poem, occurs also in Shadwell's *The Sullen Lovers* perhaps gives some support to the allegation that Dryden privately furnished Shadwell with the idea for his caricature of Howard there. A few typical lines from the 39-line poem are:

> Since all must certainly to death resign,
> Why should we make it dreadful, or repine?
> How vain is fear, where nothing can prevent
> The loss, which he that loses can't lament?
>
> . . . .
>
> We always should remember, Death is sure;
> What grows familiar most, we best endure:
> For life and death succeed like night and day,
> And neither gives increase, nor brings decay.
>
> . . . .
>
> No just and temperate thought can tell us why
> We should fear death, or grieve for them that die;
> The time we leave behind is ours no more,
> Nor our concern, than time that was before.
>
> . . . .
>
> We all must pass through Death's dead sea of night,
> To reach the haven of eternal light.[25]

These lines, suggested, I should think, by the Third Book of Lucretius (part of which Dryden was himself to translate superbly) are certainly undistinguished and often clumsy, but are not more platitudinous than is most verse on this subject. Dryden, however, was obviously in no mood to make concessions and could not resist a hit at

25. Quoted from J. Nichols, *A Select Collection of Poems* (London, 1780) II, 330-331. The greater part of the poem is also cited, as having "gained him no small Reputation," by Giles Jacob, *Poetical Register*, II, 80.

the bathos of, particularly, the line "We always should remember, Death is sure." Whether the point scored against Howard is relevant to a discussion of the unities in drama is, perhaps, another question.

Dryden's real answer to Howard's argument is in his statement—and it is no more than a counter-allegation—that "the imagination . . . will in reason be less chocqu'd with the appearance of two rooms in the same house, or two houses in the same City, than with two distant Cities in the same Country, or two remote Countries in the same Universe . . . the nearer and fewer those imaginary places are, the greater resemblance they will have to Truth." The same reasoning, he argues, applies to the unity of time, which Howard has certainly infringed in Acts II and III of *The Duke of Lerma*. "In few words my own opinion is this, (and I willingly submit it to my Adversary, when he will please impartially to consider it,) that the imaginary time of every Play ought to be contrived into as narrow a compass, as the nature of the Plot, the quality of the Persons, and variety of Accidents will allow" (and tragedy, he feels, allows greater latitude than does comedy).

Dryden's final paragraph shows that he is aware of his fault in bringing personalities into the quarrel. The opening sentence of this paragraph is not itself either gracious or adequate, if one remembers the history of the debate: Dryden would have done better to withdraw the statement in question; but the remainder of the paragraph is worthy of the great man who wrote it:

His last Assault, like that of a French man, is most feeble: for whereas I have observed, that none have been violent against Verse, but such only as have not attempted it, or have succeeded ill in their attempt, he will needs, according to his usual custom, improve my Observation to an Argument, that he might have the glory to confute it. But I lay my Observation at his feet, as I do my Pen, which I have often employ'd willingly in his deserved commendations, and now most unwillingly against his Judgment. For his person and parts, I honour them as much as any man living, and have had so many particular Obligations to him, that I should be very ungrateful, if I did not acknowledge them to the World. But I gave not the first occasion of this difference in opinions. In my Epistle Dedicatory, before my *Rival Ladies*, I had said somewhat in behalf of Verse, which he was pleased to answer in his Preface to his Plays: that occasioned my Reply in my Essay, and that Reply begot this rejoynder of his in his Preface to The Duke of *Lerma*. But as I was the last who took up Arms, I will be the first to lay them down. For what I have here written, I submit it wholly to him; and if I do not hereafter answer what may be objected against this Paper, I hope the World will not impute it to any other reason, than only the due respect which I have for so noble an Opponent.

Howard, to his credit, let the matter rest; and Dryden, to his credit, withdrew the *Defence* and, when he did have occasion to return to the question of rhyme, necessarily, in his "Of Heroique Plays. An Essay," prefixed to *The Conquest of Granada by the Spaniards*, 1672, treated it very briefly. "Whether Heroique verse ought to be admitted into serious Playes," he wrote, "is not now to be disputed: 'tis already in possession of the Stage." The only argument against it would be that "it is not so near conversation as Prose; and therefore not so natural"; but, Dryden points out, serious dramatic dialogue ought not to be too near conversation and should rather be "beyond it." "But," he adds, realizing that he had once promised not to return to this topic, "I am willing to let fall this argument: 'tis free for every man to write, or not to write, in verse, as he judges it to be, or not to be his Tallent; or as he imagines the Audience will receive it"; and he goes on to discuss the general nature of Heroic plays.[26]

The discussion between Howard and Dryden, however, had aroused too much interest to be allowed by others to drop. Mention has been made of George Williamson's demonstration that the first stages of the quarrel must be seen in the context of the Sorbière-Sprat discussion; and it would seem that by the time of the final stages, many others were contributing to the debate. David Masson long ago pointed out that a greater man than either Howard or Dryden, namely John Milton, was thinking of what had already been said on the subject when in this same year, 1668, or early in 1669, he added to the fifth issue of the first edition of *Paradise Lost* his statement against rhyme, even in Heroic verse:

The measure is *English* Heroic Verse without Rime, as that of *Homer* in *Greek*, and of *Virgil* in *Latin*; Rime being no necessary Adjunct or true Ornament of Poem or good Verse, in longer Works especially, but the Invention of a barbarous Age, to set off wretched matter and lame Meeter; grac't indeed since by the use of some famous modern Poets, carried away by Custom, but much to thir own vexation, hindrance, and constraint to express many things otherwise, and for the most part worse then else they would have exprest them. Not without cause therefore some both *Italian* and *Spanish* Poets of prime note have rejected Rime both in longer and shorter

26. See above, chap. v, p. 61.

Works, as have also long since our best *English* Tragedies, as a thing of
it self, to all judicious eares, triveal and of no true musical delight; which
consists only in apt Numbers, fit quantity of Syllables, and the sense variously drawn out from one Verse into another, not in the jingling sound
of like endings, a fault avoyded by the learned Ancients both in Poetry and
all good Oratory. This neglect then of Rime so little is to be taken for a
defect, though it may seem so perhaps to vulgar Readers, that it rather
is to be esteem'd an example set, the first in *English*, of ancient liberty
recover'd to Heroic Poem from the troublesom and modern bondage of
Rimeing.[27]

Howard was a subscriber to the Folio edition of *Paradise Lost* in 1688[28]
and according to John Toland he was a close personal friend of Milton. Toland, who had no direct personal knowledge of Milton, had
sought information from Milton's last wife, his daughter and his
friends, and had read family papers; he may therefore be believed when
in his *Life of John Milton* (1698/9), noting the folly of the licensers
in expunging from Milton's *History of Britain* passages (on the super-
stition of the Saxons) which they insisted on applying to Charles II's
bishops, he continues:

This puts me in mind of a *Reply* to a certain Person by Sir *Robert Howard*
lately deceast, a Gentleman of great Generosity, a Patron of Letters, and
a hearty Friend to the Liberty of his Country. Being told that he was
charg'd in a Book [his *History of Religion*] with whipping the Protestant
Clergy on the back of the Heathen and Popish Priests, he presently ask'd
what they had to do there? He was a great admirer of Milton to his dying
day; and, being his particular Acquaintance, would tell many pleasant
Stories of him, as that he himself having demanded of him once what
made him side with the *Republicans?* Milton answer'd, among other
Reasons, because theirs was the most frugal Government; for that the
Trappings of a Monarchy might set up an ordinary Commonwealth.
(pp. 185-186)

If Milton was indeed Howard's friend, and if in his defense of blank
verse he saw himself as answering Howard's opponent, Dryden, then

27. *The Life of John Milton* (London, 1880), VI, 634. The point was de-
veloped by Morris Freeman in his "Milton and Dryden," Ph.D. thesis, Columbia
University, 1953; and since my chapter was written, Freeman has shown that
Milton had in mind not only the arguments of Dryden and Howard but also
many of their phrases ("Milton and Dryden on Rhyme," *Huntington Library
Quarterly*, XXIV (Aug. 1961), 337-344).

28. Jonathan Richardson, *Explanatory Notes and Remarks on Milton's Paradise Lost*, 1734, cited by Helen Darbishire, *Early Lives of Milton* (London,
1932), p. 294.

there is an added grim irony in his reported answer when Dryden asked permission to turn *Paradise Lost* into a rhymed play, namely that "he would give him leave to tagge his Verses."[29]

A far less important writer than Milton, Sir Robert's brother Edward, also put in a word against rhyme in the Preface to *The Usurper*, a play which had been produced early in 1664 but was only now published, in the autumn of 1668. This in turn prompted one "R.F." to write *A Letter from a Gentleman To the Honourable Ed. Howard Esq; Occasioned By a Civiliz'd Epistle of Mr. Dryden's, Before his Second Edition of his 'Indian Emperour'* (London, 1668). The author of this very rare quarto pamphlet[30] was plausibly identified by Peter Cunningham as Richard Flecknoe.[31] Flecknoe, if he was the author, was not unwilling to make an enemy of Dryden. He begins, addressing Edward Howard:

Sir,

I Have now for some time expected an Answer from your Honorable Brother, Sir *Robert Howard,* to Mr. *Drydens* Epistle before his *Indian Emperour*; But I perceive that your Brother thinks it unworthy of his Thoughts; nor can any Ingenious Person blame Him.

After denying Dryden's charges that Howard was guilty of plagiarism in *The Duke of Lerma*, Flecknoe asks whether Dryden reserves to himself the right to borrow from others—as in his *Maiden Queen* and *Indian Emperor* and *Mock Astrologer*. Then he retraces most of the argument of the *Defence*. Flecknoe thinks that Howard's slip over "reserate" might more charitably have been taken as a printer's error—particularly as the same thing has happened to Dryden: and he quotes from the first edition of *The Indian Emperor* "And follow Fate, that does too fast pursue," corrected in the second edition to "And follow Fate, that would too fast pursue." He also reminds Dryden that he has perpetrated lines like "An horrid stillness first invades the Eare."

He defends Howard as a poet by affirming that, *pace* Dryden, Howard has had a long acquaintance with the muses (but unhappily

29. John Aubrey, *Life of Mr. John Milton* (cited from V. de Sola Pinto, ed., *English Biography in the Seventeenth Century,* London, 1951, p. 197).

30. There is no copy in either the Bodleian or the British Museum. I have used the one in the Dyce Collection of the Victoria and Albert Museum.

31. *The Gentleman's Magazine,* XXXIV (Dec., 1850), 597. Cunningham added that it was probably Flecknoe's intervention in the dispute with Sir Robert Howard that caused Dryden to satirize Flecknoe in *MacFlecknoe* as the prince of dullness in poetry, succeeded by his even duller "son" Shadwell.

as an example of his skill chooses his most recent poem, "The Duel of the Stags," which was to become the butt of the Wits);[32] and he wants to know who are the critics alleged by Dryden to have complained of Howard's style and grammar:

But in his next scolding Paragraph, he is more unhappy in his Anger, and quarrels with the Honourable Person, for saying he was now fettered in Business of more unpleasant Natures, which he will have to be State matters. But the Squire was very much mistaken, for I by accident once heard that Honourable Person complain that two tedious Suits in *Chancery* had almost deprived him of the right use of any time, and yet I think he need not be ashamed of those Services he endeavours to do his King and Country; so that either way the Squires Displeasure is very unjustly applied.

Dryden had certainly left himself wide open to *that*.

Flecknoe, however, proceeds to further insulting of Dryden; and the repetition of "the Honourable Person" becomes tedious and absurd. He does score some good hits, even if what he says is not relevant to the literary problem being discussed; he ridicules Dryden, for instance, for the notorious lines in *Annus Mirabilis* describing God as putting out the Fire of London with a heavenly fire-extinguisher. He even refuses to be placated by Dryden's final paragraph of the *Defence*, where, he says, Dryden writes "fawningly":

At the last the Squire is pleased to give him [Howard] the Title of a Noble opponent; and to this last I am confident he will Receive a just return from the Honourable Person, when ever the Squire pleases to give him cause to call him so. In the mean time, I believe the Squire cannot reasonably expect it from him, since I have heard from a very brave Gentleman, who was lately engaged to waite upon the Squire, that his cold Answer has discouraged the Honourable Person from such an Expectation.

Flecknoe concludes by expressing the pious hope that he has not become dirty from handling dirt; at least, he maintains, he has carried dirt back to its source, and he is quite confident that Edward Howard and "all other Just persons" will see him as a lover of justice and good manners!

Others of Dryden's enemies soon joined in, among them Martin Clifford, in his *Notes upon Mr. Dryden's Poems. In Four Letters*, not published until 1687 but all written by 1672, the date of the fourth letter. In the third letter, Clifford wants to know what Dryden means by his simile

32. See below, chap. ix, pp. 161-165. Blunders such as this probably explain why Pepys found the *Letter* "mighty silly" (VIII, 102).

> The brave Almanzor
> Who like a Tempest that out-rides the Wind . . .

adding, "The sense of it to my weak and shallow Understanding, is, a Tempest that out-rides it self: And if it be so, pray resolve me *whether you be not cozen'd with the sound, and never took the pains to examine the sense of your own Verses*, which is a Fault you object to others in your modest Preface." Clifford is here turning back upon Dryden his criticism of Howard; and granting that not all Clifford's examples are convincing, here and in, for example, his quoting of such of Dryden's absurdities as

> Where'er thou stand'st, I'll level at thy face
> My gushing blood, and sprout [*sic*] it at that place

he does score a point. Macdonald is not fair to Clifford in his comment that the *Letters* "abuse the *Conquest of Granada* or earlier plays in a stupid and pedantic way."[33]

Clifford would also be my candidate for the authorship of the anonymous pamphlet *The Friendly Vindication of Mr. Dryden From the Censure of the Rota By His Cabal of Wits* (Cambridge, 1673). This belongs to the series of four "Censure of the Rota" pamphlets, two of them being defenses of Dryden, two of them (namely this one and Richard Leigh's *The Censure of the Rota on Mr. Driden's Conquest of Granada*) being attacks on him. The Bodleian copy of *The Friendly Vindication* (Mal. B. 288(9)) has in a seventeenth-century annotation the attribution "by Sr Robert Howard." I can find nothing to support this attribution, either in the pamphlet itself or in the reply *Mr. Dreyden Vindicated*, by Charles Blount. Blount's gibes at the author's pretense of learning would surely have been more specific and damning had he thought Howard responsible; and he clearly believes that the author had written no original dramatic work.

The Friendly Vindication is an ironical defense of Dryden, which loses most of its force because it is so heavy-handed, and so badly written. Dryden is pictured discussing with admirers the unfair censure of him by the Rota, including criticism of the language of *Annus Mirabilis* as tautologous ("fearful hare," for example) and incongruous. Howard comes into it twice. The first allusion, in a speech put in the mouth of an admirer of Dryden, is none too clear. This

33. *Op. cit.*, p. 256.

admirer points out that Dryden had often satirized opponents on the stage, and adds:

Besides, that he had been so frankly obliging as (where he could not use a Character, or apprehended the License) to assign it to some other Poet of his Cabal, or exchange one Part for another, it may be *Club Wit* too, the better to set men forth: That this was a *Sir Positive Truth* Mr. *Dryden* had not fore-head enough to denie.

At which, there being observed a guilty variety in his Countenance—A certain Gallant stept forth and said, that what was past, was past: besides, that Mr. *Dryden* had made his submissions and recantations most in- geniously both by word and writing: that he conceived a person of Honour, had a Letter dedicated to the Fire, even by the Hangmans hands, if the injur'd should think it necessary; therefore what was done was candid enough as to that particular. If Mr. *Dryden* courted more his security than honour, he was not to be blamed.

The first paragraph, as Hugh Macdonald has pointed out, must mean that Dryden had given Shadwell the idea of the caricature of Howard as Sir Positive At-All in *The Sullen Lovers*.[34] The second presumably means that Dryden had avoided the challenge from How- ard, after the *Defence*, by writing an ignominious apology which Howard was permitted to use against him if sufficiently provoked.

The second mention of Howard occurs towards the end of *The Friendly Vindication* and is no more than a reference to the letter prefixed to *Annus Mirabilis*, as proving that Dryden often changed his ground, sometimes alleging, as here, that he wrote only for fame, sometimes pleading that he had to write for money, sometimes claim- ing that he wrote for both—"which cannot but be acknowledged an- other *quaint* variety in Mr. *Dryden*." The admirers finally give up the defense of Dryden altogether, "since Mr. *Dryden* and his Muse, are best extolled by his own Pen."

At first it may seem surprising that Dryden was ridiculed more often than was Howard for his part in this celebrated controversy. Howard, being an aristocrat and not as distinguished a writer as Dryden was by 1668, was perhaps hardly worth attacking; but he is included with Dryden and Rochester in one list of poets whom it is needless to damn in Hell because they are already damned, by their false taste, on earth. This is in Captain Radcliff's "News from Hell," the relevant stanza of which is:

> A seventh, because he'd rather chuse
> To spoil his verse than tire his Muse:

34. *Op. cit.*, p. 189.

> Nor will he let heroics chime;
> Fancy (quoth he) is lost by rhyme;
> And he that's us'd to clashing swords
> Should not delight in sounds of words:
> Mars with Mercury should not mingle;
> Great warriors should speak big, not jingle.[35]

Howard could hardly have been worried by that; he might, indeed, have thought with justice that it did him more good than harm.

Dryden, however, was, not unnaturally, cut to the quick by such criticisms as those by Flecknoe, Clifford, and the Rota. In the second edition of *Tyrannic Love* in 1672 he added a final paragraph to his Preface, in which he defends some of the lines and images that had been attacked by "little Critiques" and claims that the phrases in question were derived from Horace and Ovid. Similarly, he writes,

Some foole before them had charg'd me in the *Indian Emperour* with nonsense in these words, *And follow fate which does too fast pursue.* Which was borrow'd from Virgil in the XIth of his Æneids, *Eludit gyro interior, sequiturque sequentem.* I quote not these to prove that I never write Nonsense, but onely to show that they are so unfortunate as not to have found it.

Dryden's last words on the controversy with Howard are different again: they are in his confession in the Prologue to *Aureng-Zebe*, acted in November, 1675, and published in 1676:

> Our Author by experience finds it true,
> 'Tis much more hard to please himself than you;
> And out of no feign'd Modesty, this day,
> Damns his laborious Trifle of a Play:
> Not that its worse than what before he writ,
> But he has now another taste of Wit;
> And to confess a truth (though out of time)
> Grows weary of his long-lov'd Mistris, Rhyme.
> Passion's too fierce to be in Fetters bound,
> And Nature flies him like Enchanted Ground.

Both here (particularly in the reference to "Nature") and in his decision to write *All for Love* in blank verse, Dryden virtually admitted what too many of his admirers have been loath to admit, that in the argument over the appropriateness of rhyme in drama, Howard was, after all, right.

35. Quoted from Nichols, *Select Collection*, I, 145. I owe the reference to Carryl N. Thurber's edition of *The Committee*.

TO give a consecutive account of Howard's controversy with Dryden, it has been necessary to pass over other events in his life during the years 1664-1668. These were the years in which he established himself firmly in the two worlds of literature and politics; they were also the years in which the name Howard came, in some quarters, to be almost the symbol of charlatanism in art.

This unfortunate identification was not entirely, or perhaps even primarily, Sir Robert's fault. The Howards were a writing family; and as we shall see, Edward was to become the chief butt of the wits, for his notorious poem "The British Princes." Already in 1663 or earlier, however, Robert's elder brother Henry, the distinguished Civil War veteran, had written a play, *The United Kingdoms*; and the publisher Briscoe's *The Key to "The Rehearsal,"* from which our only knowledge of this play comes, mentions it as a work that had amused the Duke of Buckingham and his circle of satirical friends, and had failed on the stage. Buckingham had found equally risible Sir Robert's own plays; and it would seem certain that in the original form of *The Rehearsal*, written by Buckingham, probably in association with other "Wits," Howard was ridiculed as the main character, Bilboa. *The Rehearsal*, most famous of the satires on Heroic drama, was first written about 1664 (perhaps it was inspired mainly by the success of *The Indian Queen* in that year); it was probably ready for production when the plague closed the theaters in 1665.[1] It was not produced until December, 1671, by which time it had suffered a sea-change. Howard and Buckingham had become friends and indeed literary collaborators, satirizing others;[2] and the character of Bilboa had become Bayes and had been adapted to fit a more important dramatist, John Dryden, perhaps with side glances at Davenant also. A few traces of the original satire of Howard do, however, remain.

Montague Summers noticed the most obvious of these, Bayes's

1. *The Key to "The Rehearsal"* (London, 1704), p. 69; see also *A New Key to the Rehearsal* (1717); "Thomas Betterton," *The History of the English Stage from the Restauration to the Present Time* (London, 1741—probably by Edmund Curll); and Theophilus Cibber, *The Lives of the Poets of Great Britain and Ireland* (London, 1753), III, 58.

2. See below, chap. x, pp. 167-168.

boast (in Act II Sc.i): "May be, Sir? I gad, I'm sure on't: *Experto crede Roberto*";[3] and the author of *A New Key to the Rehearsal* pointed out that the line in Act V "But stay, what sound is this invades our ears?" reads like a parody of one in *The Indian Queen*:

> *Montezuma:* Hark, hark.
> *Acacis:* What noise is this invades my ears?   (I.i)

(although Dryden was laughed at by Flecknoe for a similar line, "An horrid stillness first invades the Eare"). *The Indian Queen*, and particularly the claims made in the Epilogue,[4] would seem to be alluded to again in another bragging speech by Bayes: "Now, Gentlemen, I will be bold to say, I'll shew you the greatest scene that ever *England* saw: I mean not for words, for those I do not value; but for state, shew, and magnificence" (IV.i). Of course, *The Indian Emperor* and *The Conquest of Granada* were also probably in the satirist's mind; and all three plays, and others, may have been laughed at in the character of Drawcansir and in Bayes's earlier statement of principle: "for my part, I prefer that one quality of singly beating of whole Armies above all your moral virtues put together, I gad" (IV.i) and in his explanation "I make 'em, Sir, play the battle in *Recitativo*." (V.i.)

The references to *The Indian Queen* may have been allowed to stand because of their possible relevance for Dryden; but it seems that the authors of *The Rehearsal* were willing to make a sly hit or two at Howard even in 1671, whether in possible allusions to his new play *The Duke of Lerma* or in mild ridicule of plays like *The Vestal Virgin* that could be turned into tragedy "in a trice." (Buckingham's friendship with Sir Robert certainly did not prevent gibes at James, Henry, and Edward Howard in the revised *Rehearsal*.) Is there also "show-through" from the early version of the 1660's in the extraordinary number of uses of the word "surprise," perhaps originally part of an attack on *The Surprisal*? I suspect that more was involved than ridicule of the general contemporary desire for novelty. (For that matter, Howard himself was one who had expressed this desire, not only in the Prologue to *The Surprisal* but also in that to *The Committee*.) Hence, perhaps, passages like the following, or their originals in the earlier form of *The Rehearsal*:

3. *The Playhouse of Pepys*, p. 265; George Villiers, Duke of Buckingham, *The Rehearsal*, ed. Summers (Stratford-upon-Avon, 1914) p. 19.
4. Cited on p. 78 above.

i) *Johnson* . . . Your Virtuosi, your civil persons, your Drolls: fellows
  that scorn to imitate Nature; but are given altogether to elevate and
  surprise.
  Smith Elevate and surprise! pr'ythee make me understand the meaning
  of that.
  Johnson Nay, by my troth, that's a hard matter: I don't understand
  that my self. 'Tis a phrase they have got among them, to express
  their no-meaning by. I'll tell you, as near as I can, what it is. Let
  me see: 'tis Fighting, Loving, Sleeping, Rhyming, Dying, Dancing,
  Singing, Crying; and every thing, but thinking and Sence. (I.i.)
ii) *Smith* It does surprise me, I'm sure, very much.
  Johnson I, but it won't do so long: by that time thou hast seen a Play
  or two, that I'll shew thee, thou wilt be pretty well acquainted with
  this new kind of Foppery.   (Act II)

(Compare also the scorn of the actors: "now, here, every line surprises
you, and brings in new matter"—I.ii.) There would seem to be a
relic of jesting similarly aimed at Howard and *The Vestal Virgin*
when Bayes first appears and announces that he has forgotten the
plot of his last play: "but I have a new one, in my pocket, that I may
say is a Virgin; 'thas never yet been blown upon . . . if you, and
your friend will do it but the honour to see it in its Virgin attire" (I.i).

Howard could hardly complain about personal satire in the final
version of *The Rehearsal*, then, although his dramatic practice is certainly laughed at; but one can readily believe that he did not escape
so easily in 1664-1665 when he probably received the full weight of
Buckingham's scorn.

His connection with the Bridges Street theater, as building-sharer,
also brought its minor troubles. One is described in a letter from
Howard to Sir Henry Bennet, concerning what the King wrongly
supposed to be the dismissal of the actress Mrs. Weaver:

S^r

in the abscence of Mr Killegrew; I have receiv'd his Maties Commaunds
by you; I wish Mr Killegrew had been in the way, or that I had been
thought worthy to have been heard before his ma^{tie} and your selfe had been
soe ill informd; your letter I received just now beinge too late in all particular's to have obeyd it; but the information beinge soe exactly false,
I hope you wld be pleasd not to looke upon us as person's concernd in it, for
Mrs Weaver's, three week's agoe and above, of her owne accord brought in
all her part's and warn'd the Company that after such A day which is
expird shee woud act noe more, I my selfe spoke with her twice about it,
and shee continu'd her resolution to goe; and then all her part's were

given out; since indeed shee has appeard big with Child; and now knowne
to be shamefully soe, for which many women of quality have protested
they wld never come to thee house to see A woman actinge at[5] part's of
vertue, in such A shamefull condition. this S[r] has been the cause that wee
are not troubled for the losse of her, but the first cause of her leavinge the
house came from her selfe; and truly S[r] wee are willinge to bringe the
stage to be A place of some Creditt, and not an infamous place, for all
persons of honour to avoid; if wee may be permitted; and when his ma[tle]
receives A true information; his Commaunds shall be presently obeyd;
but this S[r] as A person w[th]out any power heer I returne only as an information; as becomes

Yo[r] most humble servant
Ro: Howard.[6]

The King's interest in the actresses could indeed bring its troubles
for others, even those who, like Howard, had no official connection
with the conditions of employment of the theatrical company.[7]

Howard's flourishing financial condition in these years is well
enough indicated by a warrant of 1 April 1665, authorizing Sir John
Norton, as Receiver General for Southampton, to pay £5000 each
quarter for four quarters, plus 6 per cent interest, 3 per cent "reward"
and £50 "for charges," to Lord St. John, Sir Robert Howard, and
Colonel Norton, in repayment of £20,000 "jointly advanced for the
King's service, particularly for the Office of Ordnance."[8] In spite of
his wealth, however, Howard was not averse from marrying a wealthy
widow to increase it further (his first wife having died some seven years
before); and on 10 August 1665 he married at All Saints, Wootton
Bassett, near Swindon in Wiltshire, Lady Honoria O'Brien, daughter
of the late Earl of Thomond and widow of Sir Francis Englefield.[9]
In spite of the King's willingness to recommend the bridegroom to

5. Perhaps "al" or "all."

6. P.R.O., S.P.Dom. Chas. II, 29, 109 No. 16. The letter is not dated by
Howard.

7. Alfred Harbage, in his *Thomas Killigrew* (Philadelphia, 1930), p. 130,
unfortunately gave a wrong account of this; he was misled by a false summary
of Howard's letter in *C.S.P.D.*, 1664-1665, beginning "Sir Rob. Howard to
Sec. Bennet. Wishes he could have been heard, before the King or Mr. Killigrew had been in the way, the informations given being utterly false."

8. *C.T.B.*, 1660-1667, p. 656.

9. The date, which has often been given wrongly (Howard's own son told
Ashmole the marriage took place in 1664), is here cited from the Parish Registers, generously made available to me by the Reverend R. L. Sharp.

the bride,[10] the marriage seems to have been a complete failure; Howard certainly learned to regret it.

Sir Francis Englefield, who had died only a few months before this, had left the manor of Wootton Bassett to his wife for life (it was worth £2,000 a year), with reversion for life to his uncle Sir Thomas Englefield, then a widower and nearly seventy years of age. For good consideration, Sir Thomas in 1665 conveyed his interest to Anthony Englefield, senior, and Anthony Englefield, junior; but Howard not unnaturally wished to have an unencumbered title in the estate. Sir Thomas therefore arranged that the two Anthony Englefields should reconvey to him his interest and that they should then join with him in conveying the estate to Howard; in return Sir Thomas received from Howard £2,000, plus £400 a year for life from the manor—seemingly a generous arrangement.[11]

Marriage to Lady Honoria meant that Howard had a new home, the beautiful and historic Vasterne manor house, which formed an important part of the Englefield estate. Howard lived there for some time after his marriage;[12] but his relationship with his wife was not happy for long (it may be relevant that she was at least ten years

10. P.R.O., S.P.Dom. Chas. II, 29, 194, No. 33.

11. *H.M.C.*, Report 14, App. 6, House of Lords MSS, p. 256. Briefly, this concerns a later Englefield family dispute over property in Leicestershire which Sir Thomas conveyed to the two Anthony Englefields in return for their conveyance of Wootton Bassett; but he later married his servant and there were complications and, e.g., allegations of fraud that do not concern us here. That there was some dispute over Sir Francis Englefield's will is shown by a Chancery suit in the Public Record Office (C6/33/35), but it concerned primarily the question whether, in view of the reversion to Sir Thomas, some of the estate could be sold to pay debts as directed by the will. This, of course, would have been settled when Howard purchased Sir Thomas's interest outright.

12. His letter to Dryden of 13 August 1666, previously cited, was written from Vasterne. The manor has a fascinating history. Many years before, it had come by marriage into the possession of the famous De Spencer family; from them it had passed to Queen Isabella and to successive Queens of England, until Queen Mary gave it to an earlier Sir Francis Englefield who, a staunch Roman Catholic like all his family, had stood by her in the reign of Edward. Elizabeth I had him beheaded; but James I restored the home to the family and they had lived in it until the death of the younger Sir Francis in 1665. Howard sold Vasterne to Laurence Hyde in 1676, and it remained with the Hydes until the Meux family bought it in the nineteenth century. It still stands, and my wife and I were most hospitably entertained there in 1955 by Sir Ralph and Lady Eastwood, who also assisted us in tracing its history.

older than he)[13] and before two years had passed, their differences were a matter of state concern.

If any readers of Evelyn's *Diary* happen to remember an entry of 18 October 1666 in which Howard's name is connected, not to his credit, with actresses, they may wonder whether this throws any light on his deteriorating relationship with his wife. Such an explanation, however, now seems debatable. Evelyn, complaining of the indecency of the public theaters of the Restoration, speaks of actresses who "inflaming severall young noble-men & gallants, became their whores, & to some their Wives, wittnesse the *Earle of Oxford*, Sir R: Howard, Pr: Rupert, the E. of Dorset, & another greater person than any of these, who fell into their snares, to the reproch of their noble families, & ruine both of body & Soule."[14] Evelyn's editor, E. S. de Beer, believes, however, that this passage was not among Evelyn's original notes referring to this period but was among those added in the years 1680-1685; and he suggests that Evelyn had confused Howard's *third* wife, Mary Uphill, whom he married before 1680, with the actress Susanna Uphill, who may have been, as Downes said she was, a member of the King's Company from as early as 1663.[15] Later writers, knowing of Evelyn's comments and of a reference to Howard's "W[hore] Uphill" refusing to marry him in 1677, certainly put two and two together to make six and decided that this was the actress in question. Actually there is nothing at all to connect his third wife, Mary Uphill, with the theater. Evelyn himself *may* have confused Mary with the actress Susanna, as Dr. de Beer suggests (interestingly, Mary had a sister named Susanna—not the actress); on the other hand, Evelyn was right about the liaisons of Oxford, Dorset, Prince Rupert, and the King; and he was in a position to know the truth about the Howard family, certainly in the 1680's, since he visited Sir Robert at Ashtead in Surrey in 1684 and was a trustee for Robert's elder brother William, of whose wife and daughters he became a very close friend. It is still possible, then, that he was right about Howard's

13. Paget, *Ashtead Estate*, p. 59, also cited by Florence R. Scott, "The Marriages of Sir Robert Howard," *M.L.N.*, LV (1940), 410-415, and *R.E.S.*, XX (1944), 158-159. There is an amusing story of how in 1651 Lady Honoria attempted to deceive (of all people) Ireton, and almost won him over by timely tears; it is in Edmund Ludlow's *Memoirs* (1698), I, 381, generously drawn to my attention by Mr. A. W. G. Lowther.

14. *Diary*, III, 465-466.

15. de Beer, *N. & Q.*, CLXXXVII (1944), 215 and CXCII (1947), 446.

liaison with an unnamed actress in 1666; but there is nothing to connect the lady, if she did exist, either with Susanna Uphill or with Mary Uphill, who at first refused to marry him in 1677 but later changed her mind. Nor is there anything to connect the hypothetical actress with the breakdown of Howard's marriage to Lady Honoria.

What is certain is that the quarrel between husband and wife came to a head early in 1667. A newsletter of 19 March of that year, under the date 16 March, has an entry: "Lady Honora [_sic_][16] O'Brien, relict of Sir Francis Inglefield, has petitioned the King for relief from the ill usage of her husband, Sir Robert Howard, son of the Earl of Berkshire";[17] and Lord Chancellor Clarendon wrote urgently to Secretary of State Arlington at 10 o'clock one Saturday morning a few weeks earlier:

yours came not to me, till 11 of the clocke last night, when I was just gone to bedd, so that I could only reade it: and I was beginninge to write this morninge when the Kinge came in; yett I suppose this may be with you, before the Lady will owne beinge out of her bedd, though I thinke she sleepes uneasily:
The Kinge havinge recommended such a husbande to her, he cannot well refuse to take notice of her complainte, and give any redresse he can: He shall therfore do well to referr the examinacion of the peticon and all matters arising therupon, to my Ld. Canterbury, Ld Chamberlyne, Bpp of London, Ld Arlington, Ld Hollis, & Sec. Morrice, to heare all parties, and to compose all differences if they can, otherwise to certify the state of the case to his ma^ty. If the Lady desyres I should be one I shall submitt, though I have no mind to have any thinge to doe with the kn^t. I thinke my Ld Anglesy is her frende; if she would have him, you may add him to the number; any 3 to proceede.[18]

A note in the Entry Book shows that the petition was officially referred to the special committee of noblemen on 17 March;[19] but according to the petitioner, although "there were severall meetings & . . . some Overtures were made for a Composure by mediacon of freinds & some proposalls made," nothing was "finally setled." This is stated in the preamble to Lady Honoria's second petition, which continues:

And whereas Sr Robt Howard for about a yeare last past hath refused to Cohabitt wth yor pet^r but left her wth a few goods in a house in Lincolns

16. This spelling of the name is frequent, but "Honoria" is correct.
17. _H.M.C._, Report 12, App. 7, Sir David Fleming MSS, p. 46.
18. P.R.O., S.P.Dom. Chas. II, 29, 194, No. 33. Williamson endorsed the letter "La: Honora Howard." The date was probably 23 February.
19. _C.S.P.D._, 1666-1667, p. 566.

Inne feilds, & did allowe her for some time but £6 per weeke towards the supporting of her selfe familye & keeping of a Coach (tho: he & his Children are by yo[r] pet[rs] estate enabled to live plentifully) but for the space of six weeks last past he hath given her noe allowance at all & hath forbiden tradesmen to trust her, whereby she is exposed to much hardship & must be in a starving Condicon, & S[r] Rob[t] did declare y[t] he would put yo[r] pet[r] up in a Chamber, & y[t] she should live upon bread & water, & onely have £50 per ann[um][20] And upon severall occasions presseth yo[r] pet[r] to submitt & lye at his mercy w[ch] she dares not doe haveing already found severe and Cruell usage by him: & yet he professeth to some ho[ble] persons y[t] he would performe some proposalls but yo[r] pet[r] cannot finde y[t] S[r] Rob[t] really intends to secure to yo[r] pet[r] w[t] he hath offered. Now for y[t] S[r] Rob[t] hath £2000 per ann[um] w[th]out Impeachm[t] of Wast w[th] yo[r] pet[r] w[ch] he injoyes w[th] Lib[ty] to grant Estates of Coppy holds, & had alsoe a personall Estate w[th] other great advantages & yet is not pleased to performe agreem[ts] before Marriage w[ch] yo[r] Ma[ts] letter much inclind yo[r] pet[r] to & trusted to his hono[r] for Just performance of agreemts And for y[t] S[r] Rob[t] Howard is a member of the ho[ble] house of Comons & y[t] yo[r] Pet[r] finds that her Joynture is Conveyd by way of Morgage soe y[t] yo[r] pet[rs] freinds cannot prosecute for her releife in any ordinary Court of Justice

Yo[r] pet[rs] humble suite is y[t] y[r] Ma[ty] wilbe graciously pleased to recomend yo[r] pet[rs] distressed & miserable Condicon to y[e] Consideracon of yo[r] houses of Parliam[t] that by an Act of Parliam[t] yo[r] Pet[r] may out of her owne Estate be provided for & have the house & goods she brought S[r] Rob[t]; And y[t] such yearly maintenance may be securely setled upon freinds in trust for yo[r] pet[r] As that thereby yo[r] pet[r] may be enabled to pay her just debts & support her selfe wth necessaries suitable to her birth & fortune.

And yo[r] Petition[r] shall ever pray & c.[21]

This was the petition that Lady Honoria's friend Randall Egerton (variously called "Major General" and "Colonel") presented to the House of Commons on 27 April 1668. Grey's report of Egerton's speech giving "the substance of the petition" is: "That she was ready to starve, and fled to the House for relief; her Husband would allow her nothing, though she was worth to him 40,000 l. He pleading his Privilege, she was without remedy."[22] Howard successfully moved that the petition should be read on the following morning. Grey then summarizes Howard's speech in his own defense:

20. *Not*, as Miss Florence R. Scott had it in a very inaccurate transcription of part of this document in *M.L.N.*, LV, 412-413, "5d a week"!

21. P.R.O. S.P.Dom. Chas. II, 218, No. 63.

22. Anchitell Grey, *Debates of the House of Commons, From the Year 1667 to the Year 1694* (London, 1769), I, 147. There is also a summary of the petition in *The Diary of John Milward, September 1666 to May 1668*, ed. Caroline Robbins (Cambridge, 1938), p. 281.

The first quarrel betwixt them was because he would not give the inheritance of his estate to whom she pleased, from his own children—His wife complained to the Lords of the Council of ill usage, and said she would not cohabit with him—She confessed to Lord *St. John,* that Sir *Robert Howard* had ruined her, by giving her her will in whatever she would—He never delivered the King's Letter to her, nor had he need of it when he first addressed himself to her—When [s]he lost his plate, she confessed it to the Lords, and he forgave her—He sent her 50 l. when he heard she wanted money, and she sent it back again—She said to him, "Give me a good settlement, and if I like to stay with you, I will"—He visited her when she was sick—She has tampered with them that would ruin him and his posterity, and so she sent him word by his man; which she confessed— She said that she would ruin his son that he should never marry.

She sent him word by his friend, Sir *Charles Wolseley,* "Let him do his worst, and I'll do mine."—Serjeant *Maynard* said to him, "What, will you take away your Lady's allowance?" He answered, "Let her do her part, and he would do his". He has renounced all Privilege to her, as a Member, in any Court—She has charged him with a letter he has written —She turned him off, not he her—She charges him with having 40,000 l. with her; prays God that he and his posterity be not more the worse for her.

The remark that he had not needed the King's letter of recommendation when he made his advances to the lady was not the remark of the *compleat* gentleman, if it meant that she was ready to marry any man who offered; but perhaps it meant that she liked Howard for himself. At any rate, the House must have been impressed by Howard's defense, at least to the extent of deciding to take no action. There is no mention of the petition in the *Journals of the House of Commons,* and Milward simply records that Howard "made it very ill against her" in his speech: "but the case was not determined, and so the House adjourned."[23] Nor indeed was there any need for parliamentary decision, since Howard had renounced his privileges as a Member; the matter could be left to Chancery or to private negotiation.

Howard's final arrangement with his wife was not ungenerous, particularly if one remembers that married women under seventeenth-century law had practically no right of ownership of property. The arrangement is set out in an indenture of 20 October 1670 which has not, I think, been seen by historians of the Howard family (it is among the James M. Osborn manuscripts at Yale).

The indenture is technically between Sir Robert and Lady Honoria, of the one part, and her three trustees, Arthur Earl of Anglesey, Sir

23. *Diary,* p. 283.

Gilbert Gerrard, and Randall Egerton, of the other. Relating that "some unhappy differences have hapned" between Howard and his wife, which have gone so far that they have agreed to live apart, it provides for the payment of £8240 for Lady Honoria's undisturbed use, payment being made to the trustees through Howard's usual agents Clayton and Morris. Howard agreed not to interfere in any way with the use of the money, or any property bought with it, and guaranteed Lady Honoria's right to dispose of the money or the proceeds in her will; he also agreed not to make any claim on it should she die intestate. She was granted the unchallenged right to sue for any money due to her under her father's will or otherwise, except for the property which came to her from Sir Francis Englefield. This was the subject of a separate indenture and of separate clauses here, under which Howard agreed, roughly, to maintain the property and not to dispose of it without his wife's approval. He bound himself to consent to, and to further, any Act of Parliament that might be obtained for "the better performance" of these agreements. He then confirmed both her rights to jewelry, plate, and other goods and chattels (which he made over to her trustees by deed of gift) and her right to live apart, wherever she might choose and without interference. Other minor provisions protected her against suits that might be brought against her as executrix of Englefield's will and defined the responsibilities of her trustees.

It remains to add that both parties seem to have abided by the agreement: when Howard sold the manor of Wootton Bassett to Laurence Hyde in 1676 he did so with his wife's consent and agreed to pay her £8000 from the £36,000 that was the full purchase price;[24] and when Lady Honoria made her will on 6 September in the same year, a few days before her death, she made it, she declared, in pursuance of the power allowed her by the Indenture of 20 October 1670, and other powers and authority given to her. She asked to be buried quietly in Englefield Church, Berkshire, near her first husband, Sir Francis, with one plain black marble stone to cover them both; she made many generous bequests, and remembered her "very good ffreinds and Trustees" the Earl of Anglesey and Sir Gilbert Gerrard, and her executors "my good ffreinds Coll Randall Egerton and S^r

24. *H.M.C.*, Report 7, App. 467b (John Verney to Sir Ralph). Bod. MS Don. c. 68 f. 11, an agreement of 14 July 1676, gives some of the details of the sale.

William Turner knight," but to her second husband her feelings had not altered: "Item unto Sr Robert Howard one shilling."[25]

The earlier stages of his marital troubles with Lady Honoria were, as will now be clear, the greater part of the "Business of more unpleasant Natures" which Howard mentioned in 1668, in the course of his controversy with Dryden, as having taken up much of his time; and Dryden's scoffing at the phrase will be seen as the unkind and unnecessary gibe it was. (A more sympathetic brother-in-law might also have known, or remembered, that Howard's only surviving son, Thomas, had been ill with the dreaded smallpox late in 1667; and that Thomas's sister, the only one of Sir Robert's daughters to survive infancy, had died on Easter Monday 1668.)[26] What Dryden did know, and say, was that the petition of Lady Honoria was particularly embarrassing to Howard because it came at a time when he was developing ambitions as a statesman and was beginning to take a leading part in the angry Parliamentary proceedings of the day.

He first came into prominence in the House of Commons when in December, 1666, he was responsible for the famous "Proviso" to the Poll Bill. Briefly, although the House of Lords thought it an infringement of the Royal prerogative, the House of Commons, on 7 December, after a conference between the two Houses, passed the Poll Tax Bill with the addition of a proviso that a parliamentary committee of nine should be empowered to examine the receipt and expenditure of public money raised for the war. According to Pepys, Charles II ordered the Lord Chamberlain to round up supporters "from the playhouses and bawdy houses" in an attempt to defeat the bill; but it was passed by a majority of 118 to 83. In the long run the proviso was made a separate bill, and the King named his own commissioners, who found nothing; but at the time of the passing of the original Poll Tax Bill with the proviso, Pepys noted that it was said to have been "mightily ill taken by all the Court party as a mortal blow" and he wondered at Howard's part in it, since he was "one of the King's servants, at least hath a great office, and hath got, they say, 20,000 l. since the King came in."[27]

Had this been the only instance of Howard's acting against what the King and the Court party thought to be their interests, one might

25. Somerset House, 122 Bence.
26. Bod. Ash. MS. 243 f. 273. For Dryden's comments, see above, p. 111.
27. *Diary*, VI, 88-90 (8 Dec. 1666).

have argued that he did sincerely believe in the necessity for controlling and auditing the accounts of the King's many officers and was prepared to act in a just cause even though the King may have disapproved. Clarendon makes it clear, however, that in 1666 Howard belonged to a group who "made themselves remarkable by opposing all Things which were proposed in that House for the King's Service, or which were likely to be grateful to him, as sir Richard Temple, Mr. Seymour, and Mr. Garraway, and sir Robert Howard; who were all bold speakers, and meant to make themselves considerable by saying, upon all occasions, what wiser men would [not], whatever they thought."[28] When Howard joined the Court party shortly afterwards, he could therefore be classified by Marvell as one of the "recanters" and could earn a certain notoriety as a time-server.[29]

To a student of Howard's full career, however, the cause for wonder must be not that he "recanted" to the Court party but—as it was to Pepys—that he should ever have belonged to any other. Whether his temporary adherence to the "Country Party" was a result of political conviction, of his new friendship with Buckingham, of a temporary irritation with the King or of a growing antipathy to Clarendon, it is impossible to say.[30]

Further evidence of his importance in the House of Commons is provided by Pepys's mention a few days later of his playing a leading part in the conference with the Lords on the Bill against Importing Cattle from Ireland. The Lords, although they had to give in, felt that the Commons were making yet another attack on the Royal prerogative; Howard maintained that there was no desire to limit the King's power. Pepys thought that the Commons were right.[31]

Howard's close association with Buckingham at this time is indicated by his being chosen to carry to the King one of the Duke's letters of penitence, written when he was in hiding to avoid arrest and was in disgrace because he had fled rather than face a somewhat specious charge of treason (it depended, among other things, on the

28. Clarendon, *The Continuation of the Life of Edward, Earl of Clarendon* (Oxford, 1857), II, 321.

29. Andrew Marvell, "Further Advice to a Painter," ll. 47-58 (*Poems and Letters*, ed. H. M. Margoliouth, second edition, Oxford 1952, p. 169).

30. It is not inconceivable that he had foreknowledge of Lady Honoria's approaches to Charles II. (The official action on her first petition was only a few months after this.)

31. Pepys, *Diary*, VI, 120 (9 Jan. 1667); *Commons Journals*, VIII, 673.

allegation that he had commissioned the casting of a special horoscope of the King's nativity). Pepys also records that Howard was one of the "many of the discontented Parliament" who "did attend at the Council Chamber when he was examined."[32] The King seems to have been ready enough to accept Buckingham's explanations; and Howard himself cannot have been unwelcome at Court since he was chosen as the go-between.

There was certainly never any real question of his loyalty: after the Dutch had made their famous raid up the Medway on 12 June, a commission was belatedly issued (on 15 June) "for raising 10,000 foot and 2,500 horse; the Earl of Manchester to be general, Sir Wm. Waller, Sir Rob. Howard, and Col. Inglesby, colonels." (Howard's regiment was allotted to the defense of Portsmouth, to help "prevent the enemy from landing.") Then in December of the same year he was nominated as one of the deputy-lieutenants of Hampshire.[33]

Indeed in the eyes of Andrew Marvell, Howard was becoming *too* important—or believing himself to be so, like the hero of his own *Indian Queen* or the mad Orlando. He is accordingly one of the members of the House who are thus satirized in the "Last Instructions to a Painter," probably composed between August and November, 1667:

> Of Birth, State, Wit, Strength, Courage, *How'rd* presumes,
> And in his Breast wears many *Montezumes.*
> These and some more with single Valour stay
> The adverse Troops, and hold them all at Bay.
> Each thinks his Person represents the whole,
> And with that thought does multiply his Soul:
> Believes himself an Army, theirs one Man,
> As eas'ly Conquer'd, and believing can.
> With Heart of Bees so full, and Head of Mites,
> That each, tho' Duelling, a Battel fights.
> Such once *Orlando,* famous in *Romance,*
> Broach'd whole Brigades like Larks upon his Lance.[34]

Marvell perhaps had in mind specifically the eagerness with which Howard played a leading role in the impeachment of Clarendon in

32. Pepys, *Diary,* VII, 26 (17 July 1667); Winifred [Gardner], Lady Burgh-clere, *George Villiers, Second Duke of Buckingham* (London, 1903), p. 179; J. H. Wilson, *A Rake and His Times: George Villiers, Second Duke of Buckingham* (New York, 1954), p. 86.

33. *C.S.P.D.,* 1667, pp. 187, 190; 1667-1668, p. 92.

34. *Poems and Letters,* ed. Margoliouth, p. 147, ll. 265-276.

October of this year. The impeachment, of course, is one of the sorrier chapters in the history of the time and had its outcome been similar would have been comparable with the impeachment of Strafford in the previous reign. Charles II was not anxious to defend his chief minister, of whom he had tired; and almost any charge was good enough for the Commons, jealous of Clarendon's power and bitterly aware of his contempt for most of them (including the newer Royal favorites such as Buckingham, to whom Howard thought he owed his present allegiance). For the greater part of the time the question would seem to have been not whether Clarendon was guilty (that was taken for granted) but how best to destroy him (although he had already resigned). There was a Committee on Precedents for the Method of Procedure in Impeachments for Capital Offences; and Mr. Solicitor Finch moved, after their report had been received, that the accusation should be upon oath, with secret witnesses. Nothing but impeachment, however, would satisfy Howard, who spoke many times in the long debate conducted over a period of several weeks. "The Earl of *Clarendon* has his liberty to devise his answer," he asserted, "and so have we ours to accuse him"; and it was voted that the Committee should reduce the accusation to heads and present them to the House.[35]

His speech a few days later, on 6 November, was along slightly different lines but to the same end: "Suppose the Earl of *Clarendon* be [Innocent and] committed, 'tis no more than what a great man, the Duke of *Buckingham*, lately has been—The only injury, though clear, is imprisonment. . . . *His* inconvenience, to be imprisoned only for a few days; *Ours*, to let a person go free with such a charge. . . . If the charge be not true, every member that delivered the charge exposed to ruin. His inconvenience of imprisonment fully recompensed by his innocence."[36] He continued to oppose the suggestion that the House should proceed by common law: "We are in a higher sphere. If impeachments of this nature be not allowed, we have no way left of impeaching a great person"; "our laws and liber-

35. Grey, *Debates*, I, 11-12; *The Proceedings in the House of Commons Touching the Impeachment of Edward Late Earl of Clarendon . . . Anno 1667* (London, 1700), p. 12. The importance of the latter for a biography of Howard was first pointed out by E. S. de Beer, *Inst. Hist. Res. Bull.*, III (1925), 64. See also *The Diary of John Milward*, pp. 99-176.

36. Grey, I, 17-18, with the addition of the two bracketed words from the *Proceedings*.

ties violated by this Lord *Clarendon,* and we know not by what name to call the offence."[37]

After much technical argument, the House began trying Clarendon, as Howard had urged that it should do, under each of the heads of accusation. There was often opposition to Howard's positiveness; when, for example, he asserted (on 11 November) that "No man can deny that 'corresponding with the King's enemies' is treason. If it be not, treason has neither name nor definition," Waller rightly replied that one "might hold correspondence with the King's enemies, and not betray him to his enemies." Similarly when Howard wanted to quote an "Eye witness" of Clarendon's treason, the House was not impressed. But he was chosen to go up to the Lords and desire a free conference of the two Houses and was one of five appointed to "manage" the conference when it was eventually granted. When the Lords were not satisfied with the methods of procedure, he continued to press for the impeachment and was loud in his support of the resolution finally adopted, informing the Lords that their refusal to cooperate in the impeachment was "an obstruction to the public justice of the Kingdom." Nor could he be pacified by the message from the Lords on 3 December mentioning a long petition received from Clarendon and intimating that he had "withdrawn"; on the following day Howard scornfully denounced it as not a petition but "a scandalous, seditious, and malicious paper," maintained that all its facts were wrong, and successfully moved that it should be burnt by the public hangman. He was again chosen by the House to take the vote to the Lords and desire a further conference. When the Lords refused to concur in a vote desiring the King to issue a proclamation to summon Clarendon, Howard wanted something—almost *any*thing—done rather than leave the impression that Clarendon was too "great" for the House of Commons to do anything against him; and to the end he was continuing to urge additions to the Bill of banishment.[38]

It seems certain that the main motive for Howard's persecution of Clarendon in the House was personal (and in view of Clarendon's

37. Grey, I, 21, 31.
38. Grey, I, 45-64; Milward, pp. 133-176; *Proceedings*, pp. 80-129; *Commons Journals*, IX, 23. A footnote in Grey adds: "Sir *Robert Howard* told the Speaker, that when he carried up the reasons to the Lords, he gave not the paper of reasons to the Lords, but underhandedly let the Clerk of the Lords House transcribe it."

remark to Arlington when the King consulted him about Lady Honoria's petition, that he had "no mind to have any thinge to doe with the knight," the dislike would seem to have been mutual). At the same time it is interesting to see how even at this stage of his parliamentary career, Howard was setting himself up as the guardian of the rights of the House. The adoption of such an attitude, whether or not it is sincere, is generally sound political tactics.

IN the years 1667 and 1668 Howard's name was also constantly before the public in his capacity as a dramatist and poet. There were numerous revivals of his early plays (Pepys, for instance, saw *The Surprisal* at least five times and *The Committee* twice within a period of thirteen months, from April, 1667, to May, 1668); Howard also contributed a song to the revised version, by his friend the Duke of Buckingham, of Fletcher's play *The Chances*. This was produced in January, 1667 (Pepys saw it in February), but not published until 1682; and Howard's song was not printed with the play but survives, with the music by John Eccles, in the collection of the Clark Library in Los Angeles.[1] It again illustrates Howard's ability to write for music; the words, if not unconventional, are neat and in their way charming. Without all the repetitions of phrase made necessary by the music, they are:

> Wasted with sighs I sigh'd or pin'd
> But still her unrelenting mind,
> Unsoftn'd, left me still oppress'd;
> Her scorn and my disease encreas'd.
>
> For help another way I try'd
> To use revenge, reason and pride,
> Summon'd their forces to my aid,
> But found those lifeguards were affraid.
>
> Reason enslav'd cou'd not prevail,
> Pride shrunk, and feirce revenge grew pale.
> So sev'rall ways the squadron flies
> At the first volley of her eyes.
>
> I then resolv'd to take my flight,
> For ever from her dang'rous sight,
> But then in dreams she wou'd appear,
> As full of charmes, and as severe.
>
> At length I found I must endure
> What she or death cou'd only cure,
> At length I found I must endure
> What she or death cou'd only cure.

1. It may also be found in *A Collection of Songs set to Music by Mr Henry Purcell & Mr John Eccles* (London, n.d., ?1696) a possibly unique copy of which is in the Royal College of Music, London.

Then on 20 February in the following year, 1668, Pepys went to see the King's Company in a new play that Mistress Knepp had mentioned to him on 11 January among those planned, as we should now say, "for immediate production." The performance gave him particular pleasure, and not only because of Knepp's part in it:

Dined, and by one o'clock to the King's house: a new play, *The Duke of Lerma*, of Sir Robert Howard's: where the King and Court was; and Knepp and Nell spoke the prologue most excellently, especially Knepp, who spoke beyond any creature I ever heard. The play designed to reproach our King with his mistresses, that I was troubled for it, and expected it should be interrupted; but it ended all well, which salved all. The play a well-writ and good play, only its design I did not like of reproaching the King, but altogether a very good and most serious play.[2]

Pepys's enthusiasm is understandable (he saw the play again on 18 April) but not his interpretation of the story as designed to reproach the King with his mistresses. To be sure, the plot deals with the Duke's attempt to prostitute his daughter to a King; but the attempt fails and the story ends with the prospect of an honorable marriage. It is not impossible, of course, that the play was altered before publication in the middle of the year;[3] but it is most improbable that Howard would have wanted to criticize Charles's amours, least of all through a part played by Nell Gwyn. Interestingly, Nell had established her reputation as an actress partly through plays written by the Howards: her first leading role had been in James Howard's *English Monsieur* in December, 1666; and in 1667 she had played in *The Surprisal* and had been very successful in James Howard's *All Mistaken*. Moreover, the Buckingham faction had been keen to advance her liaison with Charles; and Howard is thought to have been anxious not to criticize but to assist.[4] Pepys, who had been told by Knepp on 11 January, when she first mentioned *The Duke of Lerma*, "that the King did send several times for Nelly, and she was with him," and who had noted that he was "sorry for it, and can hope for no good

2. *Diary*, VII, 309.

3. It was entered on the Stationers' Register on 24 June 1668. The title page and head title use the full form *The Great Favourite, Or, The Duke of Lerma*.

4. J. H. Wilson, *Nell Gwyn, Royal Mistress* (New York, 1952), p. 83.

to the State from having a Prince so devoted to his pleasure," was perhaps oversensitive on that matter and read into the play the comment that he himself would have liked to make.

Pepys was right, however, about the merits of the play, which is easily the best of Howard's serious dramas.[5] What is open to question is how much of the credit for it can be given to Howard, since, as he was quick to admit in his note "To the Reader," it is a rewriting of a play by another (probably a Jacobean dramatist).

After noting that he was only too ready to publish the play because he was "concern'd to let the World judge what subject matter of Offence was contain'd in it" (perhaps a reference to opinions, such as Pepys's, that it reflected on the King), Howard mentions that "Some were pleas'd to believe, little of it mine." He thanks these for "thinking there was any thing in it that was worth so ill design'd an Envy, as to place it to another *Author*"; and then in his second paragraph explains the circumstances:

> For the *Subject*, I came accidentally to write upon it; for a Gentleman brought a *Play* to the *King's Company*, call'd, *The Duke of Lerma*; and by them I was desired to peruse it, and return my Opinion, whether I thought it fit for the *Stage*: After I had read it, I acquainted them, that in my Judgment it would not be of much Use for such a Design, since the Contrivance scarce would merit the Name of a *Plot*; and some of that, assisted by a Disguise; and it ended abruptly: and on the Person of *Philip the III^d* there was fix'd such a mean Character, and on the Daughter of the Duke of *Lerma*, such a vitious one, that I cou'd not but judge it unfit to be presented by any that had a Respect, not only to Princes, but indeed to either Man or Woman; and about that time, being to go into the Country, I was perswaded by Mr. *Hart* to make it my Diversion there, that so great a Hint might not be lost, as the Duke of *Lerma* saving himself in his last Extremity, by his unexpected Disguise, which is as well in the true Story as the old *Play*; and besides that and the *Names*, my altering the most part of the *Characters*, and the whole *Design*, made me uncapable to use much more; though perhaps written with higher Stile and Thoughts, than I cou'd attain to.

Dryden, not in a mood to be pacified by a mere explanation, still thought it necessary to ridicule Howard's claim to the play, and early in his *Defence of an Essay of Dramatic Poesy* wrote:

5. The play has been reprinted by D. D. Arundell, in his *Dryden and Howard 1664-68* (Cambridge, 1929)—unfortunately with a claim, in the "Editorial Note," that it "is, in fact, the first attempt at drama of character since Shakespeare"!

As for the Play of the Duke of *Lerma,* having so much alter'd and beauti-
fi'd it, as he has done, it can justly belong to none but him. Indeed they
must be extream ignorant as well as envious, who would rob him of that
Honour; for you see him putting in his claim to it, even in the first two
lines.

> *Repulse upon repulse like waves thrown back,*
> *That slide to hang upon obdurate rocks.*

After this let detraction do its worst; for if this be not his, it deserves to be.

Richard Flecknoe, or whoever was the author of the *Letter from
a Gentleman to the Honourable Ed. Howard Esq.,* made a point of
trying to reply to this. If, he said, Dryden meant that the lines were
nonsense, Dryden was wrong:

But if the Squire would have it understood, that the Honourable Person
used some things in the old Play, he has acknowledged it already, and
professed that he would have used more, had not the Alteration of the
whole design deprived him of the Benefit. But the Squire having writ
down the two first lynes, what ever he means, I that have read the old Play
will assure him, that the Honourable Person used but the two first words
of it, though he has preserved the method in the beginning. (p. 2)

If Dryden meant what I take him to mean, that the lines were too
bad to be by anybody but Howard, he must have smiled at that. At
any rate, there was no mistaking his general attitude, for two paragraphs later he had written that Howard "gives me the Compellation
of *The Author of a Dramatique Essay;* which is a little Discourse in
Dialogue, for the most part borrowed from the observations of others:
therefore, that I may not be wanting to him in civility, I return his
Complement by calling him *The Author of the Duke of* Lerma." This
attack was to draw from Dryden's enemy Langbaine the perhaps over-
enthusiastic defense of Howard, "that this Admirable Poet has too
great a Stock of Wit of his own, to be necessitated to borrow from
others," together with the not unjustified rebuke to Dryden, that "had
he consulted Reason, Gratitude, or his own Reputation, he had otherwise imploy'd his time."[6]

The authorship of the original manuscript from which Howard
worked is not known. Alfred Harbage, who first drew attention to
The Duke of Lerma as an "Elizabethan-Restoration Palimpsest," gave
very strong reasons, in similarities of plot situation and of style, for
believing that the original play was by John Ford.[7] Discussing this

6. *The English Dramatick Poets,* pp. 277, 276.
7. *M.L.R.,* XXXV (1940), 287-319.

elsewhere, I have suggested that the evidence is not quite conclusive, if only because there are also many parallels with the work of James Shirley; nor can I readily overlook the fact that Moseley (admittedly unreliable) entered on the Stationers' Register on 9 September 1653 a *Spanish Duke of Lerma* which he attributed to Henry Shirley (whom we know as the author of only one surviving play, *The Martyred Soldier*).[8] I am inclined to hold to the opinion I hazarded then, that the original may well have been a play written in collaboration—which could explain not only the odd way in which certain stylistic characteristics tend to fall within groups of scenes but also the failure of the authors to publish.

One part of the play that nobody would deny to be Howard's is the prologue. It is typically "Restoration," though it was also novel enough to appeal to Pepys (whose interest in Mistress Knepp's part in it was, of course, not purely literary). Nell Gwyn and Knepp entered, as themselves, and discussed, in prose, the author's refusal to provide a prologue for his play. Then, very skilfully, the prose modulated into rhymed couplets as they expressed, in dialogue form, the kind of sentiment that was usually expressed in Restoration prologues, on the theme of "delivering" the author from his audience:

> *Nepp* Deliver him from you that nothing spare;
> Nay, you that would fain seem worse than you are,
> Out-talk your own Debaucheries, and tell
> With a fine Shrug, *Faith*, Jack, *I am not well.*
> *Nell* From you that with much Ease, and little Shame,
> Can blast a Poet's, and a Woman's Fame;
> For at first sight a well-bred Trick y'have got,
> Combing your Wiggs, to Cry, *Dam me, She's naught.*
> *Nepp* Prithee let's say no more, but run away,
> For they'll revenge themselves on the poor Play.
> *Nell* No matter, we have here one Party fast,
> I mean the Gentlemen we spoke of last:
> Though they deny't the Poet, yet we know,
> On us they freely wou'd their Claps bestow. *Exeunt.*

This shows again not only a good ear for contemporary speech and idiom but also a sound knowledge of how far one can count on the

8. *The Problem of John Ford* (Melbourne, 1955), pp. 131-139. I would now withdraw the suggestion that there may have been significance in the fact that the abbreviation "d'ee"—so characteristic of Ford—is replaced by "d'ye" in the second (1692) edition of *The Duke of Lerma*. Howard seems to have taken no interest in the printing of his plays; and the 1692 compositor modernized often.

personality of known players to "put across" given material (including the final indecency) and establish in the audience (as it did in Pepys) a willingness to listen with appreciation to what is to come. The incongruity of the humorous prologue and the seriousness of tone of the play it introduces was not the matter of concern then that it would probably be now.

The opening scene of the play proper takes us into a different world—the world of the Elizabethan and Jacobean villain-hero. The first speech is a soliloquy, in blank verse, spoken by Lerma—a complaint against the King who

> shot Ruine at me, and there lies,
> Forgiving all the World, but me alone;

and the metaphor of the "untimely frost" used to describe the King's alleged ingratitude is a reminiscence of Wolsey's farewell to his greatness in *Henry VIII* (and perhaps also of *Romeo and Juliet*), while the ensuing discussion between Lerma and his servants is modeled on the so-called "Act IV Scene ii" of *Timon of Athens* and takes over much of the sentiment and some of the imagery of that scene, as in

> See—here are the parts of my full Ruine,
> These decay'd Out-Houses shew the chief Building
> Wants Reparation.

One does not know, unfortunately, whether these Shakespearian echoes are the work of Howard (who liked such literary reminiscence) or whether they are taken over from the original play (which would almost certainly have contained many such if it was by John Ford or by James or even Henry Shirley). They continue throughout *The Duke of Lerma*, and it may be sufficient to cite one other, the *Othello* allusion in Act IV Scene i:

> And I will gladly tell you my true Story,
> Like those that with a pleasure do repeat
> The Tales of mighty Dangers they have past.

The characterization of Lerma is also in the tradition of the able but evil villain-heroes of late sixteenth- and earlier seventeenth-century drama. The type is recognizable when Lerma rejoices in the news that the King has died in torment, when he announces his program:

> I will sow Jealousie in every Breast,
> 'Tis a Rank growing weed, and will choak up
> All that shou'd spring of Love, or Confidence—

and above all when he plans to make his daughter Maria the mistress of the new King and, through her, to control the kingdom. One of his agents is his servant Caldroon, another is his kinsman, the confessor to the King, soon to become Archbishop of Toledo; and when Lerma does gain power, he uses it to oppress the people, poison the Queen Mother, and suppress all the King's true friends and advisers. The dramatist has made Lerma's villainy plain while giving him also much of the insolence, Machiavellian ability, and capacity for grim humor that win a certain respect for many of his predecessors (particularly Shakespeare's Richard III).

These qualities are well illustrated in the admirable scene (II.i) in which Lerma tries to persuade his daughter that it is her duty to her father to allow herself to be prostituted to the King:

> *Maria.* My Mother, Sir, upon her Death-bed, charg'd me
>   (When her Acquaintance grew so great with Heaven,)
>   That I shou'd still be chast; chast to all Appetites,
>   Call'd Pride, the Dropsie of Infected Souls,
>   That swell'd 'em first, then burst 'em.
> *Lerma.* Your Mother was for t'other World
>   When she preach'd thus, but I am yet for this;
>   And I must leave it in a hurry, unless thy power
>   Stops the fierce Whirlwind that is just now ready
>   To wrap me into nothing—
> *Maria.* Heaven defend my Father.
> *Lerma.* Amen, but you must help; it was
>   On purpose that Heaven made thee fair,
>   To save thy Father.

The King, bewitched by Maria's beauty, immediately decides not to take his late father's advice and not to banish Lerma; and Lerma's only fear is that Maria's virtue will prove unassailable:

> *Maria.* Heaven will defend you, Sir.
> *Lerma.* I will not trouble Heaven, when you may do't.

To this point the play moves with speed and directness, and the dialogue is in blank verse that is often splendid (as I hope the quotations have shown), even if it is occasionally spoiled by the incomplete lines that Howard presumably considered to be essential for variety and to approximate to the rhythms of speech. I suspect, then, that most of the dialogue in these early scenes is from the original play, with some adaptation and some omission.

A different tone, however, becomes apparent later in Act II Scene i, in a soliloquy by Maria that, although mainly in blank verse, seems to have a Restoration idiom and movement:

> *Maria.* What storms are risen, in my shaken breast?
>   Thoughts succeed thoughts, like restless troubled waves,
>   Dashing out one another: if I deny,
>   My Father to avoid his destiny,
>   May reach that sacred Life, which I may save;
>   If I discover this my Father dies.
>   Vertue, thou shalt protect me before heaven,
>   Though not from this bad world. Ah me!
>   The only way now left me to preserve
>   A King, and Father, is t'expose my Fame:
>   Hard fate, when Vertue is the guide to shame.

Then, as soon as Maria and the King are left alone, the dialogue is in couplets. Howard's claim in the preface that he wrote some scenes in blank verse, others in rhyme, for no other reason than "Chance, which waited upon my present Fancy," is disingenuous; he apparently composed some blank verse, but most of his additions are probably in rhyme (and since he explained that he disapproved of the portrayal of the King and Maria in the original play, his additions are most likely to be in scenes involving those characters). His dislike of rhyme was not so great, then, as to prevent his introducing it for variety and to give his audience the kind of "romantic" scene they liked in their serious plays. One is immediately struck, however, by the inferiority of the serious idiom of the Restoration to that of the earlier period; Howard does his best but there is little chance of psychological development of character once the sing-song begins and the conventional attitudes are struck:

> *King.* Those that obey may fear a slavery,
>   You now may be the Tyrant, but not I.
> *Maria.* If this, Sir, from your power does you remove
>   Against your self; there's Treason in your Love.

Another example may be quoted from the part of Act III Scene ii in which Maria, having persuaded the King to sign warrants for the virtual banishment of his loyal nobles, tells him that she has done it in his own interest and advises him how to proceed:

> Can you my heart for want of friendship blame,
>   That for your safety have expos'd my fame?

> Love to your glories, shou'd his flames resign,
> As fires their Light, when the bright Sun does shine.

It says something for Howard that in this play such artifice does not destroy the characterization already established, even if nothing is gained.

There is improvement, in this scene as in others, immediately on the entrance of Medina, brother to Maria's dead mother. Medina is particularly well drawn as the bluff and honest man who refuses to submit to such evil-doing as Lerma's, and tells even the King and Maria what interpretation the world puts upon their relationship. It cannot be without significance that all *his* speeches (with only one trifling exception) are in blank verse, and that they contain more of the Ford-like idiom than do the lines of any other character in the play:

> Yet will you turn your Eyes in to your Breast,
> And they must weep, for they will see thy heart
> So very foul, that it needs pious washing.

Similarly the speeches of the others are often most moving when Medina is involved: one example would be Maria's refusal to let the King punish him for his outspokenness:

> *Maria.* Think how the World would Curse me, when they hear
> *Medina*'s love to Vertue, lost his Life.
> He talkt to me of nothing but of goodness;
> And when he spoke of that, (as he must needs)
> He nam'd my Mother, and by chance I wept.[9]

Nor can there be much doubt that Howard has taken over without major alteration the scene (IV.i) in which Medina, having presented before Maria a Jacobean masque to expound to her the nature of her supposed evil, is astonished to find her not only gentle to him, because of the honesty of his misunderstanding, but also defiant, because of her knowledge of her own innocence; he in his turn alternates between his unwillingness to be deceived and his desire to believe that all is not evil:

9. II.ii. I should be inclined to give to the original author the credit also for the touches of grim humour, such as the comments of the noblemen on the Queen Mother's sudden illness:

> *Alcara.* These fainting fits seem as if she were
> With Child.
> *D'Alva.* With Death I fear.

> All may be Counterfeit—and yet—
> There may be such a thing as a good Woman.

The play holds our interest here and till the end. As the tide turns against him, Lerma's courage and resourcefulness earn him a certain dramatic sympathy; and the story moves rapidly as his agent to the Archbishop (formerly the King's confessor) is sent away on the pretense of being called by the Pope to Rome, but takes poison and sends to Lerma a letter from the Pope appointing Lerma Cardinal, and a box containing the Cardinal's robes. I suspect some slight bungling of the original here. For one thing, Howard refers to Lerma's donning of the robes in the original as a "Disguise" (although he also says that the old play corresponded here with fact, and that the historical Lerma did become a Cardinal). In the source, did the Confessor perhaps become the Cardinal and, before poisoning himself, send the robes to Lerma? However that may be, there is no doubting the theatrical effect as Medina and the nobles, preparing to condemn to death a man of whose villainy they have ample evidence, are confronted by a cynically amused Cardinal who can defy them to touch him and can inform them that with the Pope's consent he has chosen his own "prison," in the monastery he has built himself. Here, I feel sure, the Jacobean play ended, and ended well; but Howard, who says that it "ended abruptly," has added about one hundred lines. They begin with a valedictory speech by Lerma, significantly in couplets, defying his enemies, accusing them of hypocrisy and self-seeking, and predicting that they will destroy each other:

> May you all sink in fates for me you meant,
> And be too dull, your ruines to prevent;
> That when you're lost in this ambitious toil,
> I in my safe retreat may sit and smile.   *Exit.*

I cannot see in this, as does Alfred Harbage in his admirable comment on the play, a "hint" that Lerma "reforms";[10] and our final impression is rather meant to be Medina's:

> Methinks the greatness of his Spirit stir'd me,
> I cou'd almost forgive him.

Howard has blurred the effect by giving Lerma the superfluous farewell, and he has certainly altered the tone of the ending by allowing

10. *Cavalier Drama*, p. 249.

the King to plead his case with Maria, who has come, needlessly as it proves, to beg for her father's life. She is prepared to enter a nunnery, but the King vows that

> *Spain's* empty Throne,
> Unless from you, shall want succession

and his final words are

> Let not a smile upon a Face be seen,
> Till fair *Maria* yields to be my Queen.

Perhaps a lingering respect for history forbade Howard to end the story with a royal marriage; but obviously he is responsible for the addition of the "happy ending."

Howard wrote for the 1668 performance a topical Epilogue, spoken by Nell Gwyn, again as herself:

> Much injur'd Gentlemen, may you now please,
> You true Committee of such Grievances,
> Kindly to hear me now, and I will show it,
> We have been all ill us'd, by this days Poet.
> 'Tis our joynt Cause; I know you in your hearts
> Hate serious Plays, as I do serious Parts. . . .
>   Henceforth, against all sad and Grave intreagues
> We'll make Offensive, and Defensive Leagues;
> And for all those that dare write Tragedy
> We'll make a Law, with a huge Penalty. . . .
>   This Poet may be pardon'd, let it be said
> You did condemn before the Law was made;
> I mean, if's Play be good, I tell you True,
> He thinks it is, but pray now, what think you.

I cannot help hoping that the audience thought, with Pepys, that the play was indeed good. Much of the credit for it, of course, must go to the author of the original—but not all. In one or two minor ways Howard interfered without improving, notably by adding the parts in rhyming couplets and by tacking on a happier ending. Yet he rarely seems to have spoilt his source and he showed admirable judgment in what (apparently) he left alone. Moreover I accept his statement that he altered the "Design" and I suspect that he omitted a subplot, and that he is entitled to much of the credit for the speed and continuity of the present plot. The play also shows, again, his admirable stagecraft; and I agree with D. D. Arundell that Dryden was being rather absurd when, in his *Defence*, he said that the Author of the Duke of *Lerma* is to be excus'd for his declaring against the Unity of time; for if I be not much mistaken, he is an interested person; the time of that Play taking up so many years as the favour of the Duke of *Lerma* continued; nay, the second and third Act including all the time of his Prosperity, which was a great part of the Reign of *Philip* the Third: for in the beginning of the second Act he was not yet a Favourite, and before the end of the third, was in disgrace.[11]

The position is that whatever the historical facts, the play gives the impression of covering (and the playwright may have thought he was covering) only a short period—a matter of a few months—from the death of the elder Philip, through Lerma's brief return to favor in the reign of the new King, to his enforced retirement from Court. Had Dryden not been "an interested person," he might have paid Howard the tribute he deserves for handling history with dramatic economy and probably improving on his source, in that respect, by doing so.

However one divides the credit between Howard and the original author, *The Duke of Lerma* must be seen, as Harbage, Nicoll and Summers have seen it, as one of the best serious plays of the Restoration.[12] Perhaps we should remember also what happened only too often when Elizabethan or Jacobean plays were adapted later in the seventeenth century. Compared with *The Tempest* of Dryden and Davenant, Shadwell's *Timon of Athens*, and even Rochester's *Valentinian*, Howard's *Duke of Lerma* is a tribute not only to its adapter's craftsmanship but also to his good taste.

It would be difficult to persuade literary historians that it may have been Pepys's valuation of Howard as a dramatist, and not Dryden's, that was in accordance with general opinion at the time. Yet in 1669, the very year after Dryden's onslaught on *The Duke of Lerma*, Milton's nephew, Edward Phillips, in his *Compendiosa Enumeratio Poetarum*, named Howard, after Orrery and before Dryden, in his list of the three most distinguished living dramatists.[13]

11. Arundell, p. 211.

12. Harbage, *Cavalier Drama*, p. 249; Nicoll, pp. 137-138; Summers, *Playhouse of Pepys*, p. 178.

13. The *Enumeratio* was first published as an appendix to Johannes Buchler's *Sacrarum Profanarumque Phrasium Poeticarum Thesaurus*. I owe the reference to R. G. Howarth's article on it in *M.L.R.*, LIV (1959), 321-328.

Chapter nine. POLITICAL PROMINENCE AND
LITERARY RIDICULE, 1668: *THE SULLEN
LOVERS* AND "THE DUEL OF THE STAGS"

ON 14 February 1668, just six days before he saw *The Duke of Lerma,*
Pepys noted in his Diary the deplorably "broken" condition of the
House of Commons: "nobody adhering to any thing, but reviling and
finding fault: and now quite mad at the Undertakers, as they are
commonly called, Littleton, Lord Vaughan, Sir R. Howard, and others
that are brought over to the Court, and did undertake to get the King
money; but they despise, and would not hear them in the House; and
the Court do do as much, seeing that they cannot be useful to them,
as was expected."[1] Just how Howard was "brought over" to the interests of the King, Pepys does not say; indeed, as has been shown,
it was really there that Howard's sympathies had always lain. What
is clear is that Howard's part in the impeachment of Clarendon and
his increasing participation in the debates of the House had helped
to make him a person worth having on one's side.

On 22 November 1667 it was Howard who informed the House
of the offense of a member, Sir John Ashburnham, in accepting a
gratuity of £500 from the French wine merchants to procure a license
for them to land their French wines.[2] On 14 and 15 February 1668
he made a few contributions to the debate on the miscarriages of the
war against the Dutch, particularly the alleged failure of the English
Intelligence service and the ability of the Dutch to take advantage of
the division of the Fleet between the two commanders. Many in the
House agreed with Marvell that the Intelligence was to blame; Howard took what seems the more reasonable view and argued successfully that the Intelligence was satisfactory and that the error lay in
the dividing of the command between Albemarle and Prince Rupert.
Pepys noted that at this time the "Undertakers" were not listened to
with respect; but Milward recorded that Howard "spoke well" and
his opinion prevailed.[3] He certainly seems to have been following an

1. *Diary,* VII, 301.
2. Grey, *Debates,* I, 46; Milward, *Diary,* pp. 131-135. (Ashburnham was
expelled from the House.)
3. Grey, I, 70-79; Peter Fraser, *The Intelligence of the Secretaries of State*
(Cambridge, 1956), p. 95; Pepys, VII, 301; Milward, p. 185.

unprofitable line two days later, when, agreeing with the majority of the House that there had been neglect in failing to fortify Sheerness, he added a little sermon on the theme that "We must make the King a throne of the people's hearts, that they may hope to see them better, by presenting them to his Majesty." On the following day, however, he was both expressing his own sincere convictions and risking offense to the King when he supported the bill for triennial Parliaments and told the House once again that "if this bill be 'compelling' the King, all laws do so."[4]

On this same day, 18 February, Sir William Coventry told Pepys that Howard had had the minor triumph of providing the House with a new phrase, "the rolling out of officers," when he remarked "that for his part he neither cared who they rowled in, nor who they rowled out";[5] but that he did not appreciate the application to himself of another of the House's favorite terms, "Undertaker," is made clear by Grey's report of other debates. On 24 February, for instance, when he very properly objected in the Committee of Supply to a proposal to take action on an anonymous letter offering to give information on the sale of offices, he said that he thought "a man wants honour and courage that will not subscribe a paper he gives in" and illustrated the point by adding that he himself could in this way "be libelled for an Undertaker."[6]

He continued to work towards a more adequate "Supply" for the King: on 29 February and again on 10 March he spoke in favor of an excise duty on wine to raise money for the Crown, and on 7 March he seconded an unsuccessful motion "for the Sale of Dean and Chapters lands." He was also following the course approved by the King (who wanted a Bill of Comprehension, not an Act of Uniformity) when on 4 March he opposed the House's decision to ask for a stricter enforcement of the laws against Nonconformity.[7]

He next played a leading role in the House in the impeachment of Sir William Penn, in April. Pepys attributed the impeachment to the vindictiveness of the members and their desire to prevent Penn from going to sea in command of one section of the Fleet; and he says that "W. Coventry's being for him, provoked Sir R. Howard and his party," although the Court party proper was "all for" Penn. The charge

4. Grey, I, 82, 83; Milward, pp. 189-190. The bill was withdrawn.
5. Pepys, VII, 305.   6. Grey, I, 92.
7. Grey, I, 98-99, 109, 108, 106; Milward, pp. 202, 203, 206.

against Penn was, roughly, embezzlement, or, in Evelyn's words, "breaking bulk, & taking a way rich goods out of the E[ast] India Prizes formerly taken by my L[ord] San[d]wich." The Coventrys tried to argue that Penn was innocent because he had acted on Lord Sandwich's orders (Pepys believed, because they thought this the only way to save him); but Howard was most eager to bring Penn to judgment and would not be put off.[8]

When Penn first heard of the charges, brought by the Commissioners for Accounts, he denied them and asked for a few days to prepare an answer. Howard is reported as saying "The thing is not to be trifled with—A gentleman-like memory may forget things done so long since," and he urged that the charges be pressed. When Penn next replied that no goods were sold until Sandwich gave the King's warrant for the sale, Howard argued that "A superior officer cannot command things not relating to the war." In Penn's defense, the following day, the argument was used that there was no actual evidence of fraud and that "The law of breaking of bulk cannot reach the inferior, in a command from the superior—If you permit not this rule, all discipline is at an end," but to this, Howard, still nursing his grudge that he should ever have been called an "Undertaker" for the Court, replied:

If *Undertakers* ever were, this is one, in undertaking for a person thus charged—If you lay down common fame not to be a ground of impeachment, common fame will impeach you—Should an Admiral command a person to be apprehended, and also to pick his pocket, is this command to be obeyed; to bring a woman, and vitiate her by the way?—A man may be commanded to sink a ship, but not to rob the King . . . If this man be not impeached, I could wish Lord *Clarendon* never had been.[9]

This reads like impressive parliamentary oratory, even if many members must have wondered whether Howard's motive really was to prevent the King's being robbed, rather than to press a charge for personal reasons. At any rate, he gained the day; a committee was appointed to draw up the impeachment, Penn was suspended and "disprivileged," and on 24 April Howard was chosen by the House to carry the impeachment to the Lords and attend a conference with them. Eventually the impeachment was allowed to drop, but not be-

8. Pepys, VII, 374 (16 April 1668); Evelyn, III, 508 (24 April); Milward, p. 255.
9. Grey, I, 133-139; Milward, pp. 257-260.

fore Howard had tried to pursue the matter further by having Lord Sandwich recalled to London.[10] It will be seen that Sir Robert's enemies must have had more than a little satisfaction in discomfiting him in turn when Lady Honoria's petition was presented to the House on 27 April, even if nothing came of it.

The question of Supply in relation to the Navy arose again on 1 May, when Howard spoke in support of a proviso to a money bill, "for fixing a part of the revenue arising by subsidy of Tonnage and Poundage, for setting out a fleet every year." He told the House that he believed his Majesty's revenue was "managed with all prudence," and that he was not normally in favor of having "a Prince confined in his methods," but in the circumstances he thought that this regular charge on the Customs was reasonable and would at least ensure that the seas were not unguarded when the King's own finances were low. He asked the House to approve this measure now, and later decide on other ways of financing the Navy. The House, however, was not often in a reasonable mood where finance was concerned, and the proviso was defeated.[11]

There was much more support for Howard when early in May he spoke on his other favorite theme, the privileges of members, during the famous debate on the case of Skinner and the East India Company. The Lords had awarded Skinner £5000 damages against the Company, whose Governor then appealed to the Commons. It was alleged that since nine members of the Commons were partners in the Company, the award was a breach of privilege; and Howard contributed the thought that "the condition of Privilege of this House is not taken off by the convenience or inconvenience of the thing; if it were, some body must be judge over us—How dangerous that is, I leave you to judge." He spoke often in what developed into a quarrel between the two Houses; he was one of the six members chosen to take the Commons' message to the Lords; and on 4 and 8 May and again in December of the following year he reported back to the House on behalf of the relevant Committees.[12]

10. Grey, I, 142-146; *Common Journals*, IX, 88; Pepys, VII, 383 (27 April); Milward, pp. 279-280.

11. Grey, I, 149. Milward records that he approved of the proviso but voted against it because he thought it was brought in only to obstruct the main bill.

12. Grey, I, 150-156, 204; Milward, pp. 286-299. The quarrel ended only when the Houses adopted the King's suggestion that all record of the proceedings be struck from the official Journals.

Not even his being a member of the House of Commons, however, could protect him from literary satire; and on 2 May he received what must have been a very hard blow, when at Lincoln's Inn Fields Shadwell's play *The Sullen Lovers, or, The Impertinents* was produced, with its famous caricature of Howard as Sir Positive At-All. "Lord," Pepys wrote a few days later, "to see how this play of Sir Positive At-all in abuse of Sir Robert Howard, do take, all the Duke's [i.e., the Duke of York's] and everybody's talk being of that, and telling more stories of him, of the like nature, that it is now the town and country talk, and, they say, is most exactly true. The Duke of York himself said that of his playing at trapball is true, and told several other stories of him."[13]

Pepys himself saw the first three performances of the play (on the second, fourth and fifth) and he saw it again at least three times afterwards, without ever deciding whether it was "tedious" (2 May), "very contemptible" (4 May) or "pretty good" (24 June); he even had the inconsistency to write of it as "a play that pleases me still" (13 April 1669)! The truth is that, if only because of the character of Sir Positive, the play is very amusing indeed; Howard must certainly have wished that it had been less so, for it succeeded, and the name of Sir Positive was to haunt him for years. It is a most curious example of irony, that the literary reputation of Shadwell, who gave posterity the impression that Howard was nothing but an insufferable bore, should itself have been similarly destroyed by another of Howard's opponents, Dryden, whose portrait of Shadwell as MacFlecknoe has blinded most later critics to the fact that Shadwell also was a dramatist of unusual ability. It is all more ironical still if, as the author of *The Friendly Vindication* maintained, Dryden gave Shadwell the hint for his caricature of Howard.[14]

Shadwell justified his satire, in a preface to the play when it was published later in the year:

Perhaps you may think me as impertinent as any one I represent; that, having so many faults of my own, shou'd take the liberty to judge of others, to impeach my fellow Criminalls: I must confess it is very ungenerous to accuse those that modestly confess their own Errors; but positive Men, that justifie all their faults, are Common Enemies, that no man

13. Pepys, VIII, 8 (8 May 1668). The "trapball" is an allusion to Act III of the play (see below).
14. See above, chap. vi, pp. 112 and 118-119.

ought to spare, prejudicial to all Societies they live in, destructive to all Communication, always endeavouring Magisterially to impose upon our Understandings, against the Freedome of Mankind: These ought no more to be suffer'd amongst us, then wild beasts: for no corrections that can be laid upon 'em are of power to reforme 'em; and certainly it was a positive Foole that *Salomon* spoke of, when he said, *bray him in a Mortar, and yet he will retain his folly.*

(Even the word "impeach" may now be seen to have possibly a special relevance, coming so soon after Howard's impeaching of Clarendon and of Penn.)

The harsh judgment of Howard's positiveness and pride expressed here and in the play is confirmed by others. Pepys's statement that the portrait was agreed everywhere to be "true" has already been quoted, as have Marvell's gibes in his "Last Instructions to a Painter" and Dryden's in the *Defence* (the latter clearly inspired by Shadwell's play but hardly likely to have been dependent on it). Then, later, John Evelyn, who certainly bore Howard no political or other grudge and knew him well enough to visit him, called him "that universal pretender" and, on another occasion, "a Gent: pretending to all manner of Arts & Sciences for which he had ben the subject of Comedy, under the name of Sir Positive; not ill-natur'd, but unsufferably boosting."[15] The qualification is important, and it is an interesting fact that those who wrote about him towards the end of his life or just afterwards were more inclined to stress his liberality and patronage of letters and learning, as did Toland in 1698 ("a Gentleman of great Generosity, a Patron of Letters, and a hearty Friend to the Liberty of his Country"), and Gildon ("I have not the Honour to say much of my own knowledge of him, but I am told, that it is no small Part of his Character, to be a Patron and Encourager of Learning").[16] Shadwell, to whom the patronage obviously did not extend and who sincerely disliked the kind of Heroic play for which Howard was best known, was not concerned to make any such concessions.

Accordingly, in his Prologue he points out that his play has no song and dance, or romantic lovers:

15. *Diary*, IV, 316 (16 June 1683) and 416 (16 February 1685).
16. Toland, *Life of John Milton* (ed. Darbishire), p. 185; Gildon, in Langbaine, *The Lives and Characters of the English Dramatick Poets . . . improv'd and continued . . . by a Careful Hand* [Charles Gildon], (London, 1712), p. 75.

But if you love a Fool, he bid me say,
He has great choyce to show you in his Play.

The *literary* model for the portrait of Sir Positive was surely in Ben Jonson (on whom Shadwell so often modeled himself and whose praises are sung in the preface). Jonson's Sir Politick Would-Be, in *Volpone*, is just such another foolish fast-talking know-all:

> Peregrine. It seems, sir, you know all
> Politick.   Not all, sir. But
>   I have some general notions. I do love
>   To note and to observe.   (II.i.98-100)

Shadwell's characters are also described in the Dramatis Personae in the Jonsonian manner. Sir Positive is "A foolish Knight, that pretends to understand every thing in the world, and will suffer no man to understand any thing in his Company; so foolishly Positive, that he will never be convinced of an Error, though never so grosse." His crony Ninny is "A conceited Poet, always troubling men with impertinent Discourses of Poetry, and the repetition of his own Verses; in all his Discourse he uses such affected Words, that 'tis as bad as the Canting of a Gypsie"; and Lady Vaine is "A Whore, that takes upon her the name of a Lady, very talkative and impertinently affected in her Language, always pretending to Vertue and Honour."[17]

The first heard of Sir Positive after the play begins is that he has just discovered the wit in *The Silent Woman* and *The Scornful Lady*, has announced that "if I understand any thing in the World, there's Wit enough in both those, to make one good Play, If I had the management of 'em," and has taken an hour to say why. We are therefore ready for his entrance, which comes as the last straw on the back of the hero Stanford; Stanford has just had to endure the fulsome friendliness of Woodcock[18] and the endless platitudinous couplets of Ninny, and now has to suffer Sir Positive, who enters proclaiming:

I have made this morning a glorious Corrant, an immortal Corrant, a Corrant with a Soul in't; I'le defie all Europe to make such another. . . . But for Musick, if any man in *England* gives you a better account of that then I do, I will give all Mankind leave to spit upon me: You must know, it's a thing I have thought upon and consider'd, and made it my business

---

17. Quotations from *The Sullen Lovers* are from *The Complete Works of Thomas Shadwell*, ed. Montague Summers.

18. Understood by Pepys (VIII, 5) to be a portrait of Lord St. John.

from my Cradle; besides, I am so naturally a Musician, that *Gamut*, *A re*, *Bemi*, were the first words I could learn to speak.

The corranto has to be listened to, with Woodcock dancing to it and Ninny beating false time, and Sir Positive praising the dancing: "betwixt you and I, I taught him every step he has." Worse is to come, for Sir Positive knows all about Flanders, and indeed all about Mankind:

I'le tell thee, I will give Dogs leave to piss upon me, if any Man understands Mankind better then my self, now you talk of that. I have consider'd all Mankind, I have thought of nothing else but Mankind this Moneth; and I find you may be a Poet, a Musitian, a Painter, a Divine, a Mathematician, a States-man; but betwixt you and I, let me tell you, we are all Mortal.

(Shadwell is here alluding, of course, to Howard's poem "Against the Fear of Death," particularly the line "We always should remember, death is sure," which Dryden similarly ridiculed in the *Defence*.)[19] Stanford gets rid of Sir Positive only when his harlot, Lady Vaine, sends for him—but not before he has also told of his skill in painting:

And now you talk of Painting, either I am the greatest Fopp in Nature, or if I do not understand that, I understand nothing in the World: why I will paint with *Lilly*, and draw in little with *Cooper* for 5000 l.

Shadwell is remarkably successful in capping even his best jokes, for in Act II Sir Positive, unwilling to admit anybody's superiority to him in anything, asserts that, "if I would bend my self to 't," he would be the best pimp in town; he is already the best at debauching a woman. When this is too much even for Lady Vaine, who, seeing herself compromised by his boasts, threatens to have no more to do with him, he has an answer:

'Tis true, I said no man in *England* understood pimping better than my self, but I meant the speculation, not the practical part of pimping

—which satisfies *her*.

Act III begins:

Nay then, Cozen, I am an Ass, an Ideot, a Blockhead, and a Rascal, if I don't understand Dramatique Poetry of all things in the World; why this is the onely thing I am esteem'd for in *England*.

19. See above, chap. vi, pp. 112-113.

Emilia may burst out that she can stand no more from "you and your Crew," but the answer is a laugh and the concession *"Woodcock* and *Ninny* will be a little troublesome sometimes." Lady Vaine can only believe that anybody who finds Sir Positive unbearable must be "distracted":

> *Lady Vaine.* Great wits you know have always a Mixture of Madness.
> *Sir Positive.* . . . I found that by my self, for I was about three years ago as mad as ever man was: I scap'd *Bedlam* very narrowly, 'tis not above a twelve-moneth since my brains were settled again

—and he drags Lady Vaine off with him, though she has an assignation and tries desperately to free herself for it.

Stanford is the next victim. Sir Positive insists that Stanford second him in a duel (which he has no intention of fighting) against a cowardly clerk who commented on the failure of his play, *The Lady in the Lobster.* (Allardyce Nicoll suggests that the play in question, since we are told that a character hangs himself at the command of his mistress, is *The Indian Queen,* in which Acacis stabs himself to "deserve" Orazia's tears—but *The Indian Queen* was certainly not a failure and I think it probable that no one play is meant. A reference later in the speech is clearly to *The Duke of Lerma.*)[20] At the meeting in the fields, Sir Positive insists that his opponent sign a prepared statement:

> 'I do acknowledge and firmly believe that the Play of Sir *Positive Att-All* Knight, called the Lady in the Lobster, notwithstanding it was damn'd by the Malice of the Age, shall not onely read, but it shall act with any of *Ben Johnson's,* and *Beaumont's* and *Fletcher's* Plays.'
> *Sir Positive.* Hold, hold! I'll have *Shakespeares* in, 'slife I had like to have forgot that.
> *Clerk.* With all my heart. 'I do likewise hereby attest that he is no purloiner of other mens Work, the general fame and opinion notwithstanding, and that he is a Poet, Mathematician, Divine, Statesman, Lawyer, Phisitian, Geographer, Musician, and indeed a *Unus in Omnibus* through all Arts and Sciences, and hereunto I have set my hand. . . .'

It turns out that the victim is not in fact the expected opponent but an innocent man who has come into the fields to play trapball with his friends. Sir Positive, of course, immediately prepares to show them how to play.

In Act IV, he discourses on his skill in law and military tactics

20. Nicoll, I, 203; and see above, chap. v, pp. 79-80.

(he could "preserve Flanders from the French" with only one hundred thousand men plus another six hundred thousand and a further four hundred thousand); and then when he re-enters with Lady Vaine it is to boast of his knowledge of Latin and Greek, of painting (but he mistakes an inn sign for a Holbein) and of mathematics. Even Woodcock tries to object when told that he is in the presence of the man who also invented the cittern, but it is in vain:

> *Sir Positive.* Pox on't, I have told thee often enough of this, thou wilt still be putting thy self forward to things thou do'st not understand.

His accomplishments further include dicing, metaphysics and statesmanship:

> This very thing has made me so famous all over Europe, that I may be at this instant Chiefe Minister of State in *Russia*, but the truth on't is, *Stanford*, I expect that neerer home.

Shadwell must surely have had "inside information" and possibly he added to the text of the play between its first performance and publication (S.R. 9 September); for (i) there was a move to appoint Howard as Governor of Barbados: Lord Willoughby wrote on 22 July that "that noble gentleman was daily expected and still is," and on 11 August he asked Williamson to supply him with ships and men if war with France was apprehended and to entrust the command to him, "unless some abler person, such as Sir Robert Howard, be designed for that honour"; and (ii) at Michaelmas or earlier in this year " 'tis said the Duke of Buckingham endeavored to bring Sr Robt Howard into that place," of Secretary of State in succession to Morice, according to John Starkey writing to Sir Willoughby Aston.[21] If, then, the humor of Shadwell's play seems to lag a little in Act IV, it may do so because we do not pick up all such topical references as these.

Sir Positive goes on to boast of his rope-dancing and pastry-making and architectural skill, and his poetry ("without comparison the best Poet in *Europe*")—until he simply cannot talk fast enough to claim

21. *C.S.P. Colonial Series, America and the West Indies*, 1661-1668, pp. 593, 603; B.M.Add. MS. 36916, f. 114, first cited by E. S. de Beer, *Inst. Hist. Res. Bull.* III, 65. It was similarly rumored later in the year that Howard was likely to become one of a commission of five Lords Justices of Ireland (Andrew Browning, *Thomas Osborne, Earl of Danby and Duke of Leeds 1632-1712*, Glasgow, 1951, I, 66).

pre-eminence in all the subjects that are simultaneously named to him, "*and he goes out talking as fast as he can.*"

There must be another reference to the proposed Barbados appointment and the hopes of the greater appointment as Secretary of State in Sir Positive's boast early in Act V, which would otherwise seem altogether too absurd:

I can live so long under-water, that (but that I have greater designs on foot here) *I* would go into the West Indies to dive for Sponges and Corals.

No playgoer can have had any difficulty in following the allusions when Sir Positive blustered at Woodcock and Ninny (who have been induced by Emilia to defy him, under promise of protection):

I'le undermine all Commonwealths, destroy all Monarchies, and write Heroick Plays: ye dogs, let me see either of you do that.

There is, however, some room for doubt about the interpretation of the finale of the play. Sir Positive marries Lady Vaine and returns to tell Ninny and Woodcock to "have a care of being *Positive* another time, a man would think you might learn more Modesty of me." He congratulates the newly married couples (Emilia and Stanford, Carolina and Lovell) on their "good Fortunes," adding "for my own part, if I understand any thing in the world, I am happy in this Lady"— and then receives a letter telling him that she is a harlot, mother of one child, and pregnant again. But, of course—and it must have made a grand finale—he has the last word:

Well! this is the first thing in the World that I have met with which I did not understand: but I am resolv'd, I'le not acknowledge that: Master *Lovell*, I knew well enough what I did when I marry'd her, He's a wise man that marry's a harlot, he's on the surest side, who but an Ass would marry at uncertainty?

The unsolved problem is whether there is any specific reference here to Howard's relations with one particular woman, and whether Lady Vaine, like Woodcock, Ninny, and Sir Positive, is a personal portrait. It must be significant that neither Pepys nor Evelyn makes any attempt to name an original for the character. The identification of her with the "W— Uphill," who refused to marry Howard in 1677 but later did marry him, was first made by Anthony à Wood, or the reviser of his *Athenae Oxonienses* for the 1721 edition, who wrote of "the lady *Vaine* a Whore; which the Wits then understood to be the miss of the said sir *Rob. Howard*, whom, after he had for some time kept, he made her his Wife."[22] This looks like a guess, long after the event, although it was echoed by Theophilus Cibber and others;[23] and the further identification of Mistress Uphill with Susanna Uphill the actress is a still wilder guess, first made in the nineteenth century. E. S. de Beer, who did much to clear up this problem (following H. S. Howard's identification of Howard's third wife as Mary Uphill), does not believe that Lady Vaine is a portrait of any individual; he is probably right, although it is conceivable that Mary Uphill was Howard's mistress as early as 1668.[24] At any rate, whether Lady Vaine is identifiable or not, Shadwell may well have had some justification for associating Howard with a mistress.

There is no doubt that the poet Ninny in *The Sullen Lovers* is a caricature of Sir Robert's elder brother, Edward. Edward was already the author of three plays: *The Usurper, The Change of Crowns,* and *The London Gentleman*; and although Pepys, on 15 April 1667, judged the second of these "the best that I ever saw at that house, being a great play and serious," it was never published,[25] and the third was probably neither published nor acted. It is, then, an open question whether Samuel Butler was thinking of Edward or Robert or the whole Howard family when he wrote in his "Satyr on Rhyme" (1667?)

> Sometimes I set my Wits upon the Rack,
> And, when I would say *white*, the Verse says *black* . . .
> When I would praise an Author, the untoward
> Damn'd Sense, says *Virgil*, but the Rhime [says *Howard?*][26]

Certainly, after the portrait of Poet Ninny in *The Sullen Lovers,* Edward was damned. His three other plays, *The Women's Conquest,*

22. *Athenae Oxonienses*, II, 1018.

23. Cibber, *Lives of the Poets,* III, 58.

24. de Beer, *N. & Q.*, CXCII (1947), 447; H.S.H[oward] *N. & Q.*, CLXXXVII (1944), 281-283; J. P. Shawcross, *The History of Dagenham* (London, 1904), pp. 104-105, 239. Mary Uphill was the sixth of the eleven children of Jacob Uphill (who died on 16 June 1662).

25. This was the play in which Lacy ridiculed the Court so well in extempore additions to his part that he was arrested; and the King forbade further performances (for the minute).

26. *Satires and Miscellanies,* p. 125. Henry Howard had written *The United Kingdoms* (which Buckingham ridiculed in *The Rehearsal*); the younger brother James was the author of the successful comedies *The English Monsieur* and *All Mistaken* and a version of *Romeo and Juliet* with a happy ending.

The Six Days' Adventure, and *The Man of Newmarket,* all failed on
the stage; worse still, he published, in the very year after *The Sullen
Lovers,* "The British Princes: an Heroick Poem," which probably received more ridicule than did any other poem even in this satiric period.
The best satires included Samuel Butler's "Palinode," and the "Mock
Encomium,"[27] Martin Clifford's "To a Person of Honour on his Incomparable Poem":

> The language, too, intirely is thy own;
> Thou leav'st as trash, below thy great pretence,
> Grammar to pedants; and to plain men, sense

and Dorset's "To Mr Edward Howard, on his incomparable, incompre-
hensible Poem, called *The British Princes*":

> So in this way of writing, without thinking,
> Thou hast a strange alacrity in sinking.

Edward must have been an embarrassment to his brother Robert,
but the latter could hardly have afforded to be critical. He, after all,
had pronounced no less positively on British antiquities in his 1662
poem to Walter Charleton; and with even worse timing than Edward's, he now published, only two or three months after being
ridiculed in *The Sullen Lovers,* a very bad poem that was to become
just as notorious as "The British Princes," namely "The Duel of the
Stags."[28]

> In *Windsor* Forest, before Warr destroy'd,
> The harmless Pleasures which soft Peace injoy'd;
> A mighty Stagg grew Monarch of the Heard,
> By all his savage Slaves obey'd, and fear'd:
> And while the Troops about their Soveraign fed,
> They watch't the awfull nodding of his head . . .
> Long had this Prince imperiously thus sway'd,
> By no set Laws, but by his will obey'd;
> His fearfull slaves, to full obedience grown,
> Admire his strength, and dare not use their own.

Only one member of the herd, it appears, seemed to deserve the Monarch's suspicion:

27. Bodleian MS. Eng. Poet. e4 p. 191, where it is attributed to Waller;
Satires and Miscellanies, pp. 115-119.

28. S. R. 24 June 1668. The spelling of the title on the title page is "The
Duell of the Stags"; at the head of the poem it is "Staggs."

> In the best Pastures by his side he fed,
> Arm'd with two large Militia's on his head
> . . . and from a subject to a Rival grows.
> Sollicits all his Princes fearful Dames,
> And in his sight Courts with rebellious flames . . .

and soon they meet in single combat. Or rather, as the poet has it:

> Their heads now meet, and at one blow each strikes,
> As many strokes, as if a rank of Pikes
> Grew on his brows, as thick their Antlers stand
> Which every year kind Nature does disband

(and as if this were not bad enough, the combat is next compared to the meeting of two *oaks*). The rebel is defeated and flees:

> Now to the Shades he bends his feeble course,
> Despis'd by those, that once Admir'd his force:
> The wretch that to a scorn'd condition's thrown,
> With the Worlds favour, looses too his own.

But the defeated rebel recuperates:

> Then shook his loaded head; the shadow too,
> Shook like a tree, where leafless branches grew.

He again becomes envious of the pastures held by others and (after a bloated account of his dreams and resolutions) again engages the Monarch in battle and defeats him:

> For now, too late, the Conqueror [i.e., the Monarch] did find,
> That all was wasted in him but his Mind . . .
> Yet then he rais'd his Head, on which there Grew
> Once, all his Power, and all his Title too;
> Unable now to rise, and less to fight,
> He rais'd those Scepters to demand his Right:
> But such weak Arguments prevail with none;
> To plead their Titles, when their Power is gone. . . .
> Unhappy State of such as wear a Crown
> Fortune can never lay 'em gently down. . . .
> The faith of most, with Fortune does decline,
> Duty's but Fear, and Conscience but Design.
> The Victor now, proud in his great success,
> Hastes to enjoy his fatal Happiness;
> Forgot his Mighty Rival was destroy'd
> By that, which he so fondly now enjoy'd.

> In Passions, thus Nature her self enjoys,
> Sometimes Preserves, and then again destroys;

Yet all destruction which revenge can move,
Time or Ambition, is supply'd by Love.

A fable about a monarch at Windsor, his "Dames" and his rivals naturally seemed to invite allegorical interpretation, particularly as Howard published with the poem a fulsome dedication to the Duke of Buckingham, to whom, he said, he had "made so entire a Dedication" of himself, in one of those friendships "which are as much above the Ceremonies of the world, as the usual Practise of it":

but your Grace has a farther Title to this [the poem], being more yours than Mine; as much as an Image made well shap't and polish't, is more properly due to him that gave it that perfection, then to him that first dig'd the stone out of the Quarry; it was an ill contriv'd House within, full of Entries and unusefull passages, till your Grace was pleas'd to take them away, and make it Habitable for any Candid opinion.

At the same time when your Grace made this your own, you made me more justly yours; 'twas in your Confinement, where after some Concealment of your self, to weigh the Circumstances and Causes of your persecution, you generously expos'd your self to stand all hazards and tryals, from the assurance of your Courage, and advise of your Innocence; and as your Grace in your adversity has found the advantage of an unshaken Honour, I doubt not but your Prince and Nation will find an equal benefit in your better Fortunes, by your Council and Service, which will always be directed by such a steady vertue.

J. H. Wilson has gone so far as to date the poem May or June, 1667, take the two stags to represent Charles II and Buckingham, and write that "At the time Buckingham was in hiding under suspicion of high treason, and it is possible that Sir Robert, who was his political ally, wrote the poem to show him the fatal results of a conflict between the duke and the King."[29] I cannot follow this. How could a poem that tells of the success of a second revolt against a reigning monarch show Buckingham "the fatal results" of such a conflict? All it might do, if one argued along these lines, is either incite Buckingham to revolt or warn Charles never to let Buckingham have a second chance, and I cannot believe that this is its meaning (not with the dedication to Buckingham!).

What Howard says in the dedication is only that he took the poem to Buckingham *for revision* while Buckingham was in hiding; and C. E. Ward has drawn attention to a letter to Sir Thomas Clifford in which Howard, who had obviously been told that his poem was being

29. J. H. Wilson, *The Court Wits of the Restoration* (Princeton, 1948), p. 180.

read as a comment on the contemporary political situation, disclaimed any such intention and dated its composition much earlier. The relevant part of the letter, which is dated 26 July 1668, is:

all they can charge on mee I despise, especially in this particular wch upon my honour was writt above foure years since; and when I was retird into the Country, neither with any thoughts or acquaintance of what others did; but meerly beinge told the storie by one that livd in Windser forrest—all that I have writt was punctually between two staggs; the love of description in Poetry, and I confesse the Nurse of Fancy, were the only causes that invited mee to endeavour the description.[30]

One must agree with Ward that while Howard may have had a *possible* political situation in mind, he may be believed when he denied topical reference to any existing political rivalry.

It is surely relevant also that when the poem was parodied, it was ridiculed not for any attempted allusions to living people but for its glaring literary faults—its bathos, lack of humor, inflated and inadequate diction, ludicrous similes, and feeble moralizing. The parody was first published in an incomplete form, in 1694, as "The Duel. By *Henry Savil*, Esquire. Written soon after the Duel of the *Staggs*";[31] the complete version was printed a few years later under the title "The Duel of the Crabs" and attributed to Dorset.[32] It also survives in a manuscript version (from which I quote) where it is attributed in a penciled note to "Ld Dorset & H. Savile"—an attribution that may well be correct.[33]

The parody is remarkably clever, and all Howard's faults are neatly hit off. The basic idea of the parody will be clear from its MS title, "A Duell Between two Monsters upon my Lady Be—ts C—t with their change of Government from Monarchial to Democraticall" and from its opening lines:

> In Milford Lane neer to S^t. *Clement's* Steeple
> There liv'd a Nymph kind to all Christian People.

30. Charles E. Ward, "An Unpublished Letter of Sir Robert Howard," *M.L.N.*, LX (1945), 119-121. The letter was found among the Clifford papers at Ugbroke Park.

31. *The Annual Miscellany for the Year 1694. Being the Fourth Part of Miscellany Poems . . . By the Most Eminent Hands* (London, 1694), pp. 293-297.

32. For example, in *Poems on State Affairs*, I (5th edition, 1703) 201-203.

33. B. M. Harl. MS 6913, f. 62.

This is the Mistress Bennett of the title, who was, of course, a notorious bawd and prostitute. After ridicule of Howard's solemn setting in his park, attention is turned to his cheap moralizing:

> But yet what corner of the World is found
> Where pain our pleasure does not still surround—
> One would have thought that in this happy Grove
> Nought could have dwel't but quiet peace and Love. . . .

In fact, however, as in Howard's forest, there was discontent:

> The Gods will Frown wherever they doe Smile
> The *Crockidill* infests the fertile *Nile* . . .
> Two mighty Monsters did this wood infest. . . .
> But dire ambition does admitt no bounds
> There's no resisting 'gainst aspiring Crowns. . . .

and so, to avoid the long marches which tire their armies out as they seek each other round the "Briny Lake," they come to single combat (with, of course, much laughter at Howard's "battle"), fall in the "Lake," and are drowned. The final lines, naturally, parody Howard's last irrelevant stanza on the superiority of Love to destruction, and also his attitude to monarchy:

> Both Armies at this sight amazed stand
> In doubt who shall obey who shall command
> In this Extremity they both agree
> A *Common-Wealth* their Government shall be.

It is an odd fact that Howard's poem was often reprinted. Not only did Hills republish it in 1709, with Dryden's lines "To my Honored Friend Sir Robert Howard, on his Excellent Poems" (and by altering "Poems" of the original 1660 title to "Poem" made it appear as if Dryden had complimented Howard on this particular poem!) but also it was included in many of the anthologies of the late seventeenth and the eighteenth centuries.[34] Howard himself, however, seems to have accepted the cruel verdict, and in the remainder of his life he did not complete a single major poem or play. (Two other plays— or parts of plays—come into the story of his later life, but probably both were begun before the end of 1668.) If we remember *The Committee*, *The Duke of Lerma*, and the best parts of *Poems 1660*, we may not rejoice at his decision virtually to abandon literature.

34. For example, *A Collection of Poems By Several Hands. Most of them Written by Persons of Eminent Quality* (London, 1693), pp. 65-82, and Nichols' *Select Collection* (1780).

Looking back on the events of 1668, Howard must indeed have felt that this was his unlucky year, although it had seen the production of *The Duke of Lerma,* successful revivals of others of his plays, and some of his earliest parliamentary success. Not only had he been held up to public ridicule, not always fairly, by Dryden in the *Defence,* Shadwell in *The Sullen Lovers,* and Savile and Dorset in "The Duel of the Crabs," but also his hopes of the Secretaryship of State had been dashed, his wife was pursuing him with her petition in Parliament itself, his son, Thomas, having recovered from the smallpox, had had another long and serious illness, and his daughter had died.[35] It must have taken courage to carry on; and there was at least one other personal disaster not far ahead.

35. So Thomas Howard to Ashmole, Bod. Ash. MS 243, f. 273: "My sister yᵉ only one I had died Easter munday morning aboute four of yᵉ cloke, In yᵉ year 1668"; "In yᵉ *yeare 1668* about a month before miclemas, I had yᵉ Greatest and *longest fitt of sikenesse* I ever had, it held mee six weeks in bed, and left a *Consumption behind it.*"

Chapter ten. PARLIAMENT AND FINANCE: 1669-
SEPTEMBER 1671

IT seems that before the literary debacle of late 1668, Howard may
have written, or begun, another comedy, called *The Country Gentleman*, and that there were plans to produce it on 27 February 1669,
with the addition of a satirical portrait of Sir William Coventry, one
of the Treasury Commissioners, this portrait being in a separate scene
written by Howard's friend Buckingham. The story, which has often
been told incompletely, may be put together from references in Pepys,
the Aston Papers, and the Egerton Manuscripts.[1]

Sir John Nicholas, writing to his father Sir Edward on 3 March,
admits that he does not know all the facts but gives a convincing
account of what happened. He says there was "a new Play made by
Sir Rob: Howard called the Country Gentl in wch ye Duke of Bucks
hath incerted a part to personate Sr Wm Coventry sitting in the midst
of a Table wth papers round him to wch he can easily turne himself
round on his chaire as he pleases, such an one it seemes he hath, but
there are other circumstances in ye part likewise more abusive. there
are others personated also in that Play as i heare, my Ld Chanc^r, S^r
Jo: Dumcomb &c." Pepys makes it a little clearer, on Coventry's own
word: "He told me the matter of the play that was intended for his
abuse, wherein they foolishly and sillily bring in two tables like that
which he hath made, with a round hole in the middle, in his closet,
to turn himself in; and he is to be in one of them as master, and Sir
J. Duncomb in the other, as his man or imitator: and their discourse
in those tables, about the disposing of their books and papers, very
foolish. But that, that he is offended with, is his being made so contemptible, as that any should dare to make a gentleman a subject for
the mirth of the world." (Howard might for once have agreed with
him on *that*!)

Coventry told Tom Killigrew that if any of the actors dared im-
personate him he would cause that actor's nose to be cut; and all
accounts agree that Coventry, through a letter written by Henry Savile
as a kind of second, sent a challenge to Buckingham. Nicholas's ac-

1. Pepys, VIII, 226 ff. (1-22 March); B.M. Add. MS 36916, f. 128, 129,
133; Egerton MS 2539, f. 327^v, 328, 329^v (first cited by E. S. de Beer).

count is the only one that explains why the challenge was sent to Buckingham and not to Howard—namely, because Buckingham had "incerted" the particular scene in question; Howard must have welcomed the contribution, however, for it will be remembered that, according to Pepys, it was Coventry's support of Penn that made Howard urge the impeachment so eagerly.

Arlington heard of the challenge and told the King, who asked Buckingham on his honor whether he had received it. He admitted this, and Coventry would not deny it, and so, under an act of Henry VII which declared it a felony to conspire the death of a Privy Councillor, Coventry was sent to the Tower. Savile at first was sent to the Gate House—a distinction between his case and Coventry's that greatly angered the Duke of York and his friends—but was later removed to the Tower; and the King forbade the presentation of the play.

The sympathies of Pepys, and of many others, were with Coventry. Pepys felt that the King's action was ominous evidence of the power of Buckingham and his faction, who were depriving Charles of his only good counselors: "This, therefore, do heartily trouble me as any thing that ever I heard." To the annoyance of the King and Buckingham, Pepys and dozens of others visited Coventry often in the Tower. The two prisoners were released on 20 March—but not before Coventry had been removed from the Privy Council and the Treasury and deprived of all his offices of honor or profit. Coventry himself told Pepys that he was "weary and surfeited of business" and was glad to be out of the Treasury and away from Sir Thomas Clifford, but he did feel that he had been singled out for harsh treatment because he had refused to join the Buckingham faction and he feared the implications for the country. Charles told his sister that he was glad to have an excuse for getting rid of "a troublesome man"; and Sir John Nicholas commented to his father that Coventry would have deserved more sympathy had he not been one of those who hounded Clarendon out of the country. Howard seems to have been lucky not to be more involved than he was; but an incident such as this must have confirmed many in their political enmity to him. As for the play, it was never acted or published and has presumably not survived.

A minor personal and financial problem faced Howard in this same month when the King and the Treasury Lords finally decided to call in the patent of the Greenwax. They did so because, as the King wrote to the Lord Chancellor and the Lord Treasurer, "the Judges in the Courts of Westminster" had complained, as well they might, that the farmers of the Greenwax or their deputies were using or misusing their power by bargaining with "persons fined for great misdemeanours" and (for a consideration) releasing them "before the end of the assizes, to the obstruction of public justice, and discouragement of the justices, when it appears that the fines imposed are for the benefit of particular persons." The king wrote that if the patent for the Greenwax was willingly surrendered, "a reasonable compensation for it" was to be paid.[2] Howard saw that the family rights were well guarded. The agreement made, after months of amicable but firm negotiation lasting until 1670, was that Howard and his brothers and sister would accept £1000 per annum for the remainder of their term of thirty-one years in lieu of their previous rights under the grant. They stipulated, however, that there must be a person acceptable to them appointed to receive the Greenwax and to be responsible for the payment to them of the yearly £1000, "else they will not deal"; and they refused to have the present receiver, Brewster, even though, as Howard's counsel Ayliffe pointed out, Brewster was entitled still to receive his £40 per annum. The nominee of the Howards, "Thomas Aram, gent.," was duly accepted as Brewster's successor, at an annual salary of £150. Full precautions were taken to see that all arrears due before the surrender of the patent were paid; a guarantee was given that if the receipts from the Greenwax were for any reason inadequate to pay the annual £1000, that sum would be met from the Exchequer.[3] In October, 1672, under a further agreement, Howard took £1200 cash, together with the arrears to 24 June 1672, as a net payment for his fifth share of £200 per annum, but the shares of other members of the family continued to be paid on an annual basis.[4]

The negotiations with the Treasury concerning the surrender of the Greenwax were carried out for the family by Sir Robert, some-

2. *C.S.P.D.*, 1665-1666, p. 71; 1667-1668, pp. 86, 156.

3. *C.T.B.*, 1667-1668, pp. 500-501; 1669-1672, pp. 84, 88, 111, 146, 174, 346, 377, 386, 447, 517, 1316; 1672-1675, p. 83.

4. *C.T.B.*, 1669-1672, pp. 1077, 1316, 1333, 1341, 1348-1349; *C.S.P.D.*, 1673-1675, p. 490. In an indenture of 26 June 1671 among the Osborn MSS, Robert acknowledges Philip's right to a one-fifth share and authorizes Aram to pay it direct to him, less expenses. One has the impression that the Howards did not trust one another very far.

times accompanied by his elder brother Colonel Thomas; their father, the Earl of Berkshire, had died on 16 July 1669.[5] Only one week later, Howard suffered a far worse blow, in the death of his eldest son and heir, Robert.[6] This left only the one surviving child, Thomas.

A lighter touch is provided a few months later (8 October 1669), by Thomas Gower writing to his son William Leveson Gower at Stitnam and sending his compliments to "my Lady Jane" his wife: "I doubt not that she hath ere this received her letter in blank verse, but she is to expect another from Sir R. Howard unless his muse be out of humour, because my Lady Bathe won his money at l'hombre last night."[7] This is not the only hint that Sir Robert shared the passion of his time for gambling. On 9 May 1678 the Marquis of Worcester told his wife that he "had been to see Sir R. Howard's running horses which he would sell, but there is not one up to his weight"; and on 23 March 1676 John Verney wrote to his son Sir Ralph that "Sir Robert Howard runs his son's nag against one of Crampton's horses for 1000 l." It may not be a coincidence that it was in 1676 that Howard gave Pepys a promissory note for £400 which Pepys said he had lent him, at his "desire," "upon an occasion of your going to New-Market." (Pepys found the note among his papers in 1691, when he wrote to Howard claiming that while the sum of two hundred guineas was repaid soon after the loan, the balance was still owing.) Even so, gambling was a vice that Howard could well afford.[8]

More and more of his energies, however, were being put into parliamentary affairs. His blood pressure could nearly always be raised by the possibility of an impeachment—one of the least attractive qualities in his make-up, even if his principal motives appeared to him to be, and perhaps were, the prevention and punishment of fraud. He was thus again to the fore when, after receiving the report of its

5. The Earl was buried in Westminster Abbey. His eldest son, Charles, inherited the title; and when he died in 1679, it passed to the second son, Thomas, and then to the descendants of the fourth son, William. Robert's mother, the Countess Dowager of Berkshire, died in August, 1672, and was buried in the same vault as her husband.

6. Bodleian Ash. MS 243, f. 273.

7. *H.M.C.*, 5th Report, App., Duke of Sutherland MSS, p. 196.

8. *H.M.C.*, 12th Report, App. IX, Beaufort MSS, p. 69; *H.M.C.*, 7th Report, App., Verney Papers, p. 467a; *Private Correspondence and Miscellaneous Papers of Samuel Pepys*, ed. J. R. Tanner (London, 1926), I, 47. (Pepys, signing himself "Your old humble and most faithfull servant," points out that money did not come to him as easily in 1691 as in 1676.)

Commissioners of Account, the House proceeded in November, 1669, to examine Sir George Carteret. Carteret, as Treasurer of the Navy, had handled much of the money spent on the Dutch War, and the House suspected that there was some not properly accounted for. Howard began with a show of impartiality, but when on 12 November Henry Coventry argued that there was no evidence on which to impeach Carteret, Howard challenged "any learned man to show him a precedent that ever any man was impeached upon greater matter than this against *Carteret*, by the Commissioners," and on the following day he continued the attack, by following his old line and perhaps speaking sincerely: "Under the specious pretence of private humanity, we lose all humanity to the nation."[9] Carteret was voted guilty of many misdemeanors. Then the question of his punishment was debated, and Howard did not see how the House could do less than suspend; and the suspension was carried, if only by 3 votes (100 to 97).[10]

If Howard thought that by his hostility towards Carteret he was protecting the interests of the King, he must have been shocked when Charles told the two Houses on 4 February 1670 that "I have fully informed myself of that matter and do affirm to you that no part of those monies that you have given me for the war have been devoted to other uses." Howard fought to the last: on 22 February he led more than sixty members of Parliament in a protest against the King's protection of Carteret. Unless this was pure camouflage, one must conclude that he had a stronger sense of principle than has been allowed him by Pepys and those others who have implied that he could always be bought; and on 19 November in the debate on the motion for the King's Supply, he certainly argued that it was little use granting money unless the House took measures to see that it was properly used. But the fangs of the House had been drawn; the Commons could not proceed further against Carteret once the King had assumed the responsibility for the expenditure, and eventually all eighteen articles of accusation against the Treasurers of the Navy were expunged.[11]

One witch-hunt that Howard would not join was that against the Earl of Orrery, who in November, 1669, was accused of "raising of moneys, by his own authority, upon his Majesty's subjects; [and] defrauding the King's subjects of their estates." Howard assured the

9. Grey, I, 157-169.   10. Grey, I, 213-215.
11. *Journals of the House of Lords*, XII, 287; *C.S.P. Venetian*, 1669-1670, pp. 134, 162-163 and n., 164-165; Grey, I, 176.

House that "Lord Orrery will undergo any torture rather than the torture of not answering his charge"; and on 1 December Orrery did answer. It was resolved that accusation "be left to the law," and although there was further debate on 10 December, the whole matter lapsed.[12] Before it is concluded that Howard was ready enough to defend those whom he thought innocent, one caveat should perhaps be entered: Orrery had married Sir Robert's cousin, Margaret. On the other hand, there was presumably no such personal motive for his similar defense of Jekyll on 24 November, 1670. Jekyll had been brought to the Bar of the House, with his attorney, for threatening legal action to question an imprisonment confirmed by the House; but, as Sir Edward Dering recorded in his Diary, *"Sir Robert Howard* averring that to his knowledge Jekyll was willing to withdraw his action and would not have proceeded so far if he had known the sense of this House to be against it," a majority voted that Jekyll and the attorney should be discharged.[13]

So frequent was Howard's participation in the debates in the House at this period that one can see how he had come by his reputation of being too positive on too many subjects. Nevertheless, he was often right about the question of principle involved and he often expressed his own opinion in terms of a general principle. When, for example, in March 1670 the House received a petition from the importers of brandy and discussed the question whether brandy should be imported from Ireland, Howard thought it a good thing that England's own "hot waters" were sent to the Indies—"and suppose we had no Brandy in the world, cannot we live without it?" (The House decided not to forbid the importing of foreign brandy; and Howard was chairman of a Committee which then discussed the duty on it.)[14]

Again, to the debate on the Conventicles Bill in the same month, he contributed some sound history—"Queen *Elizabeth's* greatest power was her indulgence"—and he proposed as an alternative to the harsh bill of the Commons "a short Act to punish them that the King does

12. Grey, I, 182-186, 195-201.

13. Sir Edward Dering, *Parliamentary Diary 1670-73* [B.M. Add. MS 22467], ed. B. D. Henning (Yale Historical Publications, Vol. XVI, 1940), p. 12.

14. Grey, I, 217-219, 242; *C.T.B.*, 1669-1672, pp. 386, 392. Dering notes (p. 114) that on 8 February 1673 Howard again "moved for a bill for prohibiting the importation of foreign brandy."

not indulge, according to his own wisdom" (but the original bill was passed). He earns no credit, however, for his failure—or refusal—to see the consequences of the Lords' provisos and amendments to the bill. When these came back to the Commons, most members were, understandably, very wary of the implications of clauses which enacted that nothing in this Act or any other destroyed any rights or prerogatives Charles or his predecessors had ever had in ecclesiastical matters, "any other Law, Statute, or Usage to the contrary notwithstanding." With some parade of legal terms and history, Howard argued that the Lords were right: "we restore the King to what he had before, and no more." He was wrong, and the offensive words of the amendments were rejected. His reasoning was sounder when, at a later stage of the debate on the bill, he said that he cared not "how large mercy be, so that all our breasts may equally share of it" and told the members that they all wanted an Act of Grace from the King but were not willing themselves to pass one.[15]

A third debate to which he contributed in this month, on a different subject again, was that concerning the bill from the Lords empowering Lord Roos to marry again (he had brought charges of adultery against his wife and had obtained a divorce in the ecclesiastical court). Howard's old adversary Sir William Coventry asked with reason why a special dispensation should be granted to a rich man that was not available to a poor one, "and therefore if the thing be made an Act, would have it general." Howard replied that he thought more highly of women than to believe that Lady Roos was typical of her sex; each separate application could therefore be dealt with separately. His reasoning was not impeccable, but the bill was passed.[16] (Howard may well have known that it was hoped in some quarters that the Roos case would serve as a precedent for the divorce and remarriage of the King himself.)

He was right, however, when he questioned the action of the Lords in granting to the Duke of Richmond possession of lands in Lincolnshire and argued that "no power has a right to put a man in possession but by legal ways"; and he was also justified, at least according to modern ideas, when in yet another debate he opposed a plan for erecting new buildings in London and commented that "it was ever held by the wisest men he could meet with, that the great-

15. Grey, I, 220-222, 245-250, 418.   16. Grey, I, 253.

ness of *London*, when half was not built that now is, would be the ruin of the country. . . . We are asked abroad, whether *England* stands in *London*, or *London* in *England*?"[17] Twentieth century decentralization, if not necessarily satellite towns, would have had his whole-hearted approval.

His influence and power were obviously increasing all the time; he was a good man to have on your side, and Freschevile Hollis is reported to have said, while bragging of his introduction to the favor of the King and the Duke of York, that "there are none now greater at Court in his Majesty's esteem than Sir Robert Howard and Mr. Seymour."[18] The names of these three are also linked by Viscount Conway a few months later: "I met Sir Robert Howard, Ned Seymour, and Sir Fretchevile Hollis in the Gallery at Whitehall and was glad to see them reconciled to one another."[19] I question whether they had been enemies for long; at any rate, they were associated about this time in what was the most ambitious of all Howard's financial projects, the proposal for the farming of the Customs.

This story begins with the debate in the House on the King's debts, in the first week of November. The House formed itself into a Grand Committee on Supply to try to find sounder methods of finance than reliance on the Bankers. Howard, for one, was sure that something had to be done "that the King's fleet may not have these continual defects," but he was opposed to "the barbarous way" of a poll tax. Land-tax was also unacceptable, and the discussion therefore centered on excise. Howard proposed an excise duty on spices and linen and other such marginal articles as were not used so commonly as to make a tax on them too unpopular, and he predicted that this would bring in £100,000. On 7 November he amplified this: in fact he could see how £500,000 a year could be had, and that without customs officers. He was willing to "make good" what he had said, if the House wished. One of the Treasury Commissioners, Duncombe, immediately asked that Howard "tell us how he can make his proposals good," and an-

17. Grey, I, 290, 301.

18. *C.S.P. Relating to Ireland*, 1669-1670, p. 211 (Lord Aungier to Sir Joseph Williamson, 6 Aug.). Compare Viscount Conway to Sir Robert Harley, on 13 September 1671: "If my interest with Sir Robert Howard or Lord St. John be suitable to my inclinations and desires of serving you, I hope this which I have written will satisfy both you and me." *H.M.C.*, 14, App. II, Rutland MSS, Vol. 3, p. 324.

19. *H.M.C.*, 14, App. II, Vol. 3, p. 317 (to Sir Edward Harley, 15 Nov.).

other, Clifford, cynically reminded the House, as well he might, that "many things in gross fell away in particulars." Howard was unwilling to give details from which others might profit, but offered to be specific if the House accepted his offer; if the Treasury could find a better offer, he would not "hinder the King's revenue." The story is best continued by giving Grey's summary of Howard's speech to the House on 10 November:

[He] Returns all humble thanks to the Committee for their charitable interpretation of his proposals. Has met with difficulties enough to shake him, since he proposed the business, but hopes he shall answer their expectations in some measure. For this service he has taken care of the manufacture of the nation, that that be not impaired; exportation he has not touched at all. Brings in a paper of rates upon several things, as salts, linnens, silks, wrought and unwrought iron, sugars, fruit, spices, copper. If the Wine-Act may be let, in the method he proposes, with the Customs, etc., 516,000 l. a year may be made. Some may say, that this being farmed by one person, here may be a banking trade set up. But for advance, he will undertake that the money shall be advanced at 6 _per cent_. All the country farmers shall not sink, but this and that stand together. . . . 400,000 l. a year clear he will undertake to make good. If you like this proposition, he hopes he shall be supported by you, and that another shall not build on his foundation. He will secure the rent, and hopes he may not suffer under it, and that you will take that care of him, as is requisite for one that will faithfully serve his prince.

Not unnaturally, there were doubts. Garroway said that he did not question Howard's fair dealing, but disliked the suggestions of monopoly ("worse than the Bankers") and also the idea of a bargain and of an act putting the House under lock and key. Howard, on his dignity, replied that "he would have had his hand struck off rather than he would have drawn a Bill 'with locks and bolts.' " The House imposed the duties much as Howard had suggested but did not accept his offer to farm them.[20]

On 16 November the King and the Treasury accepted another offer of £600,000 a year for five years for the Customs and the wine and wine-licenses, "so that," as Marvell wrote to Mayor Acklam, "S^r R: H^s proposall seems broke wch though for some reasons is not perhaps to be regretted, yet now I doubt we may beside this additl excise at home on beere & the forain excise return to the other harsher ways of

20. Grey, I, 272-287, 310-313; see also _C.S.P.D._, 1670, p. 520 (Seymour to Conway).

raising mony"; but on 26 November he reported that "Those that took the Customs &c: at 600000[11] are now struck of again & S^r R: Howard Bucknall & the Brewers have them as formerly projected."[21] They were not to have them for long.

It may be worth mentioning here that Marvell about this time was responsible for a reference to Howard that, because of Marvell's deservedly high reputation, may perhaps have carried undue weight. This is in his "Further Advice to a Painter," dated by his editor H. M. Margoliouth October 1670–April 1671. Marvell writes of

> the five recanters of the Hous
> That aime at mountains and bring forth a Mous,
> Who make it by their mean retreat appear
> Five members need not be demanded here.
> These must assist her in her countermines
> To overthrow the Darby Hous designes,
> Whilst Positive walks Woodcock in the dark,
> Contriving Projects with a Brewers Clerk.
> Thus all imploy themselves, and without pitty
> Leave Temple Single to be beat in the City.   (ll. 49-58)

The identity of the "five recanters" is made clear by another of Marvell's letters at this time, in which he tells how an "obsequious" House of Commons voted to supply the King according to his occasions and adds that "*Sir R. Howard, Seymor, Temple, Car,* and *Hollis,* openly took Leave of their former Party, and fell to head the King's Busyness."[22] Since I have shown that Howard had been negotiating for the King for years before this, I can only assume Marvell to have been misled, perhaps because Howard and the others first formally declared themselves to be of the Court party at this time. The identification of the others as proposed by Margoliouth may be accepted: the "her" of line 53 is the Duchess of York, the "Darby Hous designes" would be the republican plots, Positive and Woodcock are Howard and St. John, as in *The Sullen Lovers,* and the "Brewers Clerk" is their associate in the farming of the Customs, Sir William Bucknall, the London brewer.[23]

21. *Poems and Letters,* II, 112-113, 116.
22. *Ibid.,* II, 305 (to William Popple).
23. *Ibid.,* I, 290-291. A later satire sometimes attributed to Marvell, probably erroneously, "Brittania and Rawleigh," has, in one version, a damning allusion to Howard:

The Grand Committee on Supply resumed its debates in the first week of December, when Howard confirmed the new offer of £600,000 per annum for the farming of the Customs with "the Paper Act and the Wine," and on 3 December he outlined the proposed new "paper" charges (that is, taxes or fees on charters and grants to corporations etc.) though he could not accept Garroway's proposal for a tax of £10 a time on dispensations to clergymen to hold more than one living. He also favored an increase in the Land Tax rather than take the risk of granting the King insufficient money to "set out the Fleet."[24] A newsletter of 6 December names the exact sum offered by the farmers as £610,000, with a guarantee "to advance 150,000 l. before Christmas, 50,000 l. the latter end of January, and the like at the end of February." The farmers are listed as "Lord St. John, Sir Robert Howard, Sir William Bucknall, Sir James Hayes, Mr. George Dashwood, and others"; and another newsletter of 8 December mentions "the two Forths." There must have been further aligning and realigning of forces and more bargaining in the next few months—not surprisingly, in view of the huge sums of money involved—for when the grant was finally prepared in July, 1671, it was made out to St. John, Howard, Sir John Bennet, Sir William and Ralph Bucknall, Sir William D'Oyley, John Bence, William Robarts, John Mann, and George Blacke (or Blake), and the annual rent was fixed at £480,000 for five years, payable monthly, plus £10,000 payable each New Year's Day into the King's Privy Purse.[25] The conclusion of the story is almost perfect anticlimax. The Venetian Secretary in England reported to the Doge and Senate on 25 September that the farmers,

I stole away; and never will return
Till England knowes who did her Citty burn,
Till Caveleers shall favorites be Deem'd
And loyall sufferings by the Court esteem'd
Till Howard and Garway shall a bribe reject,
Till Golden Osborn cheating shall detect. . . .

Some manuscripts read "Lee" instead of "Howard" and that was almost certainly the original reading, referring to the occasion in 1673 when Lee and Garroway betrayed their own party—allegedly for a consideration—by proposing a grant to the King of £1,200,000 instead of the £600,000 the party had previously agreed on. (Margoliouth, I, 185 and 306-307; Burnet, *History of My Own Time*, ed. Airy, Oxford, 1897, II, 15-16.)

24. Grey, I, 317, 319-321, 327; Dering, p. 20.

25. *H.M.C.*, 12, App. VII, p. 73; *C.S.P.D.*, 1670, p. 571; *C.S.P.D.*, 1671, p. 407; *C.T.B.*, 1669-1672, p. 890.

alarmed by threats of war and the consequent decrease in the Customs, petitioned the King for a reduction of their rent; that Charles granted this but, "provoked" by their further request that they should withhold, as security, part of their first cash payment, "cancelled their contract, which was all ready under the great seal." The King had had enough of farmers, and appointed a new set of six Commissioners of the Customs to act immediately. The French ambassador Colbert reported that Buckingham had told him how important it was for the King to be master of his own revenues, "en sorte qu'il fût assecuré d'en pouvoir disposer sans aucun obstacle ni retardement, pour l'execution de ce qu'il a promis, et que cependant ceux qui s'etaient rendus adjudicataires de ses principales fermes depuis la dernière seance du parlement, et entre autres Milord St. Jean et Sir Robert Howard, etaient fort devancés à l'Espagne, et le roi avait resolu de les retirer de leurs mains."[26] Perhaps Buckingham, not for the first or last time, was exaggerating; he had somewhat of a phobia about Spain, but in any case it may have been good policy to have Colbert think that Charles was still opposing the Spanish (and supporting the French) interest. There is nothing else to connect Howard at this stage with international intrigue, although there need hardly be any question that like most Englishmen he would have been horrified had he known of the Secret Treaty of Dover.

Between November, 1670, when the question of imposing fresh taxes had first led to the project of the farming of the Customs, and September, 1671, when the King finally withdrew the proposed grant, the House had given most of its time, and Howard had given much of his thought, to ways and means of raising money for the King. On the whole, he was for increasing taxes, to meet the nation's commitments, and he felt sure that Clifford was greatly overestimating the Supply already agreed to. He accordingly favored not only an excise on private brewing ("To the person that will brew, it does indeed bring him a home Excise, but then he may chuse whether he will brew or no") but also a tax on legal proceedings. He drew the line, however, at a proposed annual tax on coal, lead, and tin mines: tin and lead, he pointed out, were already taxed and where one mine might have a rich output in its first year, another might produce

26. *C.S.P. Venetian,* 1671-1672, p. 108 and n.

nothing in ten years. Besides, "the miners are lusty bodied men" and their "discontent" would be dangerous![27]

There had been one tragicomedy associated with these debates on Supply. In December a suggested "amusements-tax" on entrance money to the theater was opposed by the Court Party in the House, on the ground that "the Players were the King's servants, and a part of his pleasure," and Sir John Coventry asked his famous question "If the King's pleasure lay among the men or women players?" On 20 December Coventry was attacked in the streets, and his nose slit; and in January the House debated the two questions, of punishing Coventry's attackers and of giving precedence to this question over the important Supply bill. Howard was all for hastening the bill to punish Coventry's attackers but voted against a proposal to stop all other business until the Coventry bill had passed *both* Houses. (Seymour remarked that you need only "hire some persons to assault some Members of this House, and Supply may be hindered at any time.") Howard also opposed the move to treat all accessories to the crime as if they were principals and so remove them from the possibility of pardon.[28]

It is not surprising to find that Howard was again one of the leading speakers in indignant debates in April when the Lords presumed to call a message from the Commons "unparliamentary." On 12 April it was he who read to the House the next message, to be presented at a conference with the Lords, a message most conciliatory in general tone but concluding that the Commons "conceive there is hardly a precedent to be found" for the use by the Lords of the offensive word; and he was again to the fore on the following day when the Commons reasserted their right not to have their money bills, fixing taxes, altered by the Lords.[29] A supporter of the King he might be, and one capable of being bought; but he was also, in at least one important sense, a champion of democratic rights.

27. Grey, I, 394, 397, 409, 366; Dering, pp. 24, 41, 60.
28. Grey, I, 332-349; Dering, p. 45.   29. Grey, I, 424, 436-443, 465.

Chapter eleven. THE TREASURY, PARLIAMENT,
AND APPOINTMENT TO THE EXCHEQUER:
1671-1673

IN October 1671 Howard began a career in yet another sphere when
he was appointed Secretary to the Treasury, in succession to Sir
George Downing. That the Secretaryship was a reward for political
services rendered is likely enough, but allegations[1] that Howard had
to be bribed in 1671 to stop him attacking the Court party are fantastic, in view of all his attempts to obtain money for the King in the
preceding years and Hollis's plain statement more than a year before
that there were then none greater at Court or more highly esteemed
by the King than Howard and Seymour.[2] Moreover, since the Secretary was regularly a member of the House of Commons and was
expected to assist in seeing the financial business of the King through
the House, there can have been very few better qualified to fill the
position than a man who had frequently led the debates on the Supply,
had acted as chairman of at least one of the House's financial committees, had known enough about finance to be able to plan the farming of the Customs at the huge figure of at least £400,000 per annum,
and had been associated for years with such financial giants of the
City as Morris and Clayton. No doubt such associations had their
dangers and I should not be surprised to learn that Howard rewarded
himself in the manner of the time; yet the modern historian of the
Treasury, Stephen B. Baxter, no admirer of Howard, pays him the
tribute of saying that "there is no evidence of dishonesty" on his part
while he was at the Treasury.[3] Incidentally, when Clifford became
Treasurer in 1672, he could presumably have dismissed the Secretary,
but he allowed him to continue, and one can only assume that Clifford,
as one of the five Commissioners before December, 1672, was quite
satisfied with Howard's work.

1. See, e.g., the statements by the editor of the Calendars of Treasury Books,
William A. Shaw, in *C.T.B.*, 1669-1672, p. 939, and by Stephen B. Baxter, *The
Development of the Treasury 1660-1702* (London, 1957), p. 181.
2. A cryptic contemporary comment is that of Sir John Berkenhead to Williamson (P.R.O. S.P. Dom. Car. II, 293, No. 126): "We hear Sr Rob: Howard
has wonn all: must hee alwaies gain by being ag^t the King? You see w^t small
Game we play at."
3. *Op. cit.*, p. 182.

Both Baxter and W. A. Shaw have complained of Howard's sloven-ly methods of keeping records as Secretary of the Treasury,[4] and their opinion must be respected. Perhaps, however, two caveats may be entered. The first is, as the two historians point out, that some of the records may have disappeared (and I would add that so many official documents signed by Howard are in places other than the Public Record Office that this is quite likely); the second is that very often the Secretary who keeps poor records is the one who keeps most details in his head.

There would be no point in mentioning individually all the docu-ments of the next few years that bear Howard's signature in his ca-pacity of Secretary. They include memoranda in Howard's hand, with note, in the margin, of the name of the officer who is to attend to them, and also such inscriptions as "Abbot write this minute faire for me";[5] references from the Treasury Lords to the Master of the Ordinance, the Surveyor General, and other officials, for advice or ac-tion or report back to the Lords;[6] and letters, or drafts of letters, re-quiring people to appear before the Treasury Lords to "explain."[7] The most interesting of all these, if only because of the fame of its recipient, is one to Rochester. Addressed on the outside "For the Earle of Rochester these. Leave this at the post house in Taunton to be sent to Enmore in Somersetshire," it was written from the Treasury Chambers on 29 May 1672:

My Lord:

I will not dispute whither you or I shall receive the most advantage by our freindship but I am soe well satisfied with my share that I resolve to Continue the Contract, and will performe all that's in my pow'r to prevent your havinge the least equitable cause to breake it, and in order to soe just and advantegeous designe, I will with as much speed as I can endeaver to serve you in the particulars of your wages and pension, I cannot promise soe derectly as I wish, for the Kings affaires are at this time very pressinge, but I will doe all that is possible to assure you of the truth of what I professe to be soe really

Yo[r] most faithfull
freind and humble
servant
Ro: Howard.[8]

4. Shaw, p. lxvii, Baxter, p. 181.   5. P.R.O., Treas. Min. Bk. IV, 61.
6. For example, B.M. Add. MSS 38849, f. 66 and f. 76, and 38694, f. 34.
7. For example, one of 12 June 1672 to "Mr Norman" who has to explain "some Arreares of Hearthmony," Osborn MSS, Yale.
8. B.M. Harl. MS 7003, f. 289.

Howard's Secretaryship was probably worth rather more than £2000 a year (Baxter calculates this to have been the value of the post in the 1660's).[9] The salary was £250, payable quarterly, and for once—not unnaturally—warrants for payment were issued regularly; there was also an annual gift of 200 guineas from the King, and the remainder was made up from fees. Even without this, Howard was certainly not poor; but he continued to ask, successfully, for other privileges and sources of income. On 29 June 1672, for example, the trustees of the late Henrietta Maria were instructed "to pass a grant to Sir Robert Howard of the stewardship of the Honor and manor of Pontefract, co. York [and the manor of] Spalding with its members, with the other manors therewith granted, [and of] Barton, Barrow and Gouxhill, co. Lincoln, and Hitchin, co. Herford. . . ." The fees paid to previous holders of these offices totaled at least £27.6.8 per annum. Then on 2 July the trustees were further ordered "to pass a grant to some nominee of Sir Rob. Howard of the bailiwick of Wallingford and Ewelme, co. Oxford, and Chertsey and the Hundred of Godley, co. Surrey, now void by the death of the late Queen Mother and a certain parcel of land called the Warren lying in the parish of Ewelme, co. Oxford, formerly in grant to the late Earl of Berkshire."[10]

When Howard was confirmed in the Secretaryship after the appointment of Clifford as Treasurer late in 1672, at least one contemporary felt that he had risen too far. Perhaps, indeed, Sir John Lauder expressed the attitude of many when he wrote in his Journal:

The Lord Clifford, lately but Sir Thomas Clifford, is exalted to be great Treasurer of England . . . and the Commissioners for the Threasurie are suppressed. . . . Sir Robert Howard, commonly called Sir Positive, is made Secretary to the Treasurer. . . . My Lord Lauderdale has undoubtedly had a great hand in this extraordinary revolution; for they are on the caballe with him, and are all his confident privado'es. The old nobility cannot but repute them selves slighted when they sie thesse great offices of State conferred upon [muschroomes] upstarts. But this is a part of the absolute power of kings to raise men from the dunghill and make them their owne companions.[11]

After his appointment to the Treasury, Howard was free to give most of his time to his office duties; and when Parliament met again

9. Baxter, p. 177.
10. *C.T.B.*, 1669-1672, pp. 1262, 1267, 1367, 1368.
11. *Journals of Sir John Lauder Lord Fountainhall*, ed. Donald Crawford (Edinburgh, 1900), pp. 221-222.

early in 1673, after a break of nearly two years, he brought to the debates his new knowledge and any authority associated with it. While Parliament was not sitting, the third Anglo-Dutch war had begun; and the King had also issued a Declaration of Indulgence removing the legal penalties on both Nonconformity and Roman Catholicism. When Parliament resumed, it gave him the money he needed for the war but made it clear that withdrawal of the Declaration of Indulgence was the price he must pay; and on both these themes Howard naturally had much to say.

On 7 February, after Mr. Secretary Coventry had spoken at great length about the necessity for Supply, and Garroway had acidly remarked that he believed there would already have been a vote "if Coventry's speech had not taken off the celerity," Howard sensibly intervened by saying that "Nothing expedites the King's service more than ingenuous dealing with one another." He did not believe that delays were "hid in the breast" of any man there. Since he had had the honor to serve the King in the revenue, the "comings-in" had been more, and "goings-out" less; the war had been managed without a penny given, or borrowed; and the King was asking no more than would "save him from shame in the prosecution of the war."[12] Supply was voted, of eighteen months' assessment, not to exceed £70,000 a month.

The House then turned to the Declaration of Indulgence and there was a lengthy debate which centered on the relative powers of King and Parliament on questions of toleration. On 10 February Howard argued that the Church of England was not endangered by the Declaration; after all, not every member of the Church observed all its ceremonies. The Declaration did not threaten any man's life, liberty, or estate, and he referred to previous dispensations that had rightly not been thought grievances. "Nothing can gratify the Pope more than to say the King has no such jurisdiction. . . . It is a strange question to dispute what Prerogative is, when all Statutes make it so sacred a thing." If Papists made ill use of the indulgence, then the proper course of action was for the House to address the King; it ought not to vote his action illegal "else the Hollanders will rejoice." The House did not entirely agree with him and it was resolved both that an address should be presented to the King and "that penal

12. Grey, II, 11.

statutes in matters ecclesiastical cannot be suspended but by Act of Parliament."

In the ensuing debates on the address and on the alternative bill proposing that any indulgence should be confined to Protestant dissenters, Howard followed the line he had taken in his previous speech (and is not recorded as having said anything when the debate degenerated into petty squabbles, as it did, for example, on 22 February). When on the twenty-fourth the King returned a particularly conciliatory reply, Howard, of course, rejoiced: "We have that plainly which we have long hoped for. . . . The Answer, in its own nature, is perfectly kind, as the nature of the Prince it comes from" and he desired the House to record its thanks without a Question. (The ensuing debate, however, was again so tumultuous that the Speaker had to tell one Member, "It is not in my power to prevail with the House to hear you.") Howard was one of the Committee appointed to consider the King's Answer in detail.[13]

Howard again spoke sincerely and with far better sense than most members when the House proceeded to discuss a motion for removing all Catholics from military positions. He was no great affecter of their religion, he remarked on 28 February, but would not have the swords of gallant men taken from them. Again, on 3 March, he told the House that if its bills meant the dismissal of a man such as Sir John Harman ("We have few such"), the House was only hurting itself and its Protestant subjects. He was, of course, in the minority; and on 5 and 6 March he could only try to persuade the House not to limit too strictly the King's power to grant to Catholics pensions and rewards for positions from which they would now have to resign.[14]

He was perhaps not present in the week from 7 to 12 March, for he contributed nothing when the bill to prevent the growth of Popery was read the second and third time. On the following days, however, he continued to fight for the Supply, and against fanaticism; and on 17 March, for instance, when the debate was on the power of the Papists in Ireland, he granted that there was "no doubt but that much exorbitancy had been committed by the ecclesiastical part of Romish jurisdiction" but thought that this was still a matter to bring before the King by way of address and not a matter for a penal statute. On

13. Grey, II, 12-45, 49-68; Dering, pp. 115, 119, 126, 133.
14. Grey, II, 75, 79-80, 85-88.

19 March, when at the third reading of the Bill for Ease of Dissenters it was solemnly argued whether the bill was or was not "according to the Law of God, Law of Nations, and Complection of the Nation," Howard refused to contribute to the historical and theological non-sense talked and could only beg the House, if this was what it really wanted, to pass the bill and not leave everything in a state of chaos. The Lords, however, wanted amendments which the Commons disliked because they gave the King a discretionary power of relaxing the provisions of the bill; Howard pointed out that *somebody* had to have the power that the Commons were willing to allow; the King had power in ecclesiastical matters if anything. "Can you avoid the conduit-pipe?" he asked. "Some body must be in trust still for the peace of the nation"; and he added that, desiring that peace, he himself had been for seven years of the opinion that the laws against dissent should be relaxed.[15]

Cynics will no doubt say—indeed cynics said at the time—that it was for just such "services" to the Crown as these that Howard received his next major gift from the King.[16] As a matter of fact, the King was in debt to Howard in the other sense also: in 1672, when Parliament was not sitting and money was desperately needed for the conduct of the war against the Dutch, he had lent to the Crown at least £9000. (Order was given for repayment in 1673, after Parliament granted Supply, and he apparently then made a further loan of £3500.)[17] The new gift to Howard was the grant of the office of Writer of Tallies in the Exchequer, in reversion after Sir Robert Long's life interest. With this went also the more important position of Auditor of the Receipt, although this was technically in the gift of the Treasurer. The grants were made in March, 1673, and Howard was sworn in on 14 July, the day after Long's death.[18]

Perhaps I should record here, though without belief, a fantastic story told by John Oldmixon of how Howard came to be given the reversion of the Auditor's place. Oldmixon's version is that Howard, "one of the most active Members of the House of Commons," was

15. Grey, II, 103, 109-114, 122, 135, 163-166; Dering, p. 140.
16. Wood, II, 1018.
17. *C.T.B.*, 1672-1675, pp. 154, 162. These entries are distinct from several others ordering repayment to him of money he had "disbursed," presumably as Secretary (for example, pp. 173, 370, 414).
18. *C.S.P.D.*, 1673, p. 18; *Letters to Sir Joseph Williamson* (Camden Society, London, 1874), I, 104, 106.

for impeaching the Lord Chancellor, Shaftesbury, and that seventy or eighty Members of Parliament met "at a certain Tavern near Charing-Cross" to discuss the proceedings. Shaftesbury, however, heard of it beforehand, secured the next-door room in the tavern, and, after listening to Howard address the assembled members on the intended impeachment, sent the Drawer to tell him that a Gentleman wished to speak with him in the next room. Oldmixon continues:

Sir Robert came immediately, and, to his great Surprize, found the Lord Chancellor, who receiv'd him with a very gay Countenance, and taking no Notice of what was concerting against him, told him, He was so much his Friend that he could not help bringing him good News, which was, That the King had given him the Reversion of the Auditor of the Exchequer's Place by his Recommendation. . . . Robert replied honestly "I will very frankly own to you, my Lord, I have by no Means deserv'd this Favour at your Hands; on the contrary, I am now the main Contriver and Actor in an Impeachment against you; but it is not too late to undo all that has been done, and if your Lordship will but have Patience to stay here but a Quarter of an Hour, you shall hear how I will put an End to it."

Then, Oldmixon says, Howard returned to the next room, renewed his attack on Shaftesbury "with greater Vehemence than before," but advised the company that without proof they could not proceed and would find that Shaftesbury would easily arrange for his acquittal:

The Members finding how it was like to go, and that Sir Robert had left them, went away one after another, without saying a Word, and Sir Robert enjoy'd many Years, the Reward of his Management, the Office of Auditor. It is certain he was made Auditor July the 19th following.[19]

Oldmixon cannot even get his dates right. It is a good story but one need not call it history.

The position was worth, according to Wood, £3000 a year (the Auditor of the Receipt was entitled to £1 in the hundred as his fee on pensions etc., or 10/- if they were paid "under the title of secret service"; the official grant specifies only a salary of £316.13.4 but also mentions "the house, cloisters and gardens" attached to the office, "and all other profits thereof").[20]

19. Cited by James Ralph, *The History of England: During the Reigns of K. William, Q. Anne, and K. George I. With an Introductory Review of the Reigns of the Royal Brothers, Charles and James* (London, 1744), I, 223 n. I have not reproduced the italics.

20. Wood, II, 1018; Baxter, p. 185; *C.T.B.*, 1672-1675, p. 83. But see below, chap. xviii, p. 275.

Howard's right to such a lucrative position did not go unchallenged. The King had previously promised the Auditorship, in reversion after Long's death, to the Earl of Bristol for his youngest son Francis Digby, and Bristol had taken the precaution of receiving an assurance that he would have the reversion himself if his son predeceased him. Digby was killed in battle, and Bristol alleged that Charles, through Arlington, had then confirmed his previous promise. In spite of this, so Bristol's claim continues,

Sir Robert Howard, Knight, taking advantage of a time when his Majesty's great care and trouble could not choose but hinder him from reflecting upon so inconsiderable a thing as the said Earl's greatest concernments, and at a time when the said Sir Robert Howard made most ostentation of his pretended usefulness to his Majesty's service in the House of Commons, obtained of his Majesty by surprise a warrant for a patent for the reversion of the said place after Sir Robert Long, and got it passed the Signet before ever the said Earl got the least notice of it.

Bristol thereupon went to the Duke of York, who interposed with the King; and the King promised he would "set a stop at the Great Seal to the passing of the said patent to Sir Robert Howard till such time as the said Earl had received satisfaction for the said place by Compensation." Bristol personally thanked Charles, who assured him that "he had never intended him in this business any prejudice either in honour or interest"; but to make sure, Bristol entered a caveat that the patent might not pass until he had been heard.[21]

Obviously it was to everybody's interest that the matter should be settled by payment of compensation to Bristol, particularly if the probabilities were—as I should maintain they were—that Howard would be a far more knowledgeable Auditor of the Receipt than would the Earl. The compensation was paid before Howard took office, and on 20 June 1673 Bristol wrote a cordial note to thank Howard for "what you offer mee soe obligingly" and "the Civility of y^r proceedinge in my Concerne of the two thousand pounds."[22]

Between March, when Howard was given the reversion of the offices of Writer of the Tallies and Auditor of the Receipt, and July, when he was sworn in, Clifford had been forced to resign as Treasurer, because of the Test Act, and had been succeeded late in June by Sir Thomas Osborne, recently created Viscount Osborne of Dumblane in

21. *H.M.C.*, 79, MSS of the Earl of Lindsey, pp. 181-183.
22. B.M. Add. MS 38855, f. 105.

Scotland and shortly to become Viscount Latimer of Danby (in August, 1673) and Earl of Danby (in 1674).[23] Evelyn, for one, found Danby "of a more haughty & far lesse obliging nature" than his predecessor, Clifford; and certainly I do not get from the official documents an impression of a pleasing personality, however able he may have been.[24] Danby, like Howard, had been of the Buckingham faction, and he had been just as opposed to Clarendon, for example, as had Howard, but they were later to become bitter enemies; if they were already so, it must have been very awkward for them both that Howard was Secretary to the Treasurer when Danby was appointed. Nor would matters have improved greatly when Howard moved from the Secretaryship to his new positions in the Exchequer (Danby's brother-in-law, Charles Bertie, becoming the new Secretary). It has been suggested that Howard would have liked to retain the Secretaryship even after becoming Auditor but that Danby defeated the move.[25]

Baxter has come to the conclusion that the Auditorship of the Receipt was a sinecure; that in any case Howard could hardly have done any important work while his enemy Danby was Treasurer from 1673 to 1679; and that "even in the 1680's he does not seem to have done anything," while in the 1690's, it is implied, he was constantly ill.[26] It is, I suppose, not necessarily a contradiction of this that hundreds of official documents were addressed to him (for example, the whole volume *B.M.Add MSS 27876*), but I have seen so many papers annotated by him and bearing his signature (some of which I shall mention from time to time) that I must question Mr. Baxter's verdict. I would also suggest that it is virtually contradicted by his own account of Howard's part in the D'Oyley scandal of 1677; it is certainly contradicted by the evidence Howard produced when Danby was impeached in 1679 and also during the earlier attack on Danby in the House in 1675.[27] Such a letter as the one from Danby of 23 November 1673 "To my very loveinge freind Sir Robert Howard," asking him to pay the salary of one of the King's falconers, surely

23. *Williamson Letters*, I, 49, 67. Danby became Marquis of Carmarthen in 1689 and Duke of Leeds in 1694.
24. *Diary*, IV, 20. Compare de Beer's notes, *ibid.*, IV, 20 n. 2 and IV, 267 n. 5. Compare also Baxter's perhaps unfair verdict, p. 18, that Danby may have made the position of Treasurer worth the £20,000 a year calculated upon "but his personal standards were unusually low."
25. Browning, *Danby*, I, 110 and n. 2.
26. Baxter, p. 127.
27. See below, chaps. xii, xiii, and xiv, pp. 197-210 and 219-234.

implies personal attention by Howard to an Exchequer matter (and makes one wonder whether the enmity between the two men began as early as Baxter believes); and Danby's direction of 16 February 1674 "that all orders unassigned shall be brought in and deposited in the hands of Sir Robert Howard," who is to make three receipts and enter "the same in some book kept by him for that purpose," although it is not friendly in tone and suggests that Howard had failed to keep proper records in the past, envisages his looking to his obligations personally in future. The matter is really put beyond reasonable doubt by two letters from Robert Yard to Williamson. The first, of 21 November 1673, contains the sentence: "Mr. Floyd . . . further told mee that the warrants for your Ex^{cys} arrears in the Councell were now in Sir Robert Howard's hands, with whom he has lately had some difference, and therefore thought it necessary that I should goe and sollicite it, which accordingly I will doe"; the second, of 13 February 1674, reports that £337 is due and the warrants now "lye ready": "one reason that they were not paid already is the unkindness between Sir Robert Howard and Mr Floyd, of which I formerly told your Ex^{cy}. I have severall times spoke to Sir Robert Howard about it, though I have not had any order from your Ex^{cy} to sollicite or receive any moneys from [for?] your Ex^{cy}."[28]

What Baxter has shown is that when Danby began the practice of dictating to the Auditor the particular fund from which a Treasury order was to be met, he tried to remove what was the Auditor's last chance of having any part in the formulation of *policy* (Howard apparently attended meetings of the Treasury Board only rarely and, I suspect, only by invitation or command). We have already seen, however, that Howard did not necessarily do only what he was told, and there is further evidence in an entry in the Treasury Minute Book on 13 October 1675: "Write Sir Robert Howard to restrain him from making other payments than such as are particularly directed by letter [from the Lord Treasurer]."[29]

Other evidence that will be quoted from time to time will make it certain that Howard was active as Auditor and that he was not content to sit back and accept the salary and fees and any other incidental money that merely happened to come to him.

28. B.M. Add. MS 37999, f. 76; *C.T.B.*, 1672-1675, p. 478; *Williamson Letters*, II, 79, 149.
29. *C.T.B.*, 1672-1675, p. 341.

Chapter twelve. DEFENSE AND OFFENSE IN
PARLIAMENT: 1673-1675

PARLIAMENT in the next few years must have been in an even
more unstable and turbulent state than at any other period during the
reign of Charles II. Every great official seemed to be in danger of
impeachment, and it would have been impossible to predict whom
the House of Commons would turn on next. According to Sir William Temple, writing to the Earl of Essex on 25 October 1673, even
on the major questions such as the war with Holland and the alliance
with France there were at least four parties in the House: the ex-
tremists and the moderates (who were both for the King); those who
wanted to hold up all Supply until peace was made; and "the last
party is made chiefly to carry on the business of the *devorce,* and this
is headed wholly by *Shaftesbury* and Sʳ R. Howard, who carry it on
both with *the King,* and *Lords* and *Commons. The King* seems
sometimes very earnest in it, and sometimes cold." Temple added
that the Court party sadly lacked good men to manage its business
in the House.[1]

We do not need Temple's letter in order to understand how important the question of the succession was becoming to the nation, but
his words provide evidence that, in spite of his denigrators, Howard
did not always follow the lead given by the King (or by Buckingham).
Here we find him trying to initiate a policy for the King to adopt;
and on the other great issue of the time, the marriage of the Duke of
York to the Catholic Mary of Modena, he may well have acted in a
similar way.

In this same letter, Temple told Essex that the House had presented
to the King an address objecting to the Duke's proposed marriage
(performed by proxy later in September); according to Sir Christopher Musgrave, Powell moved for the address, and "Sir Robert
Howard expressed a great satisfaction in the motion" (to which there
were very few dissentients). Temple continued: "But many of the
House imagine the thing was not very displeasing to *the King,* becaus
Sʳ Ro: Howard promoted it; and with expressions of His not onely
desiring the Duke should not marry a Roman Catholique, but wish-

1. *Essex Papers,* ed. O. Airy (Camden Society, London, 1890) I, 130-132.

ing none of that profession might ever be marryed to any of the Royall Family."[2]

Poor Howard! If he suggested a policy that was obviously acceptable to the King, people said he had been bribed; if he suggested one that was not obviously acceptable, they said either that he had "ratted" and been bought by the opposition or that there was a secret understanding with the King that Howard should advance what were really the Royal interests although they could not be admitted to be so. The one thing that historians have not been prepared to allow him is a mind of his own. Yet on the question of Catholicism his attitude is not hard to understand: he was opposed to general persecution for the sake of persecution, but he did not like the Catholic religion and he was determined to do everything in his power to prevent it from having a say in the government of England. Then, as the threat of Catholic domination of English policy grew greater, Howard's opposition to the whole religion hardened.

Accordingly, when on 30 October the House debated whether the Test Act applied to members, Howard is reported as saying that "without a thorough care, we shall be in a worse condition for Religion than before. . . . It is necessary, that where any fountain is, it may be pure; and he would have the Protestant Religion pull up the very roots of Popery, wherever they grow."[3] Perhaps it was to these same debates that he contributed the thought recorded by Sir Francis Fane in his Commonplace Book: "Sr Robt Howard told them in ye Par^t house, y^t was time to look to there Religion, where young men of 24 years quitted there employment of great honor & proffitt to embrace ye Roman."[4]

These sentiments are in fact most unlikely to have had the King's approval. Contemporaries expected that Howard would be dismissed;[5] and among the Danby papers in the British Museum there is an undated form of suspension of Howard from his office, apparently pre-

2. *Williamson Letters*, II, 52; *Essex Papers*, I, 130, both first cited by E. S. de Beer, *Inst. Hist. Res. Bull.*, III (1925), 65. Howard's opposition to the marriage is also recorded by Dering, p. 151.

3. Grey, II, 196-197.

4. f. 178^v. The Commonplace Book is in the Library of Shakespeare's Birthplace, at Stratford-upon-Avon; I am indebted to the Director, Mr. Levi Fox, for his kindness in copying the entry for me. It may safely be dated 1673 on the evidence of the preceding and following entries.

5. *C.S.P.D.*, Nov., 1673—Feb., 1675, pp. 12-13, Bridgeman to Williamson.

pared by Danby, to be signed by the King, but never used.[6] If the King had ever thought of dismissing Howard, however, he quickly changed his mind, and by 17 November Robert Yard could write to Williamson: "Sir Robert Howard, &c. continue still in their severall places, and wee now talke no more of these matters."[7]

Charles would indeed have been unwise to suspend a man who, although he could not stomach the thought of a dominant Catholicism in England, was still one of the Crown's most loyal supporters on all other matters relating to the Prerogative and to finance. When the King asked again for Supply on 27 October, because he had failed to make a satisfactory peace with the Dutch, he promised the members "that he should be very ready to give them fresh instances of his zeal for preserving the established Religion and Laws." Not surprisingly, they were disinclined to believe him. Howard begged members to consider their own interests: if they were concerned about what would happen to any money they gave, they could easily check that: "If Money be ill managed, any body may see it; he [as Auditor of the Receipt] will give an account of it, and ask no time to do it, Registers being all in order. . . . You say the Papists have power; by this you give more way yet to have it. . . . He must be a God that can say, 'there shall be no enemies, and we shall have Peace'; and yet we do so by this negative." The Dutch would rejoice, he reminded them, if Supply were denied now; and the right thing to do was to grant the King the money he needed for the war and tackle the religious question separately, by way of a "Grievance" stated to the King. He was surely right; but the only support was from Coventry and from Finch (who, significantly, became Lord Keeper shortly afterwards). It was resolved that there would be no Supply of any sort before the expiration of the eighteen months' assessment unless "the obstinacy of the Dutch" made it necessary, nor would it be granted "before this Kingdom be effectually secured from the dangers of Popery, and Popish Counsels and Counsellors, and the present Grievances be redressed."[8]

In the ensuing debate on 3 November, Howard tried in vain to

6. B.M. Add. MS 28086, f. 11. The form could equally well be an expression of Danby's pious hopes either at the time of his own open break with Howard or when he had obtained the reversion of the Auditorship for his son Peregrine Osborne.

7. *Williamson Letters*, II, 74.   8. Grey, II, 182-214; Dering, p. 157.

dissuade the House from voting the Standing Army to be a "grievance." It was indeed, he said, a grievance—to the Dutch. Again he asked that the House avoid "any distrust betwixt the King and us, and . . . give no argument to the King to apprehend it." The right course, he maintained, was to inform the King, if they must, that there was now no occasion for the Standing Army and that it might be "a terror to the people, as you apprehend."[9] When the House returned to the subject on 7 February, after a prorogation, Howard did succeed in making modifications in the motion "that the standing forces now in this kingdom are a grievance"; he argued that a certain force was necessary, and had recently been proved so, to guard against disturbances, and the House finally accepted his arguments and resolved "that any standing forces *other than the Militia* were a grievance and that the King be petitioned to disband those that were raised since January 1, 1663."[10] I doubt whether even momentarily Charles thought of dismissing as able a supporter as this.

In expressing his own regret at the prorogation, Howard had reminded the Commons that "the eyes of all the World are upon us now, and should we not do things as amicably as possible, the censures of the people will lie as heavy upon us, as in any other thing."[11] "Amicable," however, is the last adjective one would apply to the subsequent proceedings of the House. For example, three times during 1674 and 1675 they presented addresses to the King against Lauderdale, accused of attempting to undermine government by asserting "edicts superior to law," by being Commissioner to the Army in Scotland, and so on. On the first two occasions, Howard tried to modify the wrath of the House, and support the King;[12] when the third address was presented against Lauderdale in May, however, "severall who wer look't on formerly as his great friends wer turned against him, as Sir Robert Howard, who injoyes a great place at Court, and others in the Houss who wer altogither reulled by the clergie; which gives ground of warious conjectures." There was soon "a report that Sir Robert Howard, Sir Johnne Princomb, who have verry considerable place about Court, are to get a bill of ease" but once more gossip was sadly astray: a few days later the King was again showing his faith in

9. Grey, II, 216-223.
11. *Ibid.*, II, 224, 234.
10. *Ibid.*, II, 391-399.
12. *Ibid.*, II, 243-244; III, 110.

Howard by approving his appointment as Deputy Lieutenant of Wiltshire.[13]

After the original attack on Lauderdale in January, 1674, the next member of the Cabal to come under fire was the Duke of Buckingham, accused by the Lords of immorality and by the Commons of fostering Popery. Howard had to go carefully; and he does seem to have been particularly tactful. He successfully proposed an adjournment of one day after the House had heard a statement from Buckingham on 13 January; then on the fourteenth he tried in vain for a further adjournment until the fifteenth, on the ground that the man should not be condemned before his defense had been properly considered. The House resolved to present an address to the King, to remove Buckingham from all official employment and councils. The only other assistance Howard could offer he tried to give when in February it was debated whether it would not be advisable to seek the concurrence of the Lords in the address. Howard agreed with those who argued that this was a different case from that of Lauderdale, who was (at the time) a commoner, and that the House of Lords was "the proper place" for any proceedings against Buckingham. But a motion "that the concurrence of the Lords be desired" was lost.[14]

On the very day after the first vote against Buckingham, the Commons turned on a third member of the Cabal, Arlington, who was accused (by Buckingham's friends, acting in retaliation) of promoting Popery and, by embezzling public money and otherwise, of acting against the interests of the nation. It seems to have been a particularly vindictive and unnecessary attack, and Howard, although a friend of Buckingham, tried again to modify the vehemence of the House. For example, when it was debated whether it was proper for the Commons to ask questions of a Lord, Howard pointed out that Arlington might have no opportunity to be heard in his own defense if not questioned; and after Arlington had spoken, answered questions and withdrawn, Howard defended him against the charge of having favored the Declaration of Indulgence, by recalling that Arlington had told him at the time that he had "used all his interest against it," and had added "and pray use you your's." He himself, he explained later, felt only

13. *H.M.C.*, Laing MSS, I, 402, 404 (George Scot to his kinsman James, Chamberlain to the Duke of Buccleuch); *C.S.P.D.*, March, 1675—Feb., 1676, p. 161.

14. Grey, II, 252, 265, 270, 384.

"tenderness" and "generosity" for Arlington, but as a member of the House he would not express this by advising it to desist. The accuser, Gilbert Gerrard, ought to produce his evidence. On 17 January Gerrard, "finding his evidence not ready," wanted to withdraw the charge; Howard said that the only proper way of proceeding now was by impeachment: it would be wrong to change the point of attack and try to convict Arlington on his own words (which Howard defended). He added later that he suspected that in fact there was *no* evidence against Arlington (and no doubt he enjoyed discomfiting Lady Honoria's friend, Gerrard). It would be unjust to delay proceedings: let the House have the evidence and get on with the impeachment. The House decided that there was no evidence even for removal, though a Committee was formally asked to report whether there were any grounds for an impeachment.[15] Howard surely comes out of this well (particularly if it be remembered that Arlington was thought to have been the man who opposed Buckingham's attempt to have Howard made Secretary of State). Even in a minor way he had been shown respect during the debate: he had taken "exception at being misrecited" by Sir William Coventry, and Coventry had replied that he "would not fail, in matter of candour, to any man, especially to Howard" and had asked his pardon "if he misplaced his words."[16]

The debates in the House continued with unabated vigor for the remainder of the month. Members discussed the regulating of parliamentary elections (Howard: "The expences of Elections are grown so vast, that it goes beyond all bounds, the charges considered in the country and here"), the proposals of the States General for peace (Howard: "He that is not for Peace, forgets the four Gospels") and a petition from Bernard Howard of Norfolk containing an oath he would take to bind him to be a good subject but desiring exemption from the penalty of the Law against Recusants. Courtney Poole wanted the petition thrown out "with scorn"; Robert protested that Bernard Howard was of too much "honour and gallantry" for this, unacceptable as his religion was: "This deserves not 'scorn' for a man to live quietly —It would be a good thing to be done for all other Dissenters." Robert had too good a sense of tactics to press for a Committee; the House did not accept the petition, but allowed it to be withdrawn,

15. *Ibid.*, II, 275, 280, 287, 311-312, 329.
16. *Ibid.*, II, 322-323.

with no discredit to its presenter, of whose personal merit there was general praise.[17]

The case of another kinsman came up early in February, when the House debated a proposal to send an address to the King asking him to arrange for the return from Europe to England of the lunatic Duke of Norfolk. Howard, who obviously knew more of the facts than did members of the House who relied entirely on gossip, denied assertions that the Duke was not mad but only made to appear so by Catholic oppressors, and offered to bring reliable witnesses to prove it. He asserted that Norfolk, though "as well attended as any of his quality in *England*" was "a sad spectacle, and in some measure ignominious to his family were he here, and the place where he is, is a more probable place possibly of his cure." The House twice voted for bringing the Duke back to England, though Howard said that the request for the return had been prompted by an "unfortunate difference" in the family and ought not to be favored. The Duke was still in Padua when he died later in 1677.[18]

The next victim of malice in the House of Commons was Samuel Pepys, whose election as member for Castle Rising was endangered by an accusation that he was by conviction a Papist and kept an altar and "crucifix" (possibly only a picture of the crucifixion) in his closet. Howard came into it only to protest against a proposal that Littleton be *ordered* to declare what *he* knew in the matter. Howard objected both on principle and because the evidence of the other members would be no stronger for such further support and ought not to need it. The House did not agree with him, it was ordered that Littleton and any other member must declare what they knew, Pepys defended himself adequately, no evidence was forthcoming, the debate was adjourned—and Pepys kept his seat.[19] It is doubtful whether Howard had any serious objection to Pepys (from whom he apparently borrowed £400 in the following year, 1676). Perhaps family jealousies were involved, since the Castle Rising borough was controlled by Sir Robert's Catholic kinsman, Lord Henry Howard; in 1679 Sir Robert replaced Pepys as member for the borough.[20]

17. *Ibid.*, II, 333, 356, 358; see also p. 375.
18. *Ibid.*, II, 386; IV, 222, 342-343.
19. Grey, II, 408-431; Arthur Bryant, *Samuel Pepys, The Years of Peril* (Cambridge, 1935), pp. 110-116.
20. See above, chap. x, p. 170, and below, chap. xiv, p. 222.

It is clear that Howard saw himself, not altogether incorrectly, as a guardian of legal as well as parliamentary principles, and in 1674 he often spoke on questions relating to the administration of the law. He played an insignificant part in debates in February, 1674, on the Habeas Corpus Bill (when he was for keeping legal proceedings as far as possible in open court), on the appointment of sheriffs, and on the Lords' Bill for the trial of peers; and in April, 1675, he contributed some comments (which were ruled out of order) to a debate on the bill to prevent illegal exaction of money from the subject.[21]

In view of all Howard's activities, it is not surprising that the author of the satire "A Charge to the Grand Inquest of England, 1674" (later published in *State Poems*, 1697) included him in his list of prominent members of Parliament who are to be detested for their arrogance and for being "Law-givers, Judge, and Party too":

> Room for the *Bedlam C — ns*, Hell and Fury!
> Room for the Gentlemen of our *Grand Jury* . . .
> The Foreman first, preferr'd before the rest,
> 'Cause he has learnt the Art of Prating best.
> Then *Howard, Powell, Garaway* and *Meers*,
> *Temple* and *S* — (who yet wears his Ears). . . .

The year 1674 also saw the development of another enmity, one that was to cause Howard more trouble than mere parliamentary differences or satires. This was his quarrel with his immediate superior in the Exchequer, the Lord Treasurer, Danby. The dispute is first heard of in a letter from Lord Conway to the Earl of Essex written on 17 February 1674: "Great dissention there is betweene *Treasurer* and *Sir Robt. Howard,* too long to trouble yor Excel^{ce} with the Particulars. *Keeper* [Finch] is so much concerned for *Trear.* and the unworthy dealing of *Sir Robt Howard,* that he told me last night he should never rest in quiet till he had gott *Sir R. Howard* turned out of all."[22] Writing to Conway from Ireland on 28 February, the Lord Lieutenant also referred to the subject: "The differences of Lord Treasurer and Sir R. Howard must needs make all matters of the tresury go ruggedly. As for Sir R. Howard I do not much wonder at his misbehaviour, but rather how he kept so long in the station where

21. Grey, II, 418, 434, 447, 448; III, 2.
22. *Essex Papers*, pp. 175-176. The Editor (Airy) "explains" that Howard "had now 'ratted' to the Court"!

he is."[23] One does not know what irregularities, if any, Danby may have discovered in the Exchequer or whether they were the real cause of his enmity. Some reason for thinking that they may not have been hard to find is given by a letter from Rear Admiral Richard Carter, on board the *Crown* in the Downs, to Howard's financial associate Sir Robert Clayton, on 4 April. Carter writes: "I have advice from London y^t S^r. Robt. Howard is at Newmarkett Else I should have beg'd ye favor of him to have spoke to y^u in my behalfe" and he asks Clayton whether he knows of any merchants who might wish to send goods, since "the place where I now am I can take them on board wthout any suspition if I have Notice of it before they come."[24] It hardly sounds like a proper relation between a Rear Admiral and the Auditor of the Receipt in the Exchequer, although such practices were common enough in the Navy at the time.

Certainly Danby must have been alarmed when at the end of the year the King gave to Howard's son Thomas the reversion of the place of one of the four tellers in the Exchequer.[25] Less than a fortnight later, Danby retaliated, not very satisfactorily, by having his own younger son Peregrine, Viscount Osborne of Dumblane, given the reversion of Howard's Auditorship.[26]

Matters came to a head when the House of Commons, on 27 April in the following year, 1675, considered seven articles against Danby to decide whether on any or all of them he could be impeached. Howard's position when he was asked to explain Treasury and Exchequer practices to the House was indeed invidious, unless it be believed—and I know of no evidence whatsoever why it should be believed—that Howard himself in some underhand way had assisted in sponsoring the attack. (Arlington would seem to have promoted it as a way of embarrassing the Government.)

The first article against Danby concerned Howard closely: this was the allegation that, as Lord Treasurer, Danby had "violated the method of the Exchequer," overthrown its traditional practices, and "perverted" proper methods of receipt (etc.) by taking "into his own

23. *C.S.P.D.*, Nov., 1673—Feb., 1675, p. 185. The names are in code.
24. Osborn MSS, Yale. In a later letter Carter sends through Clayton his "humble service" to Howard.
25. Bod. Ash. MS 243, f. 193; *C.T.B.*, 1672-1675, p. 633. The salary of £31 was supplemented by fees (*ibid.*, p. 281).
26. *Ibid.*, pp. 641, 868.

hands the sole power of disposing almost all the King's revenue, laying aside the Chancellor and Under-Treasurer of the Exchequer and other officers." The House wanted to know whether money could be "kept back out of the Exchequer" and not be accounted for, and on what authority such money would be paid. Howard was questioned, and replied that he was "a sworn servant to the King, in his office, and would have the questions in writing, and show them to the King, for his leave to answer." The House voted that Howard must answer, and the Speaker asked him "Whether, since the Patent [for the Customs] was granted to Mr. *Mounteney*, less money than formerly was brought into the Exchequer, from the Customs, and more money diverted from the Exchequer." His reply gives some interesting information about the defective accounting methods of the day:

Formerly the Patentee paid the money, and it was never entered into the Exchequer, as the more easy way for the persons to get their money, than when paid in the Exchequer—What is received above the pensions (which are good store) is paid by tally into the Exchequer—The pensions are never recorded—All the out-lying moneys are foreign to his office—If the Chancellor of the Exchequer should join with the Lord Treasurer in warrants for payment out of his office, he cannot pay a penny. No man can cheat in the Exchequer, they never paying any money out of method.

We may well feel that the last sentence is contradicted by the preceding ones, but the House was satisfied and voted that the first article contained no matter fit for an impeachment of Danby.[27]

The House next inquired into the conditions governing the patent for the Excise (held by a "Mr. Kent"). The patentee was obliged "to pay the money as the Lord Treasurer shall direct," and the Chancellor of the Exchequer had entered a caveat and had the patent stopped on 8 April. The Chancellor (Duncombe) was now questioned whether such a patent did not give the Treasurer the chance to dispose of money "without warrant either by the Great Seal, or privy Seal"; and Howard explained the procedure. A proper understanding of his answer demands, however, a knowledge of the Exchequer practice of issuing tallies; and with the assistance of Baxter's *Development of the Treasury 1660-1702*, I shall attempt a brief explanation.

When one of the four tellers in the Receipt received money, the Tally Court (in the room below) issued a notched hazel-wood "tally" as a receipt, the various notches indicating payments of tens, hundreds,

27. Grey, III, 49-56.

thousands, pounds, shillings and pence, and so on. The tally was split down the middle and one half (the "tally" or "foil") handed to the payer, while the other (the "counter-tally" or "counterfoil") was kept. When the foil was eventually returned through the Exchequer, the two halves were matched, and destroyed.

By a further development, tallies were issued as receipts for *loans*; the lender then received with the tally an order for repayment, bearing the same date as the tally, and loans were subsequently paid off as money became available. The repayment could be promised for a particular date and could be directed to be made by a particular receiver or on a particular branch of the revenue. The next step, however, was a tally for a *fictitious loan*. Such an official as the Treasurer of the Navy, seeking money to which the Navy was entitled, would be assumed to have made a loan to the Exchequer and would be issued with a "tally of anticipation" and an order for payment on a given date (and here, of course, there was room for bribery to ensure an earlier date of repayment). The official then had to cash these tallies of anticipation as best he could and, naturally, at a discount. Theoretically the Treasury determined the maximum discount, but in practice, not surprisingly, the cash value of the tally was often low.[28]

It will be seen that in this way the income of the Crown was always mortgaged in advance. The House of Commons itself was becoming increasingly concerned at this, and only three days before the Danby debate began had resolved to present an address to the King "to prevent any farther anticipation or charge upon his Majesty's customs of England and Ireland, it being a disservice to the King and Kingdom," although Coventry, as Secretary of State, had said that "The Kingdom may be lost for want of anticipations upon the King's revenue" and Howard had asked what would happen in time of war with a navy unprepared and "not one shilling" in the Exchequer to equip it.[29]

Now, when the Danby debate was continued on 28 April, Howard spoke at length:

He thinks himself happy that he shall say nothing here, but what he has said before in another place. As good service may arise from this Patent, as ever was done to the nation, he thinks.—Before this Patent was granted to Mr *Kent*, the Lord Treasurer sent for him, and told him, 'here are

28. Baxter, pp. 130-135.   29. Grey, III, 37-40.

debts, and there must be credits, and he would do according to the constitution of the Exchequer.' When he saw Kent's proposals to the Commissioners of Excise, he desired the Treasurer and Chancellor to do no
such thing, for the proposals would bring things to utter ruin in the Exchequer.—Says the Treasurer, 'on the one side, I may do amiss in the
Exchequer, and on the other side, I hazard the King's credit, if I do it
not'. He showed him how it might be done by the Tallies, according to
law, and all returned into the Exchequer. The Treasurer was pleased with
it, but, after this, he never knew of *Kent's* Patent, nor saw it, till he saw
it here, on the reputation of a Gentleman. The course of the Exchequer is
as ancient as the law of the land. . . . Now 'tis a question, 'whether
this Patent does not take away the legal account in the Exchequer'—Tallies
of anticipation take all things out of course in the Exchequer, without
doubt—By no constitution nor law, but money must be paid in *specie* into
the Exchequer; and what is otherwise is different from the law of the
Exchequer—Tallies of anticipation are much more usual in the former
Lord Treasurer's time, than this—Tallies of anticipation do expose the
King's accounts to interest accounts. 'What will you give us, and I'll pay
you?'—The officers will do it. He cannot tell whether the Patent was by
the Treasurer's procurement—He [Howard] has told you that his judgment was to proceed legally in the Exchequer, and he knows nothing of
passing the Patent.[30]

If the effect was not exactly to clear Danby of possible malpractice
over the particular patent, it said nothing to incriminate him either;
and the House did decide that none of the articles constituted a ground
for impeachment.

The only other time Howard contributed to this debate was on 3
May when there was a suggestion that the books of the Exchequer
should be examined by the House. *That*, he wittily remarked, might
truly be said to be stopping the Exchequer. Precedent and common
sense alike suggested that inquiry might be confined to specific sums
alleged to have been misemployed.[31]

The next proposal was that the Customs ought to be appropriated
by bill for the specific use of the Navy for three years; Howard said
that if the Customs were appropriated entirely for the Navy, " 'tis
impossible the King should live." He challenged the House to examine the King's financial position carefully "and you will not find
such an exorbitant balance as you imagine." The King had done what
he could for the Navy out of the Customs and would be just as willing
to have the accounts examined as the House was to order the examina-

30. Grey, III, 57-59.   31. *Ibid.*, III, 85-86.

tion.[32] Modern opinion, on the whole, supports Howard on this: the King was indeed constantly in difficulty (even with the secret French aid of which Howard, of course, knew nothing), because the House would not vote him sufficient Supply even for the wars it approved.

Danby may or may not have been grateful, temporarily, for Howard's share in the Commons debates.[33] Perhaps for a few months, Treasurer and Auditor did let their differences rest. What is certain is that the King continued to appreciate Howard's support: in addition to the approval, on 12 June 1675, of his appointment as Deputy Lieutenant of Wiltshire (already noted), he granted him for life, on 19 October, the office of Keeper of the Royal Game "in and about the manor of Oatlands, Surrey," with the fee of 1/– per day and 26/8 yearly for a livery (and this fee too was paid—Howard was in a position to see to that).[34]

32. *Ibid.*, III, 98-101.

33. I do not think there is any personal significance in the appearance of Howard's name on a list of "servants & Officers," in Danby's hand, dated October, 1675 (B.M. Add. MS 28091, f. 144, also cited by Browning, III, 68-71, and by E. S. de Beer, *Inst. Hist. Res. Bull.*, III, 64-65); Danby was always listing the names of members of the House who might be counted on to vote for the Court, and no loyalty to him personally is implied. Another such list, drawn up for Danby, is f. 169.

34. *C.S.P.D.*, 1675-1676, p. 354; *C.T.B.*, 1676-1679, pp. 104, 990.

Chapter thirteen. PARLIAMENT, THE D'OYLEY AFFAIR, AND TRUSTEESHIP FOR NELL GWYN: 1676-1677

PARLIAMENT had been prorogued towards the end of 1675 after the conflict between Court and "Country" parties had reached something like a stalemate, and it did not meet again until February, 1677. For Howard, therefore, 1676 began quietly and promised to be an uneventful year in which, perhaps, more attention could be paid to private concerns.

It was in April, 1676, that he sold Wootton Bassett to Laurence Hyde for £36,000, of which Lady Honoria, from whom he had now been separated for at least nine years, had £8,000 by agreement. (Clayton once again acted as Howard's agent in adjusting some of the minor details of the sale.)[1] Neither Lady Honoria's death in September of this year nor her action in leaving him only 1/- in her will can have moved him very deeply.

The growing power of Danby was probably the main danger to Howard's peace of mind; and as early as 28 April, Grace Lady Chaworth was writing in a postscript to a letter to her brother Lord Roos: "Sir John Duncombe hath lost his place [as Chancellor of the Exchequer]. . . . There is talk of Sir Robert Howard's remoove, but also that he says he will stand a suite to the King before he quits it."[2] He was indeed proving a redoubtable opponent, far harder to shift than many of higher status and rank.

Danby continued to probe into the management of the Exchequer and to be dissatisfied with what he found. He needed information about the money lent to the Exchequer, both directly and through the goldsmiths. In April, Howard was one of the referees appointed to meet three days a week to look at the goldsmiths' accounts and continue to meet until a report was finished; then on 22 December he was asked to prepare a statement of direct loans. He brought to Danby

1. Bod. Don. MS c68, f. 11. The names of Clayton and Howard are also linked in a letter written to Morris by Nic. Charlton on 8 July of this year (Osborn MSS).

2. H.M.C., Report 12, App. 5, Rutland MSS, p. 28. Lady Chaworth seems to have been well informed; she also reports Lady Honoria's death (19 September, ibid., p. 29).

"a paper book" showing three classes of loan: (1) money lent to the public offices for the King's immediate service, (2) money lent relating to public service, and (3) money lent to private persons and not relating to any public service—"which (he says)," according to the Minute, "is clearer than A.B.C." Danby does not seem to have thought so. He read the book, directed that "an alphabet or epitome be made thereof the better to illustrate the same" and desired Howard "to give an account of such persons as really lent money into the Exchequer and what was lent and what has been assigned by the bankers to other persons and not comprehended in the bankers' accounts." Howard took away "his own paper of calculation of the goldsmiths' accounts" and promised to send it back "with a state of those accounts as they came to him." When Danby reported to the King in February, 1677, however, he explained that he was unable to be specific "by reason of the uncertainty of Sir Robert Howard's certificate, which does not distinguish those who have paid money into the Exchequer or the public offices from such as have orders for fictitious loans or otherwise." Obviously Danby was not succeeding in his laudable attempt to discover just what the financial position of the nation was; and Howard as Auditor was the one who should have been able to give him exact figures for the national income and expenditure. A few months later (June, 1677) the goldsmiths themselves were called in and Danby told them they had "to discharge the King by general release." "Humbly" but firmly, they said "no." Danby thereupon directed Howard (and others) to view all their orders, tallies and other vouchers and compare these with their accounts and grants.[3]

An ominous note is sounded by an annotation in Danby's hand on a memorandum to the King in June, 1677, speaking of the necessity of having "officers" he can trust and exploring the possibility of replacing Howard by Sir Philip Warwick; nor can Howard's stocks have risen with the marriage in this same month of Danby's daughter Sophia to a grandson of the Earl of Thomond, a close kinsman of Lady Honoria.[4]

More ominous still is a simple statement of 1676: a deposition by Sir William D'Oyley, of Westminster, "that what he has informed the

3. C.T.B., 1676-1679, pp. 95, 96, 201, 451, 542-546.
4. Browning, II, 69 n., I, 244.

Earl of Danby concerning Sir Robert Howard is true."[5] There was a short lull, but then the bomb that Danby had been carefully planting blew up, although ironically it blew up under Danby's informant D'Oyley and did more damage to him than to Howard, for whom it was obviously intended.

Before this happened, Parliament resumed in February, after the long prorogation, and proceeded to argue whether it had in effect been legally prorogued or only adjourned. Howard thought it "the most dangerous Debate that may be, and from which no good consequence can arise." If Parliament had not been prorogued—and he certainly thought it had not merely adjourned, a matter of its own volition—then somebody might argue (and some did wish to argue) that it had in fact been dissolved. The House finally accepted his wise advice "to lay aside this dangerous debate" and by the reading of a bill (for regulating elections) acted as if it had been prorogued.[6]

Soon they were on to weightier subjects again and on 20 March debated a bill from the Lords "for farther securing the Protestant Religion, by educating the Children of the Royal Family therein, and providing for the Continuance of a Protestant Clergy." Howard agreed with another member that this was doing by law what had before been done by arms, in the Civil War. Then, concentrating on the provisions concerning the clergy, he argued for not making "a perpetual quarrel" with them. The bill was against the wishes of the twenty-five bishops in the House of Lords; and he did not think the House ought to try to—or that in practice it could—control the clergy by this bill, if, as was inconceivable, they desired to be "Popish."[7]

He followed this same line several times in March, April, and May, in the various debates concerning the European alliances. On 29 March, for example, he joined Williamson in opposing, unsuccessfully, an address to the King which, by specifying the alliance with Spain that the King ought to make and by promising aid if such alliances forced him into war with France, seemed to the supporters of the Court to limit the King's power too much. "Why should you do more than give the King thanks for his Answer, and tell him that you will assist him?" Similarly on 23 May, Howard spoke against any address

5. *H.M.C.*, 11th Report, App. Pt. 7, MSS of the Duke of Leeds, p. 13. (Danby became Duke of Leeds in 1694.)
6. Grey, IV, 65-72.
7. Grey, IV, 284-326. The bill "died of neglect."

that presumed to use phrases like "trusting the King." Two days later, again in vain, he tried to convince the House that the Prerogative ought not to be infringed by a specifying of particular alliances, when more general phrases would adequately express the opinion of the House. In one sense he was right, for when the address was presented, the result was that the King in his reply censured Parliament and adjourned them first to 16 July, then to 3 December.[8]

During the session Howard was seen in a completely favorable light in a little incident that threatened to show just how contemptible the House could become. Marvell, coming in to his place in the House on 29 March, stumbled on Sir Philip Harcourt's foot; and the Speaker (who had, on the previous day, gibed at Marvell for some of his comments when he opposed the Bill for Educating the Royal Children in the Protestant Religion) told the Members that it was "his duty" to inform them that he had seen a box on the ear given. Harcourt himself assured the House that Marvell's tripping over him was accidental, but the Speaker would not be satisfied: "Marvell struck Harcourt so home, that his fist, as well as his hat, hit him." Marvell had previously been unable to resist the taunt that he hoped that, as the Speaker kept the House in order, he would keep himself in order for the future. Howard brought some common sense to the argument when he hoped the House would not have Harcourt say he received a blow when he had not; Howard thought what had been said by both was "sufficient," and soon the whole matter did lapse.[9] Admittedly Howard and Marvell had voted on the same side on the bill in question; but in other ways they were poles apart politically and (although perhaps Howard did not know it) Marvell had been including him in his fiercest satires. One hopes that Marvell appreciated the assistance given him.

In September the Danby bomb exploded. On the twenty-first, Secretary Williamson noted that investigation in the Exchequer had revealed a shortage in the money held by the tellers, that Howard had allegedly known of this "& concealed it," that he had used his knowledge to blackmail the tellers into lending him money, and had then repaid one teller with the money borrowed from another, and that when discovery was threatened, he had tried "to cheat my Ld Treasurer

8. Grey, IV. 333-334, 343-347, 364, 374-388.
9. Grey, IV, 328-331.

wth false Baggs." Howard appeared before the Council and was ready to answer, but asked for a day's postponement that he might "have Counsell present"; and although the Attorney-General objected, the King agreed that the investigation should be deferred until the third council day after his return from Newmarket.[10] Howard went to Newmarket himself, and Danby wrote to his Countess on 28 September that "Sir Robert Howard is also com'd, and the King does not speake to him, so that I am here lookt upon as a much greater conqueror then I am."[11]

The inquiry was resumed on 7 November, when Howard "came in on crutches, being lately risen from the gout. The King spoke kindly to him and ordered a chair whereon he sat."[12] The Attorney-General elaborated the charges, and witnesses were produced. It was now alleged that Howard had conspired with the teller Sir William D'Oyley to conceal the deficiency in D'Oyley's bags (a deficiency of well over £7000) and that on Howard's suggestion a plumber was sent for and induced to cast pieces of lead of the size of half-crowns which were to be put into the bottom of the bags and covered with real coins. This certainly makes one doubt E. S. de Beer's sweeping claim that "there was no question of dishonesty on Howard's part";[13] indeed, as Williamson noted with an "N.B.," it was a most important point of the charge that "all this while" Howard actually certified that the missing money was in the Treasury. The only letter from D'Oyley to Howard that could be produced, however, was so vague that it did not help the prosecutors; nor can it have been other than in Howard's favor that D'Oyley had previously been suspended for a piece of sharp practice, in 1673.[14] Perhaps too the Council thought it unlikely that Howard could not have found money enough of his own to fill a teller's empty bags, if necessary.

10. P.R.O. S.P. Dom. Car. II 366, p. 375; *H.M.C.*, Ormonde MSS, N.S. IV, 377.

11. *H.M.C.*, 4, App. IX, p. 387 (also cited by Browning, II, 40). The following account of the inquiry is based on this letter and on P.R.O. S.P. Dom. Car. II 366, pp. 397-407. These documents were first cited, not quite accurately, by Florence R. Scott, "Sir Robert Howard as Financier," *PMLA*, LII (1937), 1094-1100.

12. Southwell to Ormond, *H.M.C.*, Ormonde MSS, N.S. IV, 383. A letter from Charles Hatton two weeks earlier (23 October) also mentions that Howard had gout so badly that he could not stand for long. (*Hatton Correspondence*, Camden Society, London, 1878, I, 152).

13. *Inst. Hist. Res. Bull.*, III, 65.   14. *C.T.B.*, 1672-1675, 47, 104.

Howard's defense was that he had been unwise in that he had not revealed his knowledge of the borrowing by the tellers, but that this was not a cause for dismissing him; he "totally" denied making any use of the King's money himself, and scorned D'Oyley's story that the lead had been put in the bags at Howard's own house: he successfully challenged D'Oyley to produce the men who had brought the lead there. The Clerk of the Council, Sir Robert Southwell, in a full account of the proceedings sent three days later to Ormond, wrote admiringly of Howard's speech in his own defense, though he added, fairly enough, that "it was thought he might have spared the declaring himself not to be a man that had raised any great hasty fortune."[15] At this point, the King adjourned the inquiry (because news came that the Duchess of York was in labor).

Howard's friends were optimistic when the case was resumed two days later. His witnesses having been heard, and the evidence summed up, Howard withdrew and the Council debated its decision. It was agreed that the story of the false bags "did wholly rest" on the testimony of D'Oyley, "so infamous a man" that he could not be believed. Notice had to be taken, however, of Howard's failure to impart to the Lord Treasurer his knowledge of D'Oyley's deficiency, until Danby started his own inquiries; and the Council thought it had been proved that Howard had borrowed four or five hundred pounds from a teller, though he "paid it justly again." He was held "blameable in what had passed"; yet since "no man had objected that he was to be any gainer thereby," it might be difficult to obtain a legal conviction. Moreover, he had served the King and his father well, and since it was thought that "to a man of honour nothing could be more grievous than the declaration of His Majesty's displeasure," it was proposed that the King should censure him in person. This was agreed to, "and His Majesty himself discoursed somewhat largely on the matter, chiefly to vindicate my Lord Treasurer from any imputation of malice." Danby had acted properly in notifying the King immediately of his discovery of the default; and therefore, Southwell concluded,

the King ordered that (when Sir Robert Howard and the company were called in again) he should declare His Majesty's satisfaction in what my Lord Treasurer had acted in this matter. And in the two points of Sir Robert's not declaring the want of cash when he first knew it, and the

15. *H.M.C.*, Ormonde MSS, N.S. IV., 383 ff., which is also the source of the following sentences.

borrowing that which belonged to His Majesty, that he should understand His Majesty's great displeasure, and that His Majesty should take it into his own consideration what was farther fit to be done. And this (Sir Robert and the company being called in) was declared accordingly. And so the matter ends with honour to my Lord Treasurer, and without danger of suspension or loss of office to Sir Robert Howard.

A warrant from Danby on 17 November suspended D'Oyley from office during the King's pleasure[16] but Danby can have received small, if any, satisfaction from that. Indeed, his only consolation in the whole D'Oyley scandal may have been that, although Howard was soon allowed to kiss the King's hand, "withal he was commanded to go and make his submission to the Lord Treasurer, which he intends to do."[17] It is still an open question whether he did it.

Howard himself believed, or pretended to believe, that he had been completely exonerated. The best evidence of this is a letter he wrote to Ormond on 26 November, in answer to one from Ormond dated 20 November and referring apparently to the information given him by Southwell a week before. Howard and Ormond were writing to each other because Howard had been chosen (either by the King or by the lady herself) to help Nell Gwyn to obtain money due to her from a grant of Irish property made by the King; and Ormond had been asked to assist her cause in the Irish Court of Claims.[18] In the letter in question, Ormond wrote to Howard: "I received yours concerning Mrs Gwin's concernment in the pension given her in the name of my

16. C.T.B., 1676-1679, 788, 1093. The rest of the D'Oyley story confirms all previous evidence of the man's character. The Crown took over control of most of his extensive property, to repay itself from the profits until the debt should be paid off; and in 1679 Henry Coventry paid £7000 to the Crown in exchange for the rents and fees until D'Oyley had paid the remainder of his full debt of over £12,000. D'Oyley died in 1680, and Coventry was shocked to learn that while he had been shown a marriage settlement which declared the property to be "free" (of entail or mortgage), a second one, good in law, had entailed the land to D'Oyley's son by "a never before practised artifice of a double marriage settlement"—and therefore Coventry could not touch it. (He not unnaturally wanted his £7000 back.) The Crown had allowed D'Oyley to retain the income from the property that came to him when his father Sir William senior died in 1677; when now it attempted to realize on this (since it could not touch the entailed lands), it met defeat again, for the will of Sir William senior had never been proved and therefore the property had never legally belonged to Sir William junior, and had to pass to his son! See C.T.B., 1679-1680, 175-176, and Baxter, pp. 151-156.

17. Southwell to Ormond, 13 Nov., H.M.C., Ormonde MSS, N.S. IV, 386.

18. J. H. Wilson, Nell Gwyn, Royal Mistress, p. 199.

Lord of Middlesex" but he had to say that he could not overlook prior patents, and the petition of those holding them. He suggested that Nell's pension should "be put on the Establishment" until prior rights terminated, so that everyone could be satisfied: "Be pleased to let her know all this, and that I am her most obedient servant." Then he added a postscript: "We have heard of wonders you did upon your crutches—it was no small one in that state to be so nimble. I congratulate your activity." Howard's reply was:

I would not have troubled you with the least mention of what has happened to me, were it not to justify myself why I have not thus long presented the offer of my poor services to your Excellency; but while I lay under the least accusation that could but seem to cast a blemish on me, I thought presenting such an offer to your Excellency would rather seem to beg the protection of a powerful friend than to make a clear tender of an inconsiderable servant. But since I am free from such an objection, which perhaps is by this time presented to your Excellency by indifferent persons, I would use the benefit of such an advantage which I have received by the favour and justice of so excellent a King and master only to entitle myself the better to receive your Excellency's commands, and if you are now pleased to judge anything in my power here that may be useful to your Excellency, your commands would give me the satisfaction of esteeming myself your servant by that mark of your favour, and my obedience and care in the performance should at least justify my endeavour to merit the title.

Mrs. Nelly has commanded me to present her among the number of your true servants, and does think herself so much obliged to your Excellency, that unless within a little time you command her something that she may serve you in, she swears she will pick a quarrel with you, for she vows she loves you entirely. I presume to present her own words to your Excellency that she was pleased to use. . . .[19]

Perhaps we may follow Howard's example and turn from the D'Oyley affair (about which there is indeed nothing more that can be said) to the more entertaining Nell. In February of the following year, 1678, Howard again wrote to Ormond, to tell him that "Mrs Gwin has commanded me to give your Excellency an account that as yet she cannot get the money due on her pension Michaelmas last," unless she pays one shilling in the pound plus Exchequer fees; and Howard added: "That experience that I have here makes me know that this is not for the King's interest nor honour, and therefore I know 'tis enough that I present it to your Excellency, and beg I may

19. *H.M.C.*, Ormonde MSS, N.S. IV, 70.

receive your commands by Mr. Mylius, who presents this to you."[20] Mylius, or Mulys, or Melius, or Melish, was Nell's "agent"; Howard was, in her own words, "her trustee in the business," and a confidential one.[21]

Howard and Ormond continued to do their best for Nell for nearly another two years. Not even Sir Joseph Williamson, Secretary of State, knew exactly what was involved; when he wrote to Ormond about the Dungannon estates in Ireland (which the King wished Nell to have also), he added that "Sir Robert Howard . . . is directed to give you a more particular account of his Majesty's mind and intentions in all that matter. All I know is that his Majesty told me it was a concern of his own and in a certain sense for himself." The King also promised that if the estates (in Dundalk and Carlingford) were held to be in his gift, "he will grant the same to Sir Robert Howard and his heirs."[22]

Howard, of course, was only a trustee, and a "dummy," for Nell Gwyn and her (and the King's) illegitimate son, the Earl of Burford, later Earl of St. Albans. This is made quite clear by Howard's letter to Ormond on the same day as Williamson's:

With this your Excellency will receive an account from Mr. Secretary Williamson with a copy of a warrant to Mr. Attorney-General for the prosecuting a suit against the possessors of Dundalk and Carlingford, which was begged upon discovery made of the deficiency of the title by Mrs. Gwyn. The King took the opportunity of it to cause the benefit she is to have to be added to some other things to buy an estate in land for my Lord Burford, in which His Majesty was pleased to command me to take the trust upon me to follow this business, and if effected to add to it some other things granted for the same design, and to take care for the purchasing of land as he shall please to approve and direct from time to time. So upon the promise of the King to settle it when obtained, I am ordered to give the Attorney-General the informations and direction how this estate is discovered to be of right in the King. We would not proceed to desire any grant without your Excellency's full knowledge of it, and in the meantime we only prosecute the right of the King. All farther accounts of the proceeding of this business your Excellency shall timely receive from me.[23]

20. *Ibid.*, IV, 119.
21. In Howard's absence from town, in March, the Earl of Arran had to tell Ormond that he could find no official record of Nell's pension either in her name or in Howard's; *ibid.*, IV, 132.
22. *C.S.P.D.*, 1679-1680, pp. 54-55, 196.
23. *H.M.C.*, Ormonde MSS, N.S. IV, 309.

On 15 July Howard wrote again to Ormond, telling him that the King now believed that the title in Dundalk and Carlingford was in him. In his next letter, on 27 August, he enclosed a personal letter from the King on the question of Nell's pension, and reported again that her agent Melish was "very slow in his returns"; then on 12 November he told Ormond that Melish had necessarily been replaced by a new agent and that Nell "presents you with her real acknowledgments for all your favours, and protests she would write in her own hand, but her wild characters she says would distract you. This, my lord, was her own natural notion when I showed her your Grace's kind return upon the King's letter."[24] In December Ormond wrote to the Earl of Ossory that the business was "done" as far as it depended on him and asked Ossory both to tell Howard so and to beg his pardon for not writing to him direct.[25] As late as January, 1682, however, Ormond was patiently replying to the inquiries of a new Secretary of State, Sir Lionel Jenkins, and was saying that he would do his best to settle the problem.[26]

Perhaps the most interesting feature of these documents is the way in which the personality of Nell Gwyn shows through, even when we are hearing her words only as reported by another. To the biographer of Howard, the letters also have the interest of demonstrating how little success Danby had in undermining Howard's position as a responsible officer of the Crown. The very years of the inquiry and the accusations against him are also the years in which he is acting as the confidential agent of the King in a personal matter of some importance. Before long, moreover, the tables were to be turned, and Danby himself was to face accusers anxious to remove him from office.

24. *H.M.C.*, Ormonde MSS, N.S. V, 155-156, 193, 237-238.
25. *Ibid.*, V, 246.
26. *H.M.C.*, Ormonde MSS, N.S. VI, 299, 304.

Chapter fourteen. *THE CONQUEST OF CHINA*; THE IMPEACHMENT OF DANBY; AND THE PAMPHLET WAR OF 1678-1680

ONE minor set-back Howard did suffer during the period when he was recovering from the D'Oyley scandal: "his W——— Uphill," according to a contemporary pamphlet, "now refuses to marry him."[1] This, as we have seen, must be a reference to Mary Uphill; and she cannot have refused for very long, for she married Howard, as his third wife, some time before June 1680.[2]

Meanwhile, when Parliament met late in January, 1678, it again discussed matters on which Howard had strong opinions. It resolved to present an address to the King conveying the thanks of the House for the marriage of his niece Mary, daughter of the Duke of York, to "a Protestant Prince" (William of Orange) on 4 November 1677; but it also besought him not to countenance any treaty of peace except "such a one as leaves the *French* King in no better state and condition to offend his neighbours, than he is left in by the *Pyrenean* treaty." Howard would have approved of the Protestant marriage (even though Danby played a leading part in arranging it), but he spoke once more against the attempt to limit the King's prerogative in foreign affairs. He cannot himself have been either surprised or offended at the King's caustic answer to the address. In the consequent debates on Supply, he again tried to persuade the House not to attach too many conditions to their grant and was unimpressed by the argument that the money might be ill used. He argued that an inadequate Supply might even lead Holland, feeling that England had forsaken her, to make peace on terms unwelcome to Parliament: "Let the *quantum* be appropriated, and there is no danger." After heated debate the House agreed to grant Supply; and on the following day, Howard tried to obtain as large a sum as possible. The majority of the House, however, was against him, and it was resolved that the

1. *A Seasonable Argument to Perswade All the Grand Juries in England to Petition for a New Parliament*, 1677. First cited by Montague Summers, in his edition of *Roscius Anglicanus*, p. 92.
2. B.M. Add. MS 27447, f. 460 (in which Howard refers to "the dangerous sickness of my wife").

Committee should sit for consideration of Supply for ninety ships and no more.[3]

Howard and Danby were again on the same side, for Danby about this time was trying to convince the House of Lords that England could not afford war with France and was endeavoring to get adequate Supply for the King. Yet in a list of his enemies in the Exchequer in 1678, he included Howard with Carr, Fox, Duncombe and others who "meet generally at Sir Robert Howard, sometimes at Sir Robert Carrs."[4]

There is no record of Howard's having taken any part in the debates between 6 February and 3 May 1678, and since the subjects covered included many on which he had strong opinions (for example, Supply, imports, treaties with Holland, and restrictions on the growth of Popery), this may mean that he was ill with "gout" once more.

On 3 May he is seen in a favorable light again in a personal matter—asking the House to accept the apology of a member, Goring, who had offended it. On the eleventh, however, he spoke with unnecessary malice when Pepys tried to tell the suspicious House that not one penny of the money voted for the ninety ships had been spent on anything else, and "I doubt not" to have the ships ready by 30 May as "I promised." There had been no "cheat," as some members alleged, and there was no reason for refusing further Supply. Howard should have welcomed this expert opinion but to his discredit said "*Pepys* here speaks rather like an Admiral than a Secretary, 'I' and 'we'. I wish he knows half so much of the Navy as he pretends. Now the King of *France* is greater at Sea than we, with all the preparations that are pretended." Well might Charles have asked to be defended from his friends; and indeed he did find the House's address "so extravagant that I am not willing speedily to give it the Answer it deserves," and not surprisingly he prorogued Parliament. It reassembled later in May, and Howard made minor contributions to debates on 1 and 6 June, in each case speaking on a point of parliamentary procedure; and then Parliament was again prorogued and did not meet until 21 October (and some of its problems were solved for it when in July Louis of France made peace with the United Provinces).[5]

3. Grey, V, 39-40, 61, 82, 110.
4. B.M. Add. MS 28049, f. 36, cited by Browning, *Danby*, III, 7.
5. Grey, V, 315-316, 386-390; VI, 57, 66; compare also 271, 304-305.

It was probably in this year that Howard wrote to the Earl of Rochester a letter that has been discussed by more than one of the latter's biographers. The letter, which is dated simply "Aprill: 7th," was once thought to have been written in 1672, on the theory that the play to which it refers, *The Conquest of China by the Tartars,* was abandoned when Settle's similarly named play forestalled it; but J. H. Wilson has pointed out not only that in fact Settle's play failed and would have presented no obstacle to a successful play on the same subject, but also that Rochester's serious illness to which Howard alludes was more probably that of 1678, when he was in fact reported dead.[6] (On the other hand, for what it is worth, Howard's only other surviving letter to Rochester was written in 1672.)

Howard's letter, "For the Earle of Rochester at adderbury neare Banbury in Oxfordschire," is as follows:

Though this towne is apt enough to like an ill entertainment better then A good one; yet I Cannot beleeve them soe stupid as to be insible [sic] what they shoud have lost by your death; and I am soe well pleasd with your health that I am troubled I Cannot assure you that I owe such an abundance of satisfaction to my freindship only, but must allow some share to the pleasure I promise my selfe by enjoyinge such thinges as the Doctor was pleasd to declaime against; but like an angry Impeacher; (nature beinge that great monarch for whose favours their is soe many Rivalls:) the Doctor drew up his Charge against her Cheife minister. The next satisfaction to your health; your Company will give mee; and shall be obligd to know when I may expect you in this modest towne, where the worst men and women censure the best; and the silent knave is shelterd under the Charracter of A sober person; The Criticks on men's Actions, are like the ill naturd ones of the stage, most busie where there is greatest Ingenuity; beinge Commonly more provokt by there envie then their judgment; but I forgett how ill I entertaine though upon A good subject; and am sure I shall be better by you though upon an ill one. I mean by the sceen you are pleasd to write. nor shall I repine to see how far you Can exceed mee; noe more then I doe to see others that have more wealth then I live by mee with A greater plenty; I have tooke [?] pleasure that you exceed all that can excell mee; and those advantages of my Lord Rochester must needs be pleasinge to me that is soe perfectly his

most faithfull and humble servant
Ro Howard.[7]

6. J. H. Wilson, "The Dating of Rochester's 'Sцæn,'" *R.E.S.,* XIII (1937) 455-458; Johannes Prinz, *John Wilmot Earl of Rochester* (*Palaestra,* Band 154), (Leipzig, 1927), p. 286.

7. B.M. Harl. MS 7003, f. 291.

Rochester's "Scæn of Sʳ: Robert Hoard's Play" survives in a fair copy in a very legible print-hand in B.M. Add. MS 28692, f.70, where it is followed by his *Valentinian*.[8] After the heading there is a stage direction "The Army appeares drawn up in three Battalions The Empresse Leading the maine Body, on the right hand Hyachian, on the left Lycungus," then comes the scene (268 lines in all) beginning with a speech of 35 lines by the Empress. It would appear that Howard sent Rochester a full plot.

Rochester seems to me to be trying to write in the manner of *The Indian Queen*—a manner that does not suit him (he is too good a poet) and one that Howard himself had outgrown. The opening speech by the Empress Amacoa, for example, from which we learn only that she is leading an army against the Tartars to seek revenge for the death of her father the Emperor, is all of this kind:

> This day I'le prove the Injustice of that scorne
> Men treat our Sex withall, Woman is borne
> With equall thirst of Honour and of Fame
> But treacherous man misguides her in her aime
> Makes her believe that all her Glories lye
> In dull obedience, Truth and Modesty

and the ensuing dialogue with her new general Hyachian and her new ally Lycungus contains, as her answer to the information that the Tartars are about to attack, the incredible anti-climax:

> They meet my just Revenge and their own Fate
> And have the manners not to make mee waite.[9]

Can Rochester really have written that without tongue in cheek?

The scene develops with Lycungus, incensed at the preference given to Hyachian, plotting treachery and if necessary rape, refusing to fight, and, in an address to "Eternall God," pronouncing his judgment on women:

> If for a Blessing they were sent us, why
> Have you not given them one good quality?
> If for a Curse, how are you just or wise
> To lend em your own form for a disguise?

8. V. de Sola Pinto, in his edition of Rochester's *Poems* (London, 1953), p. 183, records also a rough draft of this scene and *Valentinian* in the Folger Library.
9. Pinto, *op. cit.*, pp. 62 (ll. 8-13), 63 (ll. 73-74).

In the final lines Hyachian tells of the bravery of the Empress and learns of the treachery of Lycungus and announces that

> Noe more shall Nations in distress and thrawll
> On helpless man for Aid in Battails call:
> This Woman's Valour is above us all.[10]

It may be doubted whether Rochester ever sent the scene to Howard; and Howard's own portion of the play does not survive. Yet he must have written some part of it and did not abandon the idea of completing it some day, for nearly twenty years later, when he and Dryden, both old men, had again come into friendly association, Dryden wrote to his sons in Rome: "After my return to town, I intend to alter a play of Sir Robert Howards, written long since, & lately put by him into my hands: 'tis calld The Conquest of China by the Tartars. It will cost me six weeks study, with the probable benefit of an hunderd pounds." Dryden's enthusiasm also lapsed in time, however. This letter was written on 3 September 1697; and in December he was telling Tonson "I have broken off my Studies from The Conquest of China, to review Virgil, and have bestowd nine entire days upon him."[11] Dryden's contribution to the ill-fated drama has also not survived. The play would indeed have been an odd patch-work if it had been completed; and yet a tragedy with serious contributions from Rochester and Dryden and the adapter of The Duke of Lerma would have been worth reading.

Perhaps in 1678 what put The Conquest of China out of Howard's mind was the event that replaced all others as an object of interest for most Englishmen—Titus Oates's revelation or pretended revelation of the Popish Plot; and on 30 October, in spite of illness, Howard took part in the debate following a report from the Committee which had examined Edward Coleman, Secretary to the Duchess of York, and one of the first to be accused by Oates. At a time when, according to Grey, the debate had fallen into "a great silence," Howard spoke up:

You have been told of a magistrate murdered [Sir Edmund Berry Godfrey], and it is disputed in every street, whether it was done by Papists, or others, and they have produced reasons for both: The discovery of that would set mens minds at ease—Five hundred pounds are offered in the Proclamation; it is a poor combination that cannot give 600 l. to stifle the discovery: I would have 5000 l. reward for him that shall discover the murderers, and

10. Pinto, pp. 66 (ll. 157-160), 69 (ll. 262-264).
11. Letters, ed. Ward, pp. 93, 97.

secured to him by this House, by Act of Parliament, and if he was an actor in it, a pardon; the money to be paid to him or his Executors—I have made a motion suitable to my infirmity, and I leave it to you.[12]

There was some sense in what he said, but the House did not accept the motion.

Perhaps because of his illness, but not necessarily for that reason, Howard does not seem to have taken part in the ensuing debates of the period of panic when anyone was likely to be regarded as a Papist —or a potential one—until on 18 November ridiculous charges were brought against Sir Joseph Williamson, Secretary of State, of having signed warrants for Popish officers to receive commissions and pay. Williamson's answer was, as well it might be, that he had simply countersigned the documents as they had come from the Secretary for War; and Howard once again tried to save the House from committing an absurd mistake because of its state of religious hysteria. He pointed out that the House ought to seek, if anybody, the person who advised the King to grant the commissions, and not make a victim of an innocent intermediary; it was "hard" that Williamson should even have to withdraw while the House considered his fate. Not only did Williamson have to withdraw, however; he was also sent to the Tower and would have remained there had the House had its way. Charles had more sense and discharged him before the House sent a second address "that he may not be discharged by your Majesty."[13] It will be evident, I think, from the number of times such things happened, that Howard was one of the few level-headed members of this contentious Parliament and, particularly when it came to times of panic, much less "positive" than those who claimed to be democratic and to take seriously the responsibility of looking after the morals of the nation.

The next debate in which he took part was that of 21 November, on the bill, sent down from the Lords, for disabling Papists from sitting in either House, with a proviso exempting the Duke of York from taking the Oaths of Allegiance and Supremacy and the Declaration. There was opposition to the proviso, whereupon Howard, not unreasonably, asked those concerned, "What will hold of all you have done, if the Crown come to him? What will become of you, if an exasperated Prince come to govern, though not of so great a spirit as

12. Grey, VI, 122-124.   13. *Ibid.*, VI, 217-226, 239, 271.

the Duke?" One wonders, however, whether many were impressed by his further argument: "We all respect his person, and may hope, that, when he sees his own temper so different from us, he will embrace that here which he will never find in the Popish religion." The proviso was agreed to, but only by 158 votes to 156.[14]

Howard must have thought his star was in the ascendant, however, when on 19 December it was decided to impeach Danby. If Howard's part in the proceedings was negligible, this was probably only from a sense of tactics. (There is no evidence to connect him with the events that led to the impeachment.) Briefly, the King gave orders for the seizure of the papers of Montagu, his Ambassador in France, on alleged information that Montagu had been in private conference with the Papal Nuncio there, and two letters were held to incriminate Danby, though they had in fact been written on the King's orders, requesting money from the French in return for an English foreign policy acceptable to France.[15]

Howard reported to Ormond the vote of the Commons for impeaching Danby but he commented on it only in general terms, and in connection with a disagreement with the Lords over payment of the Army:

You may judge how great a ferment everything is in; and, in the meantime, the condition of the King's revenue in so low an estate that it cannot brook delay. I wish there were such help as you might be to incline the King to consider what is best to be done; and not put anything to the hazard of great promises. I am confident the Parliament would give him that ease that is due to his excellent nature, and I cannot but wish that all interpositions, like so many eclipses, between him and them were removed. Your Excellency knows that I have been ever of this judgment, and want but assistance to show it; for never time so pressed for determination, and I fear all things but a Parliament will be but mean help to restore such breaches as are now made. . . .[16]

In the circumstances, this can only be regarded as specious, for Howard must have known that the King would not welcome the decision to impeach his chief minister. And although he had the sense not to take part in the debate on the articles of impeachment on 21 December (or in any other debate before the prorogation of Parliament on 30 December), he must have voted for the impeachment: on the

14. *Ibid.*, VI, 240-254.
15. *Ibid.*, VI, 337-348; Burnet, p. 338 and n.
16. *H.M.C.*, Ormonde MSS, N.S. IV, 281.

twenty-eighth Sir Stephen Fox wrote to Ormond that he himself had
been "dismissed the King's service . . . though all other members
in the same vote, who were said to be put out are not so, namely, Mr.
Solicitor, Sir Phi. Warwick, Sir Robert Howard, Sir Robert and Sir
John Holmes, and others";[17] and four days earlier Lord Herbert had
told his father that "for voteing against the Treasurer" both Fox and
Solicitor Warwick had lost their places "and which Sir Robert Holmes
and Sir Robert Howard had done if there had not been two comfort-
able words *durante vita* as they say in their Patents."[18]

Danby was impeached in the House of Lords on 23 December. The
articles recited that, among other crimes, he had "Traiterously en-
croacht to himself Regall Power, by treating in matters of Peace and
War with Forreign Princes and Embassadors," tried to alienate the
people from the King, and—what must have concerned Howard
most—

That he hath wasted the Kings Treasure, by Issuing out of his Majesties
Exchequer, and several Branches of his Revenues for unnecessary Pensions
and secret Services, to the vallue of 231602 l. within two years, and that he
hath wholly diverted out of the known Method and Government of the
Exchequer one whole Branch of his Majesties Revenue to private Uses,
without any account to be made to his Majesty in his Exchequer . . .
and he hath removed two of his Majesties Commissioners of that part of
the Revenue, for refusing to consent to his unwarranted actings therein,
and to advance mony upon that branch of the Revenue for private uses.[19]

With the pamphlet from which the above is quoted was published a
letter from Danby to Montagu of 25 March 1678 commanding him,
in the name of the King, to make peace proposals to France without
the knowledge of parliament.

Danby's main crime was, probably, to have acted as the King directed him to act; but the Commons were not likely to consider that
in his favor, and only the prorogation of Parliament by the King on
30 December saved him. It could not, however, prevent a pamphlet
war, which continued to rage throughout 1679 and 1680.

17. *Ibid.*, IV, 290.
18. *H.M.C.*, 12, App. IX, Beaufort MSS, p. 79.
19. *Articles of Impeachment of High Treason and other high Crimes* . . .
against Thomas Earl of Danby . . . *As they were delivered in to the House
of Lords in the name of the Commons of England, by Sir Henry Capel, December 23. 1678* . . . (London, 1678/9). The copy cited is in the Clark
Library, Los Angeles.

One does not know what part, if any, Howard played privately in drawing up the articles of impeachment; but in connection with the allegation that Danby had interfered with the Exchequer for his own gain, one incident in which Howard's name is mentioned may be cited. This is a law case of 1685 but referring to 1678 and arising out of the marriage of Danby's daughter to the son of Lord O'Brien.[20] It was claimed that the Duke of Richmond had assigned to others part of an order charged on the fee farms, and that one part of this had in turn been assigned to O'Brien, another to the appellants Francis Terrence and Martin Drynence; and in an appeal to the House of Lords in 1685, Terrence and Drynence alleged that Danby "and Mr. Bertie, knowing that Sir Robert Howard would not pay the money out of the Exchequer upon the order, unless satisfied that the assignees were discharged, contrived to pay it out of private service money, so that neither the Appellants nor Cox might learn that it was paid till after Lord O'Bryon was dead." The appellants further alleged that when they had petitioned the King in 1678, Danby had stifled the petition and prevented their receiving satisfaction. The story has a ring of truth about it, and perhaps Howard and others did know, or thought they knew, of unwarranted interference by Danby in Exchequer matters. Undoubtedly if there was one claim on which Howard and Danby would have disagreed more than any other, it was one connected, closely or not, with the family of Lady Honoria.[21]

However that may be, it is certain that the King did his best to protect Danby. Parliament was at first prorogued until 25 February and then, on second thoughts—or, gossip said, on the advice of Danby —dissolved on 24 January and a new election ordered for early February. Howard twice wrote to Ormond during this period, but did not choose to mention Danby directly. On 21 January he told Ormond:

. . . I have been extremely ill of the gout so that I have not seen the King since the Parliament rose. I hope I shall now be able, and am resolved to discharge my duty, there being no supporting the guilt of a conscience that shall punish me more for a neglected duty than one can be punished for performing it . . . and if I continue able to wait upon the King according to my design, I may perhaps be as early as any in my account; and I hope then your Excellency will contribute to the restoration and peace of a divided nation, which I hope yet to see perfected, and a

20. See above, chap. xiii, p. 204.
21. *H.M.C.*, 11th Report, Pt. 2, pp. 254-256.

happy understanding between the King and Parliament, all other notions being but the desperate counsels of State mountebanks.

Then, on 25 January, to a letter concerning Nell Gwyn's affairs (already cited in part), he added the news of the dissolution of Parliament, saying that Ormond would know what to think about this; and he concluded, "Had I a safe way I could give you some particulars, but I forbear to add more at present."[22]

In the new Parliament of 1679, Howard was elected member for a different constituency, Castle Rising, in Norfolk, which he continued to represent until his death (except for the Parliament of James II elected in 1685). Pepys, who had previously been one of the members for Castle Rising and now had to transfer to Harwich, felt that he had in some way been betrayed. On 1 February 1678/9, he wrote to Thomas Pepys that the new candidates for Castle Rising, Howard and Sir John Baber, "are both my honoured friends, and as far as any interest of mine may bestead them, I do readily resign it to them"; four days later, however, he told Sir John Werden that "by a letter this day come to my hand I find they [Baber and Howard] have (between them) done all they could to revive all my old charge of being a Papist, and the new one of having a hand in the late Plot."[23] It is only hearsay evidence, but electioneering propaganda was no cleaner then than now.

Before Parliament sat, the King issued to Danby a pardon under the Great Seal, dated 1 March, and on 16 March made him a Marquis. This only added to the ire of the Commons, and until the King again dissolved Parliament late in May, they continued their attacks. The debates mainly concerned methods of procedure, for Danby was committed to the Tower in April; and Howard now showed his hand and took part in the debates at every opportunity.

He first spoke in the new Parliament on 21 March, ostensibly on the subject of one Bedlow, who complained both that he had not been rewarded for discovering the murder of Godfrey and that his life was not safe from attack, because "a great person" had threatened him. Howard insisted that the great person be named, and of course Bedlow named Danby. On the following day the King agreed to pay Bedlow his £500 reward as requested by the Commons but now informed

22. *H.M.C.*, Ormonde MSS, N.S. IV, 308-309.
23. J. R. Tanner, ed., *Further Correspondence of Samuel Pepys 1662-1679* (London, 1929), pp. 340-341.

them that he had pardoned Danby and "I will give it him ten times over, rather than it should not be full and sufficient for the purpose I design it."[24]

Howard's position was difficult: he wanted to do the greatest possible harm to Danby (perhaps from a sincere conviction of his guilt), with the least possible offense to the King. He therefore delivered a long and roundabout speech, contrasting the days of the Civil War when it was easy to distinguish between the King's friends and enemies (his friends being "in dungeons and prisons") with the present time when men did ill and blamed the King for it, and continuing:

If we well know the Revenue, it is in the most deplorable condition that can be. . . . As to the Treasury-part, Lord *Clifford* [Danby's predecessor] was a great man, and he left it flourishing, and in good order, and I know the King might have been supported in his necessities. I was Secretary to the Treasury, and look upon that charge as upon myself. The Revenue was then clear, and had no charge, and it was the felicity of Sir *Thomas Osborne* [Danby] to come in so. . . .[25]

It was resolved to seek a conference with the Lords, and to sequester Danby from Parliament; and on 24 March an address was presented to the King about the "irregularity and illegality" of the pardon.

On the twenty-fifth, Danby resigned as Lord Treasurer and went into hiding, and for a few days the House turned to other topics. (Howard expressed the majority opinion in the examination of Titus Oates when he resented Oates's attitude and his language but encouraged his evidence.) Danby gave himself up on 15 April and was sent to the Tower. He was asked whether he wished to insist on his pardon or to plead to the charges against him; and when he returned an answer that was branded "equivocal," some members were for postponing consideration for a few days. This did not suit Howard: "In this case I would not lose a minute. . . . I would proceed upon what is clearly before you . . . it is a favour to him to know whether he will stand upon his Pardon, or any other Plea."[26] The debate was adjourned until 5 May, when the pardon was declared "illegal and void" and the Lords were asked to make formal judgment on Danby.

On the seventh, eighth, and ninth there was much wrangling about

24. Grey, VII, 11-19.
25. *Ibid.*, VII, "50-1" (that is, 34-35, sig. D1ᵛ and D2).
26. *Ibid.*, VII, 63-64, 68, 170-171.

methods of procedure, with Howard objecting strongly to the proposal of the Lords to bring Danby to Westminster Hall (it was unprecedented and "looks like a pageant") and arguing that the refusal of the Lords to confer with the Commons on the methods of proceeding was only a way "of saving him" and that a pardon such as that extended to Danby "will, at the root, destroy any Act of Parliament."[27]

The inquiry turned to the payment of the Secret Service money, on which Bertie was interrogated. He claimed rightly that he had accounted for it to the King and hoped he would not be commanded to disclose the King's secrets without his leave. Howard had to admit that, for reasons of security, Secret Service money was not normally accounted for in the Exchequer, but he managed to get in the criticism that "This very time the Warrants for secret service were procured by Lord *Danby*, and countersigned by himself. (He took up the Secretaries places; they had little to do)" and added that "no man is so unwise, but he will keep notes of what he does." This clearly influenced the House to its decision to commit Bertie for contempt for refusing to answer questions satisfactorily.[28]

A message from the King stating the urgency of "having a Fleet at sea this Summer" gave Howard another opportunity, eagerly taken, of discoursing on Danby's handling of the nation's finances:

The Exchequer has been managed in such an extravagant way, that the Nation is at the mercy of the Money-lenders, what to do with it. Had Common Law been observed in it, things had not come to this pass. There is not a 12d. due of the Revenue to find the King bread for a year.[29]

His animosity led him to speak again on the following day (the fifteenth) and again on the seventeenth expressing his fear (shared by the majority of the Commons) that if the Bishops voted upon the impeachment of Danby, he would be acquitted. He expressed this, of course, as a concern for correct procedure. Since, according to Burnet, it was only because the King insisted on their presence that the Bishops had not already withdrawn, Howard's stocks with his sovereign must

27. *Ibid.*, VII, 199-230.
28. *Ibid.*, VII, 228-236. Compare also p. 323.
29. *Ibid.*, VII, 271 (14 May). This speech is also referred to with approval by Sir John Reresby in his *Memoirs* [1634-1689] (London, 1734), pp. 93-94. Relevant also is B.M. Add. MS 28078, f. 319, a statement of the revenue as it was when Danby resigned on 25 March. Danby has endorsed it as the statement that Howard gave "to the Lords after his mending an error of 50,000 l. on the Customs. And as it was refuted by mee." See also below, pp. 227-234.

now have been at their lowest ever, although in a letter to Ormond on 24 May he still speaks as a friend of the King. There must certainly have been some wry smiles when on 26 May in a final debate on a question of the wording of "The Narrative of the Proceedings relating to the Tryals," Howard, speaking against the use of the word "injustice" to describe what was clearly to him the "evasiveness" of the Lords, actually said: "Had I the greatest enemy in the world, I would not provoke him with ill words: He has then the advantage of me."[30]

Danby, languishing in the Tower, could defend himself only with his pen, and he wrote to the King on 21 May regretting the wrong advice, concerning the revenue, given by the new Commissioners of the Treasury—and added that they could hardly be blamed since they were guided, and the King suffered, by "Sir Robert Howard's ignorance."[31] Charles himself could act, and did; with the provocation not only of the impeachment of Danby but also of the passing of the Exclusion Bill through two readings, he prorogued Parliament on 27 May and then dissolved it. Danby, however, remained in the Tower—remained there until 1684, and did not resume his seat in the House of Lords until 1685, when the Lords finally ruled that the impeachment had lapsed with the dissolution of Parliament.

The struggle was now carried on in print, beginning with *An Impartial State of the Case of the Earl of Danby, in a Letter to a Member of the House of Commons* (London, 1679). This pamphlet, pretending to be a letter to a friend of the author who had asked what was the truth about Danby, was anonymous but was obviously composed by Danby himself.

It begins by tracing Danby's career until he became Lord High Treasurer about midsummer 1673, and implies that he was chosen by Charles because of the understanding of problems of finance he had previously shown as Treasurer of the Navy; and it argues that he kept Charles "supplied," and this without imposing any additional taxes, at a time when it was widely believed that the nation's finances would be exhausted within six months. As further evidence of his financial genius, it is stated that although the Excise was farmed for three years at £530,000 per annum, Danby "found means to resume it" and let it immediately to the same farmers for £550,000, and then,

30. Grey, VII, 279-280, 285 and n., 342-343; *H.M.C.*, Ormonde MSS, N.S. IV, 113.

31. Cited by Browning, II, 83.

when that lease expired, won £600,000 a year from the Excise until parliamentary Acts (relating to brandy, etc.) reduced it. Conceding that something had to be let slip, the pamphlet claims that Danby was right to choose the private pensions, although these too were better paid than ever before; and it is argued that he could not possibly have spent the King's money on "Secret Service" as alleged, since there was nothing left to spend after more than eight million pounds had been paid out between Easter, 1673 and March, 1679.

In politics, we are told, Danby was ever for "diminishing of the French Interest among us," "was the Chief Instrument of procuring the Marriage of the Lady *Mary* to the Prince of *Orange*," and had refused bribes from France, although in writing official letters he had necessarily had to act as the King instructed him.

Danby is exonerated from blame in the murder of Godfrey and in the concealing of the Popish Plot; in his support it is claimed that he kept the King informed of all developments but was prevented by the King from taking further action on reports of the conspiracy. The pamphlet also insists, of course, that Danby is not of Papist sympathies.

The reply to Danby's pamphlet was *An Examination of the Impartial State of the Case of the Earl of Danby. In a Letter to A Member of the House of Commons* (London, 1680). This answer is confidently attributed to Howard by Danby's biographer, Andrew Browning. Danby *pretended* to believe that Howard was not the author; if Howard did not write it, however, he probably had a hand in its preparation.

The author of the *Examination* ascribes the earlier pamphlet to Danby and claims that it begs all the important questions. It asserts that any credit for the payments to the Navy, for instance, belongs to the Commissioners of the Navy and not to Danby, who was £2747/5/11 short in his accounts and applied this money to his own use, "and was forgiven it by a Privy-Seal, bearing date the 21 of *February*, 1676." It also asserts that while no Supply was actually voted in Danby's time, the sum of over a million pounds granted in the period of office of his predecessor Clifford was paid in Danby's, and the disposition of the second half of this determined by him. Other allegations include one that he "caused many sums of money to be paid by his private direction." It is said, on very doubtful reasoning, that no honor was due to Danby for promoting competition for the farming of the Customs, and that Clifford had preceded him in the "trick" of resuming the "Farm" and re-letting it for £600,000 per annum.

A major accusation is that Danby "practic'd most upon Tallies of Anticipation, the way that has been the great destroyer of the Revenue; which is done by a fictitious Bill thrown down by a Teller for Money, when really he has it not, and he discharged by a Tally instead of an Issue; which Issue is removed from being vouch'd by Record in the Exchequer; so that when 'tis paid, or when the Interest is paid, or what Interest is paid, never appears there; so that all the vouching lyes among those that deal in Money; and if they can but agree well, there is no fence against their Combinations." The interest in such cases cannot be checked, because it can begin from *any* date; "and when the Farmers or Contracters of the Excise have advanced great Sums, the Commissioners have by their Acquittances given Vouchers instead of Records, for the Commencement of the Interest; and I have heard, (nor is it improbable) that they were all very well acquainted."

A statement of the revenue as Clifford left it (dated 10 June 1673) and a letter from the then Cashier of the Customs, Mounteney, to Howard, allegedly then Secretary of the Treasury, are quoted and the pamphlet then concentrates on Danby's behavior in state affairs generally. He is accused of having attempted "the removal of every one that was not prostrate enough to him: he began with Sir *John Duncomb* and Sir *Stephen Fox*, men of most unquestioned worth in their Employments: then brought a Charge in the Council against Sir *Robert Howard* Auditor of the Receipt, the success of which is publickly known, and might questionless have been very well guessed by this Lord; but there were two great causes that blinded his Reason: his Son the Lord *Dunblain* had the Reversion of the Auditors place, and the removal of him [Howard] with the others, had reduced the Exchequer into his uncontradicted power." Danby is similarly accused of conspiring against Arlington and Coventry; and although he is willingly acquitted of complicity in the murder of Godfrey, he is not to be allowed to plead innocence in the negotiations with France: the French interest was anything but diminished in the days when Danby alone had influence with the King and would have been greater still had not Parliament stood firm.

To this the reply was a third pamphlet, *An Answer of the Right Honourable the Earl of Danby to a Late Pamphlet, Entituled, An*

Examination of the Impartial State of the Case of the Earl of Danby
(London, 1680). In this Danby begins by saying that he does not
know who wrote the *Examination*; no doubt ironically, he asserts
that he cannot believe it could have been anyone connected with the
Exchequer, for there are so many errors of fact in it. He states, for
example, that the sum alleged to have been missing from the Navy
accounts was given to him by the King; that more of the Eighteen
Months' Tax than was stated had already been assigned, and that the
receipts had been overestimated; and that the revenue for the five
and three-quarter years ending in March, 1679, had been much less
than the eight million alleged, "and by Sir *Robert Howard*'s State
thereof, for the year 75, (which is hereunto annexed) he tells you it
amounted that year to but six hundred fifty six thousand one hundred seventy two pound, clear to the Kings use." Other errors in
calculation are mentioned; and in the Secret Service "it will appear by
Sir *Robert Howard*'s Certificates, that the Examiner is as much mistaken in his Computation *of two hundred fifty two thousand four
hundred sixty seven pound, for Secret Service, in the space of two
years and 3 months*, there being no such sum in that time." In fact
the sum was for three years, and at least £57,000 of it was for public
uses. The rest, Danby ingenuously adds, is a sum so slight that it is
not worth worrying about.

He does score a point, however, when he quotes a recent letter
(18/3/'80) written to him by Sir Philip Floyd, assuring him that
Floyd gave no statement to the author of the *Examination* and reminding him "of a Paper which I [Floyd] have seen in your Lordships hands of better Authority than any thing that I can say: Which
is a state of the Revenue presented to your Lordship by Sir *Robert
Howard*, the *21ˢᵗ* of *June*, 1673, which was two days after you entered
upon your Office, wherein having stated the Income of Ordinary
Revenue and the Expences for that year by way of Debtor and Creditor,
he finds the Expence would exceed the Income by the Sum of 1163400 l.
and there is no doubt but Sir *Robert Howard*, who was furnish'd
with all the means of making a true Calculation did take care to do
so." Danby is also able to point out that the letter (cited in the
Examination) from Mounteney to Howard as Secretary of the Treasury could not have been written on 10 November 1673, because "Mr.
Bartie was then my Secretary, and not Sir *Robert Howard*."

Danby alleges that since part of the debt to the goldsmiths had been paid during his period as Treasurer, the King's debt had actually decreased during his term, in spite of all the demands made for the Navy and generally. Finally he asserts that the *Examination* is guilty not only of constant misrepresentation on the question of state affairs but also of not sparing the King for his alleged share in the negotiations with France, whereas Danby thinks better of his sovereign than that. (If he did, of course, he was simply mistaken!)

Howard now replied in person in a fourth pamphlet, the text of which is dated 13 October 1680 although the title-page has 1681.[32] It is *An Account of the State of his Majesties Revenue, As it was left by the Earl of Danby At Lady-day, 1679. In a Letter to a Friend. Occasioned by his Lordships Answer to An Examination of the State of the Case of the Earl of Danby. By the Honourable Sir Robert Howard.* As this title indicates, Howard follows the usual practice of pretending that he is writing to an uninformed friend who has asked him "to give you as clear Satisfaction as I could, of the matter of Fact, especially relating to the Difference of the Accompt . . . which as you justly say, depends on the large Deductions set down by my Lord of *Danby*, the Charge by Tallies being seemingly agreed to on both Sides."

Noting in passing that his name has been used by Danby "ingenuously sometimes," he explains his own circumstances and attitudes:

I had before now finished this, but the Sickness of my nearest Relations, and my long continuance at *Tunbridge-Wells* this Summer, hindred me from applying my self sooner to what I resolved upon. Besides, I could not till now obtain Certificates, from such places, as were to be the sure Proofs of what I should assert; being careful to set down nothing, but what I had Vouched from the Office or Records, to which it related; not desiring to meddle with Politique Disputes, nor to endeavour to support Reason or Matter of Fact with undecent Expressions.

In detail, he comments on each of the questions discussed by Danby. Only Danby, he says, knows whether he used or kept the £2747/5/11 from the Navy accounts; but he does maintain that Danby's estimate of the revenue was wrong. He can find no record that Clifford left any charges on the fourth quarter and thinks it very improbable that

32. In Narcissus Luttrell's copy, at Harvard, the date "1681" is altered in ink to "1680.3.Nov.". Luttrell received his copy "gratis"; and he has annotated it "Ag^t ye Earl of Danby shewing how he hath misimploy'd the Kings revenue."

he could have done so. The Customs, he affirms, *were* larger in Danby's period of office, if only because during time of war the English merchant ships were "the Carriers to most parts of the World." Unfortunately unable to resist a hit at Danby personally, he adds both that "Tis . . . very true, that Mr *Charles Duncombe* did often complain to me at the Exchequer, That my Lord *Danby* did hinder and divert the Money from being paid into the Exchequer, according as the Act of Parliament did direct" and that while money in the Exchequer can be issued only under the Great or the Privy Seal, Secret Service funds particularly can be afterwards distributed by "Private Letters or Directions"—and some of these funds were in this way applied by Danby "to other uses."

On the important question of the Tallies, he agrees that the interest is subject to audit; but the *only* evidence for the auditor is the private "voucher"—and this is why the present Commissioners of the Treasury have ordered that all must now be properly recorded in formal Exchequer documents, "and no Combination of Private persons in this Method can defraud the King." Moreover—and Howard surely wins this round:

By what has been said . . . it appears, the *Weekly Certificates* in the Exchequer cannot be Proofs for Moneys dispos'd by *Talleys* of *Anticipation*: but my Lord *Danby* has been pleased to say the Cause is, That he has had out of the Exchequer some of those Certificates which have not been true, and that to the Mistake of Ten or Twelve thousand pounds in one week. I cannot imagine what my Lord means by this; for I suppose, had it been really so, I have not had so great a share in his Lordships favour, but that he would have made it appear in a more proper place, if he could have made good any such thing as is pretended.

Howard is clearly right when he asserts, against Danby, that the farming of the Excise, Customs, and Hearth-duty is wrong in principle, if only because of the "many Frauds and Bargains, that are this way sheltered" (but Howard's principles must have changed since the days when he wished to be a farmer of the Customs himself!) He seems to be on reasonably safe ground in his peroration:

And his *Majesty* I doubt not but remembers, that I gave him often notice of my apprehensions, how much the Revenue was like to suffer, by the way of *Management*; and therefore my *Proposition* to the King, to find a *Weekly Credit*, was to help pay off all Tallies, and to bring the *Government of the Kings Revenue by Specie into the Exchequer*; in which those

Frauds that had been committed, would infallibly have been avoided. Which is quite contrary to what my Lord *Danby* mentions, p. 12 *of putting the Three great Branches into the hands of Undertakers*; and a thing I never thought of. But the *Propositions* I presented to the King, I offered to prove, and could have made good, if he had thought it for His Service; which I can make appear by Men of the greatest Quality, if required of me; and to evidence that 'twas my constant judgment, *that Tallies of Anticipation would be the ruine of the Revenue*, I presented to my Lord *Danby* at Windsor, not long after he received the *Staff*, my thoughts of it; and how it was at that time in his Lordships power, to place it in the *right way of Management*; upon which he commanded me to put it in Writing, which accordingly I did; and in that *Paper* there appeared to be no difficulty, but upon the Debt due to Sir *Stephen Fox* by Tallies on the Excise, to whom I was commanded by his Lordship to impart the *Scheme*; who seeing it for the *Kings Service*, freely consented to receive his Debt by the week, by which means the *Revenue* might have been reduc'd to that way of *Management*, as would have hindred many disadvantages to the *King*, which since that has hapned.

Howard presents certificates from responsible officers in support of his figures, and calculates that the charge on the revenue as left by Danby was in fact something over two million pounds. It is still no doubt true that a deficit was inevitable and that Danby, more than any other man, had kept it within reasonable limits. Howard's pamphlet would have been better had he admitted this; as it is, it is not only scrappy and not very well written, but also, for part of the time, in the wrong tone.

It was, then, possible for Danby to reply, and he did so in the fifth pamphlet of the controversy, *The Earl of Danby's Answer to Sr. Robert Howard's Book, Entituled An Account of the State of his Majesties Revenue; as it was Left by the Earl of Danby at Lady-Day, 1679.* (London, 1680). He did not have all the better of the argument; indeed he shared Howard's ability to put himself sometimes in the wrong even when he was intellectually right.

He begins by saying that he could almost thank Howard for his pamphlet, in that he has made no new charges, has confined himself to the question of the state of the Revenue (which need not necessarily have been the Treasurer's fault), and has made some concessions:

insomuch that were it not for some expressions not so becoming a mans own Secretary to be guilty of, and that the time of publishing his Book hath not been so generously taken, as some men of Honour would have done, I should not only have forgiven but have thanked Sir *Robert* for the opportunity of clearing the integrity of my management in the Treasury, however I may have been wanting in those abilities which God hath given to himself above other men: And he ought not to blame me, but my understanding, if I could not always comprehend such Schemes and Projects of his concerning the Revenue, whereof I have some still in my custody, which I must acknowledge I do not yet understand, any more than I did when I first received them.

The first clauses are fair enough, but the gibe at Sir Positive is not; and perhaps Sir Thomas Osborne ought to have been less certain that his own financial understanding was greater than that of the protégé of the great City financiers Morris and Clayton.

Danby again puts himself in the wrong by questioning Howard's reasons for delaying his book: if Howard's relatives were not in good health, Danby quips, apparently Howard himself was. He is more convincing when he points out that Howard at least had access to the relevant documents, which are not available to one in prison. Nevertheless he believes that Howard's financial statements are full of error and that the certificates reproduced with them give true answers to wrong questions.

Danby comes closer to a legitimate defense when he pleads that Howard sought the wrong kind of statement concerning the Ordnance and Excise: what Howard ought to have obtained was a statement not only of the money the Excise and Ordnance had in hand but also of the lessening of the charges on those departments, by payment. Accordingly Danby produces a new set of calculations based on Howard's figures, as now adjusted, and his own, and reckons that the total increase in the deficit was only £158,521/7/0 over a period of five and three-quarter years, during which Parliament granted no Supply except for special purposes.

He disclaims responsibility for the payments falling due to the Fleet since his resignation; and so reduces Howard's charges of misappropriation against him to the £2,747 which, he repeats, was actually given to him. Previous Treasurers had made fortunes; he had always insisted on public inquiry into charges of fraud: "so that since the blame can only be laid upon my management (who could be no wiser than God had made me) and not upon any corrupt actings in my employment; I do not only willingly undergo Sir *Roberts* Rebukes, but do acknowledge my own failings, and hope that by Sr

Roberts good Advice his Majesty will for the future be served as he ought to be."

He agrees with Howard that Tallies of Anticipation are to be avoided if possible;

but that the Revenue must be ruined by them, I deny; or that the Interest is left to any such uncertainty as he would have believed; but that it must be by the knavery of the Lord Treasurer, Chancellor of the Exchequer, or the sworn Auditor of the Exchequer (before whom the Account is brought) if the King be wronged in what Interest he pays upon such Tallyes . . . nor do I know how it can be helpt, unless Sir *Robert* can be able to do more by his Legislative Capacity for remedy of the matter, then he will ever be able to do by his private; and if this be now the Case, as well as it was in my time, then by Sir *Roberts* rule *the Exchequer will still be no wiser than it hath been in knowing when Interest is to commence upon such Tallyes.*

This, of course, is an oversimplification, as Howard could easily have told him; and when Danby adds that the private vouchers should themselves be audited, he is not contradicting Howard at all.

Danby asks in conclusion that he should not be believed guilty till proved so and expresses his confidence (unfortunately misplaced) that he will soon be restored to favor:

And since Sir *Roberts* friend (to whom he writes) had no curiosity to enquire into those other parts of the Examiners Book which concerned the affairs of State therein mentioned, I shall repeat nothing upon that Subject, but conclude that his friend is satisfied in those matters, which are of much the greatest Concern to me; but I hope it will be taken notice of, that both the Examiner and Sir *Robert* (how much soever they may be strangers to one another) have carried on the same design against me, as if it had been with the same hand; saving that Sir *Robert* has shewed himself to be the better Accomptant, by rectifying divers Errors in the Examiners Computations, and that he has been much more civil than the Examiner in his Language.

I think it important to note that, as in the controversy with Dryden, Howard had enough good sense to know when it was pointless to say more. There, so far as he was concerned, the matter rested; and he seems to have taken no part in the new outbreak of pamphlet warfare when Danby applied for bail in 1682. Danby himself was less wise and in his old age, in 1710, republished in book form the pamphlets he and Howard had written, as *Memoirs relating to the Impeachment of Thomas Earl of Danby (now Duke of Leeds) in the year 1678*—with some discreet omissions and even occasional alteration.[33]

33. The preceding account of the pamphlet warfare is confined to the pamphlets thought to have been written by Howard and Danby themselves. There were many others. One J. B., for example, published *Some Reflections Upon the Earl of Danby* accusing him of complicity in the murder of Sir Edmund Berry Godfrey; to this Edward Christian replied; and then there was a reply to the reply; and yet another, *An Explanation of the Lord Treasurer's Letter to Mr Montagu*, tried to absolve both him and the King by arguing that the Secretaries of State were aware of the peace proposals and asked the King to make approaches to France.

Chapter fifteen. MINOR PERSONAL AND OFFICIAL
PROBLEMS, 1679-1685; AND *THE LIFE AND*
REIGN OF KING RICHARD THE SECOND

THAT Howard did not incur the lasting ill-will of the King even
during the Danby controversy is suggested by one or two grants made
to him in these years. On 6 May 1679 as Auditor he petitioned the
King "to order the Lords Com[rs] of the Treasury for paym[t] of w[t] shall
appeare by Certificate from the officers of the works to be unpaid for
the building his house, and alsoe for making such allowances to him
for his care & pains in making and keeping Registers & other extraordinary Books of the Taxes granted in his time, as hath been allowed
his Predecessors for like Services."[1] It was the kind of request that
Charles was continually receiving from his officers and granting if
he could,[2] and it was treated in the usual way: "His Maj[ty] being well
satisfyed with the Pet[rs] constant and faithfull Services is graciously
pleased to referre the consideration of this Petition to the Rt. Hon[ble]
the Lords Com[rs] of the Treasury."[3] The outcome was no doubt the
order of 28 July for payment to Howard of £745/4/0.[4] Where Howard had the advantage was that he could make sure that the grant
was charged on a particular source of revenue and paid: and the
Treasury directed that his £745/4/0 was "to be hereby satisfied by
tallies on Anthony Rowe *et al.* on their half-year's Hearthmoney farm
rent due Sept. 29 next."[5] Probably resulting from the same petition was
the order made on 2 January 1679/80, and thereafter annually, for
£200 to be paid to him "for extraordinary services performed by him
and his clerks in the office of the Auditor of the Receipt."[6]

Another petition that proved more complicated was one he made
on 12 July 1679 for the "title to the manors of Bridston and Upton in
the Hundred of Wirrall, Cheshire." On the advice of the Attorney-
General, the Treasury Lords recommended that since the lands had

1. P.R.O., S.P. 44, Entry Book 55, p. 13.
2. Florence R. Scott, *P.M.L.A.*, LII, (1937), p. 1097, seems to have misunder-
stood the petition.
3. S.P. 44, Entry Book 55, p. 13.
4. *C.T.B.*, 1679-1680, p. 152.   5. *Ibid.*, p. 789 (1 March 1679/80).
6. *Ibid.*, p. 389; 1681-1685, 7, 674, 1027.

long been out of the King's actual possession and had yielded no profit to him, the petition should be granted, with a reservation of part of the rent.[7]

The title that Howard sought in this petition must, I think, be the one discussed soon afterwards in the correspondence of the Paston family. On 21 December 1679, a Sunday, the Countess of Yarmouth's agent Taylor wrote to her telling her that one Steel had entered a caveat against the granting to Howard of the title to certain lands. Steel said that he had bought the estate from the Earl of Derby (who himself renounced the title and claimed only "a remaynder at Domesday Q^{r}"); Taylor accused Steel of "oppression and Fraud," demanded to know how much he had paid Derby and whether he did not know that "the Estate was in the King." The King solved it all by giving special orders to the Lord Chancellor to affix his seal to Howard's patent on the following Monday; and so Taylor tells the Countess very proudly, "I have saved you 5 ginneys in Sr Roberts hands wch hee would have given to m^{r} sollicit^{r} to noe purpose wch I hope you will send for them for mee to gett those other Records ready to avoyd any Scrupell or Doubt."[8] This enables us to date confidently on the same day, 21 December 1679, an undated letter from Howard to the Countess:

Madame

When I waited on my Lord Chancellor yesterday morninge I found the Patent was not brought engrost from the Pattent office, and that-morninge alsoe A Caveat was putt in from Steel. my Lord therefore tooke the opportunity to send word that the pattent was to be brought to the seale to-morrow in the afternoone; and then any one from m^{r}. Steel might be heard; but told mee privately that the king had been soe kind to mee as to Commaund him what-ever pretentions or Caveats there was to seale it; for who-ever opposd it I should have his title, and accordingly my Lord promist to seale it on munday in the afternoone, but for forme sake woud appoint Steel an houre, after this I tooke care and sent away Taylor to the Pattent office with my Lord Chancellors Recepe; soe that it will not faile I hope to be seald [word erased] to morrow in the afternoone; of which you shall not faile to have notice, this is the full account at present which can be given yor La^{p} from

Madame
yo La^{p}'s
most humble and faithfull
Servant
Ro: Howard

7. C.S.P.D., 1679-1680, p. 195; C.T.B., 1679-1680, 249.
8. B.M. Add. MS 27447, f.443.

[P.S.] my wife presents her humblest servise to yor La^p and hopes my writinge will excuse hers.⁹

Whatever Steel's rights may have been, it seems that he had little chance against this kind of autocracy. There was, however, another objection, from an unexpected quarter. The consent of the Dean and Chapter of Chester had to be obtained; and Taylor, fearing that Steel might attempt to bribe them, sought and was given the permission of the Countess to go to Chester himself and see what he could do. He went, and was not well received.

At this stage, the Earl of Yarmouth obviously used his influence with the Dean and Chapter on Howard's behalf, for on 6 June 1680 Howard wrote to the Earl from Mitcham, in Surrey:

My Lord
 Y^r letter found mee in such a confused condition by ye dangerous sickness of my wife, that I am not able to write more then that I readily promise fourty pounds or if you please more shall be setled on ye church of Chester for ever whatever y^r Lord^pp undertakes for me in y^t affaire concerning ye graunt of ye Estate possest by mr Steele shall be made good by my Lord y^r Lord^pps

most faithfull & humble
servant
Ro: Howard

There is a postscript "pardon ye confusion I am in that can write noe larger butt what you doe I will make good" and Yarmouth has added a formal signed statement undertaking that Howard will pay the £40 a year "for ever."¹⁰

The bribe—if it was that—worked, for on 27 June the Dean and Chapter of Chester wrote to Yarmouth accepting the offer:

We having understood . . . your gracious inclination and promise of setling fourty pounds per annum for ever upon our poor Cathedrall (out of the lands now possessed by Mr Steele, when recovered from him by Sr Robert Howard or your selfe) doe in this paper returne your lo^p ye most humble and hearty thanks of the said Dean and Chapter.

They add, however, mention of "our feares that Mr Tailor (who hath taken a great deal of paines to trouble both himself and us) hath miserably mistaken his Groundwork, as our counsell does informe us"

9. B.M. Add. MS 27447, f.311.
10. B.M. Add. MS 27447, f. 460 (a copy, only, of Howard's letter).

and they assure Yarmouth that they "have alwayes disowned and discouraged his [Taylor's] intermedling with ye affayres of our Church."[11] It must have been poor consolation to Taylor that he received a separate letter from his friend the Dean regretting that he could not prevail on the Chapter to omit from the letter to Yarmouth one expression "which I believe would not be pleasing";[12] Steel's only consolation can have been the realization that in this company he was hopelessly outgunned from the start.

During the period of these minor trials, Howard wrote several letters to Ormond concerning the major problems, of the second dissolution of Parliament in May, 1679, and the King's illness. Of the former he wrote on 15 July predicting, correctly, that the new Parliament "will be most the same" and that the King's readiness to dissolve hostile parliaments would more probably breed displeasure than compliance; "and," he adds, "the effect of that may be a demand of a prefixed time of sitting, which is the greatest shake to the prerogative, and was the fatal acquisition of that Parliament that built a civil war upon the Triennial Bill. But I will hope the best, and since there is no salvation but by the love of the King and his happiness, 'tis reasonable to believe that argument joined to that fatal memory will quiet all loyal minds from letting their resentments overrule their reason and experience."[13] Of the King's serious illness a month later he wrote with genuine sympathy:

On Monday last I went to Windsor and found the King newly out of a fever. . . . In the morning, being Tuesday, I was with him two hours and found him so well that it overjoyed us all . . . on Thursday I returned to Windsor, where I found the King had a fit on Tuesday night, but lessened. . . . Wednesday he continued well . . . on Thursday I waited on him and found him continue so, and I left him yesterday being Friday, in a perfect restored condition. . . . I find that both city and country were sensible how much depended on his well being. I hope it will make such an impression that all will tend to good and to a happy accommodation between the King and Parliament, which is not only the wishes but I hope will be the zealous endeavours of all good men. I believe the King has contributed much to his recovery by that extraordinary calm temper that he has shewed in all his sickness, and in those fits, which are of great pains and uneasiness, he never changed from that calmness that he had in health.[14]

11. f.463.   12. f.465.
13. H.M.C., Ormonde MSS, N.S. V, 155-156.
14. Ibid., V, 193-194 (27 Aug. 1679).

Again, on 12 November, after the King had prorogued the new Parliament more than once, before it could transact any business, Howard told Ormond of the alleged plots against the lives of the King and Shaftesbury—adding somewhat incongruously that if Sir Robert Peyton were "burned with the Pope" as seemed probable, "it may be a motive to induce all persons to hate unbecoming violences." He did see, however, that the King would be wiser to call Parliament together: "I fear that if the King depends to subsist by his own revenue without further help, he will be deceived in that opinion." Money voted by previous parliaments would soon come to an end; and there was no limit to the calls on the revenue.[15]

Another of Howard's letters about this time was written, unexpectedly enough, to Samuel Pepys. Howard had been approached by a Mr. Wormell who, as Howard explains:

had been the officiate under Dr Outram heer in Westminster these many yeares, and has now desird mee to make it my request to you for your favour to him in the enclosd particular, wch I causd him to write; as I promisd him I have now presented it with my desires in his behalfe, if noe other more weighty obligation lies upon you; wch I submitt to you and remain S^r

yor most faithfull & humble servant
Ro: Howard.[16]

Wormell wanted Pepys to support a former naval chaplain, a Mr. Wells, for a living, in the mistaken belief that Pepys had obtained one for him before. In his reply to Howard, Pepys corrects the misunderstanding but says he will offer his support if Wormell still wishes him to do so and thinks it of value.[17] One has the impression that the two men, Howard and Pepys, not now friends, are trying to do the decent thing that others may not suffer.

This brief exchange of letters may, however, have given Pepys the courage to use Howard's name when he did seriously need help himself. In May, 1679, Pepys was imprisoned in the Tower, until such time as he should be formally tried on charges of treason, including the charge brought by the notorious adventurer, "Colonel" John Scott, that he had conspired to sell to France maps of the coast of England. The servants of Charles, Earl of Berkshire (who had died in Paris in 1679) gave Pepys written statements that they had heard Scott say to

15. *Ibid.*, V, 237-238.
16. Bod. Rawl. MS A181, f. 41.   17. Bod. Rawl. MS A194, f.47.

the Earl, when the latter suggested that a map should be sold to the
King of England, that he had a better buyer;[18] and Pepys then wrote
to a kinsman of Berkshire and Howard, namely Gray of Stanford,
asking him to give Howard any relevant information about Scott's
duplicity. Gray eventually replied to Pepys, from Paris, on 18 September 1680:

> Thogh I have ye honour to be very nerely related to Sr Robert Howard
> as Cosen Germaine, yet my long absence from England has depriv'd me of
> ye happines of being so well knowne to him as my nearnesse of blood requires or as by inclination I have allwayes desird. so y^t w^t would have
> been before a presumption in me to have acquir'd his acquaitance
> by way of Letter, is now become a duty seeing y^u are pleas'd to desire it of
> me upon so just an account as to cleare ye innocent. . . . assure y^rselfe
> y^t I should have had no difficulty to have obey'd y^r commands in this particular to any person w^tever, much more y^u may Imagine to one of y^t worth
> & honour as my Cosin Sr Robert Howard. I here send you w^t I write w^th
> a flying seale to ye end y^t you may see it, & I wish from my hart it may
> prove as serviceable to you as I intend it. . . .[19]

The enclosure, addressed to Howard, was not sent on. In it Gray
tells Howard that justice demands that Pepys be cleared of the accusations Scott has made against Pepys and others in England. Gray himself has been "soe unfortunate" as to see Scott often in Paris and can
vouch for his villainy. Scott not only showed him the map in question but also said he had drawn it himself, had already received an
offer for it from the "Prince de Condy," and was having the information
on it translated into French to get a better price for it.[20] Fortunately the
charges against Pepys had been finally withdrawn in June, a few months
before he received Gray's letter and the enclosure to Howard. (There
was no evidence to support the charges; and Pepys's former servant
John James confessed on his deathbed that he had committed perjury
when he accused his master of Popery.) Had the occasion not been
so very serious for Pepys, one could almost find it in one's heart to
wish that he *had* needed the letter: it would have been pleasant to see
Howard making amends, however indirectly, for one or two of the
things he had said against Pepys in the House of Commons.

Howard's main interest during these months when Parliament
was not sitting must have centered on the purchase of his new home,

18. Bod. Rawl. MS A188, f.268, 270, 272.
19. Bod. Rawl. MS A188, f.280.   20. *Ibid.*, f.278.

the manor of Ashtead in Surrey. He bought the estate in 1680 from Henry Howard, Duke of Norfolk,[21] and built on it a new house which is described in detail by Evelyn, recording a visit on 10 May 1684:

I went to visite my Brother in Surry, caled by the Way at Ashstead where Sir Robert Howard Auditor of the Exchequer entertain'd me very civily at his newly built house, which stands in a very sweete-park upon the downe, the avenue south though downe hill to the house exceedingly pleased me: The house is not greate but with the out-houses very convenient: The staire Case is painted by *Verrio* with the storie of *Astrea,* amongst other figures is the picture of the Painter himselfe, and not unlike him; The rest well don; onely the Columns did not at all please me; There is also Sir Roberts owne picture in an Oval, the whole in fresca: there is with all this one greate defect, that they have no Water save what is drawne with horses from an exceeding deepe Well. Hence I went to Wotton that night.[22]

The house was pulled down in 1790 (and the site is now occupied by a school); but F. E. Paget records that "the stair-case has been described to the writer by one who knew it in her childhood, as made of oak, handsomely carved in the fashion of the time. She also remembers the fresco-paintings, broken up when the house was pulled down, and the plaster on which they were painted, being scattered over the fields, as a top-dressing of lime rubbish."[23] One portrait of Howard, by Kneller, was still in the new house (which replaced Howard's original home) when Paget published his book in 1873, but it seems to have disappeared since.

Paget also records that Howard built an "Island Pond," to remedy the lack of water of which Evelyn complained, and planted extensively. (A famous lime-tree "supposed to be the finest in England" and said by local tradition to have been planted in commemoration of a visit paid by the Prince of Orange, lasted until 1871, when it was blown down in a gale.)[24]

Howard would seem to have entertained extensively at Ashtead; and perhaps to improve the approaches he sought and was granted in July 1681 a special license "to enclose the highway from Ebisham

21. B.M. Add. MS 6167 ("Symmes's Collections for Surrey"), f.49. I think Florence R. Scott is mistaken in connecting the purchase of Ashtead with the petition to the King on 6 May 1679.
22. *Diary,* IV, 376-377.
23. *Some Records of the Ashtead Estate,* p. 66.
24. Paget, p. 67, citing "the local newspaper of Jan. 17, 1871."

[Epsom] to Ashtead, Surrey, and instead thereof to lay out another highway."[25]

During the summer of 1680, however, he was mostly at Tunbridge-Wells, probably because of his wife's illness; and apparently he spent his spare time composing a different kind of literary work again, for in November, 1680, there is mention in the Term Catalogues (I. 417) of his new book, *The Life and Reign of King Richard the Second. By A Person of Quality*. (Although it bears the date 1681 on its title page, it must have been published in the previous year.)[26] Howard's authorship was finally acknowledged in 1690, when his name was printed on the title page of his *History of the Reigns of Edward and Richard II* (which incorporates this earlier life of Richard II, as revised for the second time).[27]

It was natural enough that Howard should be interested at this time in the story of another King of England who had planned to rely on the help of a foreign monarch rather than on an unco-operative Parliament that accused him of wasting money granted to him. On the whole, however, there is surprisingly little comment on the story of Richard, and the reader—wisely—is often left to draw his own parallels and conclusions. Howard shows few of the gifts of the distinguished historian and—although he seems to have read Shakespeare —does not give a fully convincing portrait of the character of Richard himself; but the history is readable, is modestly presented, and shows an appreciation of the value of original sources, even if Howard went to no particular trouble to find them.

The preface "To the Readers" claims only that "the *Compiler* (for he as little *affects*, as deserves the *Title* of an *Author*)" has set down fact as found in "the *best Authors*, without obtruding his own *Fancies* or *Dreams* under the Notion of *History*." He mentions two sources in particular: Henry Knighton's *De Eventibus Angliæ* (in *Historiæ Anglicanæ Scriptores Decem*), described as a contemporary account of Richard's life until 1395; and Thomas Walsingham's *History*, covering the years 1273-1422. "To these cheifly is the present work Indebted, and in most *material passages*, they are Cited, and their *very words*

25. *C.S.P.D.*, 1680-1681, p. 358. Compare E. W. Brayley, *A Topographical History of Surrey* (London, 1841), IV, 393.

26. A copy in the Rare Book Collection of the Library of the University of Texas once belonged to, and bears the autographs of, Hurd and Robert Browning.

27. See below, chap. xvii.

strictly Translated, yet still not omitting to consult other the most credible Historians that have wrote of those times."

After giving a few facts about Richard's birth and youth, and announcing that he inherited his mother's beauty rather than his grandfather's "Prudence" or his father's "Spirit and Conduct," the history soon becomes rather episodic, and there are digressions and occasional side-comments that quickly make it clear that *this* author has no Papist sympathies. Narrating, for example, that Richard had to pay for eternal prayers for the soul of Haule, slain at mass in Westminster Abbey, Howard adds "though one would have thought dying, in their Opinion, a Martyr, he might have had no great *need* of such everlasting *Orisons*"; and the story of Wat Tyler's rebellion gives him occasion to praise "that good man" Wyclif, who was wrongly blamed for it: although "*all Papists* so furiously condemn him to this day as a *wicked Heretick*, . . . we justly own him as one of the first and most eminent *Authors* of the Reformation in Doctrine." Howard's treatment of the rebellion is interesting evidence of his political beliefs: he sees that Richard had given provocation enough by imposing unjust taxes and by spending money on pleasure and corruption, thereby making himself contemptible in the eyes of his subjects, but Tyler's demands for equality are branded "extravagant" and there is not a word of blame for the revocation of the pardons granted to the peasants or for the execution of Ball.

Richard's great fault is seen as his fondness for minions such as Suffolk (the suspicion of homosexuality is mentioned, though Howard would rather not "charge an *English Prince* with such a *detestable suspicion*"). It is related that when Parliament demanded the expulsion of Suffolk, Richard threatened to do without Parliament and rely on the King of France, but he was reminded that he could be deposed if he did not govern according to law. (Howard's political theory here corresponds exactly with his practice in the Revolution of 1688.) Richard gave in, and Suffolk was impeached; but he and other minions were soon back in favor with a King whose "*Youth* and *Weakness* rendred him too much disposed for such Impressions" (p. 94). Howard does not, however, claim to be positive about everything; "it seems" that the Judges "proceeded against their Consciences" in answering the questions proposed to them by the favorites; and the Citizens offered to let troops into the city "whether more out of *Fear* or *Love*, I cannot say."

The struggle between King and Parliament in 1388 is naturally given special attention. Howard relates that Parliament met in 1388 "though the King used many means to *dash* or *defer* the same"; and he gives in full, translated into English (he says for the first time) from Knighton, the articles of impeachment of these earlier royal favorites—and predecessors of Danby? Again any such inference is the responsibility of the reader; but it may be significant that Richard is not given nearly enough credit for his humanity in having sentences of hanging, drawing and quartering altered to beheading, and in having the judges banished instead of executed.

It is the weakness of Howard's book that, in the tradition of the annalists, he gives as much attention to a story of how a young woman in London acted as the celebrant at Mass or to the alleged prodigy of fighting swarms of gnats on one of the King's manors, as to the King's insistence, when he attained his majority, on appointing his own officers and seizing the liberties of the city—restored on payment of a fine of £10,000. A certain wisdom, however, is apparent again in some of the comments—such as the one on the common people, "who though sometimes they may be deceived by *Finesses* and *Craft*, are yet generally *shrewd Guessers* at *Right* and *Wrong* in Matters of *Fact*, and *Transactions of common life*."

The growing tyranny of the King (who is held personally responsible for the murder of Gloucester, among others) and the hopelessness of the situation when Parliament was controlled by the royal favorites Bushy, Bagot and Green, are well shown; but Howard maintains that such a state of affairs could not last long, for "there is still an *over-ruling Providence* that can *blast all Projects*, though never so *subtlely laid*, if not founded on *Equity*, and carried on with *Justice*" (pp. 164-165). So he comes to the well-known story of the banishment of Mowbray and the Duke of Hereford, and gives *"the most probable account thereof*, that I can meet with"; this means making Mowbray the villain, who misrepresented Hereford to the King, and whose death exactly twelve months after giving the order for the murder of Gloucester is a cautionary instance of poetic justice.

The case against Richard is shown to have become stronger every day: English possessions were lost, England was invaded by the Scots, and money that had been exacted from the English people was wasted on the private pleasure of the monarch, so that he "became first hated, and afterwards contemptible, and drove many of his Subjects to an Inclination to Revolt, as resolved rather to run the hazzard of a speedy ruine by Rebellion, than to perish by such a lingring Death of slavery." (I would point out again the parallel with the later situation of 1688.)

Hereford is presented as a splendid tactician, who gave it out when he returned to England that he was seeking to regain only his Duchy of Lancaster and measured his steps carefully before marching first on London, where he was well received, and then west. The execution of Bushy and Green is seen as "Politick" even if it had not been also just, "for partly because it was so grateful to the People; and partly because it excluded all hope of the Kings Pardon; It became a great ingagement to all the Dukes followers, to adhere more firmly to him for the future." (Howard was to see it differently in later years, as an illustration of the way "new-gotten *Power* is commonly endeavour'd to be preserv'd by Destruction.")[28]

Richard's losing of the advantage by his dilatoriness and weakness is adequately related, followed by the acceptance of his "resignation" by Parliament and the unanimous granting of Lancaster's claim to the vacant throne. Howard even prints in black letter the terms of Richard's renunciation of the Crown: "Thus far the Record, word for word Translated out of the *Latine* and *French*, and the *English* recited in the Old Words, and obsolete spelling as it stands in the Rolls remaining in the Tower, the same being attested to have been Examined and found to agree therewith" (p. 236). Richard, he adds, had outlived his honor, but he is exonerated from blame for such rebellions as those of Aumerle against the new King.

Howard does not know which of the accounts of Richard's death is correct: the story that he was deliberately starved "seems wholly fabulous," the tradition that Exton slew him on a hint from Henry IV "likewise seems a little Romantick," there is no evidence to support Walsingham's version, that Richard "voluntarily starved himself," and the Scottish tradition that Richard escaped from prison, lived "divers years" and is buried in Stirling, must be wrong, because

28. *Historical Observations upon the Reigns of Edward I.II.III. And Richard II* (1689), p. 157.

the body of Richard was shown in St. Paul's with the face exposed. "So different," he concludes weakly, "is the Report of Fame touching this *unhappy* Prince's *exit* out of the World, who lived therein about 33 years, and *Reigned* 22 years and 3 months."

I do not suppose that Howard knew of the famous earlier occasion when a version of the history of Richard II had been played at the instigation of a group of rebels in the hope that it would provide a model for supporters of Essex; and so devoted an adherent of Charles II would not have wished to compare him seriously with Richard. But Charles *was* trying to protect a favorite, Danby, from the just anger of a legally elected Parliament, and he *was* trying to do without that Parliament by proroguing it as often and as long as he could. Howard was not stupid, nor was Charles: the history was there, and he who ran might read. After the death of Charles, however, Howard perhaps saw different parallels and lessons in the story of Richard; certainly his interpretation of it was different when he rewrote it in 1689 and 1690.

Meanwhile, the Parliament that had been elected in 1679 met to transact business on 21 October 1680; and Howard took part in a debate on 27 October on the subject of petitions. Shaftesbury, leader of the Country Party now in power and now first regularly called "Whigs," had, as Burnet put it, "set on foot" petitions for the calling of Parliament to protect both the King and the Protestant religion; and the King had issued a proclamation banning them. Howard thought the King had been badly advised: "Saying prayers, and meeting together, at this rate, may be a riot towards Heaven"; and the House resolved that it was "the undoubted Right of the Subjects of *England* to petition the King for the calling and sitting of Parliaments."[29]

On 6 November Howard spoke again in the debate on the Exclusion Bill ("A Bill to disable James Duke of York from inheriting the Imperial Crown of England") which only for the prorogation would have been passed by the "Little Westminster Parliament" dissolved in 1679. Howard, like many other members of the House, was in a difficult position once again because of the combination of Royalist and anti-Catholic sympathies. He argued, therefore, in fairly general terms: "What is moved is of a strange nature. To talk of the

29. Grey, VII, 369-370.

King's death is not usual in Acts of Parliament. If you shall say, such an one shall succeed the King, by name, it will be a fine invitation to him to endeavour to succeed. [Howard was almost certainly thinking of Monmouth.] This is not language to be put into a Bill. It is the King's life we all depend upon, and I hope this House will show the World how little they are for a Commonwealth, and shame them that have said to the contrary." He thought it would be best to enact simply that *all* successors must be Protestant. It was resolved, however, that the exclusion extended to the Duke of York only, and the Bill was ordered to be committed.[30]

It is a pleasure to state that there is no record of his having taken part in any debate between 9 November 1680[31] and 7 January 1681— for this means that he may not even have been present in December during the disgraceful impeachment of Stafford for his alleged part in the alleged Popish Plot.[32]

The King, of course, rejected the Exclusion Bill and recommended that the Commons consider "all other means for the preservation of the Protestant Religion." According to Grey, Howard said in the ensuing long debate that "Whoever is for the Bill, and against the Duke's succeeding, etc. I shall believe is for the King, and whosoever is against the Bill, I shall believe is against him." A contemporary newsletter quotes him as saying even more succinctly "those that scruple the excluding the Duke would not scruple at the excluding this King." He opposed, however, as a restriction on the King, a proposal that Parliament should name a Council to rule England if the Duke should succeed. The House resolved "That, untill a Bill be passed for excluding the Duke of *York*, this House cannot give any Supply to his Majesty without danger to his Majesty's Person, extreme hazard to the Protestant Religion, and unfaithfulness to those by whom this House is entrusted." Curiously enough, the debate got on to Tallies of Anticipation: Howard now told the House, as he had just told the world in his pamphlet against Danby, how he had predicted long ago in the 1670's that "the way of anticipation could ruine the Treasury." This time the Commons agreed with him, and it was resolved that

---

30. *Ibid.*, VII, 429-430.   31. *Ibid.*, VII, 437-438.
32. See *Ibid.*, VIII, 114 and n. He can hardly have been one of the four Howards, kinsmen of Stafford, who, Burnet says, voted against him; Burnet was probably referring to the vote of the House of Lords.

"no person shall hereafter lend or procure any money by anticipation."[33]

By now, however, the King had had more than enough; and a few days later, Parliament was again dissolved.

The new Parliament was summoned to meet at Oxford (where presumably Charles hoped that the Whigs would miss the moral support of the Londoners) but he dissolved it after a week. Howard was present and took part in one debate, on 26 March. The Lords had rejected the impeachment by the Commons of Fitzharris, an Irish Catholic, for a "malicious and treasonable Libel" upon the King, and had directed that he should be tried at Common Law. Howard, though "glad we are off from one great thing, viz. 'the Exclusion of the Duke of *York* from the Succession of the Crown as the best means to preserve the Protestant religion,'" thought that the case of Fitzharris was important too and that the Lords were concerned not with questions of law but with saving Fitzharris—and that, he maintained, was no service to the King. Even the French ambassador was allegedly involved—and Howard was suspicious that it was all only a way of stopping Fitzharris from revealing what he had to reveal about plots against the Protestant religion: "Therefore I move, that, in the wording of your Vote, you will not only say, 'That the Lords rejection of this Impeachment is not only a subverting the Constitution of Parliament', but 'of the Protestant Religion' also; and I hope you will do this with the same calmness of mind that every man does wish that loves his religion." The House, perhaps calmer than Howard, was content to call it "a denial of Justice, and a violation of the Constitution of Parliaments."[34]

It is not surprising that Howard now exercised less influence in the House; he was getting old (he was fifty-five) and, more important, the Whig party was now in the majority. It did not remain in power for long, however; the attempt to convict Shaftesbury of treason failed in the summer of 1681 but the election of Tory sheriffs more than counteracted the Whig juries, and when Shaftesbury fled in 1682, the

33. Grey, VIII, 235, 279-280, 284-285; *H.M.C.*, 12, App. IX, Beaufort MSS, pp. 112 ff.

34. Grey, VIII, 335-338. Fitzharris was tried, condemned, and executed. His "Libel" is published as Appendix XIII in William Cobbett's *Parliamentary History of England* (London, 1808) IV, cxxiii-cxxviii.

Tories were again at the helm, even though no other Parliament was ever called in Charles's reign.

Howard may well have had mixed feelings about the part played in the rout of Shaftesbury by Dryden's magnificent satire *Absalom and Achitophel*; but, ironically, the names of the brothers-in-law are found linked in 1681, for the first time for many years, in an anonymous satire *A Modest Vindication of the Earl of S——y*, which ridicules the Earl by using the standing joke that he had been a candidate for the throne of Poland and says that he will need such wonderful ministers as

> *Seignioro Roberto Howardensko* Our Chancellour,
> *Jean Drydenurtzitz* Our Poet Laureat, and
> *Tom Shadworiski* His Deputy.[35]

There is little to narrate of Howard during the remainder of Charles's reign. That he continued to act personally as Auditor of the Receipt is shown by official letters addressed to him by the Secretary to the Treasury, Henry Guy, asking him, for example, to attend meetings of the Treasury Board.[36] With Parliament not sitting, however, Howard must have been freer from responsibility than he had been for some time; and one hopes that it was a relief to him not to be involved in the actions of his royal master and the Tories when they demanded that the boroughs surrender their charters and when men like Essex, Russell and Algernon Sidney were driven to suicide or executed following the "discovery" of the Rye House Plot. (His later *History of Religion* and the documents associated with it do indeed indicate that Howard disapproved of much in the last years of the reign of Charles II.)

That he spent at least the summers at Ashtead is suggested by sundry references. He entertained Lord Effingham there in July, 1681, and Evelyn in May, 1684; Evelyn also found him at the home of Sir Stephen Fox in Chiswick (perhaps on his way to or from Ashtead) on 16 June 1683. On 3 August 1682, however, *The London Mercury* recorded that "Sir *Robert Howard* and his Lady going to the Bath for their Healths sake, the said Lady in her passage thither was taken very sick of a Distemper her Ladiship has been some time af-

35. First cited by Macdonald, *Bibliography*, p. 223.
36. B.M. Add. MS 856, f.95 (5 Dec. 1681); see also f.93.

flicted with, and being carried to the next Gentlemans House, dyed in a Convulsion."[37]

On 1 June 1683 Howard appointed his deceased wife's brother-in-law, William Duncombe, to the living of Ashtead—not to the delight of Evelyn, who had a very low opinion of Duncombe and complained that he came only once a year to the parish of Wotton, of which also he was rector.[38] A much more important family occasion was the wedding of Sir Robert's only surviving son Thomas to Diana Newport, daughter of Francis Lord Newport and later Earl of Bradford, on 31 August 1683.[39] The marriage settlement dated 25 August was largely concerned with the Ashtead estate.[40]

In return for Diana Newport's marriage portion of £5,500, Sir Robert agreed to pay Thomas £500 a year as rent for Ashtead so long as he, Robert, should live and remain unmarried. (That the rent might be better secured, the prebend and parsonage of Stoke in Nottinghamshire, and other lands and tithes in the counties of Nottingham and Lincoln, were made over to Andrew Newport, Sir Robert Clayton, and John Stanier as joint trustees.) On Robert's death or marriage, Ashtead was to become the property of Thomas for life, then of Diana for life, and then of their heirs. Sir Robert and Thomas further jointly covenanted to spend £1,500 in the purchase of other freehold property in England, within three months of Thomas's marriage to Diana Newport; and Robert bound himself, should he die unmarried, to bequeath all his real and personal estate (over and above £500 for legacies and funeral expenses) to Thomas and his heirs. If Robert married again, he covenanted to pay to Thomas or his heirs £3,000, within three months of the marriage, and to make over to Thomas and his heirs not only Ashtead (with "all the household stuff and furniture" there) but also all the lands and tithes in Nottinghamshire and Lincolnshire. Finally it was specified that so long as Thomas and Diana chose to reside with Sir Robert, he must

37. Evelyn, *Diary*, IV, 376-377, 316; *London Mercury*, No. 35, 3 Aug. 1682, first noted by Florence R. Scott, *N. & Q.*, CXCII (1947), 316.

38. E. S. de Beer, *N. & Q.*, CLXXXVII (1944), 19; J. P. Shawcross, *The History of Dagenham*, p. 105; O. Manning (cont. Wm. Bray), *The History and Antiquities of Surrey* (London, 1809), II, 635.

39. Florence R. Scott, *N. & Q.*, CXCII (1947), 17. Malone in a manuscript note wrongly gave the date as 4 September 1682 (Osborn, p. 143).

40. There are at least two surviving copies, one of them in the Elford Hall collection of the Birmingham Public Library.

maintain them and their children and their servants, at Ashtead or in Westminster or in London (and even provide stabling and hay and provender for their horses, not exceeding six coach-horses and three saddle-horses); and if they chose not to live with him, he was to pay them a further £300 a year in quarterly instalments.

It seems to have been a generous enough arrangement on Sir Robert's part, and it was carried out. Thomas and his bride lived at Ashtead whenever they chose, from 1683 until Sir Robert did marry again, in 1693; and they had undisturbed possession thereafter.

The death of Charles II on 6 February 1685 marked the end of Howard's long service to the Stuart Kings; and it might well have seemed that his political career had also come to a stop. In fact, however, he was later to play his part in the placing of another monarch on the English throne; and as an elder statesman of some distinction he was to serve William III for several years after the Revolution of 1688.

Chapter sixteen. ECLIPSE AND TRIUMPH, 1685-1690: THE REIGN OF JAMES II, THE REVOLUTION OF 1688, AND THE FIRST YEARS OF WILLIAM AND MARY

THE first reference to Howard during the new reign is made by Evelyn only ten days after the death of Charles II. Evelyn notes: "I din'd at Sir Rob: *Howards Auditor* of the Exchequer, a *Gent*: pretending to all manner of Arts & Sciences for which he had ben the subject of Comedy, under the name of Sir Positive; not ill natur'd, but unsufferably boosting: He was sonn to the late Earle of Berkshire."[1] The sequence of entries in the Diary makes it clear that Evelyn was at the time in London and that therefore the reference is to Sir Robert's London home and not to Ashtead. Howard's frequent presence in London was made necessary by his Auditorship, which, being for life, could not be touched by the new monarch; and that he continued to act in person is made certain by the surviving documents bearing his signature. Many such are among the uncalendared state papers of James II's reign, in the Public Record Office, beginning with one of 5 March 1685;[2] and there are the regular Treasury Orders for payment of the annual £200 "on the usual and accustomed allowance for extraordinary service performed in his office."[3]

Not unnaturally, however, in the official papers of the reign there seem to be no references to him in any other capacity; and he was not elected to the subservient Parliament which first sat in May, 1685 (the members for Castle Rising then being Sir Nicholas L'Estrange and Sir Robert's son, Thomas Howard).

Curiously enough his comedy *The Committee* seems to have gained a new lease of life. For example, there is record on 8 April 1686 of a Lord Chamberlain's warrant for payment of £15 for "The King & Queene & a Box for yᵉ Maydes of honoʳ at yᵉ Comittee," and on 17 November £20 was paid for a performance of the play "at White-

1. *Diary*, IV, 416 (16 Feb.).
2. See, for example, P.R.O. S.P. 31, Nos. 55, 70, 113. (The papers were in process of being calendared and re-numbered in 1955 and these may be the old numbers.)
3. *C.T.B.*, 1685-1689, pp. 42, 1104, 1111, 1690, 2149; see also pp. 258, 354, 442, 467.

hall," while in July there was a performance at Oxford (during which Anthony Leigh offended the King by some gags he interpolated while playing Teg).[4] Perhaps satire of the earlier Puritans was to the taste of the Catholic monarch, even though he attempted to win their successors to his side in politics.

Minor evidence that Howard was still a person of standing is provided by his having been chosen, with the Marquis of Worcester and two others, as one of the trustees to whom Lord Thomas Howard conveyed his estate by deed of 8 December 1688 for payment of the debts of his brother the Duke of Norfolk. (The Duchess later alleged, when the Duke was trying to bring in a bill to divorce her, that she had always had to oppose both Lord Thomas and Sir Robert, who had bought "great bargains" from the estate; she also alleged that the Duke had asked her many times "to quit her interest" in Castle Rising, which Sir Robert had long wanted to buy.)[5]

Far more important is a letter Sir Robert himself wrote early in December to the Prince of Orange, who had landed in the West in November and was still patiently waiting to see which way the wind would blow, James as yet not having made any clear move. The letter presumes that Howard is well known to the Prince of Orange and can only mean, I think, that he had been one of the inner circle of supporters who worked for the "Revolution," as he had formerly been one of the group which worked behind the scenes for the Restoration of Charles II.[6] Indeed, Sir John Dalrymple, who first printed the letter, called it "the most material" of all the letters written to William at the time.[7]

4. P.R.O. L/C 5/147, pp. 125, 260, cited by Nicoll, I, 351; Summers ed., *Roscius Anglicanus*, p. 146.

5. *H.M.C.*, 13th Report, App. Pt. 5, MSS of the House of Lords, p. 238; *C.S.P.D.*, 1700-1702, Appendix, pp. 567-569.

6. The unsigned letter, in King William's Chest in the Public Record Office, was rightly identified as Howard's by Miss H. C. Foxcroft, on the evidence of its reference to his late wife's brother Richard Uphill (though she was rather astray on the facts about the women of the Uphill family); *The Life and Letters of Sir George Savile, Bart., First Marquis of Halifax* (London, 1898), II, 20 and n.

7. *Memoirs of Great Britain and Ireland, from the Dissolution of the last Parliament of Charles II till the Capture of the French and Spanish Fleets at Vigo* (London, 1790), II, 254. Dalrymple not unnaturally was unable to identify the handwriting (which is in fact unmistakable to one who knows it) and could only say that the document was obviously written by "a person of condition."

Halifax, who had been ordered by James to go with Nottingham and Godolphin on an embassy to William, had discussed with Howard (a fact itself significant) the difficult situation in which he now found himself. The famous "Trimmer" was the last man to wish to be identified absolutely with the lost cause of the Stuart King, and he told Howard that he was sorely troubled by James's order. Howard therefore wrote to William, from London, that he himself told Halifax that he

had reason soe to doe, for he woud give very unhappy suspitions that he was engag'd in A designe to give A stop to your Highnesses advancinge to this place, by the delays of A Treaty, and the mistaken notion of an accommodation, for I plainly told him that nothinge of that woud be endur'd, for there was noe roome left for trust, and every thinge must be built upon new foundations; he seemd then fully to agree with mee, and assurd mee he woud not Act soe, as to deserve the least censure of this nature.

After mentioning a second visit from Halifax, who reported further developments, Howard continues:

I perceivd by this hast that they were reduc't almost to A dependancy on this designe; and therefore by the advise of some considerable persons heer, whose Interest in the Citty and Parliament will be very great, I have presumd to give your Highnesse this account, that you may not only be prepared to judge of his proceedinges, but alsoe that you may be presented with the generall sense of things heer as neer as I can Collect them; and I may presume to assure your Highnesse that any delay causd by the notion or pretence of A Treaty will cast A dampe on the spirits of people who are new raisd with the mighty expectation of your advance. . . . as your Highnesse has come to redeeme us from the threatninge misery of Popery and slavery, wee can never suffer the name or trust of Power in any other person. . . . wee have reason to suppose that you will find little opposition from force, and therefore all other Artifices will be attempted; which wee doubt not but your great Judgment and prudence will prevent.

The Citty keep themselves prudently quiet, but are very well inclind and resolvd upon your approach to appeare in your assistance, which I receive now from A considerable person of it,[8] who alsoe beleives that if I can gett release by that time of this fitt of the gout that has now held mee this three weeks that I may probably be of some use to them.

Youre Highnesse will have An account of the Duke of Norfolkes appearinge very considerable in that Country.

Lastly give mee leave to present to your Highnesse the person I send this by, Mr Richard Uphill; he is my wives brother that died; at present

8. Clayton perhaps?

A cornett of horse in the Kinges Army who has been ready to embrace any occasion that I shoud derect him in to serve your Highnesse; I have soe good an opinion of him in all respects that I usd him in this businesse; and humbly desire your Highnesse to beleeve that in any thinge you Commaund him he will not deceive your expectation.[9]

That William did take Richard Uphill into his service is indicated by the description of Uphill on his tombstone (he died on 26 February 1718) as "Standard Bearer to their late Majesties King William, Queen Mary and Queen Ann."[10] The confidence placed in Howard himself, to be proved many times during the new reign, is perhaps nowhere better illustrated than by a letter of 17 December from the Mayor, Aldermen, and Commons of the City of London, in Common Council, to William, thanking him for his endeavors to preserve "Religion lawes & liberties," offering him their full support, and acknowledging receipt of "your Highnesses gracious Letter of the 16th: instant by the hands of two hon:[ble] persons S[r] Rob[t] Howard & M[r] Powle." The letter (which also thanks William for communicating his "gracious purposes to this city, & for the assurance of your kindnes & Protection to us," tells him that "an extraordinary guard of our city forces" has been ordered to be in arms, and offers to welcome him in the City) makes it clear why on the following day William was able to enter London without opposition and receive the famous "invitation" to call a representative Parliamentary convention.[11] Indeed, if other evidence may be believed, Howard had been staunch to the point of refusing James money from the Exchequer when he sought it before finally fleeing from capital and kingdom.[12]

One of Howard's first recorded acts after the Revolution was to stand surety for £1,500 for his son Thomas, that he might take over the office of Teller in the Exchequer of which he had been granted the reversion fourteen years before. Thomas Howard's sureties (his father-in-law Viscount Newport for £1,500, Clayton and Alderman Duncombe for £500 each, and himself for £3,000, in addition to his father's £1,500) were found sufficient and he began his duties as Teller

9. P.R.O. S.P. 8/2, No. 46.
10. Shawcross, *History of Dagenham*, p. 104. See also p. 239.
11. P.R.O. S.P. 8/2 (King William's Chest), f.43.
12. Ethel M. Richardson, *The Lion and the Rose* (London [1922]), p. 403— citing a manuscript note by Colonel James Grahame. I have not, however, found this book reliable elsewhere where Sir Robert is concerned.

and no doubt moved into the London house that was granted with the office and was repaired for him.[13]

Sir Robert was, of course, a member of William's first Parliament. (He was again elected for Castle Rising, and his son Thomas transferred to Bletchingley, for which he was a Member from 1689 to 1698; after his father's death, Thomas again represented Castle Rising.) Parliament met on 22 January 1689 and for some days debated the question whether James II could be said to have abdicated and whether the Throne was vacant. In the Grand Committee, Howard made a long speech, in which, significantly, he compared and contrasted the situation in 1689 with that in the time of Richard II. (He had just been revising his History of that reign.) James, he maintained, was like Richard in his desire to pack Parliament and so on, but had gone even further in that he wanted his own way not only "in the Laws Temporal, but in the Laws of the Church too, thereby to influence our souls as well as our bodies." There must, he argued, be *some* way of facing the situation that now confronted Parliament and nation; and in his view when a King "acts by his Will, and not by the Laws, he is no King; for he acts by Power and Tyranny." "I have heard," he added in an eminently quotable phrase,[14] " 'that the King has his Crown by Divine Right', and we [the people] have Divine Right too; but he can forfeit, if he break that pact and covenant with his People, who have Right, by reason of their Election. . . . The Constitution of the Government is actually grounded upon pact and covenant with the People. . . . I am of opinion 'that *James* II has abdicated the Government.' "[15] The Commons resolved accordingly, but the Lords could not accept the word "abdicated," and the dangers of the doctrine of election were pointed out: could Parliament, for example, elect another to the throne if there was an undoubted legal heir? The Lords were happy to agree that it was inconsistent for a Protestant kingdom to be governed by a Catholic king, and in the ensuing conference of the two Houses, Howard spoke very well on the theme that since the Lords acknowledged that James could not be king, they ought to admit that the throne was vacant (he was cynical on the

13. C.T.B., 1685-1689, pp. 2146, 2151; 1689-1692, p. 1259.
14. See, for example, the citation of it by Leopold von Ranke, *A History of England Principally in the Seventeenth Century* (Oxford, 1875), IV, 495, and C. B. R. Kent, *The Early History of the Tories* (London, 1908), p. 356.
15. Grey, IX, 19-20.

subject of James's "pretended" male heir); and if the throne was vacant, then somehow something *had* to be done: "Your Lordships, it seems, cannot agree with us to supply the Gap; and we must not do it ourselves, by Election, which is the only Way left to provide for our Settlement: So that, upon the Whole, nothing remains but to break up in Confusion, and so leave the Nation to extricate itself, as well as it can, out of the present Distraction: But then at whose Door that will lie, I must leave to your Lordships thoughts."[16] Grey also reports him as having said in the Commons on 5 February that arguments which were "good in quiet times" were not necessarily adequate now: "All things are not so clear as we could wish; but let us preserve ourselves, which must be our supreme Law."[17] It was indeed a time, if ever there was one, when practice was more important than very inconvenient theory; the Lords came into line, and William and Mary were declared to be joint monarchs of the kingdom.

Howard, perhaps not unexpectedly and not altogether unjustifiably, seems to have regarded himself as one of the grand old men of the Commons, and spoke more frequently, and with more authority, than in the last Parliaments of Charles II; and on 13 February 1689 his statesmanship at long last received official recognition when he was appointed by the King to the new Privy Council.[18] (One of his first official duties was the pleasant one of appending his signature to a circular to the Governors of colonies, ordering them to proclaim the new King and Queen, to administer the oath of allegiance and to continue all officers in their employments).[19]

Sir Edward Harley even reported to Robert Harley on 16 February that Howard was one of the five new Commissioners of the Treasury; but he was not in fact one of those appointed in April. He may have acted temporarily, in the emergency; or Harley may have confused the Treasury Commission with the committee appointed to report on the revenues of the kingdom (a committee from which Howard did report to the House on 1 March that the annual revenue was only £150,000, besides the additional duties on sugar and tobacco).[20]

16. Cited from Ralph, *History of England*, II, 47-48. See also Cobbett, V, 96-97.
17. Grey, IX, 62-63.
18. Narcissus Luttrell, *A Brief Historical Relation of State Affairs* (Oxford, 1857) I, 502. This is, of course, a contemporary account.
19. *C.S.P. Col., America and West Indies*, 1689-1692, p. 7.
20. *H.M.C.*, 14, II, Rutland MSS Vol. 3, pp. 428, 430.

Anthony à Wood was apparently first responsible for the statement, repeated parrot-like by Theophilus Cibber, that, having been appointed to the Privy Council, Howard was from that moment a "so fiery and passionate abhorrer of all Nonjurors that he disclaimed all manner of Conversation and intercourse with any of that character." I think Wood has overstated his case and certainly he has given a wrong impression—of bigotry. On 25 February, for example, when the House's leave was asked "to bring in a Bill for taking away the Oaths of Allegiance and Supremacy, and to insert others," Howard remarked "I would have an Act to take away any obligation to take the Sacrament upon accepting any Office; it is a prophaning the Sacrament"; and while he was in favor of the Oath of Allegiance and wanted to add the words "as is taught by the Doctrine of the Church of England" to a clause in the Bill of Indulgence specifying that Quakers and Nonconformists "must not write nor speak against the doctrine of the Scripture," he also said "To tell a man, 'he shall forbear to write against a thing' is no hardship; but 'that he shall not believe it' is." To take a final example, he told the House on a later occasion that "I would not shut a man out of the Government, that is willing to come in, both Clergy and others: I am so far from taking advantage of Omissions, that I would restore all."[21] (He did still feel that such men *ought* to "come in" by taking the Oath of Allegiance.)

William's first Parliament met regularly throughout 1689 and in the first few months of 1690; and while Howard occasionally seems to have missed a debate (probably through illness) he spoke frequently —indeed with almost embarrassing frequency—and was not always satisfied to speak only once to the question. He did not invariably carry the day (at least twice other Members suggested that he was not speaking to the point, and he does seem to have spoken sometimes at undue length); but he was very influential. It would be tedious and unnecessary to itemize his contribution to every single debate; but the following summary does, I believe, indicate the direction of his thought.

In the first place, he seldom lost an opportunity of praising William or of reminding the House of what it and the nation owed to the new King. If a single thought had to be chosen from all his speeches of

21. Wood, II, 1018; Cibber, III, 57-58; Grey, IX, 111; IX, 260 (17 May 1689); X, 69 (24 April 1690).

this period, it would certainly be his argument for giving William revenue for life and not merely for three years (it having been suggested that the shorter period would ensure the regular meeting of Parliament): "I never will speak against a Triennial Parliament [but] when a Popish King has received such testimony of kindness from the Parliament as to have the Revenue for Life, if a Prince, come in to save your Religion and Laws, should not have the same confidence, it will be thought a great coldness. It will be a matter of great rejoicing beyond sea, if we come up with more chearfulness to that King who would have imposed upon you what this King has delivered you from." This King, he told the House on another occasion, was indeed unlike others: "He has been so far from breaking your Laws, that he has not so much as bowed them"; and he wanted the King to be given full credit for his desire to regulate abuses in collecting the Hearthmoney and for his offer to dispense with it if necessary. He summed it all up when he said, on 1 June, that he was glad that he now stood in a Parliament where he could speak for King *and* Country, and not be thought to speak against the one when he spoke for the other.[22]

Secondly, as one of the King's chief supporters in the House, he worked unceasingly to obtain Supply, and put to Parliament other requests William wished to make (for example, for a financial settlement on his great soldier Schomberg). On the question of Supply, Howard not only urged the granting of revenue for life and adequate Supply for the wars in Ireland but also went to some trouble to get over the minor difficulty that the tallies had been struck in the name of James II.[23]

Thirdly, for all his admiration of the King, he was still a guardian of the rights of Parliament and of the subject, and was always quick to speak on questions of procedure of any kind. When, for example, on 22 May 1689 a bill was brought in to suspend the Habeas Corpus Act for a time in an emergency, Howard defended the bill as necessary, but added, "I am sorry the condition of affairs makes it necessary." "I think," he said, "it gives great veneration to the *Habeas Corpus* Act, that it cannot be suspended but by Act of Parliament" (not by the Judges); and he was surely not exaggerating when he said that if the executive or judiciary power to dispense with the Act

22. Grey, IX, 126, 138, 129, 277; compare also 421, 485, and X, 75.
23. *Ibid.*, IX, 226, 184, 121.

had existed "when the Prince of *Orange* was upon his design . . . many might have been clapped up (and the happy change prevented) and myself one." Again on 18 June when it was proposed to except Lord Chief Justice Herbert from the Bill of Indemnity with a proviso that the King might pardon him, Howard was all for mercy but pointed out that since the executive's Dispensing Power was precisely what Parliament had been objecting to, the only proper course was to except Herbert and then petition the King that he be pardoned. On 4 November he drew attention to the folly of taking James II's power to dispense with penal laws as good precedent in Common Law. His sense of Parliamentary propriety made him anxious not to give precedent for the Lords to interest themselves in money bills; but he was not so tied by precedent as to find it impossible to receive a petition from the Sheriffs of the City of London ("Pray be pleased to admit the Petition; if it be not for you, throw it out. Nobody knows yet what it is"); and he was not as old-fashioned as some members when he thought that *if* the proceedings of the House were to be made public, then they might as well be printed and thus published accurately.[24]

Finally, he was most anxious that all the wrongs of the previous reign should be righted, whether this meant giving justice to those who had been denied it or bringing to justice those who had done wrong. The latter was the more dangerous, and Howard came to think so himself. He argued strongly for excepting from the Bill of Indemnity men like Jeffreys (who had committed murder in the name of the law but without legal authority) and the Bishop of Durham (of whose illegal proceedings Howard had had personal experience when one of the trustees for the Duke of Norfolk), but he was man enough to say later, on 26 November, "I have rather been too warm upon persons formerly." He had certainly supported the Committee of Grievances, and had had much to say about the exceptions from the Act of Indemnity: and even after his apology, he made one very bad blunder in trying to add a second amendment to a bill for restoring the rights of those Corporations which had been coerced into surrendering their charters during the last years of Charles II and the reign of James. Sacheverell's first amendment was to disqualify from office for seven years every municipal officer who had been a party to the sur-

24. *Ibid.*, IX, 269, 342-343, 396, 295; X, 145, 56; IX, 145.

render; Howard's second clause was that if any person disqualified by this provision should presume to take office, he should be fined £500 and be disqualified for life from holding any public employment whatever. "I have abhorred what was done in the late times," he concluded, "but rather than no mark of incapacity shall be put upon these men, I would part with the whole Bill." The two clauses were not only rejected eventually but also torn from the parchment containing the bill. Howard had tried here as always to act on principle, the principle he enunciated in another debate: "I do not speak to chill the charity of any body [but] King James has abdicated the Crown, and if we lump them in, who have helped to lump him out, you say King *William* has done all the wrong, and they none." The principle of being too just to be merciful, however, is a dangerous one and Howard, as we have seen, admitted it. He had shown himself in a better light when in brief but deeply felt words he had supported the bill from the Lords annulling the attainder of Lord Russell: "I cannot name Lord *Russel* without disorder. I would neglect all things to read this Bill a second time"; and he has won even the admiration of Macaulay for his stand in trying to have the 1685 sentence on Titus Oates declared illegal.[25] When Howard began to speak on this he was hissed by some of the Tories, whose opposition to Oates was based on personal and political grounds; and he commented, "Such Gentlemen as did it I shall not be reconciled to, unless they love whipping and perpetual Imprisonment [part of the punishment of Oates], and no confirmation of the Popish Plot." He hoped that "Gentlemen of the Church of England" were not of the opinion that Jeffreys in a civil court was entitled to deprive a clergyman of his canonical habit. Oates could still be tried for perjury—Howard did not oppose *that* —but the 1685 judgment had been declared illegal and ought to be reversed. Howard and others were delegated to inspect the Lords' Journal to find out whether the Lords had in fact confirmed the judgment of the Court; on 11 June he reported to the Commons that the Lords had found no defect in it, but he added: "Having said thus much, I should not have troubled you with it, had I not thought it as great a thing as could come in Parliament." He retraced the history of the Oates case (and that of another defrocked and imprisoned

25. *Ibid.*, IX, 256, 384, 456, 519, 324; 152 (compare 171); Macaulay, *History of England* (London, 1849), III, 388-389, 517, 522.

clergyman, Samuel Johnson); and concluded with the moving words: "*Oates* is the least of my thoughts, but to have *Oates*'s Judgment confirmed, and we all reproached for it, that sticks with me. Unless we are grown fond of *Jeffreye*'s Judgment, which condemns all we have done. I move for a Bill to repeal this Judgment." The Commons did declare the sentence on Oates (and Johnson) "cruel and illegal," but the Lords would not agree with them; "and in the end," as C. B. R. Kent puts it, "the wretched man was forced to be content with a pardon and a pension."[26] Nevertheless, as Macaulay saw, Howard's speech and the ensuing verdict of the Commons were a triumph for the principle that judicial bodies must decide on judicial grounds, no matter how contemptible the private character of the accused.

26. Grey, IX, 286-294; *The Early History of the Tories*, p. 402.

IN 1690 Howard finally admitted his authorship of the earlier *Life* of Richard II by publishing the fuller work in which it was incorporated, *The History of the Reigns of Edward and Richard II. With Reflections and Characters of their Chief Ministers and Favourites. As Also, A Comparison between those Princes Edward and Richard the Second, with Edward the First, and Edward the Third. Written in the Year 1685. By the Honourable Sr Robert Howard . . . London . . . 1690.* The statement that the work was written in 1685 cannot be wholly true, in view of references to the reign of James II, and was presumably included to protect the author in case of any complaints that his political philosophizing was not in every detail adapted to the situation of 1689-1690 (although it was certainly all intended to be in favor of the Revolution and of William). Nevertheless the recension of the original *Life* of Richard probably was begun in 1685, when Howard had more leisure time owing to his not being then a member of Parliament.

An earlier edition of the expanded (1690) work, one which Howard claimed to be unauthorized, had been brought out by a different publisher in the previous year, under the less apt title *Historical Observations Upon the Reigns of Edward I.II.III. And Richard II. With Remarks upon their Faithful Counsellors and False Favourites. Written by a Person of Honour . . . London . . . MDCLXXXIX.*

Of these two publications Howard said, probably truthfully, in the Preface to the later one:

I was much surpriz'd to see an imperfect Copy of this steal into Publick, far from my Knowledge or Intention: for I was sensible it wanted Consideration in point of History. There were many material Things which I intended to have added, and others to leave out as unnecessary to my design: considering therefore that my best and most correct Performances cou'd hardly challenge merit, I thought it just to myself, and others, to endeavour that they might need the least Pardon; and that my owning now the Publishing of this, may rather be lookt upon as an effect of Necessity than Confidence.

The 1689 edition is very careless indeed, and obviously had not been checked by the author. I should imagine that it was set up from an unrevised manuscript by a compositor who could not always read his copy. There are even omissions like "Sir ——— Bushy" (on p. 140) only three lines after he has been called "Sir John Bushy"; or again (on p. 174) it is said of Edmund Crookback that "for his Deformity he was put by the succession and   given to Edward I" and we have to turn to the 1690 edition (p. 163) to find out that the missing words are "the Crown."

It may be sufficient if I list briefly the principal differences between the 1689 and 1690 editions and then concentrate on the latter.[1] In the revision, then, Howard was concerned

1. to clarify and improve his phrasing (although not every clumsy sentence was improved)

2. to correct oversights, compositor's errors, and other errors of fact (for example, on p. 185 Edward III had been said to be the son of *Henry* II)

3. to give additional information that had now become available from further research (for example, dates and names, but sometimes such changes involved reinterpretation of character or the writing of whole paragraphs, as in the account of the capture and execution of Gaveston)

4. to draw additional parallels between earlier and later times wherever possible (for example in 1690 he was anxious to add, to the account of the way the Barons took arms against Gaveston: "By this it may be observ'd, that it was presum'd, when a King violates his Oath and Contracts with his People, that they had a Right to endeavour to Relieve themselves; and to take Care of the Administration of that Power, that he had so much abused and forfeited"—p. 44)

5. to reinterpret and to omit such philosophizing as was dangerous in the light of the Revolution (for example, the italicized phrase in the following, from p. 36 of the 1689 edition, was omitted in 1690: "Limited Power (for so they call Laws observ'd) is but the Fetters of a Prince, and they need be worn no longer than he submits to publick Notions, *which are nothing but unsolid Fancies*"; and 1690 omitted "All new-gotten Power is commonly endeavour'd to be preserv'd

1. The first half of the book was revised more carefully than the second.

by Destruction; and the Execution of the Unfortunate, is call'd a Justice"—p. 157).

A hostile biographer would assert that Howard was a time-server; another might simply say, as Dr. Johnson once said of Dryden, that if he changed, he changed with the nation; but perhaps a friendly one ought to suggest that events had forced Howard, and many others, to rethink their political philosophy. Even in 1681 Howard had stressed the fact that the people of England had been given cause enough to rise against Richard II; when first revising this in 1685 he had seen more clearly that there was an element of hypocrisy in Henry IV's invented title to the Crown; now in 1690 he had come to feel that the hypocrisy of the title was only part of the story, *because* "Parliament did not seem to proceed upon this pretended Title . . . but by way of Election" (p. 163) and so was able to add that "This Ceremony seems to shew that Right which can never be separated from the People."

Not surprisingly, the 1690 volume is dedicated to William. Howard, not often at his best in his prefatory material, begins:

Such as have Dedicated their Writings to Princes, have usually presented them in Characters that rather shew'd what Excellent Princes might be, than what they were; and so resembling one another, that most of them seem'd flattering Copies, and very few like the Originals.

I esteem it therefore a very great Happiness to be freed from Flattery, by being only Just to You, since of no less a Nature are Your Actions, than to make it almost impossible for any to Approach You with that Servile Prejudice to Themselves and Princes.

One hopes that even the grim William managed a smile at that. Howard goes on to say that William has saved Englishmen from virtual slavery, by using his royal power for preservation and not, like "our late Princes," for destruction. (It will be noticed that—as one had suspected from the lack of reference to him in the last years of Charles II —Howard had come to take a very critical view of the king in whose interests he had done so much.)

The preface begins with the passage, already quoted, disowning the "imperfect" edition of 1689, and states that "the Scheme of this was digested in the Year 85." He says that he became "very much affected with" the similarity between contemporary events (i.e., of the last years of Charles II and the short reign of James II) and the earlier reigns, in that kings relying on their favorites made the inevitably vain attempt to "subdue" the law of the land; "and I then expected to see a Revolution resembling theirs." (It is difficult to decide of which period exactly Howard *is* speaking—1685 or 1688.) His next paragraph explains what one particularly wishes to know—why he had changed his opinion of Charles II—and the answer is the simple one, that he had since learnt of Charles's growing inclination towards Catholicism and France:

When K. *Charles* had prepar'd things ready for Popery and Slavery, he seem'd no longer useful to those that eagerly waited to assume that Power that the Papists had guided him to make ready for them; and as his Actions were like those misguided Princes [Edward and Richard], I believe, his Death as much resembled theirs, and was equally as violent.

(Howard is here referring to the widely held belief, mentioned also, for example, by Burnet, that Charles was poisoned, at the instigation of the Duchess of Portsmouth or even of his brother.)

James II, of course, committed not only the sins of the earlier kings but also the worse one of trying to impose Catholicism on the nation —a danger that two Parliaments had anticipated and tried to avoid by passing a bill excluding him from the throne. "I was a Member of both those Parliaments," Howard notes, "wherein the Debates seem'd to me very clear, and almost unanimous, and they were too well justified by the Popish Successor when he came to the Crown." Indeed, had not William intervened, "we had practis'd *Passive-Obedience* against our Wills, and in our Souls and Bodies felt the Misery of that Doctrine, the Encouragement of Destruction."

Howard here recognizes that the publication of his work in 1689 had involved him, willingly or not, in the controversy concerning the doctrine of Passive Obedience, which may be traced back at least to 1681. In answer to a sermon delivered in that year by George Hickes, Samuel Johnson published in 1682 his influential *Julian the Apostate*, to which Hickes in turn replied with the anonymous *Jovian* in 1683.[2] The pamphlet war spread, with Hickes, John Bennet, and later Dr. Sherlock arguing both that the religion of an heir to the throne was not in itself a legal reason for exclusion and that the duty of the subject was one of passive obedience to the sovereign prince, while John-

2. The titles are explained by the arguments from Christian precedent. Johnson argued that the early Christians, so far from practising passive obedience, tried to hinder Julian's succession; Hickes replied that the Christian subjects of Julian did practise it when they did not resist his successor Jovian.

son led the attack and maintained that the true Christian must defend his religion. Accordingly in 1683 Johnson had entered on the Stationers' Register his answer to Hickes's *Jovian*, entitled *Julian's Arts to undermine and extirpate Christianity*. This, however, he suppressed, probably because of the execution of Lord Russell; he was nevertheless examined by the Privy Council and although at first liberated on bail, later imprisoned because of the earlier *Julian the Apostate*, which was ordered to be burnt by the public hangman. On release he wrote still other pamphlets and was again arrested, and ordered to be degraded from the priesthood and whipped through the streets. In 1689, as we have seen, Parliament decided that this judgment on Johnson and that on Oates were illegal; and although Johnson's hopes for a bishopric were never realized, William did later give him a yearly pension. In 1689, then, he was at last free to publish *Julian's Arts,* and also another pamphlet written earlier, *Remarks upon Dr. Sherlock's Book, Intituled The Case of Resistance of the Supreme Powers Stated and Resolved, according to the Doctrine of the Holy Scriptures*; and Hickes was probably the author of the statement of the opposite case, *The Doctrine of Passive Obedience. By a Layman of the Church of England* (1689).

This, then, is the background to the next section of Howard's 1690 preface, in which he continues:

But yet we see a History of this Doctrine of *Passive-Obedience*, new put forth, which is no better then an Arraigning this present Government, and all those that contributed to this happy Change . . . but I leave that zealous History under the Execution it has received from the Excellent Mr. *Johnson*, in his short Reflections upon it, which can receive no greater a Character, than to be like himself and his other Writings, both which were Victorious in the midst of all his barbarous Persecutions.

Howard next announces that he will treat the depositions of Richard II and Edward II "by the People in their Representatives, presuming they had a Right to reassume that Power which was derived from them, when any Prince forfeited the Trust they had placed in him, and acted contrary to his Executive Office." He will show how the people informed Edward II that if he did not abdicate, they would not elect his son as King; "nor," Howard adds, "has this Electing of Kings been so unusual in England, since seldome any Government has had more broken successions." This is the crux of the matter;

Howard is concerned to deny not only the Divine Right of Kings, claimed by the later Stuarts, but also the contention that the recognition of William and Mary marked the introduction of a *new* principle, the elective one, into the English monarchy.

In his detailed examination of the doctrine of Passive Obedience as enunciated particularly in *Jovian*, Howard finds many inconsistencies, even allowing for the fact that Hickes was writing before James actually became King. What good are laws that protect us against tyranny, he asks, if we are not prepared to enforce them? The right of self-preservation, which his opponents do not deny, must surely include preservation against a tyrant; and Howard cannot agree that resistance to such a ruler does more harm to a country than any ruler can do. Starting from Hooker's thesis, in the *Laws of Ecclesiastical Politie*, that law derives from a social contract between ruler and people, Howard argues that the right given to a ruler is given by the people as a form of self-defense and therefore cannot possibly have been intended to be unlimited; the ruler has "only an Executive Power committed to him by the People," a "derivative Power." The doctrine of Divine Right is ridiculed as postulating a King "dropt down from Heaven to Govern a People intentionally created for him, and he therefore accountable to none but GOD"; it cannot be supported from Scripture, Howard maintains, whereas the story of David is clear evidence for the theory of contract. For that matter, he adds, paraphrasing his own famous remark in the House of Commons, "every Man has alike a Divine Right to his Life, Freedom, and Estate"; and both ruler and ruled forfeit their rights if they fail to obey the law. The preface then concludes by scoring a point:

But I hope this late Happy Revolution has satisfied every undesigning Heart beyond all Arguments, and shew'd the Falseness of their Reasons, as well as prevented the Mischiefs of their Doctrine; since contrary to their Assertions, we have seen Opposition with much less expence of Blood, than Submission wou'd have suffer'd to be spilt; and Arbitrary Tyranny chang'd into a Limited Monarchy.

Too much (though not all) of Howard's argument depends on a premise (the social contract) which his opponents would simply deny; and one has the uneasy feeling that facts used in the earlier *Life of Richard II* to demonstrate one thing are now being used with the same facility to prove another. Nevertheless the case is stated fairly well and demanded to be (and was) taken seriously.

The work proper begins with a humorless discussion that, unfortunately for Howard, falls comically short of the work of which it reminds one irresistibly by similarity of subject matter, namely, the superb opening of Marlowe's *Faustus*. Howard explains why he chose history as "the most useful Study." He first considered divinity, but thought the Gospel covered that "fully and clearly"; differences of religious doctrine arise, he maintains, "more by the Zeal for this World than the other," and—given time—he could trace most of these to their source. (We shall see that he did have time to do this a few years later.) Philosophy was rejected next, apparently for the reason (logically irrelevant) that he questioned the motives of those engaged in "the endless and useless Searches of Subtleties and nice Distinctions"; but he gives some eleven pointless pages to a demonstration of his knowledge of the fluctuations in the reputations of Plato and Aristotle. Of mathematics he knew only enough to regret that he had not made it his entire study; and so he chose history, primarily because it provided precedents for the problems of his own time. How Shadwell must have smiled if he read these pages! They would have served unaltered for another Sir Positive scene as good as any he had invented.

Howard begins with the story of Edward II and his favorite Gaveston, and takes the view that the Lords were anxious for obedience but felt entitled to take action when the King, by recalling Gaveston from banishment, broke his contract with the people. The execution of Gaveston led to a truce, but it was only temporary, and in time the King regained power and used it so arbitrarily as to cause his own ruin. Howard is no champion of Edward's Queen, who "plac'd her loose affections upon *Roger Mortimer*" and "while she condemn'd those Diseases that made the Nation sick, . . . made Rebellion the Cure"; she too is seen as corrupted by power and contemptuous of the law. Parliament, of course, is admired for its actions in deposing Edward for maladministration and in *electing* his son in his place. Even Howard, however, must have had his doubts about the Commission that was sent to Edward II when the son refused to accept the Crown without his father's consent; we are told that the Commission demanded the King's consent, saying that if it was not given, "the

People wou'd chuse a King that had no Relation to his Blood." The deposed King's sufferings are depicted with sympathy, and he is said to have discovered too late "that injur'd People with as much want of Tenderness will Revenge their Wrongs, as they shew'd in the Oppression." Howard does not know whether the violent murder of the King was at the instigation of the Bishop of Hereford's deliberately ambiguous "Edoardum occidere nolito timere bonum est"; he contents himself with the observation that "Ecclesiastical Riddles are dangerous, and sometimes their Expositions of Texts are no other."

The story of Richard II is much as before but with some change of emphasis. The King committed the same error as did Edward II by allowing himself to be persuaded by his minions that he must use power against his and their enemies; he not only failed to recognize the merit of loyal Englishmen but also contemplated ways of packing Parliament, and by putting pressure on the Judges and, Howard thinks, bribing them, succeeded in getting the notorious opinion that the King could "disannul the Proceedings" of Parliament since he was "above the Law: A Maxime very much us'd in the late Times, and must be always, when *Arbitrary Power* is design'd." The King came to see reason, confessed his errors, and agreed to meet the Lords; but with "Fatal Mutability" he changed his mind, and the Lords then threatened to choose a new King. Richard thereupon delivered up his power, and Parliament condemned the favorites to perpetual imprisonment and forfeiture of their estates; but not even the execution of some of them, Howard adds, "could deter others, in our late Times, from being wretched Copies of such miserable Originals." (This was added in the 1690 edition.)

After this, the Coronation Oath was renewed and fealty sworn again by the Lords; but when Richard became twenty-one, he vowed that he would rather "rely on the Protection of *France*, than thus to be made servile to those he ought to Command." Howard must comment on this:

'Tis not unworthy of an Observation, how frequently the *French* have been prevalent in *England*: And always in such Prince's Times as have given so much Power to Ministers and Favourites, as made them considerable enough to be corrupted. . . . The People always judg'd right in this, and Parliaments (as *Comines* observes) were never corrupted in themselves or Judgments, and always perceiv'd the Dissimulation of the *French*

. . . . *France* can be but of little use to us, but we may be too much for them.

The French diplomat, the Earl of St. Paul, is blamed for fanning Richard's anger against Gloucester, but it was the royal favorites who finally told him how the murder should be carried out. Bushy, Bagot, and Green are seen as infamous for their leadership of "the terrified House of Commons," which voted "That any One that shou'd be Convicted of opposing the King's Power and Regality, shou'd suffer as a Traitor" (and Howard does not pause to consider the implications of this for his own doctrine of the supremacy of Parliament). Hereford's claim that he returned to England only to recover his inheritance is described as a "modest mask" and it is said that his "Popularity gave him an Interest in Power, and his Descent from a King the Pretence to use it." The usurper, then, is not the hero of the story; indeed Richard could have become that, with the right advice, but "He had been so long accustomed to follow the Counsel of others, that he knew not the way to use his own. . . . The love of Absolute Greatness in Opinion, more than real and true Greatness in itself, has hindred Princes from seeing the Defects and Designs of mean and interested Flatterers." Accordingly Richard, on bad advice, yielded to Lancaster and resigned; and Parliament, proceeding not upon the claimant's pretended title "but by way of Election," chose Lancaster as the new King.

The work concludes with a comparison between Edward I and Edward III, on the one hand, and Edward II and Richard II, on the other. The former pair inherited troubled kingdoms but won great victories and gave their people security; they were wise themselves but listened to good advice from others, were fair but merciful, made good laws and abided by them, and gave the nation value for the great Supply granted them; the latter pair inherited settled kingdoms, but would rather have made slaves of their own subjects than of the people of any other nation; they were "submissive when oppos'd and fierce when submitted to," claimed to be above the law, and wasted the nation's money on favorites who cost more than ever victory did. The latter pair, then, were the rulers who were finally forsaken by their subjects. It need hardly be added that the implication of Howard's whole book is that William of Orange belongs in the tradition

of Edward I and Edward III, while James II repeated all the errors
of Richard II and Edward II.

It will also be clear that Howard's main defects as an historian are
his preaching from his text, his tendency to see history as he wishes
to see it (though not always), his failure to appreciate some of the
wider issues, and the episodic quality of his narrative. His virtues are
those of the commentator who can point out a striking parallel; his
respect for documentary evidence (when its existence has been brought
to his notice); and, in spite of an occasional awkwardness in style,
the general readability of his prose.

There was, of course, a reply to Howard from the supporters of
the doctrine of Passive Obedience. This was the anonymous *Animadversions on Mr Johnson's Answer to Jovian, in Three Letters to a
Country-Friend* (by William Hopkins, Prebendary of Worcester). In
the prefatory matter to this, dated July 1690, Howard's preface to his
history is mentioned, as having almost persuaded Hopkins *not* to
reply to Johnson: for how, he asks, can one convert ordinary people
if one of Sir Robert's "Birth, Education, Parts, and Figure in the
World" can be so imposed on? Howard has been "misled" by Johnson not only in his preface but also in "a long *Speech*, which he made
almost in the words of it to a very full House of Commons, on that
memorable day which was appointed for the great debate of *the disabling Clause*." Howard is also accused of taking even his Biblical
quotations and his knowledge of Aristotle from others, without acknowledgment. Only after some pages of this kind of thing does
Hopkins remember that he is supposed to be answering Johnson; and
indeed he says little, or nothing, of which opponents of the Passive
Obedience theory needed to take notice.

Howard, however, felt obliged to reply, and did so with some merit
in *A Letter to Mr. Samuel Johnson, Occasioned by a scurrilous Pamphlet, intituled, Animadversions on Mr. Johnson's Answer to Jovian, in
three Letters to a Country-Friend. At the End of which is reprinted
the Preface before the History of Edward and Richard the Second, to
the end every thing may appear clearly to the Reader, how little of
that Preface has been answered. Both written by the Honourable Sir
Robert Howard. London . . . 1692.*

Howard begins by expressing his indignation at being accused of
resigning his judgment to Johnson, and says that "none sure but a

nameless Author, would have ventur'd to such a Liberty as he has taken, to allow me no use of Judgment, and to charge me with want of Morals and Religion." Johnson, he says, will confirm that he and Howard were not personally acquainted "till some time after this Revolution." He admits two minor errors in his book but has not much difficulty in answering the charge that he stole material from particular authors. He then repeats that William saved England from tyranny, and quotes from the Prince's Declaration his intention to preserve the law of the land and avoid chaos, adding:

I hope by this Account I have shewed my nameless Adversary, that the Safety and Honour of this Government was procur'd and founded against his Principles of *Passive Obedience,* which had they been as sacredly ob-serv'd as he would have them, our Redemption had never been effected, and perhaps he had been better pleased.

Howard denies that he saved his own eyes "the drudgery" of seeking relevant quotations in the Bible, and quaintly proves that the search would be neither drudgery nor beyond him, by quoting several texts relevant to the question of covenant between king and people; he also successfully refutes the charge of blasphemy (Hopkins did take a statement out of its context). He concludes by explaining that his pamphlet has been delayed only by his illness and "aversion to Quar-rels of this Nature." The reprint of the 1690 preface follows.

The *Letter to Mr. Samuel Johnson* would seem to have been hur-riedly prepared and is of no great importance. It was, however, prob-ably adequate for its purpose; and there Howard again had the sense to let the matter rest.

Chapter eighteen. ILLNESS, REMARRIAGE, AND
OFFICIAL DUTIES: 1690-1694

THE trust placed in Howard by William and Mary is perhaps nowhere better shown than by Mary's action, on 10 July 1690, in nominat-
ing him as a member of a commission to inquire into the recent conduct of the Fleet (in particular the virtual defeat off Beachy Head).
The King was in Ireland;[1] Mary, not trusting many and considerably
worried by all her responsibilities in a difficult time, was paying Howard a great compliment in thus choosing him as one of the commissioners, who had unlimited power to examine the conduct of every
officer from the admiral down, to inquire into charges of embezzlement, "and to administer an oath to all and every such person or
persons as they shall think fit." The warrant was issued on 12 July,
and on the thirteenth all five commissioners left London to carry out
their duties; as early as the sixteenth they were reporting from Sheerness.[2]

Again, on 29 July Howard was given the command of all regiments
and troops of militia cavalry, under the general command of Marlborough; and on 9 August these, "well mounted and equipt," were
reviewed by the Queen, who "thank'd them by the lord Marlborough
for their readinesse and good affection to her service."[3]

Financial business, both personal and official, also must have taken
a great deal of his time and energy. He had not been slow to obtain
from the Treasury a warrant for money due to the Farmers of the
Post Fines but paid direct by the county sheriffs to the King during
the years 1682-1687 (the sums involved for the successive years being
£1,336, £1,182, £870, £2,111, £1,929 and £2,394, with some odd
shillings and pence);[4] other Exchequer problems, however, were not
as easy. The appointment of the Commissioners for Public Accounts
meant much extra work for him,[5] and even more troublesome was

1. Howard had made a few minor contributions to the long debate on the
Regency Bill, in May.
2. Luttrell, II, 74; *C.S.P.D.*, May, 1690—Oct., 1691, pp. 62-63; *H.M.C.*, 12th
Report, App. V., Rutland MSS, p. 129; *H.M.C.*, MSS of A. G. Finch Esq.,
Vol. 2, p. 364. The admiral, the Earl of Torrington, was finally declared innocent but was not given the command again.
3. *C.S.P.D.*, 1690-1691, p. 82; Luttrell, II, 88-89.
4. *C.T.B.*, 1689-1692, pp. 573 *et seq.*   5. See, e.g., Luttrell, II, 193-194.

the fact that his own salary, fees, and perquisites were necessarily examined, and reported on in "A list of excessive fees exacted and taken by officers that have great salaries for the execution of their places, for which no legal precedent appears to justify the same." The relevant part of the report (in the form of answers by the Commissioners to the queries of the House of Lords) begins:

The Officer of Writer of the Talleys and Counter Talleys in the Exchequer is of late erection, he being properly the Clerk of the Lord Treasurer, or Commissioners of the Treasury, in which office there appears not to have been more than 6 persons from the first institution thereof.

In the time of King James I . . . there was allowed to that
officer the yearly sum of   91.13.4
And for a Clerk per annum   9. 0.0

                  In all   100.13.4

Which continued to the time of Sir Robert Long . . . with the
yearly salary for life, of   316.13.4

And the house in the Cloisters, which had formerly belonged to Sir Walter Mildmay, Chancellor of the Exchequer, and Under Treasurer thereof.

This office is now possessed by the Honble. Sir Robert Howard, knight, by virtue of two Commissions, one from Lord Clifford and the other from Lord Viscount Osborn . . . ; and by Letters Patent of King Charles the Second . . . he has the like yearly
salary as Sir Robert Long of   316.13.4

And the house which was granted to the said Sir Robert Long, is also to him granted for life, with the augmentation of his salary, by the present Lords Commissioners of the Treasury, for extraordinary attendance, the yearly sum of   200. 0.0

                  In all   516.13.4

But the said Writer of the Talleys, notwithstanding this salary, claims and takes several fees, upon the receipts and issues of the public revenue, as Auditor of the Receipt, which appears not to be any office now in being. And as Writer of the Talleys and Counter Talleys (which is the only office granted to him) to a great value
. . . they amount in one year to more than, per annum   6,000. 0.0

Besides other payments for the entries of letters patent, privy-seals, warrants, certificates, and imprest accounts.

And besides a Yearly pension paid to him by the Paymaster of the Army, by verbal order, out of money deducted from the
soldiers' pay, the sum of   1,500. 0.0

And besides a yearly New Year's Gift, paid by the said Pay-master of the Army, 120 guineas, computed, at 20 d. to the guinea   130. 0.0

There follows an itemized account of the fees which made up the £6000 per annum—so much per cent on pensions and annuities and tallies on sale of lands, so much per cent on the payments of the Treasurers of the Wardrobe and Works, and so on.[6]

The report of the Commissioners, who not only questioned "whether any fees can be legally taken by Officers that have salaries for the execution of their offices," but also often had to correct accounts submitted to them by Howard, cannot have been very pleasant reading for him, even though the Commissioners wholeheartedly endorsed the opinion he had frequently expressed that "the striking of Talleys of loan before the money is actually lent" was an evil that should and could be avoided.[7] Here, at any rate, he had been proved right and Danby wrong.

Both Houses busied themselves with the report for some time, but in the long run little or nothing was done about it. It will be seen that Howard's income from salary and fees was estimated by the Commissioners at more than £8,146 per annum; and had anything come of it, he must have been concerned at the resolution of the Commons on 12 December 1691 that, with only specified exceptions, "the Salaries, Fees, and Perquisites of all officers under the Crown . . . exceeding 500 l. *per ann.* shall be applied to the use of the War." If he was present on that day, he had the sense to keep quiet, as he had also done on 3 December, when his son Thomas felt compelled to explain the mention of annual sums of £50 and £100 paid respectively to himself and to his mother's kinsman Mr. Kingsmill: "Both have had Pensions from King *Charles* paid all this while. . . . I owe all to the Protection of the Government, but nothing to the Bounty of it."[8] The pension was still being paid in December, 1692. Similarly, Sir Robert's £200 per annum for extraordinary services was paid regularly for the rest of his life, and on 18 September 1693 he was even granted an additional £500 a year "for managing the business on the Million Act . . . he to reward his clerks as he thinks fit out of said 500 l. *per an.*"[9] The one diminution to his income following the report of

6. *H.M.C.*, 13th Report, App. V., MSS of the House of Lords 1690-1691, pp. 422-425.

7. *Ibid.*, pp. 425, 409.

8. Grey, X, 191-197. Kingsmill's pension was the one for payment of which Sir Robert had asked Godolphin's help on 25 June 1689. See above, chap. i, p. 8.

9. *C.T.B.*, 1689-1692, pp. 1917-1918, 1930; *C.T.B.*, 1693-1696, pp. 7, 452, 560,

the Commissioners was the loss of the £1,500 per annum paid to him by the Paymaster of the Forces on the verbal command of James II, in lieu of Exchequer fees. Howard told the Commons on 9 December 1693: "I had 1500 *l.* from Lord Ranelagh. I was not so saucy as to refuse the King's favour. But I surrendered the Grant" and Ranelagh added, "I had verbal directions from the King to pay 1500 *l. per annum* to Sir *Robert Howard*, and it was paid till *December* 1691; and then *Howard* delivered it up, and no more notice was taken of it."[10] It is clear that he could well afford not to put himself in the wrong by disputing a pension, large as it was, which could be regarded as exceptional even in those days; the greater part of his income, to which he was entitled according to the customs of his time, could not be touched until the whole system of public finance was overhauled.

Like many another wealthy man, however, Howard had found that there was one thing he could not buy—health. For years now he had been a sufferer from what was called gout; and early in 1691 the question of his successor as Auditor was being eagerly canvassed. On 20 March, Godolphin, as First Lord of the Treasury, wrote to tell the King that "Sir Robert Howard was very ill last week with gout in his stomach" and to remind him both that the position was of the greatest importance and that although the reversion had been granted by patent, probably not good in law, to Peregrine Osborne, the King had in fact the grant of one of Howard's *two* positions.[11] The importance of Howard's position as Auditor is even more strongly emphasized by the fact that it was apparently dangled as a prize before a far greater man, Robert Harley, who, in a journal entry referring to his political career in the years after 1690, writes that "During that time I had many overtures made to me, sometimes to be Secretary of State and very earnestly to accept Sir Robert Howard's place as Auditor of the Exchequer, who then lay ill. I was offered to *have it made easy to me*. . . ."[12]

1268, 133; 1696-1697, p. 340; 1697-1698, p. 212. See also 1693-1696, p. 1288; April-Sept., 1697, p. 215; 1697-1698, p. 370.

10. *C.S.P.D.*, May, 1690—Oct., 1691, p. 340; *H.M.C.*, 13th Report, App. 5, MSS of the House of Lords, p. 407, and 7th Report, App., MSS of the Earl of Denbigh, p. 219a; Grey, X, 357. This, incidentally, is the last time Grey mentions Howard.

11. *C.S.P.D.*, *Addenda* 1689-1695, pp. 169-170.

12. *H.M.C.*, 15th Report, IV, Portland MSS IV, 451.

Howard was still ill when on 31 July he wrote another letter to the King:

May it please your Ma^ty:

It has been A great afliction to mee that by soe longe A fitt of the Goute I have been hinderd from waitinge on your Ma^ty; but while I live the affection and Duty I have to your Person and Goverment, shall never faile of there attendance, when ever any occasion requires it;

That which now happens to be the cause of givinge Your Ma^ty this trouble, I have communicated to my Lord Godolphin; with whose approbation and opinion I humbly present it, and to whom I have committed this to be safely conveyd to your Ma^ty.

The businesse (which I have receivd from very good Intelligence by particular freinds of mine) is A designe carry'd on by A very great Party, that the war both by Sea and Land shoud be manag'd by A Committee of parliament, and this Intelligence seems to be made good, by the manner of the proceedings of the Commissioners for accounts; who Act soe unlimited, and in many things exceedinge there Pow'r, that it seems plainly to be A Method in order to such A designe; and as formerly an Abjuration of any other Pow'r has been refusd, this seems an Abjuration of your Ma^tys.

I am likewise inform'd that the same Partys will make all the strength they can to oppose the givinge of Excises, and this present Parliament has appeard very refractory in that matter, without which twill be very difficult to carry on the war, or to discharge the debts in Peace;

I humbly submitt it to your ma^ty's consideration whether A new Parliament may not be A prevention of such design's, and probaly [sic] proceed sooner to the businesse of mony then this, where the contrivance is already layd for many things to preceed the givinge of it. I hope I need not beg your ma^tys pardon for this presumption, since you have been ever pleas'd soe gratiously to receive the testimonys of the sincere duty and service of

your ma^tys
Most faithfull and most
obedient subject
Ro: Howard.[13]

In his own letter to the King, however, Godolphin hopes that the King will not expect *him* to tell Howard that his proposals are extravagant, "or ever answer him seriously on any similar occasion"; when he sees the King, he will tell him why he thinks Howard proposes a new Parliament at this time.[14] Godolphin obviously means that Howard wanted to avoid the kind of resolution of Parliament,

13. P.R.O. S.P. Dom. King William's Chest 9, No. 141, also cited in Dalrymple III, 187.

14. *C.S.P.D.*, May, 1690—Oct., 1691, p. 481.

prompted by the report of the Commissioners for Public Accounts, that was in fact passed, as we have seen, on 12 December.

William, who listened to all, committed himself to none, and made up his own mind, declined to dissolve parliament, but Howard was right in asserting that the existing House of Commons would not give the King all the money and all the freedom desired for the conduct of the war against France. Howard still fought in the House for what he thought William would want, and in a Grand Committee on Supply, on 19 November, he vainly opposed a move to advise the King on the exact number of men in the army considered necessary for the peace of the realm and the successful prosecution of the war. He could not see any danger of an army enslaving the people of England "under a King that has courage. . . ."[15]

Although Howard was in the House again on 3 December,[16] one has the impression that more and more of his time may have been spent at Ashtead, partly, no doubt, because of his illness. Luttrell has one amusing reference that suggests that Sir Robert whiled away some of his spare hours in amateur scientific experiment, for which he had apparently inherited his father's passion: "Sir Robert Howard has tryed to destill spirits from wheat, and has brought it to great perfection, to make it as strong as brandy it self."[17]

Another family reference that arouses speculation is an entry by Thomas Howard that on 16 January 1692 he paid to his aunt, Lady Elizabeth Dryden, "in charitye," the sum of £5.[18] G. R. Noyes has pointed out that the entry does not necessarily mean that she was destitute; perhaps, he suggests, the money was "to distribute in charity or because of some sudden emergency, such as illness."[19] It also does not mean that Robert had washed his hands of his sister's affairs (although I suspect that he had had no direct contact with her husband John Dryden for many years); Thomas at this time was keeping the accounts of the Ashtead estate and frequently paid money at his father's direction.

Thoughts of the old association with Dryden must certainly have

15. Grey, X, 175 ff.
16. *Ibid.*, X, 191-197.   17. Luttrell, II, 307 (Nov., 1691).
18. Cited from Thomas's "Book of Expenses" by G. Thorn-Drury, "Some Notes on Dryden," *R.E.S.*, I (Jan., 1925), 83.
19. Noyes, lvii, n. 3.

been revived by the publication in 1692 of Howard's *Five New Plays*, announced in the *London Gazette* for 26-30 May as "the Second Edition Corrected."[20] It consists of the *Four New Plays* of 1665 and *The Duke of Lerma* of 1668, each play having a separate new title page dated 1692. The text, although it differs from the earlier volumes in very minor ways, all explicable as compositor's changes, shows no signs of authorial revision. The 1692 edition (there were different issues) was printed for Howard's original publisher, Herringman. It is a handsome folio, with a portrait of Howard engraved by White after the painting by Kneller, but it may not have sold very well, for the 1700 "edition" is only a reissue by Herringman of the 1692 one, with a cancel title-leaf. (Tonson printed a "Third Edition," duodecimo, in 1722.)

It will be remembered that Howard's other publication of 1692, his *Letter to Mr. Samuel Johnson*, was said by the author to have been delayed by his own great indisposition; and there are very few references to his activities during the year. He cannot have been completely confined to his bed, however, for on 31 May he issued a certificate of money due under his third wife's will to Bridget Darcy, widow of John Darcy.[21]

In the autumn he entertained the Queen to dinner at Ashtead;[22] but in November and December he was back in London. On 12 November, when the House debated the activities of the Fleet under Russell during the previous summer, Howard wanted to know why the victory was not followed up (and why the Fleet was not as effective as in Cromwell's time). The explanation given by Sir John Ashby, who was called to the Bar of the House, was that the further movement of the Fleet had been made impossible by the shallows; and on 20 December Howard handsomely made amends for any implications in his earlier remarks, by seconding the successful motion that Russell

20. Cited by Sybil Rosenfeld, *P.M.L.A.*, LI (1936), 137.

21. P.R.O. Treasury Papers, TI, XVIII, No. 56. It appears that Mary Uphill had a pension, payable in the Exchequer, of £200 per annum, for nineteen and three quarter years from Midsummer 1672, and had bequeathed it to John Darcy, one of her executors; Howard's certificate is for the last instalment, after which Bridget Darcy was granted a new annuity. I have not been able to trace any record of the granting of the original pension to Mary Uphill or of her will.

22. Luttrell, II, 574, 577. (Luttrell says "at Carshalton" but that is probably an error for nearby Ashtead.)

"in his Command of the Fleet during the last Summer's Expedition, has behaved himself with Fidelity, Courage, and Conduct."[23]

He apparently took no part in the 1693 debates on the Fleet; for this, however, there may have been a special and most unexpected reason, namely that on 26 February he married, for the fourth time. His wife was Annabella Dives (or Dyve), described by Luttrell as "maid of honour to the princesse, aged about 18."[24] Annabella was the daughter of John Dyve or Dives, who had been a clerk under Howard in the Exchequer but on 1 March 1692 had become Clerk to the Privy Council.[25] Dives had not been a poor man (the Commissioners for Public Accounts had reported that his salary as Secretary to the Prize Office, under patent of William and Mary, was £500 a year) but of course there would have been many to say that Annabella, after the death of her father, had married the aging statesman for his money. The courtship certainly aroused the mirth of the wits, and Sedley wrote a poem for the occasion:

Mars. Cupid, I hear thou hast improv'd
    Thy little Art of War;
    Old Men conceit they may be lov'd,
    And Cripples win the Fair.

False powder'd Beaux at distance kill,
    And every Fop writes Songs:
Musick imploys her utmost Skill,
    And to thy Camp belongs.

Cupid. Great God of War, why shou'd not I
    As well as you advance,
And by new Ways make Lovers dye,
    While you bomb Towns in *France.*

William and *Louis* are your Pride,
    Belle Dives, and *Stowel* mine,
Whose Batteries Men can less abide
    Than those upon the *Rhine.*[26]

23. Grey, X, 245, 291.
24. Luttrell, III, 45; but Luttrell erred in saying that Howard was "aged 70"; he was sixty-seven.
25. *C.T.B.,* 1693-1696, p. 399; Luttrell, II, 373; *C.S.P.D.,* 1691-1692, p. 387; 1693, p. 13. Dives died before the end of the year.
26. *The Poetical and Dramatic Works,* ed. V. de Sola Pinto (London, 1928), I, 39-40. Professor Pinto thinks that "Stowel" is Lady Margaret Cecil, who married John, Lord Stowell, in 1691.

Other, anonymous, wits were even less polite and one could not resist, in his satire "The Pensioners":

> Let noble sir Positive lead the Van,
>   That only all-doing unerrable Man,
> What pity it is that his Life's but a Span?
>   Which nobody can deny.
>
> He's fain to be helped to get up and ride,
>   Whene'er his fair Wife he is pleased to bestride,
> Yet he'd rule the World was it ten times as wide,
>   Which nobody can deny.[27]

There is no evidence whatever that the marriage was unhappy. Annabella was cultured: according to Henry Purcell's widow, dedicating *Orpheus Britannicus* to her in 1698, she was one of Purcell's most talented pupils and he wrote many of his compositions for her (and she repaid the debt by erecting the monument to him in Westminster Abbey). Howard himself not only referred to her in his will four years after the marriage as "my most dear and affectionate wife," but also appointed her his executrix and left her all his property; and it is of course not surprising or to her discredit that she married again after his death.[28] That there may even have been a child of the marriage is suggested by a letter from Sir Christopher Musgrave to Robert Harley on 4 September 1694: "For Sir Robert Howard to show to the world in one year a book and a child is next a miracle, his age considered."[29] Howard's failure to refer to any child in his will, though not necessarily conclusive if the baby was a girl, would strongly suggest—as would the absence of any other reference—that any child of the marriage must have died in infancy.

Sir Robert's unexpected marriage so late in life must have been a blow to the son of his first marriage, Thomas. Thomas's right to the Ashtead estate had been guaranteed under his marriage settlement; and in the nine and a half years between his marriage to Lady Diana in 1683 and his father's fourth marriage, in 1693, he and his wife and his father had often been at Ashtead together. (They played cards—

27. *Poems on Affairs of State* (London, 1704), III, 330.
28. For Purcell, see below, pp. 299-303. Annabella's second husband was the Reverend Edward Marten. She was buried at Hammersmith on 7 September 1728. (Chester, *Westminster Abbey Registers*, p. 243).
29. *H.M.C.*, 14, II, Portland MSS, Vol. 3, p. 554. The book was Howard's *History of Religion*.

and when Thomas lost to his father he repaid himself out of the Ashtead accounts!) In keeping the accounts, Thomas entered as "by order" most payments authorized by his father. Significantly there are no accounts for a few months after 14 January 1693, around the time of Sir Robert's marriage.[30] After it, the Ashtead property was in Thomas's undisputed possession, and since he had been thus provided for, he was not included in his father's will.

There was, however, no final break between father and son, although they no longer lived in the one home in Surrey. They are mentioned together, for example, by Luttrell on 21 June 1694 as having subscribed the huge sum of £18,000 to the new bank, the Bank of England, and again in a list of nominees under the Million Act. This Act of 1693, described by Maurice Ashley as "the first instance of the Government borrowing money directly from the public on a long-term basis and not as a mere anticipation of revenue from a few rich men,"[31] authorized a kind of official lottery, under which annuities were paid on nominated lives. The original plan was that contributors were to receive 10 per cent for the first eight years, and thereafter 7 per cent; and the dividends of annuitants who died were to be added to the dividends of the nominators of the survivors, until only seven were left. (Later contributors accepted a flat 14 per cent, without "benefit of survivorship.") Thomas Howard, of "Ashted," paid the exceptional sum of £200 on the life of his son Thomas, then aged five; Sir Robert, "of St. *Margarets Westminster*" invested the normal £100, on the life of his wife Annabella, her age being given as twenty and "the Place of their Abode" as "New Palace-Yard, Westminster."[32]

Howard was officially responsible for the administration of this Act.[33] Perhaps his duties in this connection are part of the explanation of his apparent absence from Parliament in the early months of 1694 (Grey does not mention him from 9 December 1693 until the *Debates*

30. From information in the possession of, and generously communicated to me by, Mr. A. W. G. Lowther.

31. Luttrell, III, 332; Ashley, *England in the Seventeenth Century* (London, 1952; second edition, 1954), p. 183.

32. *A Particular Accompt of the Moneys Paid into the Receipt of Exchequer, Upon the late Million Act, for the Benefit of Survivorship . . . Examined by the Right Honourable Sir Robert Howard, Kt. Auditor of the Receipt of Exchequer; And Printed by his Direction. London . . . 1694.* (Yale University Library).

33. Luttrell, III, 96.

end with the report on 25 April 1694); he was certainly well paid for his work, as is shown by the warrant (already cited) for payment of an annual £500 to him and his clerks for their additional duties under the Act. Other surviving documents show that his ordinary functions as Auditor were still carried out in person and he managed yet another grant of £150 a year for himself and his clerks (the clerks to be rewarded at Howard's "discretion") for their responsibilities under the statute governing tonnage duties.[34] In addition to all this, he was one of the Privy Counsellors appointed on 27 June as "Commissioners of Appeal for prizes during the present war."[35]

Whatever else had been said of Howard, it could never have been said that he lacked energy; and in this same year he perpetrated one of the worst of his tactical blunders by publishing a *History of Religion* which he actually thought—or said he thought—contained nothing of a controversial nature! Perhaps the claim that one was writing the simple truth was not quite as fantastic in the days of rationalism as it now seems; even Jonathan Swift at about the same period asserted that there was nothing in *A Tale of A Tub* to which any true Church of England clergyman could take exception, and John Dryden had written in the closing lines of *Religio Laici* that

> Faith is not built on disquisitions vain
> The things we *must* believe, are *few* and *plain*.

Howard might have reflected that only a few years after writing *Religio Laici* Dryden had proceeded to believe something quite different from what in 1682 he had found "plain"; for that matter, he should have remembered the fate of his own history of Richard II. The positiveness in Howard's make-up, however, had not decreased with age. He even claimed to be surprised when he discovered that there is no such thing as an uncontroversial history of religion. He had, in fact, brought all the angry hornets of theological controversy buzzing round his head.

34. P.R.O. Treasury Papers, TI. XXVII, No. 72; *C.S.P. Treasury Papers, 1556-1696*, p. 390; *C.T.B.*, 1693-1696, p. 724.
35. *C.S.P.D.*, 1694-1695, p. 204; July-Dec., 1695, pp. 111-112.

Chapter nineteen. THE HISTORY OF RELIGION, 1694, AND THE SUBSEQUENT PAMPHLET WAR

THE HISTORY OF RELIGION was published in 1694 as "Written by A Person of Quality," but the authorship was widely known and was soon admitted by Howard, in one of his replies to those who attacked him. The *History* has an extraordinary Preface, of which the following passages will give an adequate representation:

There is nothing contained in it [the main work] of a Polemical or Controversial Nature; no Dispute, or Arguments upon any Controversy; the World has been stuffed with too many (useless) Wranglings of that kind already.

The Subject of the following Discourse, arises from *Matter of Fact*; How Religion has (from the beginning) been managed by Priest-Craft of the Heathens, to mislead the *Vulgar* and *Prophane* (as they are pleased to term them) into a Blind Implicit Obedience, to their Inspired and Divine Authority; Teaching the Belief of many Gods, or *Divine Powers*, and Appointing so many various Ways of Superstitious Devotions. . . .

They [the Priests] invented two great Assistances, *Mystery* and *Persecution*: by the Mystery, to prevent the Use of *Understanding*; and by Persecution, to punish any that should attempt to break out of the *Brutal Pound*, and use their Reason. . . .

All these Practices of the Heathens I have endeavour'd, and I believe *very plainly*, to make appear, that they are retained and followed to this day, in what is called the *Church of* Rome. . . . they have made it a terrible Thing for Men to trust themselves, or their own Reason, in any thing relating to Religion; 'tis with them, an equal Crime for the *Prophane Vulgar* (as the Heathens also called them) not to submit their Understandings to God, and their Priests. . . .

Nothing has given a greater Blemish to the Christian Religion, than the Controversial Writings of the Learned. . . . The Consideration of this, ought (in my Opinion) to induce those that are Guides and Teachers, to make our Way plain and easy, to follow the clear and uncontested Methods of the Gospel, to win and excite People chiefly to the Love of God, and to encourage rather than distract. . . .

In short, I must publish it to the World, that I like such Sermons as Dr. *Tillotson*'s, now Arch-bishop of *Canterbury*: where all are taught a plain and certain Way to Salvation; and with all the Charms of a calm and blessed Temper, and of pure Reason, are excited to the uncontroverted indubitable Duties of Religion.

The Preface may be a serious tactical error but is so good a summary of the main work that the latter may now be treated very briefly. Beginning with the statement that "There never was yet any Country, or Society of Men, but did own some Religion," Howard asserts that (although there has been a change from polytheism to monotheism) in all instances from ancient times to the contemporary "Church of Rome" the worship of images (and later of saints "as Patrons and Mediators") was begun by the priesthood. The increase of saint-worship, he thinks, coincided with the growth of "the Practice and Profession of Monastic Life" in the fourth century A.D.; but he quotes from Hesiod, Plato, Cicero, and Plutarch to give what he considers earlier examples of the same kind of error. His main aim, of course, is to suggest that Roman Catholic doctrine is no better than primitive religion; and therefore the Catholic doctrine of Purgatory (with quotation from Bellarmine) is compared with the Mohammedan Paradise and with Roman notions of Heaven and Hell (as seen in Virgil), with the implication that all these show the same childish modeling of the after-life on the pattern of mere earthly desires and fears.

The New Testament he examines to show that it, on the contrary, introduces no new mysteries, but solves existing ones: "the whole Aim of our Saviour in the Gospel, is to use a Clearness of Direction for Practice" (parables, for instance, are only to make principles "familiar"). Priests alone, then, are responsible for mysteries and for persecution, "the heavy Rod to awe and terrify men from questioning their Doctrine"; they "must know the Folly and Falshood of what they teach; they cannot believe things to be true, which they themselves invent" (and he gives Indulgences as his contemporary example).

Having so far concentrated on "Mystery," he turns (on p. 82) to develop his theory of "Persecution." The religion of Mahomet, originating in "Destruction and Fierceness of Rage," has become, according to Howard, "peaceful and tolerant"; the history of Christianity has been almost exactly the opposite. He blames St. Dominic for beginning the Christian persecution for heresy ("and from his Order chiefly the Inquisitors have been chosen ever since"); and he deplores such persecution not only because he traces it to the love of power among priests but also because he cannot conceive that those who practice it believe sincerely that it will convert the erring. *Verbal* recantation it may achieve, but such a "Victory is indeed a Service to the Priests Power, but none to God, or the Suffering Person."

"Error" is his next theme; and this he sees as "no Sin, because it comes not from the Will and Intention"; "if a Man does not mix a Vice with his Opinion . . . his Error in Opinion cannot be a Crime, nor any Foundation of a Punishment." Salvation surely cannot depend "upon a controverted Point," and to believe that it could do so "seems ridiculous"; the Gospel "most certainly contains all things necessary to Salvation. And if this particular Question, What Substance it was that is administred in the Sacrament, had been so very necessary to Salvation, our Saviour would certainly have deliver'd it in a plain Instruction and Precept."

He therefore regrets all unnecessary disputes such as the one concerning the doctrine of the Trinity. On the other hand, he thinks religious teachers necessary:

The Knowledge of Religion is not born with us, nor infused into us; and therefore is to be learned . . . The Unlearned must of Necessity, in some things place a Confidence in those, whose proper Imployment and Learning qualifies, and assists them to make a true Translation of the Holy Scriptures. . . .

But, he insists, these guides are not infallible and every man may therefore still use his own judgment.

It will be apparent that the so-called *History of Religion* is not really a history at all, but an anti-Catholic tract in which history is brought in to support the main arguments about priestcraft and persecution. The merit is in the style; on the whole, the work is well written and some things are well said. The weakness is in Howard's thinking: he hardly seems to be aware either that his own doctrine of the adequacy of the Gospel is itself a religious position, open to discussion in the light of Reason, or that the final pages on the necessity for teachers of religion come perilously close to giving his case away. Above all, in supposing that he or anybody else could write anything on the subject of theology which could be above argument, he showed a naïveté that would seem almost incredible were it not that this is the folly of which all philosophies of the "reasonable" and "natural" are in fact guilty.

Probably the first reply to Howard was *The Scorner Incapable of True Wisdom. A Sermon Before the Queen At White-Hall, October 28. 1694. By Francis Atterbury, Student of Christ-Church, and Chaplain in Ordinary to Their Majesties. London . . . 1694.* This sermon, on the text (Proverbs xiv. 6) "A Scorner seeketh wisdom, and findeth it not," complains that scorners have always felt that all religion, like their own, was "a Convenient Trick and Pretence onely; invented by Cunning men to keep silly People in awe, to make Princes Reign safely, and the Priesthood Live Easily." Such a man, Atterbury argues, relies only on "Right Reason . . . by Right Reason always meaning his Own." A scorner suffers from four handicaps, the first two invariably, the others normally: a proud temper, a suspicious one, false wit, and sensuality; and "as soon as he has touch'd on any Study, he immediately seems to himself to have master'd it; is as Positive in his Opinions, and as hardy in his Assertions, as if the Thoughts of his whole Life had been directed That way only." The use of "Positive" itself probably suggested to the congregation that Howard was meant,[1] and this in turn implies that the charge of sensuality also was aimed at him; sensuality, Atterbury avers, will always make a man dislike principle and religious doctrine. At any rate, there is no doubt who is attacked in the following paragraph:

And he may put the Thoughts, which arise in him upon This occasion, together; and make a Book of 'em, if He pleases; and then tell us, that This is a sober Enquiry after Truth; and a free discussion of the Point in debate; but there is nothing of that in it. He thinks of Truth just as a man does of his *Enemy*, with Spite and Anger, and a Design only of finding out whatever may blast and expose it. This is a strange contumelious way of treating Divine things, and would tempt a Good man to return the affronts done to Vertue and Piety, by opening the Characters of Those who do 'em; in which we should always find, that Sensuality and Loosness of Life had a very great and particular share. But Some Men, who Write pretended *Histories of Religion*, are beholding to the Real Religion of Others, that Their Histories are not written.

After this, Atterbury's prayers, for all who are in error, only add to the impression of most un-Christian hypocrisy.

The ensuing controversy is a fit subject, in its fullest detail, rather for the historian of theology than for a mere biographer of Howard. In fact, the next pamphlet to be published connected Howard's *History* with the Socinian controversy, which has a bibliography of its own too lengthy even to be listed here. Briefly, however, the facts are these.

The pamphlet was *The Charge of Socinianism against Dr. Tillotson Considered . . . To which is Added Some Reflections upon the Second of Dr. Burnet's Four Discourses, concerning the Divinity*

1. Compare pp. 289 and 290 for evidence that the nickname was still used.

and Death of Christ . . . *To which is likewise Annexed, A Supplement upon Occasion of a History of Religion, lately Published, Supposed to be Wrote by Sir R.—— H——d . . . By a True Son of the Church. Edinburgh . . . MDCXCV.* Tillotson had published several sermons trying to clear himself from the charge that his doctrines were Socinian (as the Socinians claimed they were); this pamphlet alleges that his denial is in vain, and that Burnet and Howard (who is never once mentioned by name) are of the same party. It is also alleged (quite unjustly, on the whole) that Howard's *History of Religion* is no more than a crib from *Great is Diana of the Ephesians*, written by Charles Blount and published anonymously in 1680. (With true argumentative logic, when it is admitted that Blount says idolatry was instituted by "Civil Princes," and Howard says it was instituted by priests, the allegation of indebtedness is not withdrawn but they are jointly accused of inconsistency!) The further charge that Howard attacked Catholicism not to reform religion but to "undermine Christianity it self" is also manifestly absurd. The anonymous pamphleteer writes better sense both on the question of respect for the priesthood (Christ himself, it is suggested, was a priest) and when he says that all such men as "Sir Positive" "decry all *Mystery* as being a Subterfuge for *Ignorance*: And plead their *Ignorance* as an excuse for not Believing in *mysteries*!" Soon, however, he again descends to personal abuse, asserting that "neither *Possitives* nor *Poslings*" would ever be thought modest or humble or free from ingratitude; and "Posling" is found guilty of "turning his father out of Door." None of the attempted answers to the pamphlet mentions this allegation, which must refer to the arrangement by which Ashtead was left in the undisturbed possession of Robert's son Thomas after Robert's marriage to Annabella Dives. The answers do make it their business to reply to the next accusation, that Posling's action "may serve as a *Fescue* to Sir *Positive*; he having not long before assisted in the same sin against a Neighbour, who never injur'd him; and who had done more for him than all the Friends and Relations he had in the World." (This is taken to refer to the virtual expulsion of James II—and, of course, its claim that James had done much for Howard is easily ridiculed.) Two even more fantastic assertions follow—that in any truly Christian country, the punishment for such blasphemy as Howard's would be death, and that men like Howard "are against *Monarchy* in *Heaven* or on Earth."

When another pamphlet in the war *Archbishop Tillotson Vindicated from The Charge of Socinianism* (London, 1696)[2] took the side of Tillotson but nevertheless attacked Howard, the latter must indeed have felt like the bear when Hudibras fell on him. He had been abused by Tillotson's enemies; now one of Tillotson's friends was repeating the charge that the *History of Religion* ("written by *Sir Positive At-All*, a very great Reformer, and very notable Man") ridiculed the Christian religion, and was further claiming that Tillotson had been grossly misrepresented.

Religious controversy being what it was, Howard and his friends had to publish a reply. Their answer, which must have been in preparation before *Archbishop Tillotson Vindicated* reached print, was *A Twofold Vindication of the Late Arch-Bishop of Canterbury, And of the Author of "The History of Religion". The first Part defending the said Author against the Defamations of Mr. Fr. Atterbury's Sermon, and both those eminent Persons against a Traiterous Libel, titled, "The Charge of Socinianism against Dr. Tillotson consider'd". In two Letters to the Honourable Sir R. H. The second containing Remarks on the said Sermon, and a Reply to the same Libel . . . By Another Hand. London . . . 1696.*

To this volume is prefixed, with no separate heading, a long letter from Howard to the publisher. In this Howard acknowledges the favor of the receipt of the two principal "Letters" when they were ready for the press, and expresses his satisfaction in the answers given by their authors to "two extraordinary angry Men, Mr. *Atterbury* and Mr. *Monroe.*" (The latter was Alexander Monro, former Principal of Edinburgh University, whom Howard and his supporters wrongly believed to be the author of *The Charge of Socinianism against Dr. Tillotson Considered.*) Howard says that he does not know Atterbury personally but does regret his improper use of the pulpit to vent "a Passion unsuitable to Christianity, or common Morality"; yet, he continues, Atterbury "seems to have a Christian Consideration that hinders him from writing some Body's Life; if he means mine, I will free him from his tender Christianity, and own that I writ the *History of Religion*; and . . . I shall not be displeased at any Truth that he

2. Variously attributed to Leslie and to Sherlock.

can write." After saying that he thinks Monro is satisfactorily dealt with by others in the succeeding two letters, he adds:

A Friend of mine, of Quality and Learning, told me, he ask'd a Minister [of the Church of England] why he was displeas'd at the *History of Religion?* he answer'd, that they were whipt upon the Backs of the Romish Priests; I could not but wonder how they got up there to receive the Lashes of the others.

Then, avowing that he will not exchange insults but, in the process, doing so, he ends the letter:

I will conclude with an Assurance, that I shall not take it ill of any one that shall offer Reasons unclogg'd with Passion against any thing I have writ; and if I cannot clearly answer them, I will submit and acknowledg my Error; and that any one may have the freer Invitation, I own that the *History of Religion* was writ by,
Sir,
Your true Friend, and most humble Servant,
Ro. Howard.

There follows a separate title page for the main work, but it in turn is followed by a letter "To the Publisher" ostensibly from the author of the two principal letters of the pamphlet, "N.S." In this, N. S. begs the publisher to allow him to say that he has received from Howard an answer to the libel that Howard was indebted for many favors to James II: "He avows, that His Majesty, both when he was King, and while he was only Duke of *York,* never did him any Favour, nor made him the Offer of any: but on the contrary, shew'd to him all the Unkindness, that Occasion and Opportunity (at any time) enabled him to express." N.S., sadly lacking in a sense of humor, announces that if favors had been offered to Howard by James, they might well have been accepted "either as part of the Reward, due to his Services; or as His Majesty's *Royal Munificence,* to Wit and distinguishing Abilities," rather than as bribes. Indeed, he writes:

King *James,* Father *Petre,* and the *Nuncio,* knew better things, than to fling away their Money on a Person, whom his Vertue, more than his Fortunes, had set so much above the reach of Bribes. . . . You and I, Sir, have nothing so much valued by us, as the Friendship and Esteem of a Fortitude, Constancy, and Vertue so extraordinary; nor any thing that we desire so much, as the long Life and Prosperity of a Friend, whom with so much reason we value and love.

One can only hope most fervently that Howard was not directly responsible for so unctuous a spoiling of a perfectly good case.

It must nevertheless be admitted that N.S. seems to know a good deal about Sir Robert. In the first of the two major letters, he begins by saying that he saw the *History of Religion* before Howard "gave way, that it should go to the Press." He confesses that he was at first worried lest the "Priest-craft" attacked by Howard might include all Christian priests; but when he went over the book carefully, as he thought was due to the subject and an author "whose Pen had always hitherto been successful," he saw that the argument "had been conceived in the last Reign; and by occasion of the danger we were in, from Popery." This is why it is particularly stupid of Atterbury to call it treasonous now; and he offers to brief Atterbury for the Life of Howard that he refrained from writing:

I can tell him, that . . . the Author of the *History of Religion*, has a good degree of Charity to the Poor, and as great of the Vertue of Liberality to the Learned: I can inform him, of your Compositions to the Theater, which made your younger Years so famous; and of the (unanswerable) Defences you have since made for the Nation's Rights against Arbitrary Power and Tyranny. I dare not, I confess, tell him of your Posts of Trust and Honour: for he will be unreconcileably alienated, when he knows, that to all your other Naughtiness, you are a *Williamite* too.

It is conceivable that this was the sincere endeavor of a friend to come to the rescue of an old man who had taken to heart the strictures of an opponent; nevertheless these compliments, as Juliet said to Paris, "will be of more price, Being spoke behind your back, than to your face." N.S. blunders again when, after easily convicting Atterbury of hypocrisy and lack of religion in the uncharitable remarks about Howard, he becomes insulting in the same way himself. He concludes by assuring Howard that he, who has done so much for the nation, need not be worried "at the Sawciness of an obscure Academick."

The second "Letter," dated 17 July 1695, joins issue with *The Charge of Socinianism against Dr. Tillotson Considered*, which N.S. wrongly attributes to Monro and which he says has appeared since the previous letter. He now adds further information about the *History of Religion*: that in the manuscript the title was *The History of Religion, as it has been abused by Priestcraft*; that the publisher wanted the shorter title, lest the victims refuse to read the book; and that it was published against the author's "Inclination," since he now thought it "not so necessary or seasonable." "As to your Book," N.S. writes to

Howard, "his general Charge against it, is; that 'tis designed against all Religion, and especially all *Positive* (or revealed) Religion: from whence he takes occasion to Nick-name you *Sir Positive*; or as he writes (according to the High-land Orthography) *Sir Possitive*." This, unless it be wilful misunderstanding or camouflage, does perhaps suggest that N.S. was not, after all, a mere pseudonym for Howard. For the rest, a few good points are scored against Howard's opponent (for example, for taking Howard's "innoscence" as equivalent to "innocence," and for defending religious persecution) but the intellectual confusion is, on the whole, no less than before.

The second part of the pamphlet, written in an inferior style to the first, again interests us mainly in so far as it gives information about, or indicates attitudes to, Howard. It also is divided into two main sections, the first answering Atterbury, the second the pamphlet attributed to Monro. "Positiveness," Atterbury is told, even if it were a characteristic of Howard, as it is not, "would be less odious in him, whose excellent Natural Parts, and all desirable Advantages of Study and Conversation, make it as probable for him, as any Man breathing to come to the knowledg of the Truth, whatever is the Object of his Inquiry," than it would be in "young" Mr. Atterbury. Unfortunately Shadwell was no longer alive, to say what he thought about that— or about the description of *Absalom and Achitophel*, of which Atterbury had written a Latin translation, as a work "which an old canker'd Poet stuff'd with Common-place Wit, and mercenary dictated Scandal." Perhaps more soundly, it is neatly if unnecessarily pointed out that on Atterbury's own showing, he, being "young and robust," is more likely to be guilty of sensuality than is Howard, now in his old age; and once again it is demonstrated that it is not religion that is restraining Atterbury from writing Howard's Life, since it has not restrained him from delivering "a scandalous Sermon"—against a Privy Counsellor at that. "And what a noble Theme," the pamphleteer exclaims, would not the life of Howard be for "a Man that had a Genius capable!"

The Roman and Grecian Orators prodigally wasted their Eloquence on meaner Subjects than the unshaken Loyalty of Sir *R.H.* during the Troubles of K. *Charles* the First, and Second, his Faithfulness to his Country during the Reign of King *James*, his Courage and Wisdom in defending the happy Choice of the People, and the Right of our present successful Deliverer, our just and lawful King *William*.

Perhaps it is because of this outburst that the author of this second part of the pamphlet thinks it necessary to separate the two halves of his contribution by a letter to the publisher, informing him, and us, that the author is not a friend of Howard, who "hardly knows my face," but "a poor Priest" who conceals his name lest he lose his curacy —although his manner would have been sharper than it is had not the publisher intervened. (This letter, incidentally, is dated 4 November 1695.)

It is with something like a sigh of relief that we come to the final item in this mixed bag of a pamphlet, the reply to the anonymous Edinburgh author erroneously thought to be Monro. Again the theological argument ebbs and flows: a point will be made, only to be thrown away in the following paragraph (indeed one wonders whether any reader would have changed his mind because of anything said in *any* of these pamphlets). Howard is congratulated on being in good company when his name is linked with Tillotson and Burnet; it is even suggested that he is one of the best models for a young man to imitate, as a happy conjunction of Christian and philosopher. He is easily defended against the charge of plagiarism from Blount, from whom he had no need to learn in any way. The main line of defense, however, is that Howard does not wish to force any man's belief in the matter of religious mysteries: "only he would not have them who are good at believing, force others to believe more than they can, in spite of their Senses." There is also further praise of Howard personally. If he is proud, it is said, he "has more in him to excuse the Fault than most Gentlemen have, and many a Priest that I know, is proud of less"; *he* "never arriv'd at that arrogant height of Positiveness, as to determine" other people's beliefs; and finally (except for the Postscript affirming the pamphleteer's intention of placing the *History of Religion* next to his Bible and the Book of Homilies!):

The Author of the History's share in the Revolution, is so far from blemishing, that it adds a new Lustre to his bright Honour. He that could be content in the prime vigorous Years of Life, to seek his Fortunes with an unhappy dethron'd Prince, has now evidently shown to all the World, that his Soul is devoted to serve the Crown with his private Interest, or any thing else, but the Extirpation of the Protestant Religion, and the utter Ruin of his Country.—But that the late King had laid such Obligations on the Author of the History, as to do more for him than all the Friends he had in the World; the Libeller rubb'd his Forehead hard when he ventur'd on that Lie; for nothing was more known through the whole Court, than that the late King number'd him, and us'd him, as one that could not be brought to sacrifice the Religion and Laws of his Country to the Arbitrary Lust of a Priest-ridden Tyrant.

The next arrow was fired from a different direction again—by Alexander Monro, who, not unnaturally, was indignant at the general agreement that the main attack on Howard had been written by him. He therefore now found it necessary to publish *A Letter To the Honourable Sir Robert Howard, Occasioned by a late Book, Entituled, A Two-fold Vindication Of the late Archbishop of Canterbury, And of the Author of the History of Religion* (London, 1696).

In this Monro explains that he wrote to Howard on 13 April 1696 protesting against the identification; and he prints Howard's reply:

Sir,
   Your Letter found me very ill in a fit of the Gout, yet I was unwilling (notwithstanding my pain) to seem so uncivil as to give you no Answer. In short, Sir, the two Treatises were sent to me, before they went to the Press, to peruse; And by reason of the kindness show'd to me and the great abilities I saw in them, I prefix [*sic*] a short preface to them, having also the opportunity to say something to Mr. *Atterbury*, who, in a Sermon at *Whitehall* before the Queen, had ventur'd to treat me very ill. But when these Papers were brought, I neither knew nor was told from whom they came: But the first seems to say that you did not keep your own Secret, but that it got abroad among many that you were the Author. And the second sets down your name, and tells you at the beginning that I hardly knew his face. This, I confess, made me take it for granted that it was yours. But if it is not, which I believe upon your affirmation, I confess, I think, they ought to ask your pardon, which if ever I know them I shall invite them to do. For your Printed Paper, there is not a little in it that concerns any thing I ever knew or said. As to your Person, I am so far from having any quarrel or animosity, that I am rather sorry that this Letter should find you in restraint. I wish you all freedom and remain,
                         Sir,
April 13[3]   Your humble Servant,
   1696   Ro. Howard.

Monro, for his part, says he can prove that another wrote *The Charge of Socinianism against Dr. Tillotson Considered*, and he adds that he did not even set eyes on *The History of Religion* until April, 1696, and (doubtful compliment) that he had never heard of Howard's name until *A Twofold Vindication* was put into his hands by a friend.

3. An error, corrected elsewhere, for "14."

Howard allowed Monro the last word; sufficient damage had been done already. All the old charges, of knowing everything and being too positive about it, had been revived, with some reason; and Howard must have realized that he had indeed rushed in where angels feared to tread. As in the earlier controversies, however, he did know when enough had been said. He therefore refrained from further theological argument, even when in 1696 he was goaded by Edmund Elys, "sometime Fellow of Baliol College in Oxford," in *A Letter To the Honourable Sir Robert Howard*. Elys said that he might have been milder in his expressions had he known when he wrote that Howard was the author of the *History of Religion*; but love of truth forced him to publish, and to record his dislike of Howard's argument. Elys concluded by beseeching *"the only wise* God" to convince Howard of all his errors. Even when taunted so far, however, Howard kept silent; and without any assistance from him the Socinian controversy raged on.

THE story of the remainder of Howard's life, although not without its problems for the biographer, may be told briefly and with a certain pleasure, since during this period his name was again amicably connected both with the theater, for which he had in different ways already done much, and with his brother-in-law John Dryden.

Late in 1694, Betterton, Mrs. Barry, Anne Bracegirdle, and other leading players, desiring to break away from Rich and the other patentees of the theater in which they had become famous, sought the assistance of Howard and Dorset in procuring a separate theater license. On 17 December the parties were instructed to wait on Dorset at Howard's house in Westminster. Through the good offices of these two, the King was persuaded to grant the actors their license; and on 4 April 1695 they opened as the "New Theatre" in Lincoln's Inn Fields, with William Congreve's *Love for Love*.[1]

The theater was also indirectly responsible for the reconciliation of Dryden and Howard, through the agency of John Dryden junior, then resident in Rome. The younger Dryden's play, *The Husband His Own Cuckold*, published by Tonson in the summer of 1696, bore the particularly apt motto from the *Æneid* "Et pater Æneas et avunculus excitet Hector"[2] and was dedicated to his uncle, "the Right Honourable Sir Robert Howard," in a letter dated from Rome 20 August 1695:

I am confident I cou'd not chuse a more indulgent Foster-Father; and tho' my very Name bears an accusation against me, yet I have the honour also to be related to the Muses by the Mothers side; for you your self have been guilty of Poetry, and a Family Vice is therefore the more excusable in me, who am unluckily a Poet by descent. . . .

You, Sir, have prudently known how to make the best use of your Excellent Talent in this kind, by applying it to your diversion, and the unbending your Mind. By these means, you have happily given our Country a great Poet in your Writings; and at the same time have not omitted the more necessary part of giving her a Great States-man and Heroe; to which Eminency your Birth, Courage, and Capacity have equally rais'd you. . . .

1. Nicoll, I, 335, 370 (citing P.R.O. L/C 7/3 and 7/1); Downes, *Roscius Anglicanus*, p. 43; "Thomas Betterton," *History of the English Stage*, p. 93.

2. Perhaps, as is suggested by William Frost, *Dryden and the Art of Translation*, pp. 63-64, Virgil's line came to the son's mind because of his father's very different adaptation of it in *MacFlecknoe* (ll. 173-174).

The son here made amends for the unnecessary gibe by his father published thirty years before; and Dryden and Howard rose to the occasion.

The full circumstances were explained by John Dryden senior in a preface to the play. The son had sent his comedy from Italy to his father, to try its fortune upon the stage. The father had hesitated, because "to confess the truth, I thought it not worthy of that honour," although he did not wish to be discouraging; and the son had guessed the truth:

And therefore in my absence from the Town last Summer, took the boldness to Dedicate his Play to that Person of Honour, whose Name you will find before his Epistle. It was receiv'd by that Noble Gentleman with so much Candor and Generosity, as neither my Son nor I cou'd deserve from him. Then the Play was no longer in my power, the Patron demanding it in his own right, it was deliver'd to him. And he was further pleas'd, during my Sickness, to put it into that Method in which you find it; the loose scenes digested into order, and knit into a Tale. As it is, I think it may pass among the rest of our New Plays; I know but two Authors, and they are both my Friends, who have done better since the Revolution. . . . If it shall please God to restore him [the son] to me, I may perhaps inform him better of the Rules of Writing; and if I am not partial, he has already shewn, that a Genius is not wanting to him.

The play was acted in February, 1696, at Lincoln's Inn Fields. It is not particularly meritorious, being derivative both in plot and in characterization (for example, the comic butt is Timothy Shallow, of Shallow-Hall, in the North, a Justice of the Peace and member of the Quorum); and the elder Dryden's claim that it was at least free from the contemporary evils of poor characterization, and of buffoonery passing for wit, is hardly substantiated (except, possibly, for the sketch of the prevaricating father, old Landy). Yet if Howard did put the play "into method," as Dryden said he did, by weaving loose scenes together, he deserves some praise, for although the comedy has three plots, related by little more than setting and coincidence, the action flows smoothly, the story holds the interest satisfactorily, and it all seems well adapted to stage presentation. Given the three conventional plots (two of them of wives anxious to cuckold husbands, the other of cross-wooing and disguises that hero may wed heroine), the *construction* cannot easily be faulted.

The author, his father, and his uncle all emerge with credit from what could have been a difficult situation; and it is a special pleasure to find Howard again mentioned in Dryden's letters as a friend. In a letter to Tonson, for instance, when the time for the production of *The Husband His Own Cuckold* was approaching, Dryden wrote: "Meeting Sir Ro: Howard at the play-house this morning, and asking him how he liked my Seaventh Eneid, He told me you had not brought it: He goes out of town tomorrow, being Saturday, after dinner. I desire you not to fail of carrying my manuscript for him to read in the Country. & desire him to bring it up with him, when he comes next to Town."[3] Even closer association is implied by a postscript to another letter to Tonson, of 26 May 1696, concerning payment for his son's play: "Sir Ro: Howard writt me word, that if I cou'd make any advantage by being payd in clippd money; He would change it in the Exchequer."[4] This was at the time of the revision of the currency when everybody was anxious to get rid of the clipped coins before they ceased legally to have their full face value; and although the kind of transaction proposed by Howard was going on all the time (Dryden would presumably have received the clipped coins at a discount), it was illegal, and one of the Exchequer clerks was in serious trouble in 1697 for doing just what Howard was offering to do here.[5] The friendship, once renewed, continued, as is shown both by Dryden's reference to "that excellent person Sir Robert Howard" in the Dedication (to Mulgrave) of his translation of Virgil in 1697 and by the fact that Howard subscribed five guineas for one of the plates in it (Plate 87, on p. 511).

Dryden does not say at which "play-house" he met Howard when they discussed the Seventh Æneid; probably it was Lincoln's Inn Fields, but if it was Drury Lane, then Howard may have been attending rehearsals of the new operatic version of *The Indian Queen*, with music by Henry and Daniel Purcell. Heroic drama, in a sense, began in opera, with Davenant; now, in a sense, it ended in it.

I would conjecture (as against Summers) that it was this operatic version of *The Indian Queen* that was referred to on 10 December 1694 in the quarrel between Betterton's group and the patentees, when it was alleged that Betterton had been paid £50 "to gett up yᵉ Indian

3. *Letters*, ed. Ward, p. 79. The probable date of the letter is November, 1695.
4. *Ibid.*, p. 82.
5. Baxter, p. 158. See below, p. 311.

Queen tho he hath not yet done itt." Summers is no doubt correct, however, when he points out that the first production of the opera must have been later than the beginning of April, 1695, since the names of Betterton and his colleagues were missing from the cast.[6]

One would dearly like to know what share, if any, Howard and Dryden had in the preparation of the opera, for the words of several new songs were written for it, including one of the most famous of all Purcell's songs, "I attempt from Love's sickness to fly." No evidence whatever is known to me for thinking that the new lyrics were written by Dryden (even though Purcell had set others of Dryden's works to music); and I have found little enough to suggest that they were by Howard either. The manuscript of the opera, which is in the British Museum (Add. MS 31449), neither hazards any opinion about the authorship nor affords any evidence, by handwriting or otherwise. Equally unhelpful are the printed score; the 1695 volume *The Songs in the Indian Queen: As it is now Compos'd into an Opera. By Mr. Henry Purcell* (published without Purcell's authority, but with reasonable accuracy); H[enry] P[layford]'s 1696 *Deliciæ Musicæ, Being, a Collection of the newest and best Songs, With the Additional Musick to the Indian Queen, by Mr. Daniel Purcell, as it is now Acted at His Majesties Theatre* (this additional music being for the Masque of the Fifth Act, which the manuscript in no way distinguishes from the work of Henry Purcell); the 1697 *A Collection of Ayres, Compos'd for the Theatre, and upon other Occasions By the late Mr. Henry Purcell;* and the 1698 *Orpheus Britannicus. A Collection of all The Choicest Songs for One, Two, and Three Voices, Compos'd by Mr Henry Purcell.*

This last volume, however, has a most important dedication by Henry Purcell's widow (he had died on 21 November 1695), to "the Honourable Lady Howard," namely, as the dedication itself proves, Sir Robert's wife, Annabella:

. . . Your Ladiship's extraordinary skill in Musick, beyond most of either Sex, and Your great Goodness to that dear Person, whom you have sometimes been pleased to honour with the Title of Your Master, makes it hard for me to judge whether he contributed more to the vast Improvements You have made in that Science, or Your Ladiship to the Reputation he gained in the Profession of it: For I have often heard him say, That

6. Dryden, *The Dramatic Works*, ed. Montague Summers (London, 1931-1932), I, 204.

as several of his best Compositions were originally design'd for Your Ladiship's Entertainment, so the Pains he bestowed in fitting them for Your Ear, were abundantly rewarded by the Satisfaction he has received from Your Approbation, and admirable Performance of them, which has best recommended both them and their Author to all that have had the happiness of hearing them from Your Ladiship.

Another great advantage, to which my Husband has often imputed the success of his Labors, and which may best plead for Your Ladiship's favourable Acceptance of this Collection, has been the great Justness both of Thought and Numbers which he found in the Poetry of our most refin'd Writers, and among them, of that Honourable Gentleman, who has the dearest and most deserved Relation to your Self, and whose Excellent Compositions were the Subject of his last and best Performance in Musick.

. . . Your Ladyship having generously prevented my intended Performance of the Duty I owe to his Ashes, by erecting a fair Monument over them, and gracing it with an Inscription which may perpetuate both the Marble and his Memory. Your Generosity, which was too large to be confin'd either to his Life or his Person, has also extended it self to his Posterity, on whom Your Ladiship has been pleas'd to entail Your Favours, which must, with all Gratitude, be acknowledg'd as the most valuable part of their Inheritance, both by them, and

Your Ladiship's

Most oblig'd, and most Humble Servant,

Fr. Purcell.

This dedication proves that it was Lady Annabella Howard who erected the monument to Purcell in Westminster Abbey (and not only makes nonsense of the statements by Brayley that Lady Elizabeth Dryden "was the patroness of Purcell" and erected the monument, but also renders most implausible his belief that the inscription "is supposed to have been written by Dryden").[7] It certainly shows that Howard's relations with Purcell were even closer than Dryden's; and if the widow's remark that Howard's "Excellent Compositions" were the subject of her husband's "last and best Performance in Musick" applied at all to the composition of the words of the new songs in *The Indian Queen*, then it would support Howard's authorship of them. Nothing would be gained, however, by pressing the argument so far: all one can say is that Howard's claim is at least as strong as anyone else's. It may also conceivably be relevant that both in

7. E. W. Brayley and J. P. Neale, *History and Antiquities of the Abbey Church of St. Peter Westminster* (London, 1818-1823), II, 218. The inscription is "Here lyes Henry Purcell Esqr Who left this Life And is gone to that blessed Place Where only his Harmony can be exceeded. Obiit 21mo die Novembrs Anno Aetatis suae 37mo Annoq. Domini 1695."

Orpheus Britannicus and in the earlier, 1695, edition of *Deliciæ Musicæ* (Book I, pp. 8-12) there is another new song, "Love thou canst hear," described as "a single Song. Words by Sir *Robert Howard*":

> Love thou canst hear tho' thou art blind;
> Leave my Heart free, oh! pitty me,
> Leave my Heart free, oh! pitty me,
> Oh! pitty me, since *Cloris* is un-kind.
>
> She is un-constant as she's bright;
> Her Smiles on ev'ry Shepherd fall;
> And as the Sun uses his light,
> She vainly loves to shine on all.
>
> I thought her fair like new faln Snow,
> When whiteness innocence inclos'd.
> Like that, she sully'd seems to show
> When to Loves melting heat expos'd.
>
> The powerfull Charms shall now be try'd;
> This Fury from my Breast to chase,
> I'le summons Scorn, Revenge and Pride,
> At least her Image to deface.

(This setting out, however, does less than justice to the way the words, and the repetitions of them, lend themselves to music and to the pattern of verses and refrain.)

For the libretto of *The Indian Queen*, the text of the play was severely cut (lines and whole speeches being omitted—and the play not losing so very much in the process); but the text was followed carefully where it was used. Significantly, too, all the elaborate stage directions and the stage "business" were meticulously preserved. Act IV of the opera is made up entirely from the dialogue of the original Act IV, with only one new song

> They tell us that you mighty Powers above,
> Make perfect your Joys and your blessings by Love . . .

(and that, incidentally, not in the manuscript version); elsewhere, songs and dances and further spectacle are added. In Act II, for instance, after the entry of Zempoalla, "Fame" is introduced, in the person of Mr. Freeman, to sing, with chorus, of the glories of Zempoalla:

> I come to Sing great Zempoalla's story
> Whose beauteous sight
> So Charming bright
> Outshines the Lustre of glory;

and "Envy" and his Followers reply:

> What Flat'ring noise is this,
> At which my Snakes all hiss;
> I hate to see fond Tongues advance,
> High as the Gods, the slaves of Chance—

and they continue to alternate. The words of the original songs (for example, the incantation of the conjurer Ismeron, "You twice Ten Hundred Deities") are preserved, but Purcell wrote new music for all of them; the new ones are fitted in from time to time, as is, in Act III:

> I attempt from Love's sickness to fly—in vain,
> Since I am my self my own Feaver and Pain;
> No more now, fond Heart, with Pride, no more swell
> Thou canst not raise Forces enough to rebell:
> For Love has more pow'r and less mercy than fate,
> To make us seek ruin, and love those that hate.

These words might almost be called a paraphrase of what Zempoalla says at length towards the end of the original Act III; and again and again one is struck by the ease with which the adaptation is thus made. From the declamation, in heroic couplets, of the play, it is the shortest possible step to rhymed recitative or song. Similarly, in Act V, there is no difficulty in substituting a fuller song, plus chorus, for the original one of the Chief Priest, preparing to offer sacrifice; and it is a simple matter to replace eight lines of Montezuma's final speech with Daniel Purcell's full hymeneal masque.

Perhaps, as Chase once said, an opera lacks one quality of the good Heroic play—the appeal to the understanding,[8] but I cannot feel that the dialogue of the first *Indian Queen*, for all its stress on Love and Honor, had progressed far beyond an exchange of platitude; and evidence has been quoted to show that the play had been popular for its spectacle and other operatic qualities and not for any intellectual content. It therefore lent itself well to adaptation into an opera; and with the magnificent Purcell music (one trio of which Benjamin Britten has recently used to fill a gap in the score of *Dido and Aeneas*), the opera would need no more apology in a modern repertoire than does *Dido and Aeneas*, or *The Fairy Queen*.

The years 1695, 1696, and 1697 seem to have been busy for Howard

8. L. N. Chase, *The English Heroic Play* (New York, 1903), p. 212.

both as Auditor of the Exchequer and as man of letters—extraordinarily so when one remembers that he was now seventy years old and, as he told Alexander Monro in the letter of 14 April 1696, seriously ill and in constant pain with gout. Perhaps his illness, paradoxically, gave him more time for writing and publishing; for in 1696, as if the theological controversy and the interest in the new version of *The Indian Queen* were not enough, he had the *Poems* of 1660 reissued, with a cancel title page, by Francis Saunders. (Hugh Macdonald, noting that copies of this issue are rare, suggested that possibly only a small stock of the original sheets remained.[9] That would be further evidence that Howard's verse had its share of popularity in its day.)

Perhaps, too, an important political action in 1696 led to his writing yet another pamphlet. In early spring of this year, Howard was one of the many members of Parliament who signed "the Association of 1696"—an agreement, on a precedent from the reign of Queen Elizabeth, to defend William, as "rightful and lawful King," against such enemies as the Jacobites and to revenge him should he meet death by violence. Over one hundred members of the two Houses refused to sign, largely because of the difficulty involved in the term "lawful"; and Howard's old enemy, Danby, was one who opposed the Association as needless.[10] Howard has been credited with the authorship of an anonymous pamphlet published in the following year, 1697, in which the issues arising from the Association are discussed.

This is *A Free Discourse Wherein the Doctrines Which make for Tyranny Are Display'd. The Title of our Rightful and Lawful King William Vindicated. And the unreasonableness and mischievous Tendency of the odious distinction of a King de Facto, and de Jure, discover'd. By a Person of Honour . . . London: Printed for John Lawrence at the Angel in the Poultrey, and Richard Baldwin near the Oxford-Arms in Warwick-Lane. 1697.* The names of the two publishers have no great bearing on the question of authorship, although it may be relevant that of the three books advertised for sale by Baldwin at the end of the *Free Discourse*, one is *The History of Religion* and another the *Twofold Vindication* (neither of which bore the name of its publisher).

Two of the few surviving copies of *A Free Discourse* bear manuscript annotations ascribing the work to Howard. On the title page

9. *Dryden*, p. 9.   10. Browning, III, 204.

of one, in the John Rylands Library, Manchester, "A Person of Honour" has been amplified, in what appears to be a contemporary hand, to "Sr Robt Howard";[11] the second, among the Thomas Hollis books at Harvard (and there by about 1764) has an annotation on the title page "This was writt by Sr Robert Howard."[12] The alternative ascription to Defoe, adopted in the catalogue of the Yale library and in the first edition of Wing's *Short-Title Catalogue*, seems to trace back to little better than a bookseller's guess.[13]

A case against Howard's authorship of *A Free Discourse* could be based on the style, which is even more colloquial than Howard's earlier prose, or perhaps colloquial in a different way. The author has, for example, a fondness for the exclamation "Well!" and affects plain language (the Divine Right of Kings, for instance, is "so wicked and odious" as to appal him; and "I can't see," he will write, "wherein this Declaration comes short"). He also takes imagery from fowling, as I think Howard never does; and his knowledge of European (particularly Scandinavian) history also seems to me beyond Howard's usual range of reference.

Yet the argument is so close to what Howard had said before and what we should expect him to be saying now, so great a knowledge of Parliamentary debates is shown, and so apt a reference is made to many an event that we know Howard to have been concerned in, that I am inclined to accept the attribution of *A Free Discourse* to him.

The writer begins by claiming to have been always true to his King and Country, although others have notably not been so, "from towards the latter end of King *Charles* the 2d, to this present time. Under the screening shelter of that Prince, Popery and Arbitrary Power were favour'd . . . till the twin Monsters were thought arriv'd at that fulness of prodigious Stature, as no longer to need his Life, for their Concealment or Protection." It is then recalled how the judges in the time of his successor, James II, ruled that a king could dispense with the law if necessary; and the doctrine of the necessity

11. I am indebted to the Librarian, Professor Edward Robertson, for his courteous answers to my inquiries on this question.

12. W. P. Trent, "News for Bibliophiles," *Nation*, XCVIII (1914), 207, said the annotation was possibly in Hollis's hand. It is demonstrably not so and is probably earlier.

13. The copy in the Firestone Library at Princeton is bound up in a volume of "S^r. R. Howard's Tracts" (bound, I should think, in the eighteenth century). The *Twofold Vindication*, not all certainly by Howard, is included.

of passive obedience even to a tyrannical king, as expounded in *Jovian* and other pamphlets of the time, is deplored. It is argued, with reference to the reign of Richard II and then to modern Europe, that tyranny follows a set pattern; the treaty of Dover and the attempt on the charters of the corporations are cited as examples from the reign of Charles II; and it is noted that after an inaugural speech that promised well, James II soon showed out in his true colors as another potential tyrant.

From James, England was rescued, at the invitation of many Englishmen, by William, "whom God and his own Vertue prompted to attempt our Deliverance." James, by leaving his kingdom, "did, as it were, Sign and Seal his own Abdication"; and the Lords and Commons then "settled the Crown and Royal Dignity on King *William* and *Queen Mary*, the exercise of Regal Power, on their glorious Deliverer only. Thus did they restore the Old Constitution of redem'd *England* in King, Lords, and Commons."

The author reveals an intimate knowledge of the debates in the Commons, and of the quarrel between the two Houses, on the question whether the throne was "vacant"; and he demands to know how otherwise the matter could have been settled: the position was exactly "as when the Original Contract was first made, the People choosing their Ruler, and agreeing the Laws, by which he should rule them." (This, it will be remembered, is the argument of the Preface to Howard's 1690 *History of the Reigns of Edward and Richard II.*) The pamphleteer knows that the *phrase* "original contract" is not acceptable to all, since it is modern and is not found in statute or public document, but he asserts the necessity of the *thing*. The decision in such a case must always rest with the people—as, he adds, Johnson has proved.

He indulges in a great deal of rhetoric on the inconsistency of people who are willing to obey a king only because he is a king *de facto*—pointing out neatly how inconsistent they are when, refusing to recognise a ruler as king *de jure*, they join him to make laws. Such Englishmen he would rather not have. He then recounts the actions of William from the time of his arrival in England, insisting that William put pressure on nobody; pressure was put on him to take over the reins of government. In this way, he leads up to the main problem, of the right of the House of Commons to demand that men subscribe to the "Association."

He recalls that the House of Commons once prayed to God that Charles II would not meet a violent death, "tho' (as 'tis thought) they were not heard"—and again it will be remembered that Howard did believe that Charles died unnaturally, perhaps of poison. The House had also vowed vengeance on the Papists should they be guilty of the murder of Charles—and is not William's life more precious still? Nor has the author any doubt about the moral and political rightness of revenge in such a context: he cannot for one minute admit any validity in the argument of those—particularly Anglican clergymen—who refuse to sign the Association, on the ground that it would commit them to an un-Christian act of vengeance:

It was a very sharp Reflection, and, I would very fain perswade my self, an unjust one, that of Mr. *Dryden, For Priests of all Religions are the same*; but it grieves my Soul to think, that so necessary an order of Men, Protestants, as well as Papists, should be so generally given to oppose the Proceedings of the State.

Old and Crazy is the Body, I cannot say, which I carry about with me, but which is carried about for me; but yet, I am in hopes, that it will hold out, till all His Majesties Subjects represented by the Commons, be taught the necessity of Subscribing the Association of the House of Commons, for, I well remember, how before the end of their last Sessions, they set their own Members a day to Subscribe it, or declare their Refusal.

The appropriateness of this to Howard, as an aged M.P., and its inappropriateness to Defoe, will, I think, be clear; and it would hardly be surprising if towards the end of his life, Howard was even more inclined than before to believe that people ought to do what Parliament told them.

At the conclusion of the *Free Discourse*, the author denies that he wants the Association to be *imposed* on the clergy, although he thinks such imposition would do "no great harm"; but he does think that the clergy ought to be forced to consider the implications of their refusal to subscribe and be made to realize that those who do refuse cannot expect the same favorable treatment as those who sign. He tells a story from Venetian history to prove that there are times when clergymen must be forced to acknowledge the right of the secular power to govern the state; he asks why the French should be expected to recognize William's legal rights if the English will not recognize them; and he concludes with the affirmation that if the reluctant clergymen and others could be compelled to "associate"—"and a very little compulsion will doe, for the most backward of them, are only a little knavish, or so, not obstinate"—nobody would lift a hand against William again.

Howard's authorship of *A Free Discourse* cannot be regarded as certain and is hardly a matter of great importance in any case. It may well be, however, that he did have this last burst of literary energy in 1697; another outcome of it may have been his decision to put his old unfinished play *The Conquest of China* into Dryden's hands, with the request that he adapt it for performance.

One other possible product of his pen must be mentioned. Also in 1697, a new, third, edition of the Earl of Mulgrave's *Essay on Poetry*, first published in 1682, was brought out by Francis Saunders. With the *Essay* were printed "several other Poems," and the volume had a fulsome dedication by Nahum Tate, "To the Honourable Sir Robert Howard, One of His Majesty's Most Honourable Privy-Council, &c":

Sir,

The Collecting into One Volume Several Choice Poems that were first Printed *singly*, met with so kind Reception as encourag'd the Publishing of the following Pieces *together*. Amongst the Former your celebrated *Duel of the Stags* made a Principal Figure; as indeed it will always shine a fixed Star in the highest Orb of English Poetry. Great and Eminent as you are in other Stations, yet I hope, Sir, you will not disdain to be Regis-ter'd amongst the Sons of *Apollo*. The Off-springs of your Muse are so Beautiful, that *Great Britain* is proud of 'em; and if you are not equally pleas'd with 'em, 'tis the first Instance of your Indifference towards any thing that does Honour to your *Country*. She glories that your Genius has not been confin'd to any single Walk of Poetry, but travers'd all its Provinces, and (like *Heracles*) every where erected Pillars and Trophies, to be gaz'd upon with wonder by Posterity. Nature and Art are equal sharers in all you Write; and whatever the Subject has been, Invention, Spirit, Manly Sense and Judgment are never wanting to adorn it. You are, Sir, deservedly Admir'd for the Ingenuity of your *Own* Works, and no less for your generous Candour to the Performances of Other Men. You are no rigid Censurer of their *Faults*, but their *Excellencies* never escape your Observation. This is the Noblest Part of *Criticism*, as requiring not only a discerning Apprehension, but a Goodness of Temper which is not always found in Persons of Wit.

But, Sir, besides the Honour you have done the Muses in their own Faculty, you have further advanc'd their Reputation, by shewing the World, that a Poet can likewise be a *Statesman* and *Patriot* of his Country. To your Knowledge in all the *Liberal Sciences*, you have acquir'd that Nobler Skill in the *Constitution* of our Government, and exerted it upon all Occasions in behalf of English *Liberty* and *Property*. You have not contented your self with the private Exercise of Justice and Generosity, but have shewn a Publick Spirit, employing your great Sense and Sagacity in matters of *National* Importance. What you have written with relation thereunto, and what has been spoken by you in Debates of Vastest Consequence, had no small Influence on the Settlement of our State. These are inviting occasions for Panegyrick, but above my small Capacity: Wherefore I return to my first Design of presenting to you the following *Collection* of Poems; amongst which I know but One that needs any Apology. But I have atton'd for That, by procuring to be here Publish'd an *Ode* on her late Majesty (never before Printed) which, perhaps, is the Truest *Picture* of her *Virtues* that has been drawn. I was only permitted to know that the Author is a Person of Quality; which appears by that easy and agreeable *Air*, by that *Justness* and *Decency*, both in Thought and Expression, that shines through every Stanza.

Sir, I shall no farther trespass on your precious Minutes, only to beg Pardon for this Address, and Permission to Subscribe my self,

> Your Honour's
> most Devoted
> Humble Servant,
> N. TATE.

Hugh Macdonald, no doubt finding Tate's praise of the "Duel of the Stags" hard to take, suspected "a little leg pulling . . . unless Tate was extremely dull."[14] I think that Tate was extremely dull; there were no depths of flattery to which he would not sink, as his "Poem on the Late Promotion of Several Eminent Persons in Church and State" adequately shows. This is the poem to which he refers in the preface as the only one in the volume that needs apology. The more interesting question is surely whether he is not hinting heavily that Howard is the "Person of Quality" who is the author of the anonymous "Ode on her late Majesty (never before Printed)," the virtues of which make up for the deficiencies of his own poem. What is certain is that if it is Howard's, the "Ode in Memory of Her Late Majesty Queen Mary" does him no credit. It begins:

> Long our divided State
> Hung in the Ballance of a doubtful Fate,
> When One bright Nymph the gath'ring Clouds dispell'd,
> And all the Griefs of *Albion* Heal'd.

14. *Dryden*, p. 217.

> Her the United Land Obey'd,
> No more to Jealousies inclin'd,
> Nor fearing Pow'r with so much Virtue join'd. . . .

From such versifying and the unblushing assertion that Queen Mary had charmed the wind to stillness when a wind was all that France needed to make possible an invasion of England, the ode descends even further, to the suggestion that the smallpox, after two hundred and fifty years of minor victories, had, in seizing Mary, won a major one. It ends with a brief history of the England of the past sixty years:

> Unhappy Isle, for half an Age a Prey
> To fierce Dissension or Despotick Sway,
> Redeem'd from Anarchy to be Undone
> By the mistaken Measures of the Throne;
> Thy Monarchs meditating dark Designs,
> Or boldly throwing off the Masque,
> (Fond of the Pow'r, unequal to the Task).

From this, and worse, England had been saved by "something Cælestial . . . Of matchless Form and a Majestick Mien," namely, of course, Mary, who had now, to England's sorrow, retired too soon "to her Native Heaven."

One would have wished to end the story of Howard's literary career with something better; and indeed one cannot be certain that he perpetrated the "Ode." The sentiments, however, while not unique, are identical with those he expressed elsewhere, and the style is not unlike him. If Tate really did not know who wrote the poem, his suspicions were, to put it mildly, understandable.

In any case, Howard does seem to have been playing till very late in life the favorite seventeenth-century role, of the gentleman who wrote with ease—and only in his spare time. It is only fair to him to add that except for the periods when his illness must have been so severe as to make scribbling one of the few possible occupations, he had little spare time, for he was still kept busy at the Exchequer—busy in a way that must surely have tried his failing resources.

Reading through the State Papers for the years 1696 and 1697, one is impressed by the amount of work that was being referred to Howard and still attended to by him personally. The major problems were the revision of the currency, with the calling in of the old coinage and issue of the new, and the attempt to put the national credit on a firm footing. As Dalrymple pointed out, at this time the country's ability to repay its debts was so uncertain that "the exchequer tallies sold from 20 to 30 *per cent* discount, according as their terms of payment were more or less remote, and bank notes at 20 *per cent* discount."[15] Other methods of restoring credit having failed, it was decided that the Exchequer should issue "40,000 l. worth of indented bills of Credit, bearing interest at the rate of three pence a day per 100 l."; a quarter of the issue was allotted to each of the four Tellers of the Receipt, for sale at face value to any willing purchaser. Even the editor of the Calendars of Treasury Books, Shaw—certainly no admirer of Howard—admits that "the more technical side of the operation, the form and wording of the Bills, the printing, checking, keeping of counterfoils and entry books, accounting, cancelling, reissuing etc. were outlined mainly by Sir Robert Howard . . . in conjunction with William Lowndes, Secretary of the Treasury."[16] Lowndes was ordered to wait on Howard and "adjust the method with him." The plate for printing the Bills was delivered to Howard by the Treasury Lords in person on 24 June and he was asked to have a press in the Exchequer itself.[17] Yet in this same year he was again so ill that there was speculation on his successor.[18]

Then, as if all this were not enough, his troubles were added to by the disclosure in May 1697 of another serious deficiency in the Exchequer. A shortage of between £25,000 and £27,000 was discovered in the accounts of John Peters, clerk to Guy Palmes, one of the four Tellers of the Receipt. Howard was not actually incriminated as he had been in the otherwise similar D'Oyley scandal many years before; but he must have been made to feel very uncomfortable, not only because the deficiency had come about in part at least from Peters's attempts to help his friends by replacing clipped coins with new ones— exactly what Howard had offered to do for Dryden in May, 1696— but also because the fraud would have been revealed sooner had Howard as Auditor exercised the proper supervision.

15. *Memoirs*, III, 86.

16. *C.T.B.*, 1695-1702, *Introduction*, p. cxlii. Incidentally, the scheme was a failure.

17. *C.T.B.*, 1696-1697, II, 9, 31. On 2 June 1697, however, the Treasury Commissioners complained of the "dilatory proceedings" of the printers Howard had chosen.

18. *H.M.C.*, MSS of the Duke of Buccleuch, Vol. II, Pt. 2, p. 412 (23 Sept. 1696).

The full account was given by William Lowndes, as Secretary to the Treasury, to Blathwaite, Clerk of the Privy Council, on 4 June 1697. Noting that the Treasury Commissioners had discussed the matter with the Lords Justices of England and now desired it to be reported to the King, Lowndes drew attention to the fact that there were already precautions against fraud, in that the Auditor of the Receipt had to certify a weekly account, and the actual cash had to be locked up each day by the Clerk of the Pells and Deputy Chamberlains. Nonetheless, he wrote:

It is obvious to my Lords that the said accounts taken by the Auditor and by him certified weekly to the Treasury do frequently contain payments for which he gives the Teller credit although such payments are not actually made but only directed and in such cases the King has no discharge in his Exchequer by the voucher or receipt of the party for the money; and that this hath happened because the vouchers have not been examined for a long time as they ought to have been as well by the orders of the Exchequer as by the directions of the . . . Act. My Lords did indeed by an authority bearing date the 2d of March last appoint Mr. Peter Humes (a very skilful and trusty person) to examine the said vouchers; but it being properly the duty of the Auditor, and he insisting upon it, Mr. Humes was not permitted to perform that service which would easily have obviated the inconvenience since accrued.

But fresh complaints being made my Lords entrusted myself and Charles Twitty, who is clerk to Sir Robert Howard, to examine the said vouchers for divers weeks past and we have found that Mr. Palmes and Mr. Peters his clerk are wanting in their vouchers about 25,000 l. and that the persons who complain for want of their money are those interested in the payments for which these vouchers are wanting.[19]

The minutes of the proceedings of the Lords Justices, recording the discussion with the Treasury Commissioners on 28 May, indicate that the feeling against Howard was justifiably stronger than the tactful Lowndes later implied:

Part of this blame was laid upon Sir Robert Howard for not observing the ancient rules of the Exchequer, though they are enforced by a late act of parliament; but he continued to certify the payments made, when the orders were issued and entered in the pells, without examining the vouchers, to ascertain whether the money were paid or not, as he ought to do every week. Instead thereof, he had obstructed the officer appointed by the

19. *C.T.B.*, April-Sept., 1697, pp. 200-201. See also pp. 20, 28, 170. The chief complainant was Lord Irvine. The details of the shortage in the office of Palmes and Peters are given also by Baxter, *Development of the Treasury*, pp. 157-164.

Treasury to examine the vouchers, though of late he had consented to name one to join with Mr. Humes in that service, so that it was hoped the methods of the Exchequer would be better established, and every one think themselves under a stricter tie to discharge their duty, by the example to be made of this failure.[20]

Peters was dismissed and apparently never re-employed (although Palmes wished to engage him again); Palmes was suspended but reinstated when the seizure of Peters's effects, the calling upon sureties, and the raising of money by Palmes and his father had finally met all or most of the debt; and stricter regulations were made to govern the operations of the Exchequer in future.[21] (A little reading in the official documents of the period shows that it was certainly not the only department with defalcations: the Excise in 1697 was almost as bad.) Howard not only retained his office as Auditor but also— incredible as it might seem to one who did not know the earlier story of the D'Oyley affair—"became a suitor to the king" in March, 1697 (the very month in which Humes had been appointed to examine the proceedings of the Auditor, and been obstructed by him) for further leases in reversion! Sir William Trumbull, writing to Lord Willoughby of this on 23 March, added that "the King is disposed to gratify him"; but either a legal difficulty or the Palmes-Peters trouble apparently foiled Howard's hopes. Nothing, however, could repress him for long; and on 15 June, only eleven days after Lowndes's report from the Treasury Lords to the Privy Council of the Auditor's share of the blame in the Peters case, he was asking the same Treasury Lords for "a consideration" for the "extreme laborious and difficult" work that he and his clerks had done on the orders under the Salt Act and on the Exchequer Bills: "he leaves it, if my Lords please, to be referred to and examined by Mr. Lowndes: which my Lords consent to"! It is almost an anti-climax to add that Lowndes was apparently on Howard's side and that the request was granted; on 29 June there is record of a money-warrant "for 1,400 l. to Sir Robert Howard . . . for his own and his clerks' pains and services."[22]

In a more important sense, however, Howard's strength *was* failing; and perhaps it was his awareness that he could not live much longer that led to these final attempts to add to his fortune. This had already been substantially increased when Philadelphia Lady

20. *C.S.P.D.*, 1697, p. 177.   21. Baxter, pp. 163-164.
22. *C.S.P.D.*, 1697, p. 69; *C.T.B.*, April-Sept., 1697, pp. 45, 225-226.

Wentworth, widow of Thomas Lord Wentworth, died in May 1696, naming Howard, in her will of 2 April, as one of the three executors who were to share the residue of her property equally, after paying specific bequests totaling about £12,350. The other executors were Sir William Smith and Edward Northey, so that Luttrell was perhaps dividing by two instead of by three when he wrote on 9 May that "The lady Horatio Wentworth is dead, leaving 8000 l. per ann. to sir Robert Howard and Mr. Northey, of the Temple, after some legacies paid." I am unable to offer an explanation of the bequest, but the sum involved was so considerable as to form a significant part even of Howard's wealth. That is shown by the way he worded his own will, which he signed on 26 May 1697. After declaring in the usual formula but none too accurately that he was "in perfect health and of a sound and disposeing mind and memory" and requesting that his executrix should determine the manner of his burial, he gave the details of Lady Wentworth's will and left his share of that estate "unto my most dear and affectionate wife dame Anabella Howard and her heirs for ever." (Ashtead, of course, was already Thomas's.) He then bequeathed to Annabella all the rest of his estate, real and personal, and appointed her his sole executrix.[23]

On 3 September an insurance policy was taken out on Howard's life for one year—one of the first life insurance policies recorded in England. On 2 December Luttrell noted "Sir Robert Howard lyes at the point of death"; yet on 13 December he was appointed one of the commissioners of appeal in Admiralty cases, and Henry Purcell's widow would seem to have had no reason to suspect any approaching calamity when she alluded to Robert in her dedication to Annabella of *Orpheus Britannicus*.[24] That he was seriously ill, however, is suggested by the paucity of the references to him personally in the first half of 1698.[25]

23. Somerset House, 84 Bond; Luttrell, IV, 56; Somerset House, 201 Lort. Luttrell (IV, 423-424) estimated the bequest to Annabella at £40,000.

24. Luttrell, IV, 313; *C.S.P.D.*, 1697, pp. 510-511.

25. One of the few references, as Florence R. Scott first pointed out, shows the continued good will to him of the family of his deceased third wife, Mary Uphill. It is a memorandum of the Treasury Commissioners on 5 February, P.R.O. Ind. 4621, desiring the Commissioners for Customs to inquire into a petition by Lady Boteler, who asked for assistance in her duties as executrix of her late brother and in particular "in preserving a Cargoe of considerable value in the *Ship Benjamin* now arrived from the East Indies, Given to Sr Robt

His illness did not earn him the sympathy of all who knew of it: on 20 August when the Duchess of Leeds wrote to her daughter-in-law the Marchioness of Carmarthen "about this business of Sir Robert Howard's death, of which I find nothing," her only interest was whether her son Carmarthen would be able to demand the succession of the Auditorship of the Receipt.[26]

Howard died on Saturday 3 September 1698. He was not, as Luttrell had it, "aged near 80" but he was seventy-two, and, by seventeenth-century standards, a very old man. The burial was early on 8 September, when Howard was interred among his ancestors, in Westminster Abbey, "in St John Baptist's Chapel, at the entrance thereof"; and Luttrell adds that the interment was private.[27] No memorial was ever erected, and only a nineteenth-century gravestone records the names of all buried in the Chapel.

Other necessary formalities were attended to immediately. The will was proved on the day before the funeral; and Christopher Montagu was appointed by the Treasury Commissioners to the position of Auditor of the Receipt and Writer of the Tallies, on Monday 5 September, when Clayton officially informed them that Howard had died on the preceding Saturday.[28] Carmarthen naturally contested the appointment: he was particularly sensitive to the claim that Howard had held the position by gift of Danby when Treasurer: "as to my father's admitting Sir Robert Howard, he was the last man in ye world to have been admitted, if it were in his power"! But Christopher Montagu surrendered his patent to his brother Charles; Charles Montagu remained Auditor of the Exchequer; and Danby, Howard's great enemy in life, thus, ironically, met defeat in a matter arising directly out of his enemy's death.[29]

Howard, herselfe, her Brother Mr Rich: Uphill and her Sisters Mrs Duncomb and Mrs Uphill by will of her Brother Mr Jacob Uphill who dyed in this voyage homeward." Miss Scott cited the document, from the Calendars, in *N. & Q.*, CXCII (1947), 316.

26. *H.M.C.*, 79, MSS of the 12th Earl of Lindsey, p. 61.

27. Chester, *Westminster Abbey Registers*, p. 243; Luttrell, IV, 423-424. A document dated 31 August 1698—only three days before Howard's death—bears his signature in a stenciled form. (It is in the possession of Mr. A. W. G. Lowther.)

28. *C.T.B.*, 1698-1699, pp. 2, 108-109.

29. *H.M.C.*, MSS of the Marquis of Bath, III, 264; B.M. Add. MS 28086, f.80 and *passim*; *C.S.P., Treasury Papers*, 1697-1701/2, pp. 240-241; *C.T.B.*, 1699-1700, p. 209; *C.T.B.*, 1702, I. 32-52, 967. The dispute continued until 1703.

Annabella, for her part, seems to have gone efficiently about the task of ensuring that she received all money due to her as Howard's widow. In January, 1699, Lowndes gave orders for payment to her of £300 owed on an allowance of £150 per annum to Howard and his clerks; and as late as 1701, arrears of £2,276 were also being paid on the Howard-Berkshire farm of the Post Fines. When, however, in April, 1699, Annabella invited the Treasury Lords to take official action to ensure that money payable to others through Howard, as arrears of annuities, might be paid through her, the Lords quite properly asked her to "release the order . . . on the book in the Exchequer" that the money might go direct to those entitled to it.[30] She also fought and won a law case for the money due under the insurance policy taken out on Howard's life for one year on 3 September 1697 (his death on 3 September 1698 having created a nice problem of legal interpretation). In all, she seems to have been a wife of whom her husband could be proud.

The dead man's reputation was not cherished by all, however. If there was one maxim that the seventeenth and eighteenth centuries did not believe in, it was *de mortuis nil nisi bonum*. From 1699 onwards, the various volumes of *Poems on Affairs of State* were reprinting the "Session of the Poets" and other attacks upon Howard's literary pretensions; the publishers also had no intention of forgetting the parody on "The Duel of the Stags."

On the other hand, throughout the eighteenth century the anthologies of "the most celebrated poets" normally contained Howard's verses and he is well represented (albeit by "The Duel of the Stags" among other poems) in Nichols's *Select Collection of Poems* as late as 1780. Nor was he forgotten as a playwright: Robert Walker could safely include Howard's name in a prospectus of a volume of celebrated tragedies, comedies, operas and farces, in 1735,[31] and *The Committee*, in particular, continued to be republished and acted throughout the eighteenth century and, in Knight's adaptation, into the nineteenth.

The custom among literary historians of referring to Howard in terms of little but contempt may be traced, I suspect—in spite of all

30. *C.T.B.*, 1698-1699, p. 246; *C.T.B.*, 1700-1701, p. 205; *C.S.P.*, *Treasury Papers*, 1697-1701/2, pp. 283-284.

31. Cited by R. M. Wiles, *Serial Publication in England before 1750* (Cambridge, 1957), pp. 19-20.

the parodies and attacks in his own day—to Scott's 1821 description of Howard's poems as "productions of a most freezing mediocrity." Others may prefer to date it from Theophilus Cibber's 1753 statement that Howard had no greater claim to literary renown than to have been Dryden's brother-in-law.[32] What is certain is that it is as Dryden's brother-in-law and opponent, only, that he has been known in our time to most students of literature; and to have been Dryden's opponent, it is normally implied, is to have been not merely wrong but also wrong-headed—even if in the long run Dryden admitted that it was he himself who was in error! The one greater injustice, I suggest, and it has been too often perpetrated, is to speak of "Dryden's *Indian Queen*" or to insinuate that since Howard by hypothesis could not write a scannable line, he cannot have had a large share in any such play.

The main aim of all the preceding pages has been to argue that the truth is different. Howard was a minor poet, to be sure, but he wrote some passable poems and translations, and Purcell, for one, was not too proud to set his words to music. He was also a minor dramatist, but he helped to create Heroic drama; he wrote one of the best comedies of his time, in *The Committee* (and this before Dryden or Etherege had contributed significantly to Restoration drama); and he had some share (at least) in one of the best tragi-comedies of the age, *The Duke of Lerma*. In religious and political controversy, he was not the ablest writer of his day, but he had to be taken seriously; and in literary controversy he did, after all, hold his own with Dryden.

Moreover, had he never written a line, the man who was one of the leaders of the Court Party in the House of Commons for something like thirty years; served as a Privy Counsellor under William and Mary; was a great power in public finance, even if he was often unscrupulous, during three reigns; played a leading role in the impeachment of Clarendon and in the first impeachment of Danby; and as one of a trusted inner group worked both for the Restoration of Charles II and for the Revolution of 1688—this man, I hope it will be agreed, has his place in history.

32. Scott, *Dryden*, XI, 6; Cibber, *Lives of the Poets*, III, 58.

Bibliography of Printed Sources

1. Works by, or attributed on reasonable grounds to, Sir Robert Howard.

a. Major works, in chronological order

Poems. 1660. ("A Panegyrick to the King," Songs and Sonnets, *The Blind Lady,* "A Panegyrick to Generall Monck," and translations of Virgil and Statius)

Four New Plays. 1665. (*The Surprisal, The Committee, The Indian Queen, The Vestal Virgin*)

The Duke of Lerma. 1668.

"The Duell of the Stags." 1668.

An Examination of the Impartial State of the Case of the Earl of Danby. In a Letter to A Member of the House of Commons. 1680.

An Account of the State of his Majesties Revenue, As it was left by the Earl of Danby At Lady-Day, 1679. In a Letter to a Friend. "1681" [1680].

The Life and Reign of King Richard the Second. "1681" [1680].

Historical Observations Upon the Reigns of Edward I. II. III. And Richard II. With Remarks upon their Faithful Counsellors and False Favourites. 1689.

The History of the Reigns of Edward and Richard II. With Reflections and Characters of their Chief Ministers and Favourites. As Also, A Comparison between those Princes Edward and Richard the Second, with Edward the First, and Edward the Third. Written in the Year 1685. . . . 1690.

A Letter to Mr. Samuel Johnson, Occasioned by a scurrilous Pamphlet, intituled, Animadversions on Mr. Johnson's Answer to Jovian, in three Letters to a Country-Friend. . . . 1692.

Five New Plays. 1692. (The plays of *Four New Plays* and *The Duke of Lerma*)

A Particular Accompt of the Moneys Paid into the Receipt of Exchequer, Upon the late Million Act, for the Benefit of Survivorship. . . . Examined by the Right Honourable Sir Robert Howard, Kt. Auditor of the Receipt of Exchequer; And Printed by his Direction. 1694.

The History of Religion. 1694.

The Indian Queen (operatic version). 1695.

A Twofold Vindication of the Late Arch-Bishop of Canterbury, And of the Author of "The History of Religion". . . . 1696.

Poems. 1696. (A reissue of the 1660 volume.)

A Free Discourse Wherein the Doctrines Which make for Tyranny Are Display'd. The Title of our Rightful and Lawful King William Vindi-

cated. And the unreasonableness and mischievous Tendency of the odious distinction of a King de Facto, and de Jure, discover'd. . . . 1697.

b. Shorter poems

"Nature's Changes" [n.d.]
"To my worthy Friend, Dr. Charleton." "1663" [1662].
"Against the Fear of Death." [Between 1660 and 1668.]
"Wasted with sighs I sigh'd or pin'd." [1667.]
"When I drink my heart is possessed." 1667.
"Love thou canst hear." [1695.]
"Ode in Memory of Her Late Majesty Queen Mary." 1697.

c. Plays begun but probably not completed, and not extant

The Country Gentleman. 1669.
The Conquest of China by the Tartars. [1678?]

2. *Other principal printed sources, cited in the text or notes.*

ADDISON, JOSEPH, AND STEELE, RICHARD *The Spectator* No. 335. London, 25 March 1712.

The Annual Miscellany for the Year 1694. Being the Fourth Part of Miscellany Poems . . . By the Most Eminent Hands. London, 1694.

ANONYMOUS *Archbishop Tillotson Vindicated from The Charge of Socinianism.* London, 1696.

——— *The Charge of Socinianism against Dr. Tillotson Considered.* London, 1695.

——— *A Companion to the Theatre.* London, 1740.

——— *An Explanation of the Lord Treasurer's Letter to Mr. Montagu.* London, 1680.

——— *The Key to 'The Rehearsal.'* London, 1704.

——— *A Modest Vindication of the Earl of S——y.* London, 1681.

——— *A New Key to 'The Rehearsal.'* London, 1717.

——— *A Seasonable Argument to Perswade All the Grand Juries in England to Petition for a New Parliament.* "Amsterdam," 1677.

Articles of Impeachment . . . against Thomas Earl of Danby. London, 1678/9.

ARUNDELL, D. D. *Dryden and Howard 1664-68.* Cambridge, 1929.

ASHLEY, MAURICE *England in the Seventeenth Century (1603-1714).* The Pelican History of England, Vol. 6. London, 1952. Second edition, 1954.

ATTERBURY, FRANCIS *The Scorner Incapable of True Wisdom.* London, 1694.

B., J. *Some Reflections upon the Earl of Danby.* London, 1679.

BAKER, DAVID E., cont. REED AND JONES *Biographia Dramatica; Or, a Companion to the Playhouse.* London, 1812.

BAXTER, STEPHEN B. *The Development of the Treasury 1660-1702.* London, 1957.

"BETTERTON, THOMAS" [E. CURLL?] *The History of the English Stage from the Restauration to the Present Time.* London, 1741.

BLOUNT, CHARLES *Great is Diana of the Ephesians.* London, 1680.

—— *Mr. Dreyden Vindicated, in a Reply to the "Friendly Vindication of Mr. Dreyden."* London, [1673-1674].

BOTTKOL, J. M. J. "Dryden's Latin Scholarship," *M.P.,* XL (1943), 241-254.

BOYLE, ROGER, EARL OF ORRERY *Dramatic Works.* Ed. W. S. Clark. London, 1937.

BRAYLEY, E. W. *A Topographical History of Surrey.* London, 1841.

BRAYLEY, E. W., AND NEALE, J. P. *The History and Antiquities of the Abbey Church of St. Peter, Westminster.* London, 1818-1823.

BREDVOLD, LOUIS I. *The Intellectual Milieu of John Dryden.* University of Michigan Publications in Language and Literature, Vol. 12. Ann Arbor, 1934. Reprinted 1956.

BROWNING, ANDREW *Thomas Osborne, Earl of Danby and Duke of Leeds 1632-1712.* Glasgow, 1944-1951.

BRYANT, ARTHUR *Samuel Pepys: The Years of Peril.* Cambridge, 1935.

BURNET, GILBERT *History of My Own Time.* Ed. Osmund Airy. Oxford, 1897.

BUTLER, SAMUEL *Satires and Miscellaneous Poetry and Prose.* Ed. René Lamar. Cambridge, 1928.

Calendar of the Proceedings of the Committee for Advance of Money.

Calendar of State Papers, Colonial Series, America and the West Indies

Calendar of State Papers Domestic.

Calendar of State Papers Relating to Ireland.

Calendar of State Papers, Treasury Books.

Calendar of State Papers, Treasury Papers.

Calendar of State Papers Venetian.

CAREW, THOMAS *The Poems of Thomas Carew.* Ed. Rhodes Dunlap. Oxford, 1949.

CAUSTON, H. K. S. *The Howard Papers.* London, 1862.

CHARLETON, WALTER *Chorea Gigantum.* London, 1663.

CHASE, L. N. *The English Heroic Play.* New York, 1903.

CHESTER, J. L. (ed.). *The Marriage, Baptismal, and Burial Registers of the Collegiate Church or Abbey of St. Peter, Westminster.* London, 1876.

CIBBER, COLLEY *An Apology for the Life of Mr. Colley Cibber.* London, 1740.

CIBBER, THEOPHILUS *et al. The Lives of the Poets of Great Britain and Ireland.* London, 1753.

The Proceedings in the House of Commons Touching the Impeachment of Edward Late Earl of Clarendon . . . Anno 1667. London, 1700.

CLARK, W. S. "Dryden's Relations with Howard and Orrery," *M.L.N.,* XLII (1927), 16-20.

CLIFFORD, MARTIN *Notes upon Mr. Dryden's Poems. In Four Letters.* London, 1687.

—— (attributed) *The Friendly Vindication of Mr. Dryden From the Censure of the Rota By His Cabal of Wits.* Cambridge, 1673.

COBBETT, WILLIAM *Parliamentary History of England from the Norman Conquest in 1066, to the year 1803.* London, 1808.

COLLINS, ARTHUR *The Peerage of England.* London, 1714. Third edition enlarged.

CUNNINGHAM, PETER "Dryden's Quarrel with Flecknoe," *The Gentleman's Magazine,* XXXIV (1850), 597.

DALRYMPLE, SIR JOHN *Memoirs of Great Britain and Ireland.* London, 1790.

DARBISHIRE, HELEN (ed.). *Early Lives of Milton.* London, 1932.

DAVIES, GODFREY *The Restoration of Charles II.* London, 1955.

DAY, C. L. *The Songs of John Dryden.* Cambridge, Mass., 1932.

DAY, C. L., AND MURRIE, ELEANORE B. *English Song-Books 1651-1702.* London, 1940.

DE BEER, E. S. "The Dictionary of National Biography," *Institute of Historical Research Bulletin,* III (1925), 64-65, and XVIII (1939-1940), 95-96.

—— "The Dramatist Sons of Thomas Earl of Berkshire," *N. & Q.,* CLXXXVII (1944), 19, 214-215.

—— "The Third Wife of Sir Robert Howard," *N. & Q.,* CXCII (1947), 445-447.

DERING, SIR EDWARD *Parliamentary Diary 1670-73.* Ed. B. D. Henning. Yale Historical Publications, Vol. XVI, 1940.

DOBRÉE, BONAMY *Restoration Tragedy 1660-1720.* Oxford, 1929.

DOWNES, JOHN *Roscius Anglicanus, Or an Historical Review of the Stage . . . from 1660 to 1706.* London, 1708 [i.e., 1711?]

—— *Roscius Anglicanus.* Ed. Montague Summers. London, 1928.

DRYDEN, JOHN, JR. *The Husband His Own Cuckold.* London, 1696.

DRYDEN, JOHN, SR. *The Works of John Dryden.* Ed. E. N. Hooker and H. T. Swedenberg. California, 1956.

—— *The Works of John Dryden.* Ed. Sir Walter Scott. London, 1808.

—— *The Dramatic Works of John Dryden.* Ed. Montague Summers. London, 1931-1932.

—— *The Letters of John Dryden.* Ed. C. E. Ward. Durham, N. C., 1942.

—— *The Poems of John Dryden.* Ed. James Kinsley. Oxford, 1958.

—— *The Poetical Works of John Dryden.* Ed. G. R. Noyes. Cambridge, Mass., 1909; revised, 1950.

—— *The Poems of John Dryden.* Ed. John Sargeaunt. London, 1935.

—— *An Essay of Dramatic Poesy.* Ed. D. Nichol Smith. London, [1900].

—— *Annus Mirabilis.* 1666.

—— *Astræa Redux.* 1660.

—— *Aureng-Zebe.* 1676.

—— *A Defence of an Essay of Dramatique Poesie, being an Answer to the Preface of The Great Favourite, or the Duke of Lerma.* (Prefixed to the second edition of *The Indian Emperour.*) 1668.

—— *Of Dramatick Poesie, An Essay.* 1668.

—— *Of Heroique Plays. An Essay.* (Prefixed to *The Conquest of Granada by the Spaniards.*) 1672.

—— *Poems on Several Occasions.* 1693.

—— *The Rival Ladies.* 1664.

—— *Tyrannick Love.* 1672.

—— *The Works of Virgil.* 1697.

ELIOT, T. S. *Poetry and Drama.* London, 1951.

ELLIS, GEORGE *Specimens of the Early English Poets.* London, 1790. Third edition, 1803.

ELYS, EDMUND *A Letter To the Honourable Sir Robert Howard.* London, 1696.

Essex Papers. Ed. O. Airy. Camden Society, N. S. Vol. LXVII. London, 1890.

EVELYN, JOHN *The Diary of John Evelyn.* Ed. E. S. de Beer. Oxford, 1955.

FIELDING, HENRY *The Tragedy of Tragedies, or, The Life and Death of Tom Thumb the Great.* London, 1731.

FLECKNOE, RICHARD (attributed) *A Letter from a Gentleman To the Honourable Ed. Howard Esq; Occasioned By a Civiliz'd Epistle of Mr. Dryden's, Before his Second Edition of his "Indian Emperour."* London, 1668.

FOXCROFT, H. C. *The Life and Letters of Sir George Savile, Bart., First Marquis of Halifax.* London, 1898.

FRASER, PETER *The Intelligence of the Secretaries of State & Their Monopoly of Licensed News 1660-1688.* Cambridge, 1956.

FREEMAN, MORRIS "Milton and Dryden on Rhyme," *H.L.Q.,* XXIV (1961), 337-344.

FROST, WILLIAM *Dryden and the Art of Translation.* New Haven, 1955.

GARDNER, WINIFRED, LADY BURGHCLERE *George Villiers, Second Duke of Buckingham.* London, 1903.

GENEST, JOHN *Some Account of the English Stage, from the Restoration in 1660 to 1830.* Bath, 1832.

GREY, ANCHITELL *Debates of the House of Commons, From the Year 1667 to the Year 1694.* London, 1763, 1769.

HARBAGE, ALFRED *Annals of English Drama 975-1700.* London, 1940.

——*Cavalier Drama. An Historical and Critical Supplement to the Study of the Elizabethan and Restoration Stage.* London, 1936.

—— "Elizabethan-Restoration Palimpsest," *M.L.R.,* XXXV (1940), 287-319.

—— *Thomas Killigrew.* Philadelphia, 1930.

Hatton Correspondence. Camden Society. London, 1878.

HEYLYN, PETER *Cosmographie.* London, 1652. Second edition, 1657.

HICKES, GEORGE *Jovian.* London, 1683.

—— (attributed) *The Doctrine of Passive Obedience. By a Layman of the Church of England.* London, 1689.

The History and Proceedings of the House of Commons, From the Restoration to the Present Time. Vol. I, 1660-1680; Vol. II, 1680-1695; Vol. III, 1695-1706. London, 1742.

The History and Proceedings of the House of Lords. From the Restoration in 1660, to the Present Time. Vol. I, 1660-1697; Vol. II, 1697-1714. London, 1742.

Historical Manuscripts Commission, Reports.

HOPKINS, WILLIAM *Animadversions on Mr Johnson's Answer to Jovian, in Three Letters to a Country-Friend.* London, 1691.

HOTSON, LESLIE *The Commonwealth and Restoration Stage.* Cambridge, Mass., 1928.

HOWARD, CHARLES *Historical Anecdotes of Some of the Howard Family.* London, 1769.

HOWARD, EDWARD *The British Princes: an Heroick Poem.* 1669.

—— *The Change of Crownes.* Ed. F. S. Boas. London, 1949.

HOWARD, HENRY *Indications of Memorials, Monuments, Paintings and Engravings of Persons of the Howard Family.* Corby Castle, 1834.

H[OWARD], H. S. "The Dramatist Sons of Thomas, Earl of Berkshire," *N. & Q.,* CLXXXVII (1944), 281-283.

—— "Sir Robert Howard, K. B.," *N. & Q.,* CLXXVII (1939), 7.

HOWARTH, R. G. "Edward Phillips's *Compendiosa Enumeratio Poetarum,*" *M.L.R.,* LIV (1959), 321-328.

HUNTLEY, F. L. *On Dryden's "Essay of Dramatic Poesy."* University of Michigan Publications in Modern Philology, No. 16, 1951.

HYDE, EDWARD, EARL OF CLARENDON *The History of the Rebellion and Civil Wars in England.* Oxford, 1704.

—— *The Continuation of The Life of Edward, Earl of Clarendon.* Oxford, 1857.

[JACOB, GILES] *The Poetical Register: Or, the Lives and Characters of All the English Poets, with an Account of their Writings.* London, 1719-1720.

JOHNSON, SAMUEL (17th cent.) *Julian the Apostate.* London, 1682.

—— *Julian's Arts to undermine and extirpate Christianity.* London, 1689.

—— *Remarks upon Dr. Sherlock's Book, Intituled The Case of Resistance of the Supreme Powers Stated and Resolved, according to the Doctrine of the Holy Scriptures.* London, 1689.

JOHNSON, SAMUEL (18th cent.) *The Lives of the Poets.* London, 1779-1781. Reprinted, 1938.

The Journals of the House of Commons.

The Journals of the House of Lords.

KENT, C. B. R. *The Early History of the Tories.* London, 1908.

LAMB, CHARLES *The Complete Works and Letters.* New York, 1935.

LANGBAINE, GERARD (the younger) *An Account of the English Dramatick Poets. Or, Some Observations and Remarks On the Lives and Writings, of all those that have Publish'd either Comedies, Tragedies, Tragi-Comedies, Pastorals, Masques, Interludes, Farces, or Opera's in the English Tongue.* Oxford, 1691.

—— *The Lives and Characters of the English Dramatick Poets. Also An Exact Account of all the Plays that were ever yet Printed in the English Tongue . . . improv'd and continued . . . by a Careful Hand* [Charles Gildon]. London, [1712]

LAUDER, SIR JOHN, LORD FOUNTAINHALL *Journals of Sir John Lauder Lord Fountainhall.* Ed. Donald Crawford. Edinburgh, 1900.

LUTTRELL, NARCISSUS *A Brief Historical Relation of State Affairs from September 1678 to April 1714.* Oxford, 1857.

MACAULAY, THOMAS BABINGTON *The History of England.* London, 1849.

MACDONALD, HUGH *John Dryden. A Bibliography of Early Editions and of Drydeniana.* Oxford, 1932.

MANNING, O. (cont. W. BRAY) *The History and Antiquities of Surrey.* London, 1809.

MARVELL, ANDREW *Poems and Letters.* Ed. H. M. Margoliouth. Second edition, Oxford, 1952.

MASSON, DAVID *The Life of John Milton.* London, 1859-1894.

MILWARD, JOHN *The Diary of John Milward, September 1666 to May 1668.* Ed. Caroline Robbins. Cambridge, 1938.

MONRO, ALEXANDER *A Letter To the Honourable Sir Robert Howard.* London, 1696.

NICHOLS, J. (comp.). *A Select Collection of Poems.* London, 1780.

NICOLL, ALLARDYCE *A History of English Drama 1660-1900.* Fourth edition, Cambridge, 1952.

NOYES, G. R. "'Crites' in Dryden's *Essay of Dramatic Poesy,*" *M.L.N.,* XXXVIII (1923), 333-337.

OLIVER, H. J. *The Problem of John Ford.* Melbourne, 1955.

OSBORN, JAMES M. *John Dryden: Some Biographical Facts and Problems.* New York, 1940.

OSBORNE, THOMAS, EARL OF DANBY *An Answer of the Right Honourable the Earl of Danby to a Late Pamphlet, Entituled, An Examination of the Impartial State of the Case of the Earl of Danby.* London, 1680.

—— *The Earl of Danby's Answer to Sr. Robert Howard's Book, Entituled An Account of the State of his Majesties Revenue.* London, 1680.

—— *Memoirs relating to the Impeachment of Thomas Earl of Danby (now Duke of Leeds) in the year 1678.* London, 1710.

—— (attributed) *An Impartial State of the Case of the Earl of Danby.* London, 1679.

[PAGET, F. E.] *Some Records of the Ashtead Estate, and of its Howard Possessors: with notices of Elford, Castle Rising, Levens, and Charlton.* Lichfield, 1873.

PARSONS, A. E. "The English Heroic Play," *M.L.R.,* XXXIII (1938), 1-14.

PEPYS, SAMUEL *The Diary and Correspondence of Samuel Pepys F.R.S.* Ed. Richard Lord Braybrooke. London, 1885.

—— *The Diary of Samuel Pepys*. Ed. Henry B. Wheatley. London, 1923.

—— *Further Correspondence of Samuel Pepys 1662-1679*. Ed. J. R. Tanner. London, 1929.

—— *The Private Correspondence and Miscellaneous Papers of Samuel Pepys*. Ed. J. R. Tanner. London, 1926.

PETERSSON, R. T. *Sir Kenelm Digby*. London, 1956.

PHILLIPS, EDWARD *Compendiosa Enumeratio Poetarum*. London, 1669.

PINTO, V. DE SOLA (ed.). *English Biography in the Seventeenth Century*. London, 1951.

P[LAYFORD], H[ENRY] *Deliciæ Musicæ, Being, a Collection of the newest and best Songs, With the Additional Musick to the Indian Queen, by Mr. Daniel Purcell. . . .* London, 1695-1696.

Poems on Affairs of State. London, 1697, 1699, etc.

PRINZ, JOHANNES *John Wilmot Earl of Rochester*. Palaestra, Band 154. Leipzig, 1927.

PROUDFOOT, L. *Dryden's 'Aeneid' and Its Seventeenth Century Predecessors*. Manchester, 1960.

PURCELL, HENRY *A Collection of Ayres, Compos'd for the Theatre, and upon other Occasions By the late Mr. Henry Purcell*. London, 1697.

—— *A Collection of Songs set to Music by Mr Henry Purcell & Mr John Eccles*. London, [1696?].

—— *Orpheus Britannicus. A Collection of all The Choicest Songs for One, Two and Three Voices, Compos'd by Mr Henry Purcell*. London, 1698.

—— *The Songs in the Indian Queen: As it is now Compos'd into an Opera. By Mr. Henry Purcell*. London, 1695.

RALPH, JAMES *The History of England: During the Reigns of K. William, Q. Anne, and K. George I. With an Introductory Review of the Reigns of the Royal Brothers, Charles and James*. London, 1744.

RANKE, LEOPOLD VON *A History of England Principally in the Seventeenth Century*. Oxford, 1875.

RERESBY, SIR JOHN *The Memoirs of Sir John Reresby*. London, 1734.

RICHARDSON, ETHEL M. *The Lion and the Rose*. London, [1922].

ROSENFELD, SYBIL "Dramatic Advertisements in the Burney Newspapers," *P.M.L.A.*, LI (1936), 123-152.

S., N. (*et al.*) *A Twofold Vindication of the Late Arch-Bishop of Canterbury, And of the Author of "The History of Religion."* London, 1696.

SAINTSBURY, GEORGE *Dryden*. London, 1881.

SANDERSON, WILLIAM *A Compleat History of the Life and Raigne of King Charles*. London, 1658.

SAUNDERS, FRANCIS (comp.). *A Collection of Poems by Several Hands. Most of them Written by Persons of Eminent Quality*. London, 1693.

SCOTT, FLORENCE R. "The Dramatist Sons of Thomas, Earl of Berkshire," *N. & Q.*, CXCII (1947), 17.

—— "Lady Honoria Howard," *R.E.S.*, XX (1944), 158-159.

—— "The Marriages of Sir Robert Howard," *M.L.N.*, LV (1940), 410-415.

—— "Sir Robert Howard as Financier," *P.M.L.A.*, LII (1937), 1094-1100.

—— "The Third Wife of Sir Robert Howard," *N. & Q.*, CXCII (1947), 314-316.

SEDLEY, SIR CHARLES *The Poetical and Dramatic Works.* Ed. V. de Sola Pinto. London, 1928.

SHADWELL, THOMAS *The Complete Works.* Ed. Montague Summers. London, 1927.

—— *The Sullen Lovers.* London, 1668.

—— (attributed) *The Medal of John Bayes.* London, 1682.

SHAWCROSS, J. P. *The History of Dagenham.* London, 1904.

SHEFFIELD, JOHN, EARL OF MULGRAVE *An Essay on Poetry.* Third edition, London, 1697.

SMITH, D. NICHOL *John Dryden.* Cambridge, 1950.

SMITH, J. H. "The Dryden-Howard Collaboration," *S.P.*, LI (1954), 54-74.

The Souldiers Catechisme. London, 1644.

STEPHEN, SIR LESLIE, AND LEE, SIR SIDNEY (eds.). *The Dictionary of National Biography.* London, 1917, etc.

STROUP, T. B. "Philosophy and the Drama," *T.L.S.*, 19 Jan. 1933, p. 40.

——"Scenery for *The Indian Queen*," *M.L.N.*, LII (1937), 408-409.

SUMMERS, MONTAGUE *A Bibliography of the Restoration Drama.* London, [1935].

—— *The Playhouse of Pepys.* London, 1935.

—— *The Restoration Theatre.* London, 1934.

SWIFT, JONATHAN *"A Tale of a Tub" With Other Early Works.* Ed. Herbert Davis. Oxford. Reprinted, 1957.

SYMONDS, RICHARD *Diary.* Ed. C. E. Long. London, 1859.

THORN-DRURY, G. "Some Notes on Dryden," *R.E.S.*, I (1925), 83.

THURBER, CARRYL NELSON, (ed.). *Sir Robert Howard's Comedy "The Committee."* University of Illinois Studies in Language and Literature 7, 1921.

TOLAND, JOHN *The Life of John Milton.* London, 1698.

TRENT, W. P. "News for Bibliophiles," *Nation,* XCVIII (1914), 207.

VENN, JOHN AND J. A. *Alumni Cantabrigienses.* Cambridge, 1922-1927.

VILLIERS, GEORGE, DUKE OF BUCKINGHAM *The Rehearsal.* Ed. Montague Summers. Stratford-upon-Avon, 1914.

WARD, CHARLES E. "An Unpublished Letter of Sir Robert Howard," *M.L.N.*, LX (1945), 119-121.

WASSERMAN, EARL R. *The Subtler Language.* Baltimore, 1959.

WILES, R. M. *Serial Publication in England before 1750.* Cambridge, 1957.

WILLIAMSON, GEORGE "The Occasion of *An Essay of Dramatic Poesy*," *M.P.*, XLIV (1946), 1-9.

Letters to Sir Joseph Williamson. Camden Society. London, 1874.

WILMOT, JOHN, EARL OF ROCHESTER *Poems.* Ed. V. de Sola Pinto. London, 1953.

WILSON, JOHN HAROLD *The Court Wits of the Restoration.* Princeton, 1948.

—— "The Dating of Rochester's 'Scaen,'" *R.E.S.*, XIII (1937), 455-458.

—— *Nell Gwyn, Royal Mistress.* New York, 1952.

—— *A Rake and His Times: George Villiers, Second Duke of Buckingham.* New York, 1954.

WING, D. G. *A Short-Title Catalogue of Books Printed in England, Scotland, Ireland, Wales, and British America, and of English Books Printed in Other Countries, 1641-1700.* New York, 1945-1951.

WINTERBOTTOM, J. A. "Hobbesian Ideas in Dryden's Tragedies," *J.E.G.P.,* LVII (1958), 665-683.

WOOD, ANTHONY à *Athenae Oxonienses. . . . The Second edition very much Corrected and Enlarged. . . .* London, 1721.

Index